The Malfunction of US Education Policy

The Malfunction of US Education Policy

Elite Misinformation, Disinformation, and Selfishness

Richard P. Phelps

ROWMAN & LITTLEFIELD
Lanham • Boulder • New York • London

Published by Rowman & Littlefield
An imprint of The Rowman & Littlefield Publishing Group, Inc.
4501 Forbes Boulevard, Suite 200, Lanham, Maryland 20706
www.rowman.com

86-90 Paul Street, London EC2A 4NE

Copyright © 2023 by Richard P. Phelps

All rights reserved. No part of this book may be reproduced in any form or by any electronic or mechanical means, including information storage and retrieval systems, without written permission from the publisher, except by a reviewer who may quote passages in a review.

British Library Cataloguing in Publication Information Available

Library of Congress Cataloging-in-Publication Data

Names: Phelps, Richard P., author.
Title: The malfunction of US education policy : elite misinformation, disinformation, and selfishness / Richard P. Phelps.
Other titles: Malfunction of United States education policy
Description: Lanham, Maryland : Rowman & Littlefield, 2023. | Includes bibliographical references.
Identifiers: LCCN 2022055371 (print) | LCCN 2022055372 (ebook) | ISBN 9781475869934 (cloth) | ISBN 9781475869941 (paperback) | ISBN 9781475869958 (ebook)
Subjects: LCSH: Education and state—United States. | Mass media and educators—United States. | Educational publishing—United States. | Education—Standards—United States. | Educational change—United States.
Classification: LCC LC89 .P49 2023 (print) | LCC LC89 (ebook) | DDC 379.73—dc23/eng/20221116
LC record available at https://lccn.loc.gov/2022055371
LC ebook record available at https://lccn.loc.gov/2022055372

Contents

Preface: Protecting Endangered Theses	ix
Introduction: The Cartel Alliance and Honest Terminology	1
Chapter 1: The View from 2001	11
Chapter 2: The Triumph of Strategic Scholarship	37
Chapter 3: The Education Establishment Cartel	63
Chapter 4: Linchpin of the Cartel Alliance: Koretz, Cannell, and the Ghost of Test Security	83
Chapter 5: The Education Reform Cartel	97
Chapter 6: A Dense Web of Common Core Confederates	119
Chapter 7: The Permanent Education Press: A Breed Apart	133
Chapter 8: The View from 2023	155
Conclusion: When What Is Left Out Is More Important	165
About the Author	175

This book is dedicated to those willing to pay the high price for telling the truth—Manuel Alfaro, Wayne Bishop, Adele Cothorne, Myron Lieberman, Erich Martel, Sandra Stotsky, and those others of whose sacrifices I sadly remain unaware.

Preface

Protecting Endangered Theses

I work to protect endangered theses. Not species, theses. Endangered theses are neither animal, plant, nor archaea. They are information—in books, articles, presentations, databases—unwanted by people in positions of power and unprotected from predation. As with efforts to preserve from extinction a diversity of seeds and plants we might find useful later, it is in society's interest to preserve from suppression and dismissal a variety of scholarly research evidence, much of which we paid dearly to produce.

It is not, however, in any individual scholar's interest. Ambitious and selfish individual scholars seek to thicken their curriculum vitae, accumulate credentials, honors, and awards, and win promotions, preferably at prestigious institutions. They win in this competitive environment by maximizing their perceived individual scholarly production in comparison to the rest of the field (Al-Janabi, 2022; Association for Psychological Science, 2021b; Green, 2019; Levitt, 2014).

Unfortunately for society, some of the most effective techniques for advancing an individual scholarly career work directly counter to society's interest in the preservation and diversity of evidence (Oransky, 2015; Tiokhin, Panchanathan, Smaldino, and Lakens, 2021).

A key component of our faith in progress is the corollary belief that our base of knowledge continually expands—that is, we know what we already know, and we are always learning more. This continual expansion of knowledge requires both that the historical accumulation of knowledge be preserved, and that new knowledge be disseminated.

A key component of our faith in democracy is the corollary belief that citizens and policymakers can easily access a wide variety of policy-relevant information needed to make responsible political decisions.

In US education research, however, the public and policymakers lack access to much of that accumulated wisdom. Important policy-relevant information is routinely suppressed, misrepresented, or otherwise removed from consideration. Overly powerful gatekeepers manage to focus the fleeting or fickle attention of policymakers and journalists.

Small, organized groups of aggressive, profusely resourced scholars replace a centuries-old, worldwide storehouse of knowledge with their own narrow and highly selective body of work. Not only are they not punished for their information suppression; they are rewarded for their net reduction in society's understanding with money, sinecures, and fame.

Whereas fallacious and even fraudulent education research and information are remarkably well tolerated in US education circles, however, decorum dictates that exposing fraudulent research is rude and offensive and so is strongly discouraged (Byrne, 2019; Crocker and Cooper 2011; Lukianoff and Strossen, 2022b; Phelps, 2019b, 2021d).

How Scholarship Is Supposed to Work

How do we know things? Of course, we all know about the experimental method, one of the medieval age's most profound legacies. Even today, centuries after Aristotle, Roger Bacon, and Ibn al-Haytham, the experimental method is widely regarded by scholars as the best method for determining truth—the "gold standard" of scientific inquiry. Some economists and political scientists publicly concur (Greene and Forster 2002; Kemple, 2013), even while they may dismiss or demean a century's worth of experimental work in psychology, the single social science discipline that has been conducting experiments by the tens of thousands for over a century.

Though inarguably valuable, experiments are like a championship game. Just two or, at most, a few, contestants, compete directly in a controlled match to determine a winner. But, first, a winnowing process must reduce a wider range of challengers to the smaller number. How fair is that process?

Regarding such social decision-making, historians of science often invoke the writings of the philosopher John Stuart Mill (1978) of utilitarianism fame. Free speech advocates Greg Lukianoff and Nadine Strossen (2022a) showcase "Mill's Trident,"[1] which

> holds that, for any given belief, there are three options:
>
> 1. You are wrong; in which case freedom of speech is essential to allow people to correct you.

2. You are partially correct; in which case you need freedom of speech and contrary viewpoints to help you get a more precise understanding of what the truth really is.
3. You are 100% correct. In this unlikely event, you still need people to argue with you, to try to contradict you, and to try to prove you wrong. Why? Because if you never have to defend your points of view, there is a very good chance you don't really understand them, and that you hold them the same way you would hold a prejudice or superstition.

Science, and our understanding of the world advances by such continuous challenges (see also Shermer, 2022; Staddon, 2017; Van de Calseyde and Efendić, 2022). As the erudite theorist Karl Popper (1959) wrote: "In so far as a scientific statement speaks about reality, it must be falsifiable: and in so far as it is not falsifiable, it does not speak about reality."[2]

Popper (1934, 1959) characterized scientific progress as a dialectic.[3] Truth is temporary—only what we believe based on all the evidence available until new evidence arrives to challenge it. New evidence might prompt a new scientific consensus, relegating the old evidence and old consensus—now-apparent errors that seemed true and reasonable at one time, and may well have helped us to progress—to the historical record.

According to Popper, we do not ever know anything for certain, but we can get closer to truth if we allow what is currently accepted as fact to be challenged. It is only through surviving those challenges—outlasting rival ideas, as it were—that propositions grow successive coatings of legitimacy, just as a pearl grows larger in response to continuing irritations.

Popper (1945, 1963) also understood that an "open society" was necessary for the dialectic to function. In societies where some evidence and some researchers are unwelcome or deliberately suppressed, scientific statements remain unfalsifiable. (See Chan, Jones, Jamieson, and Albarracín, 2017; Grove, 2022; Kudesia, 2021; Leslie, 2021; Staddon, 2022b; Stephens, 2017.)

Scholarship can be additive or subtractive. When funders, the media, or other powers bestow an outsized advantage in the open "marketplace of ideas" to certain scholars, they:

- help those scholars to promote and disseminate their work, and
- provide them a platform for misrepresenting the work of others.

Popper's version of scientific progress can work where given a chance. It is not typically given that chance in US education research. There, a wide variety of mechanisms stand ready to suppress unwanted information and stifle debate (APS, 2017; James G. Martin Center, 2021; Randall and Welser, 2018; Taswell et al., 2020).

In a truth-seeking, knowledge-accumulation culture, corrections to the scholarly record should occur frequently, even decades after. Such is a prominent topic of discussion in the hard sciences and psychology (Besançon, Bik, Heathers, and Meyerowitz-Katz, 2022; Calin-Jageman, 2022; Edwards and Roy, 2016; Heathers and Grimes, 2022; von Hippel, 2022). US education research, however, rarely corrects the record, so popular falsehoods may persist permanently. A journal article is considered forever final once just a few handpicked reviewers like it.

Incentives push scholars to produce more. People are so busy trying to produce more, they are unwilling (and may feel annoyed when asked) to fix existing errors. We're all in a race ... to what? To get ahead as individuals and small groups, sell our brands, and thicken our CVs. Not to get things right. (See Hilliard, 2022; Renstrom, 2022; Staddon, 2018.)

In his widely publicized 2021 book, *The Constitution of Knowledge*, journalist Jonathan Rauch (2021a) argues that a Popperian open marketplace of ideas generally benefits knowledge—people will know more where information is free to be expressed—but it is not sufficient for progress. Free speech, for example, can be used in intolerant ways, to misrepresent rival researchers and evidence or to stifle, threaten, or demean dissenters.

A truly open society must not only allow challenges to prevailing orthodoxies but seek them out, promote them, and protect them, lest they be forever stifled. (See also Nossel, 2020; Teles, 2021.) As Carl Sagan (1987) put it:

> You all know ... what these rules are. ... arguments from authority have little weight. ... contentions have to be demonstrable. ... experiments must be repeatable. ... vigorous substantive debate is encouraged and is considered the lifeblood of science. ... serious critical thinking and skepticism addressed to new and even old claims is not just permissible, but is encouraged, is desirable, is the lifeblood of science. There is a creative tension between openness to new ideas and rigorous skeptical scrutiny.

Just as with any consumer goods market, however, an unregulated market for ideas naturally tends toward concentration. An unregulated monopoly (or duopoly in US education's case) restricts entry to competitors, stifles innovation, purchases political favors, and raises prices and lowers quality to what the market will bear. Indeed, that aptly describes US education research and policy in its current state; it has congealed into a duopoly of domineering groups who insist that any considered policy information must emanate from or progress through them.

To overcome the inadequacy of the open marketplace of ideas, Rauch insists that there must be some way for alternative information to be considered, whether the dominant information brokers like it or not. In his words

(2021b), "Defending the truth against its many attackers is not easy. We need shared values and rules and institutions." (See also Lukianoff and Strossen, 2022c; Sagan, 1987; Teles, 2021.)

His preferred "reality-based community" requires (Rauch, 2021b, p. 4):

"The fallibilist rule: No one gets the final say."[4]

"The empirical rule: No one has personal authority."[5]

As neither rule even remotely describes elite behavior in US education research and policy, one may safely surmise the absence of a "reality-based community." Indeed, Rauch describes virtually the opposite of US education policy's current culture, where elites usually assume the "final say" in matters based on "personal authority."[6]

How US Education Scholarship Works

Earlier in my career, I managed a project at the US General Accounting Office (1993).[7] It was extraordinary both in its scale, scope, and quality. The GAO (and, thus, the American taxpayer) invested much money and effort to ensure its quality, but none to publicizing it later. GAO policy at the time was to conduct research studies for its one and only client—the US Congress. Once a study was reported to Congress—simultaneous with the publication of a summary report—the GAO's job was done. Zero dollars were spent on marketing.

In the ensuing years, other studies were conducted on the same topic that were orders of magnitude smaller in investment, scale, and quality, but heavily promoted (e.g., Beatty, 2008; Chingos, 2012; Harris and Taylor, 2008; Harris, Taylor, Levine, Ingle, and McDonald, 2008; Hoxby, 2002; Monk, 1995; Picus, 1994, 1996; Picus and Trailli, 1998; Picus, Adamson, Montague, and Owens, 2010; Stecher and Klein, 1997). Several scholars took advantage of their publicity platforms to either dismiss or grossly misrepresent the GAO study and elevate their own studies in comparison.

Some might blame "publish or perish" culture for this behavior. So, it may be, but only in part. After all, the individuals involved possessed free will. More important to my mind, their opportunistic behavior exposed three more frightening lessons:

- they got away with it, almost effortlessly;
- they faced no adverse consequences; and
- to the contrary, some were well rewarded.

Over two decades of dishonest GAO study attacks and dismissals, I was granted but one opportunity to directly defend it, in the back pages of an education finance journal (Phelps, 1996a; Monk, 1996). That seems to have stopped continued misrepresentations from the one person involved in that one case, but others continued apace. (For stories of similar editorial frustrations, see Besançon, Bik, Heathers, and Meyerowitz-Katz, 2022; Calin-Jageman, 2022; Davis, 2022; Esposito, 2017; Hilgard, 2021; Morris-Suzuki, 2022; Taswell et al., 2020; Tourish, 2019; Williams, S., 2021.)

Anyone thoroughly surveying the research literature on the topic today might find the GAO report itself and several papers I built off it. But they would find more publications from more credentialed scholars at prestigious institutions denigrating it, either directly or indirectly, via claims that any research on the topic prior to theirs either did not exist or was inferior. Anyone believing that scientific consensus is possible in US education research would surmise that the dishonest misrepresentations must be correct as they are more numerous (Phelps, 2015e).

I write in past tense, but perhaps I shouldn't. The many misrepresentations of the GAO report remain available at the click of a mouse. They were wrong twenty-five, ten, and five years ago. They remain wrong today. Those responsible could correct the record now in the electronic versions of their publications or add errata statements. In a truth-telling, knowledge-accumulation culture they would (Kleinert and Wager, 2011; Taswell et al., 2020).

After several years of Sisyphean struggle defending the GAO study, I decided that straightforward scholarship in US education research was pointless (Phelps, 2019b).[8]

I also sympathize with complaints of too much research, more than can be absorbed or effectively considered (Anonymous Academic, 2017; Altbach and de Wit, 2018; Bauerlein et al., 2010; Biswas and Kirchherr, 2015; Blaine, Brunnhuber, and Lund, 2021; Eveleth, 2014; Sanders, 2021; Vedder, 2018;). According to Ware and Mabe (2012, p. 5):

> There were about 28,100 active scholarly peer-reviewed journals in mid 2012, collectively publishing about 1.8–1.9 million articles a year. The number of articles published each year and the number of journals have both grown steadily for over two centuries, by about 3% and 3.5% per year respectively. The reason is the equally persistent growth in the number of researchers, which has also grown at about 3% per year and now stands at between 6 and 9 million, depending on definition.

In the abstract of his article, "Plea to Publish Less," Navinder Singh (2022) wrote,

Recent research (Fortunato et al. 2018) has shown ... the 19th and the first half of the 20th century saw major scientific discoveries. But from the second half of the 20th century, the number of publications far exceeds the number of impactful discoveries. Does an exponentially growing number of publications indicate an element of pathological research? Pressure to publish a large number of papers has led to the phenomena of overproduction, unnecessary fragmentations, overselling, predatory journals (pay and publish), clever plagiarism, and deliberate obfuscation of scientific results so as to sell and oversell.

Suppose a reduction in scholarly output were to occur. The social ideal would retain that of the highest quality and accuracy and dispose of the rest. But who decides which is highest quality? In the past few decades, well-organized groups of educationists, economists, and political scientists have repeatedly boasted that their education research is the highest quality and declared the rest dispensable, not even worth considering.

To be found among their designated detritus: over a century's and a world's worth of education research conducted by psychologists, program evaluators, and government agencies, including the military.

In US education policy research, unless one has ample resources to defend and promote it, one's work is probably destined for obscurity, and certainly so if it runs counter to prevailing preferences or treads on the presumed territorial domain of those in power (Levitt, 2014). Quality of work is irrelevant. It is simply not true that the best research and the best ideas always win out. In most cases in US education research, they don't stand a chance.

It is not too unlike a criminal gang environment, where one cannot protect oneself from gang predation except by belonging to one (Afonso, 2013; Perry, 2015). There are no police and no courts. For the independent scholar, there exist few opportunities to defend one's work from others' misrepresentations. Meanwhile, a metastasized mass of incentives leads ethically flexible scholars to exaggerate their own contributions while belittling others'. In this environment, whomever has more access to more information dissemination channels always wins. As Oransky and Marcus (2017) put it:

> They're not the kind of gangs that smuggle drugs and murder people. But people looking closely at the scientific literature have discovered that a small number of scientists are part of a different kind of cartel—ones that band together to reference each other's work, gaming the citation system to make their studies appear to be more important and worthy of attention.

Oransky and Marcus know best the "hard" sciences, where scholarly gangs may indeed be "small in number." In US education policy research, such groups pretty much run things, controlling or influencing virtually all the information channels that matter.[9]

Instead of producing more ineffectual scholarly research, then, I have devoted myself to countering the pervasive information suppression in US education research and policy—to protecting endangered theses and challenging those who endanger them.

On my own time, I assembled a long list of contact information for scholars and organizations that could provide viewpoint diversity for researchers and journalists. I contacted scholars who claimed a lack of research to inform them of relevant research that they had missed (either accidentally or deliberately). For two decades, I continually published bibliographies of research on topics that some educationists claimed had none.[10] (See, for example, Phelps, 2003, 2005c, 2005d, 2007, 2008/2009a, chapter 3.)

Reacting to gross misrepresentations—from "both sides"—of the research literature on the effects of educational testing I managed the publication of two book compilations, with chapters written by some of the world's foremost, genuine authorities on the topic (Phelps, 2005b, 2008/2009a). The latter was published by, arguably, the world's premier authority on cognitive testing, the American Psychological Association (APA). Later, I conducted a meta-analysis (2012b) and meta-regression (2019c) on the topic after reading over three thousand relevant studies.

To little noticeable effect. US journalists ignored all of it and continue to promote celebrity scholars' single studies as definitive, along with their "no previous research" claims (Beresini, 2015; Oransky, 2015, Oransky and Marcus, 2016).

My first lesson in trying to raise a journalist's awareness of the wider research literature occurred during the 2000 presidential election campaign. The press was all over the testing issue, close to uniformly condemning standardized testing in general, and the testing program in the state of Texas in particular. (Candidate George W. Bush had been governor of Texas.) Every week seemed to release a new anti-testing book written by an activist or education professor.

To help balance coverage of the topic, I sent some policy-relevant and time-sensitive research to a nationally known advocacy organization to use as it saw fit, but then heard nothing from them for weeks. I wrote to inquire what had happened to what I sent. It was an innocent question; I wanted to know if I should bother communicating with them in the future.

I received a reply from a report author. He wrote that he had been a senior editor at a national education news publication (*Education Week*) and had inquired about me at both his current organization and among his colleagues at his former news publication. No one at either place had heard of me. Ergo, anything I sent them was not worth wasting any of their time on. What I had sent them didn't matter because I didn't matter.

The following two decades would reveal many more occasions of elite US education journalists dismissing information from those they considered beneath their lofty station, and their concurrent infatuation with celebrity scholars.

Even the Republican Party education policy advisors, ostensibly predisposed to favor testing, ignored the reference materials I and others provided. They, too, ignored a century's worth of research in psychology, program evaluation, and the military—and joined the anti-testing educationists in claiming "no previous research."

Other like-minded independent researchers and activists and I then developed the eclectic online journal, the *Nonpartisan Education Review*, now in its eighteenth year.[11] It is a place for the truly independent who do not fit, and do not wish to fit, into the mold of one of the prevailing policy research cliques. To stay independent, however, we take no money from vested interests and operate on a shoestring, doing all the work ourselves.

It shows. Our website is neither fancy nor kept up to date with the latest software. We have no money for public relations and press releases and produce no panel discussions or conferences with complimentary coffee and snacks. Over eighteen years and over a hundred publications, no journalist has ever referenced any of it to my knowledge.

I cannot speak for the others who have supported our effort. For my part, I cannot think of anything more essential to do, despite the frustrations. Which is why I continue despite being "canceled" by the only two groups in education policy research many journalists and policymakers pay attention to, and despite their decades-long character assassinations (Rauch, 2020; Vogels et al., 2021; Wood, 2020).

It is sometimes said that university professors and other scholars, such as those at think tanks, give up lot to work in a lower-paid profession (Bright, 2021, p. 118). But that assumes that they could have, or would have wanted to, become rich just because they happened to be smart. It takes more than just smarts to get rich. Besides, some scholars do get rich.

But getting rich is not everyone's goal. For some it is being considered the smartest, for others, being the most influential or getting the most attention (Fox, 2016a; Frank, 1998, 1999; Labaree, 2021). Not everyone can be considered the smartest or most influential, though, and some are willing to fight for it more than others. In fields where ethical standards are ambiguous, unenforced, or trumped by ideology, the more ambitious willing to cut ethical corners will always win.

Sure, there remain many scholars, probably most, primarily motivated by improving everyone's lot and making the world a better place. But, these days, to stand out from the crowd, one must actively promote one's "brand," belong to a mutual promotion group, and fetch enough funds to do both to noticeable

effect (Green, 2019; Hilton, 2022; Lawrence, P. A., 2003, 2007; Levitt, 2014; Rubin, 2014).

Take off the rose-colored glasses with which many of us have viewed scholars—say, teddy bear–like Albert Einstein or funny Richard Feynman—and consider what is generally the case in US education research. It is not pretty. Comparatively, the "hard" sciences may still be somewhat successful at holding off the barbarian hordes attempting to subvert all scholarship to selfish ends; at least, some of them are trying.

The same cannot be said for most of the "social" sciences. And US education research, the focus of this book, long ago succumbed to barbarian conquest. Its knowledge production is less like Plato's Academy and more like *Survivor*, complete with tribes, ostracism, backbiting, betrayals, a few winners, and many losers.

NOTES

1. Lukianoff, of the Foundation for Individual Rights in Education (FIRE); Strossen, formerly of the American Civil Liberties Union (ACLU).

2. "Falsifiable" may have been a poor word choice. In Popper's use, the word means something like "challengeable" or "testable." That is, for a proposition to be considered true, it must be capable of being challenged or tested through normal scientific processes, such as an experiment. Sleigh (2021) takes Popper to task, essentially, for what may be a poor word choice by blaming him for the behavior of scientific nihilists and moral relativists who assert "In order to know if a theory could be true, there must be a way to prove it to be false" (i.e., there is no universal truth).

3. "Hegel's Dialectics," https://plato.stanford.edu/entries/hegel-dialectics/.

4. "You may claim that a statement is established as knowledge only if it can be debunked, in principle, and only insofar as it withstands attempts to debunk it. That is, you are entitled to claim that a statement is objectively true only insofar as it is both checkable and has stood up to checking, and not otherwise. In practice, of course, determining whether a particular statement stands up to checking is sometimes hard, and we have to argue about it. But what counts is the way the rule directs us to behave: You must assume your own and everyone else's fallibility and you must hunt for your own and others' errors, even if you are confident you are right. Otherwise, you are not reality-based."

5. "You may claim that a statement has been established as knowledge only insofar as the method used to check it gives the same result regardless of the identity of the checker, and regardless of the source of the statement. Whatever you do to check a proposition must be something that anyone can do, at least in principle, and get the same result. Also, no one proposing a hypothesis gets a free pass simply because of who she is or what group she belongs to. Who you are does not count; the rules apply to everybody and persons are interchangeable. If your method is valid only for you or your affinity group or people who believe as you do, then you are not reality-based."

6. With the exception of managed and contrived debates held within the confines of otherwise exclusive, censorial groups.

7. The General Accounting Office is now called the Government Accountability Office, maintaining the same acronym.

8. Had I been working as faculty, my university would have incentivized me to continue treading a typical scholarly path, publishing as many studies as I could, thus adding to society's ever-expanding mountain of sometimes brilliant but ultimately ineffectual research. I wasn't working in academe, though, and so felt little compulsion to spend time producing more work that would be ignored, suppressed, or misrepresented by the profession's information gatekeepers.

9. C. Thi Nguyen (2018) distinguishes "epistemic bubbles" and "echo chambers," and warns against inadvertently merging the two. US education research culture itself, however, often merges them:

> But there are two very different phenomena at play here, each of which subvert the flow of information in very distinct ways. . . . Both are social structures that systematically exclude sources of information. Both exaggerate their members' confidence in their beliefs. But they work in entirely different ways, and they require very different modes of intervention. An epistemic bubble is when you don't hear people from the other side. An echo chamber is what happens when you don't trust people from the other side. . . .
>
> In epistemic bubbles, other voices are not heard; in echo chambers, other voices are actively undermined. The way to break an echo chamber is not to wave "the facts" in the faces of its members. It is to attack the echo chamber at its root and repair that broken trust. (Nguyen, 2018)

10. For many years, I maintained and updated a web page titled "Organizations and Individuals to Contact for Testing Information." Eighteen pages and hundreds of hyperlinks. I tried to get journalists to pay attention, without any success of which I am aware.

11. https://nonpartisaneducation.org.

Introduction

The Cartel Alliance and Honest Terminology

US education policy is a "morass," according to the late Myron Lieberman (2007), because the public and policymakers are thoroughly misinformed on policy issues, unfamiliar with the full range of policy-relevant knowledge. Policymakers then set misinformed policy, typically skewed in favor of the vested interests who have managed to focus their attention.

The vested interests have money and organization, and the power and influence they accrue. The many more who are unaffiliated and unorganized—but independent—lack both.

Education insiders can bristle when encountering the term "education establishment." It is, perhaps, overused to the point where it has become for some an indiscriminate pejorative. It is not intended to be so here. Its more general meaning describes organizational configurations across a variety of fields. Here's a helpful definition from William Kristol (2022):

> A collection of people, institutions, and ideas which are not all powerful but are dominant to the point of being all-encompassing. The establishment can be, every once in a while, circumvented or leapfrogged. But it cannot be successfully opposed.

Kristol described how certain "collections of people, institutions, and ideas" can both dominate a political party and from time to time be replaced.[1]

By now, it should be obvious to all that there exist two US education establishments (or, *cartels*): the traditional, stand-pat, leave-us-alone collection of education school professors, teachers' unions, and administrator associations; and the group of self-titled "education reformers"—a collection of think tanks, economists and political scientists, charter school chains, wealthy foundations, and Republican and "Democrats for Education Reform" politicos.

The Education Establishment Cartel

A century ago, policy-relevant education research was conducted largely by academic psychologists and program evaluators working in state or school district "research bureaus." Teacher training was separate, managed in state and local "normal" schools on the apprenticeship model. This separation gradually diminished in mid- to late-twentieth-century America, as teacher training institutions became their own colleges and then universities,[2] and other universities established their own graduate schools of education. Today's teacher colleges not only train new teachers, most award master's and doctoral degrees in education, and conduct most US education research, for better or worse.

Our country lost much education research independence by combining those research and training functions. Education schools now vest a self-interest in certain research results, particularly on two issues they may legitimately perceive as threats to their autonomy—school choice and (externally administered) standardized testing.

Also, over time, education schools have nurtured an increasingly intolerant ideological dominance of Rousseau-ian egalitarianism and constructivism[3] (Anomaly and Winegard, 2019; Asher, 2018, 2019; Farkus, Johnson, and Duffet, 1997; Levine, 2006, 2007; Stanley, 2001; Stone, 1996; Stone and Clements, 1998; Wilson, N., 2019).

Representing the traditional education establishment most often in these pages is the community of educational testing experts centered on the Center for Research on Education Standards and Student Testing (CRESST), headquartered at UCLA's education school since the early 1980s, but long including other institutional affiliates, such as the Rand Corporation and the education schools at the Universities of Colorado, Southern California, and Pittsburgh.[4] Still other institutions, such as the education schools at Stanford, Harvard, and Arizona State universities have belonged for briefer periods.

For decades, from the 1980s and into the 2000s, CRESST was the only federally funded research center on the topics of educational standards and testing, and the recipient of many millions of taxpayer dollars.

Two themes have dominated CRESST research: (alleged) problems with testing and claims—hundreds of them—that little research existed on testing's effects (Phelps, 2020c).[5] Those themes proved popular among the wider population of education professors and administrators, as evidenced by the frequent election of CRESST principals to leading positions in influential education organizations.[6]

Power begets more power. In time, CRESST principals and allied colleagues captured agenda and content control of several other public- and foundation-funded research organizations, such as the Board on Testing and Assessment

of the National Research Council,[7] the National Academy of Education,[8] the International Academy of Education,[9] the World Bank's Program on Learning Assessment,[10] and the journal *Educational Assessment*.[11] For decades, they have controlled the content of the education policy chapters in NCME's encyclopedic tome, *Educational Assessment* (Ho and Polikoff, forthcoming; Koretz and Hamilton, 2006) and, more recently, in the profession's practice guidelines, the *Standards for Educational and Psychological Testing* (AERA, NCME, and APA, 2014).

The Education Reform Cartel

This second group is most conveniently circumscribed top down by the elite membership of the Koret Task Force on K–12 Education,[12] so-called because it was partly funded by the Koret Foundation[13] while housed at Stanford's Hoover Institution.[14] GOP policymakers tend to put their policy faith in academics, particularly economists.

Stanford University affiliated current or former members have included Eric Hanushek, Caroline Hoxby, Terry Moe, and the late John Chubb. Harvard University affiliated current or former members have included Paul Peterson, Tom Loveless, and (again) Caroline Hoxby. Brookings Institution affiliates have included Tom Loveless (again) and the former director of the US Department of Education's Institute of Education Sciences (IES), Grover "Russ" Whitehurst. Paul Hill of the University of Washington (Ultican, 2020) and Chester "Checker" Finn of the Thomas B. Fordham Foundation[15] rounded out the crew.

In turn, they have in two short decades disseminated a prodigious bounty of their progeny of former students and staff throughout the troposphere of education research and policy.

Like the older education establishment, the education reformers have leveraged their power, organization, and influence to subsume control over most other high-profile education policy venues on the conservative or reform "side of the aisle." Cartel members control agenda and content of education research at most national think tanks, including the Brookings and Hoover Institutions, the Academy of Political and Social Science (APSS), the American Enterprise and Manhattan Institutes, the Program on Education Policy and Governance (PEPG) and the Center for Education Policy Research (CEPR) at Harvard University, and the Center on Reinventing Public Education at the University of Washington (near the Gates Foundations).

In turn, Harvard and Stanford folk established control of the Institute for Education Policy at Johns Hopkins University and the Annenberg Institute for School Reform at Brown University. They control the education agenda and content of groups' many audio and video outlets and publications, as well

as their own popular magazines, *Education Next*, *Education Post*, and *The 74*. They even have their own graduate school: the Department of Education Reform at the University of Arkansas, near the headquarters of the Walton Family Foundation.[16]

To hear some of them tell it, they comprise the totality of education reform expertise.

Their power, however, derives ultimately from the almost complete (if blindly naïve) trust granted them by the vast panoply of national, state, and local conservative and Republican Party–aligned politicians and groups, who erroneously believe that the Reform Cartel works to support their interests. More accurately, the Cartel works diligently to preserve its information monopoly so that it may continue to pursue its own interests.

The Permanent Education Press

Three types of journalists populate the US education beat. First are the local reporters in cities and states who attend school board meetings and interview local superintendents, principals, and teachers, anchoring their reportage in the here and now with individuals their readers and listeners may know as neighbors. Second are the (often young) journalists working at a regional or national outlet who may be assigned to the education beat because more experienced journalists consider it low status and avoid it (Savage 1989). Some of the best, most insightful investigative pieces have come from this group, and it can be frustrating to see such journalists move on to other beats soon after they have demonstrated promise with a breakthrough education story or two (e.g., Dudley, 2016; Layton, 2014).

Third are the journalists of the "Permanent Education Press." They have large regional or national audiences and remain on the education beat for life. That loyalty to education topics should have advantages: they get to know the subject more deeply and, by following it over time, can compare against evolving backgrounds and changing contexts.

Disadvantages? They get stuck in ruts . . . deeply (Feldon, 2007). It is common for Permanent Education Press members to rely on "go-to" sources on topics, thus skewing their coverage toward those sources' particular knowledge base, preferences, and biases, in some cases over decades. Getting comfortable with the familiar over time often means neglecting the unfamiliar—the other sides of stories.

Some in the Permanent Education Press minimize their sourcing effort even more through long-term relationships with go-to *groups*—typically think tanks or research centers—where they can find, all conveniently in one place, alleged experts across some variety of education subtopics, but

who operate interdependently. Moreover, Permanent Education Press members tend to mimic and reinforce each other, habitually relying on the same sources and habitually ignoring others.

Finally, some members of the Permanent Education Press long ago sacrificed any pretense of independence from the monied interests in education policy. Throughout their careers, these journalists collect paychecks from a variety of institutions with clear self-interests: foundations, advocacy groups, research centers, and private companies. Some move freely back and forth between media outlets with varying degrees of independence from their sponsors. A comfortable acceptance of their own mercenary status may help explain why their go-to sources' obvious conflicts of interest are so often left unmentioned in their stories.

The decade of the 2000s saw these three groups—Establishment Cartel, Reform Cartel, and Permanent Education Press—combine forces into a single powerful juggernaut of information dissemination (and suppression): the "Cartel Alliance."

Terminological Rigor

Extrapolating from ample experience, if any members of the Cartel Alliance review this book they will lean heavily on "tone policing" to critique it. The language will be unacceptable, hyperbolic, and full of ad hominem attacks (simply because a person quoted is identified) (Delborne, 2015; Krauss, 2021; Lukianoff and Strossen, 2022b; Phelps, 2019b; Rohrer, 2019).

To establish a wider base of support for some "hyperbolic" terms, such as "dishonesty" and "fraud," independent sources are cited below. US education research and policy is suffused with both, and many who could do something about it instead accept it or join in to reinforce it. (See also Appendix 1, "The Enablers" online, https://educationpolicy.us/Malfunction/App1.pdf.)

A lie can be classified as "blatant" or "bold-faced" when the perpetrator presents, as a fact, information he or she knows to be wrong. But blatant lies are not the most common type of dishonesty in the education policy world, though they certainly exist there as they do in most social circles (Jack, 2017; Pascual-Ezama, Prelec, Muñoz, and Gil-Gómez de Liaño, 2020). Three other types of "intellectual dishonesty" bloat US education policy discourse and through their frequency alone do more damage:

- *Fabrication*: presenting certain information as factual when he or she does not know that it is (i.e., "just making it up" "out of whole cloth")[17]
- *Suppression*: hiding information or steering the public in a self-interested direction and away from information that would be relevant and informative[18]

- *Exaggeration*: liberally applying adjectives and adverbs to embellish positively the work of one's group and negatively the work of others

The products of these behaviors typically exceed the threshold for classification as "misinformation," and belong in the more harmful and intentional category of "disinformation" (APS, 2022; Calo et al., 2021; Jack, 2017; Reeves, 2021; Serwer, 2022). As Charles Blue (2022) puts it:

> Unlike misinformation, which often arises from grassroots opinions and ideas, disinformation is imposed by higher sources and carries an official imprimatur. This is part of its insidious power.

In his *Psyche* article, "The Virtue of Honesty Requires More Than Just Telling the Truth," Christian B. Miller (2021) proposes:

> There is little controversy that honesty is a virtue. It is an excellence of character. It also promotes trust, fosters healthy relationships, strengthens organisations and societies, and prevents harm. . . . Sadly, though, honesty . . . is largely absent from academic research.

Shane Snow (2021), an entrepreneur with feet planted simultaneously in the worlds of entertainment, public relations, and journalism, writes:[19]

> Intellectual Honesty is about having high standards for the truth. . . . It's not just about not lying; it's about stating the truth when you know it, hiding nothing, twisting nothing, leaving nothing out. . . . Intellectual Dishonesty . . . is a sort of blanket term for being dishonest without necessarily straight out lying. It's the failure to apply high standards for truth.

Richard Reeves (2021) brings it on home to the Cartel Alliance in citing Bernard Williams (2002):

> As Williams notes, the authority of academics is rooted in their truthfulness in both these respects: "they take care, and they do not lie." The same can (or at least should) be said of journalists and judges.

Are they picking nits? Are we being overly righteous about common, harmless human tendencies to embellish or evade? Ivan Oransky and Adam Marcus (2016) of *Retraction Watch* summarized the results of a survey conducted several years ago by Bouter, Tijdink, Axelsen, Martinson, and ter Riet (2016):

> Researchers in the Netherlands asked working scientists around the world to rank a list of 60 misbehaviors by their impact on truth, trust in science, how

often they occur, and how preventable those actions might be. They then devised a ranking for these behaviors that combined how often they occur and their impact—a sort of on-base plus slugging average that measures their overall effect on the field.[20]

Not surprisingly, fabrication of data scored the highest for its effect on truth and public trust in science. But those cases are quite rare—and detected cases are, by definition, even rarer. As a result, it didn't even make the top five.

Rather, "our ranking results seem to suggest that selective reporting, selective citing, and flaws in quality assurance and mentoring are the major evils of modern research," the authors wrote in *Research Integrity and Peer Review*.

US education policy research encourages "cherry-picking" evidence and citations, in a serious impediment to the proper functioning of civic institutions, and to be found aplenty within the Cartel Alliance.

As for *fraud*, another behavior common in education policy research, its definition is simple: an attempt to gain something of value by deceiving others (Chen, 2021; Fanelli, 2019).

Is there fraud in scholarly research? In the online science magazine *3 Quarks Daily*, Thomas O'Dwyer (2021) recalls some of the nominations from an informal poll of candidates for modern history's "greatest scientific fraud." Andrew Wakefield's bogus vaccination-causes-autism article probably led to many unnecessary deaths. The infamous early 1900s Piltdown Man hoax may not have killed anyone, but "it took 41 years before the forgery was finally proven in 1953, over which time it led paleontology down many false pathways and time-wasting controversies." (See also Biagioli, 2020; Byrne, J., 2019; Daly, 2019; Eliason, 2020; Fanelli, 2009; Glina, 2012; Lawrence, F., 2022; Ritchie, 2020, 2022; Schoenleber and Buhlinger, 2016.)

Certainly, the United States' Council for Tobacco Research (CTR) deserved its nomination (Eliason, 2020; Glanz et al., 1996; Oreskes and Conway, 2011; Proctor, 2012). O'Dwyer continues:

> From 1954 onwards the CTR was the tool of Big Tobacco's campaign against evidence that cigarettes kill. Clarence Cook Little, its chief scientist, notoriously promoted cigarette-friendly science, securing millions of dollars in cash for compliant researchers. . . . Twenty-seven Nobel laureates took money from Big Tobacco, and every major university was showered with cash.

O'Dwyer also summarizes an article by medical school professor Ferric C. Fang and two co-authors (2012) titled "Misconduct Accounts for the Majority of Retracted Scientific Publications." The authors searched through a biomedical database with over twenty-five million articles and retrieved 2,047 that had been retracted:

A detailed review of all 2,047 biomedical and life-science research articles . . . revealed that only 21.3 percent of retractions were attributable to error. In contrast, 67.4 percent were attributable to misconduct, including fraud or suspected fraud (43.4 percent), duplicate publication (14.2 percent), and plagiarism (9.8 percent). . . . The percentage of scientific articles retracted because of fraud has increased 10-fold since 1975.

Biomedical research devotes far more attention to and demonstrates far more concern for research integrity than does US education research (Gunsalus, Marcus, and Oransky, 2018; Staddon, 2022a). That retractions are few and far between in our education research journals should be cause for concern, not celebration.

NOTES

1. In the US Republican Party, for example, "Reaganism" replaced, wholesale, an earlier configuration of more politically liberal Republicans of the Eisenhower-Nixon-Ford era. Likewise, "Trumpism" replaced Reaganism with populism. Each establishment change left some party members behind; those remaining adapted by abandoning or recanting earlier convictions and adopting new ones.

2. E.g., the state of Illinois' normal school, founded in the mid-nineteenth century, is now called Illinois State University, located in the town of Normal, Illinois.

3. According to Richard Fox (2001), constructivism can be

summarised *en masse*: (1) Learning is an active process. (2) Knowledge is constructed, rather than innate, or passively absorbed. (3) Knowledge is invented not discovered. (4a) All knowledge is personal and idiosyncratic. (4b) All knowledge is socially constructed. (5) Learning is essentially a process of making sense of the world. (6) Effective learning requires meaningful, open-ended, challenging problems for the learner to solve.

4. https://cresst.org.

5. See also: https://nonpartisaneducation.org/Review/Resources/OtherCRESST_BC.htm; https://nonpartisaneducation.org/Review/Resources/DanielKoretz.htm; https://nonpartisaneducation.org/Review/Resources/LauraHamilton.htm.

6. The large American Educational Research Association (AERA), for example, elected CRESST affiliates as president in 1975, 1985, 1987, 1995, 1999, 2002, 2003, 2006, 2008, and 2015. See https://www.aera.net/About-AERA/Who-We-Are/AERA-Past-Presidents.

7. https://sites.nationalacademies.org/DBASSE/BOTA/index.htm.

8. https://naeducation.org/our-members/.

9. https://www.iaoed.org/index.php/about-iae.

10. https://blogs.worldbank.org/team/marguerite-clarke. See also Clarke, 2013.

11. https://www.tandfonline.com/action/journalInformation?show=editorialBoardandjournalCode=heda20.

12. https://www.hoover.org/research-teams/k-12-task-force.

13. Other funders include the Lynde and Harry Bradley Foundation, Mrs. Edmund W. Littlefield, Bernard Lee Schwartz Foundation, Inc., Tad and Dianne Taube, and the Taube Family Foundation. See: https://www.hoover.org/research-teams/k-12-task-force.

14. https://cepa.stanford.edu/who-we-are.

15. Originally intended to fund charitable works in Dayton, Ohio, until management was subsumed under curious circumstances by two board members named Finn—the father and grandfather of one Chester A. "Checker" Finn Jr. (Phelps, 2018c).

16. https://edre.uark.edu/.

17. The Department of Health and Human Services' Public Health Service Policies on Research Misconduct 42 CFR 93 includes this: "Research misconduct is defined as fabrication, falsification and plagiarism" (NIH, 2022).

18. To be complete, some commentators classify these as lies, such as "lies of omission," or as fallacies, such as the "fallacy of suppressed evidence" (Carroll, 2015).

19. I find his blog a useful source because it addresses political tactics, types of honesty and dishonesty, and logical fallacies, all in one place.

20. For those unfamiliar with the American sport of baseball, the authors are referring to a metric that combines the frequency of "hits" with their magnitude. Hits that get more "bases" count for more than hits that get only one base.

Chapter 1

The View from 2001

> "It's easier to fool people than to convince them that they have been fooled."
>
> —Mark Twain

Is US education better off than it was twenty years ago? Have the past couple of decades of national education policies made our schools better? Has education research improved and become more useful in recent years?

Emphatic affirmatives rebound from those who advised US politicians on education policy throughout the period. To hear them tell it, US education research and policy are now vastly improved. Where once were darkness and ignorance, now are light and wisdom. One of those scholars described the transformation to a US congressional committee in 2011 (Hoxby):

> Americans can point to so little educational improvement over the past four decades that we, as a nation, have begun to believe that very little improvement is possible. Contrast this with medicine or almost any other field of applied knowledge. If we were offered the choice between a medical procedure that relied on today's knowledge versus the knowledge of 1970, we would—all of us—choose today's. We would probably be ambivalent about today's schools versus the schools of 1970.
>
> The difference between education and medicine is not that improvement is impossible in education but possible in medicine. . . . The difference is that education has not, until recently, benefitted from rigorous, scientific research.

The presidential election in 2000 bore special significance for US education policy. Unlike in most previous presidential elections, education entered front and center on the campaign stage and in news coverage. The No Child Left Behind (NCLB) Act, then passed at the end of 2001. The Institute of Education Sciences (IES) was formed in 2003.

Economists got involved in a big way in policy development in subfields largely new to them, such as testing and measurement and curriculum and instruction. A small, select group of scholars was effectively granted a two-decades-long information dissemination monopoly to channel their preferred version of education policy truth.

They represented a new type of education researcher: more Republican than Democrat, more economist than psychologist, more public policy school than education school, more quantitative than qualitative, more academic than practitioner, and primarily housed at Harvard, Stanford, the University of Washington (near the Gates Foundation), the University of Arkansas (near the Walton foundations), a smattering of other universities, and almost all the familiar national think tanks.

They were, and continue as, the education policy brain trust for the Republican Party, for the "Democrats for Education Reform" wing of the other major party,[1] and for many mostly politically conservative organizations. To plug one large hole in their academic background, they incorporated a complementary group of highly placed education establishment specialists in standards, testing, and measurement.

This alliance of scholars captured all the country's highest level and most generously funded sinecures—the education chairs at all the think tanks that mattered, memberships on the relevant government advisory committees and the most prestigious education research honorary societies, tenured chairs at a gaggle of the country's most prestigious universities, and a surfeit of government and foundation funding on education policy topics.

The "Matthew Effect" derives its name from New Testament text in the Gospel of Matthew about those who have more getting more—the rich get richer.[2] The scholars in this new alliance did not just get more, though; they got everything. Like a Tambura or Krakatoa blackening the policy sky worldwide, they blocked any other light from peeking through and competing with theirs (Lauer et al., 2017; Merton, 1968).

Cartel Alliance members had the education policy stage to themselves for twenty years, during twelve years of Republican administrations and seven years of an accommodating US Department of Education under the sympathetic direction of President Obama's friend and a Democrat for education reform, Arne Duncan (Stotsky, 2019a). As Republican president George W. Bush's secretary of education Margaret Spellings said of Democratic president Barack Obama's education policy, "He is saying a lot of things that sound all too familiar to me. I want to sing right along" (*Education Week*, 2009; McGuinn, 2016, pp. 2–3).

With Joseph Biden's election as president, and his education staff appointments and professed priorities, however, some observers watched for reversion to a more traditional federal policy agenda favoring the education

establishment. Simultaneously, the real and perceived failures of the reformers' programs, such as NCLB and Common Core, have left those who naively thought the programs would work dispirited.

Some education insiders have recently urged sympathetic policymakers to seize the moment and reverse policy direction, particularly on the two topics considered most threatening—school choice and standardized testing (e.g., Bryant, 2021; New Meridian, 2022). With education establishment types apparently back in charge, now may be the most opportune time for them to throttle back federal support for school choice programs and to end or, at least, substantially reduce federal standardized testing requirements.

Just as the early 2000s was a hinge point in the evolution of US education policy so, too, could be the early 2020s. If so, it is worth asking now, how well did the Cartel Alliance do the past twenty years? Have they left our country's education system better off than it was before? They insist, yes.

This book explains how they're wrong.

Education Policy Formation in Action

In the early 2000s, George W. Bush emerged the victor of a close and controversial presidential contest. His campaign had focused on education policy in general and testing in particular, probably the first time in US history the latter topic had received such attention. True to his word, immediately after assuming office he began designing education programs.

We know the result: No Child Left Behind and the Institute for Education Sciences—large disruptions to the prevailing equilibrium in US education policy, particularly in the relationship between the federal, state, and local governments.

There was also the nontrivial matter of the NCLB Act's testing and accountability provisions. The federal government added the responsibility of another testing program to the agendas of fifty state education agencies, tens of thousands of school districts, and a quarter million public (and public charter) schools.

Huge impacts to come, and along the way, the president needed policy advice.

The United States is the wealthiest and, arguably, the most technologically advanced nation on earth. One might suppose that policy formation at the highest governmental level would reflect that in its level of sophistication, thoroughness, and efficiency.

The primary decision makers, of course, were elected and appointed officials of the Republican Party persuasion, as the nation had elected one of theirs as president. He, in turn, appointed US Education Department (ED) leaders. All consulted their regular education policy crew—who served on

retainer. The Republican version of education policy advisor skews heavily toward academic economists—working both in academia and think tanks—and current and former congressional staff.

Given the massive and far-reaching effects of, first, NCLB, second, the IES and, several years later, the Common Core initiative, one would think that no expense would be spared, no effort restrained, no stone unturned to get the policies right.

Instead, the Republicans' regular policy guys—who knew little about educational testing, standards, curriculum, or instruction—asked some other guys whom they thought might know something, who then asked some guys they knew, and the regular policy guys ended up believing a small group of people with credentials that implied they knew a lot. That group told the GOP's policy wonks that no relevant knowledge existed, or none that was any good anyway. They should start an education research literature on these topics from scratch.

For all effective purposes, that concluded the search for policy-relevant research evidence. Believing that there was no useful information in the research literature to guide them, the president and Congress adapted a testing program from the president's home state of Texas for the country. Why not? Wasn't one testing program just the same as any other?

Thus, the oddly idiosyncratic Texas program became federal policy. Texas's was more a weak school monitoring program than a genuine education accountability program. Most other states had more sensible and effective programs, most of which have now been discontinued.[3]

This grand federal imposition was initiated by the self-described party of smaller government (Pullman, 2017; Robbins, 2016).

Because the Republican policy advisors knew so little about educational testing, standards, curriculum, or instruction, they were forced to either rely on scholars outside their circle or dig deep into the research literatures themselves, which would take time. Being in a hurry, they chose the former option.

As they were experts in research, including presumably the methods of statistical sampling, one might have supposed the Republican policy advisors would have carefully surveyed a representative sample of scholars and scholarship. They did not.

Instead, they threw their lot in with a small homogenous group of education professors affiliated with the Center for Educational Standards and Student Testing (CRESST),[4] for two decades prior the only federally funded research center on those topics.[5] CRESST members were certainly highly credentialed; indeed, they were arguably the most highly credentialed group of scholars in their field, at least partly as a result of twenty years of taxpayer largesse.

Perhaps in part because of their safe and privileged positions—tenured professors, with large and dependable federal funding at their disposal under minimal oversight—most CRESST members had also developed a peculiar habit, the "dismissive review." They dismissed *en masse* research conducted by thousands outside their circle. Dismissals took the form of declarations that previous research on a topic did not exist or that it was too poor in quality to be worth considering. Typically, the other research and researchers were not identified, giving the public no help in finding them (Phelps, 2021a, 2021b).

Meanwhile, CRESST members and close allies generously praised and frequently referenced each other's work, thus forming a "citation cartel" (Bogazzi, 2017; Davis, 2012; *Enago Academy*, 2018; Fister, 2017; Oransky and Marcus, 2017).

Censorial behavior now pervades the activities of both groups, the GOP advisors and CRESST. They hide information they do not like. "All the research" tends to be the relatively small proportion done within their group. Most of those who might provide contrary information are ignored, dismissed, or ostracized. Those too famous to be simply ignored may be insulted and demonized (Delborne, 2015; Jilani, 2018).

Their declarations of a void in humanity's pile of accumulated knowledge should have struck genuine experts as absurd. Those familiar with the relevant research literatures could have been found in psychology departments, in government agencies, in the heterodox margins of education school faculty, in firms doing the actual work, or working as reference librarians. The policy guys either didn't talk to them or didn't believe any they talked to.

The research void myth overlooked consideration of these facts:

- The social science field with, by far, the longest and deepest history in education research is psychology.
- Psychologists invented standardized testing and remain the most knowledgeable of its development, implementation, and effects.
- Psychologists had been conducting, with great frequency, (mostly experimental) research on educational testing, standards, and accountability for over a century.
- Program evaluators working in or for local and state education agencies had been conducting, with some frequency as required by state "sunshine laws" and "sunset provisions," research on educational testing, standards, and accountability.

Nonetheless, the GOP advisors chose to believe the CRESST research literature deniers and apparently, most still believe twenty years on. GOP advisor claims continue of their being the first and only to research certain topics that had, in fact, been studied for a long time. Some now label their

own "first" studies conducted in the past couple of decades as "early" studies in a new, "more rigorous" research literature they claim to be building from scratch.

One may be inclined to grant the GOP advisors some leeway for being naïve and trusting. But more well-rounded researchers would have been more skeptical. Besides, the GOP advisors seemed all too eager to believe, perhaps because pretending that no previous research existed dramatically shortened their paths to claim expertise: if no previous research exists on a topic, then one's study comprises all there is to know, and one is the world's foremost expert.

Meanwhile, a vast multitude of relevant knowledge was not considered in the federal government's policy formation (Phelps, 2012a, 2012b).[6]

One may recall the testimony before the US Congress quoted earlier. To refresh the mood, here's another advocating before Congress (in 2013) renewal of the original legislation, the Education Sciences Reform Act (ESRA), that had created the Institute for Education Sciences (IES) earlier in 2003:

> Until ESRA and the creation of IES, education research was allowed to function at standards that would never pass muster with public health, employment and training, or welfare policy, let alone with medicine or agriculture. (Kemple, 2013, p. 1)

The speaker stews all education research in the same pot, not distinguishing, for example, the propaganda emanating from mainstream US education professors from that conducted among psychologists, from outside the United States, from the honest, heterodox, and often persecuted scholars working inside US education schools, and so on. Continuing,

> the paucity of good evidence in education, and the inability to effectively communicate lessons from the little scientific evidence that did exist, left us with a legacy of reinventing the wheel and chasing fads rather than building a reliable and useful track record of what worked, what did not work, for whom and under what circumstances. (Kemple, 2013, p. 1)

Ironically, the new researchers would spend much of their time over the past two decades to "reinventing the wheel and chasing fads" (e.g., fads such as value-added measurement [VAM], socio-emotional learning, and "deep learning") rather than building on the accumulated reliable and useful track record to be found largely in the work of psychologists and program evaluators.

US education research has borne an "awful reputation" in some circles for a long time (Kaestle, 1993; Labaree, 1996; Levine, 2007). As with the congressional testimony quoted earlier, the blanket dismissal of all education

research conducted earlier or outside of their group appealed to that negative stereotype. Like many stereotypes, there lies some truth within it, but also misleading generalization.

Mainstream US education research should be read skeptically. But poor quality is only part of its problem. Bias constitutes a much larger part, emanating from both ideology and group self-interest. Biased education research can appear obviously of poor quality, or it can appear to be of satisfactory quality but dishonest, with fudged numbers, false factual claims, and the surreptitious substitution of the definitions of terms hidden underneath reasonable sounding text (Phelps, 1994, 1996b, 1998, 2003, 2005f, 2015a, 2015g, 2016e).

It requires time and patience, and a deep grounding in the subject matter, to recognize the falsehoods in cleverly disguised dishonest research.

"Top" yet gullible economics and political science academics were taken in by biased education research, even while claiming to dismiss all of it. The "no previous research" grift is a case in point. The previously quoted researcher claimed in the same 2013 testimony that

> since its inception, IES has funded and released findings from 90 studies that meet the widely agreed-upon "gold standard" for research, the randomized controlled trial. That's 89 more such studies than all of IES's predecessors combined. (Kemple, 2013, p. 1)

Perhaps this statement could be made literally true by narrowly defining "IES predecessor," but the more general point is preposterous. This new group of Cartel Alliance researchers did not initiate randomized controlled trials in education research. Unlike economics and political science, psychology has long been an experimental science. Thousands of randomized experiments in education had been conducted by psychologists, education practitioners, and program evaluators going back a century (e.g., Phelps, 2011a, 2012b, 2019c).[7]

Yet, at the same 2013 congressional hearing, the chair of the IES's oversight board, the National Board for Education Sciences, and dean of the Harvard Graduate School of Education congratulated their efforts at "pushing the field" to adopt new and better methods:

> One concrete example of this has been the push for randomized controlled trials (RCTs), which are considered the gold-standard of research and often used in the field of medicine. Prior to IES's leadership, RCTs were rarely conducted in education and not valued among many researchers. (Long, 2013, p. 3)

Meanwhile, in his own self-congratulatory paean to the importance of high-quality research and his group's alleged unique possession of same, the

founding director of the Institute of Education Sciences (IES), listed "things we know now about education that we did not know 15 years ago," thanks to his group's efforts (Whitehurst, 2011).

Included were the "spacing effect," which had been studied frequently by psychologists from the late nineteenth century through the 1980s (Dempster, 1988; Weinstein, 2018) and the "testing effect"—the learning advantage of testing over restudy—which was described by Aristotle in ancient Greece (Hammond, 1902) and by Edward Thorndike in the early twentieth century— "The active recall of a fact from within us is, as a rule, better than its impressions without" (Larsen and Butler, 2013).

Looking online in IES's own research library, the Education Resources Information Center (ERIC), for sources on the effects of testing retrieves 2,675 pre-2002 documents.[8]

According to psychologists Larsen and Butler (2013):

> The first empirical demonstration of the mnemonic benefits of testing in a controlled experiment occurred just over a hundred years ago (Abbott 1909). Over the next 30 years, educational psychologists became interested in applying this phenomenon to the classroom. (Gates 1917; Jones 1923–1924; Spitzer 1939)

Larsen and Butler would go on to describe other experimental studies conducted over the following several decades (see also Roediger, Putnam, and Smith, 2011, pp. 2–3).

While the economics and political science GOP advisors condemned as worthless all previous education research, they blithely accepted the dismissive claims about the educational standards and testing research literature from the one small group of education researchers they welcomed into their fold—those from CRESST—prompting some questions:

- The entire professional group of education researchers does work so awful it is unworthy of attention, except for a particular small subgroup whose work in that subfield is the best in the world?
- Almost all education research is terrible, but that conducted on the topics the economists and political scientists did not understand well enough to judge is totally trustworthy?
- No education research conducted by education school professors should be trusted, except for that which was conducted in the crucially most topical subjects for 2001: educational standards, testing, and accountability?
- The work of an entire professional group is execrable, except for that work from those who rose to the top of one pile, which should be accepted without question?

Apparently, these glaring ironies escaped the GOP policy advisors' notice. The below list summarizes the long-term trends in testing research and policy.

Capsule Summary: History of Testing Research and Policy in the United States

(1890–1950) Psychologists develop and study educational testing
(1920–1980) Education schools diverge from origins in psychology
(1970+) Some ed school professors suppress positive research on testing
(2000–2003) Ed testing becomes high profile issue; economists interested
(2001+) Economists believe ed school professors; ignore psych research

Neither in the early 2000s nor since would the GOP policy wonks consult the vast research literature on educational testing, standards, and accountability amassed by psychologists, program evaluators, the military, or hundreds of other countries. They would later claim as nonexistent equally large research literatures in curriculum and instruction.

This theme would play out again and again. In a perceived policy void, the policy advisors felt free to suggest public policies based on the relatively paltry collection of recent research within the Cartel Alliance. Whether out of ignorance, naivete, or disinterest, the politicians—the policy*makers*—would go along, without diversifying perspectives or evidence. No second opinions for them.

This blind trust in an extraordinarily small and homogeneous group contrasts sharply with what could have happened with a truth-seeking information retrieval process that respected Mill's and Popper's falsification challenges and Rauch's fallibilist and empirical rules. (See also *The Economist*, 2022.)

The Missing Memo

The first assignment in the first course in the Harvard Kennedy School's master's in public policy program used to teach students how to write a memo properly. Assume one works on the staff of an elected official or other policymaker. A memo should be to the point, but still thorough. It should summarize all available evidence and present all possible choices. Preferred options may be indicated, but only with justification.

Limiting a decision-maker to consideration of only one's preferred options or, even worse, only one's preferred evidence, not only insults their intelligence, but also impedes their flexibility and sets them up for embarrassment later when an ill-informed policy fails, or they are informed, likely by their political rivals, of the options they hadn't considered. Indeed, misinforming a policymaker can induce not just suboptimal policy, but widespread harm.

Yet, for over two decades, the education policy advisors that key policymakers at the federal level—in both the executive and legislative branches—chose to trust have restricted the information provided to a trickle of the available flow. Ignorance, arrogance, and ambition may have each played a role. The trickle of information allowed through just happened to benefit the advisors' careers. Ironically, some of these information-stifling advisors now teach at the Harvard Kennedy School.

Ultimately, the structure of the federal education policy advisement system (if it can even be called a system) circa 2001 relied on too few advisors and, even among them, too little *independent* advice. US federal education policy is poor in large part because federal education policymakers are poorly informed. A wider diversity of viewpoints and evidence was and is desperately needed (APS, 2017, 2021c; Graf, 2014; Güllich, Macnamara, and Hambrick, 2021; Kauffman and Konold, 2007; Teles, 2021).

On the Republican Party side, policymakers assume that their advisors are *their* advisors—the select few they can trust in an otherwise hostile left-leaning education research world. Unfortunately, this trust long ago devolved into unquestioning complacency.

Superficially, the advisors' credentials seem legitimate—faculty appointments at Harvard, Stanford, and other prestigious universities, membership on prestigious national and international advisory committees, and frequent appearances in the media as sources of expertise. Their status exhibits plenty of "face validity."

Look closer, however, and other aspects of their status should have seemed a bit off (Burnett, 2016; Cuban, 2010; Dunning, 2011; Dunlovsky and Rawson, 2012; Fazio, Brashier, Payne, and Marsh, 2015; Feltman, 2015; Fitzhugh, 2010; Fox, 2016b; Frank, 1999). They would:

- Write on topics for which they had neither any training nor any experience.
- Declare research literatures hundreds of studies and a century deep nonexistent.
- Claim expertise in subject areas despite not having read the research literature or talked to those working in the field.
- Move from topic to topic quickly and effortlessly, while implying expertise in each.
- Present a limited and homogenous background—graduate school in economics or political science—essentially training in the statistical analysis of data sets.

Think of the research methods employed by detectives and prosecutors to solve a criminal case: interviews aplenty from a variety of perspectives,

reviews of historical and financial documents and records, detailed observations of the scene of the crime, observations of suspects, historical reviews of similar, relevant past cases, and so on. If understanding a case is important, "no stone should be unturned" in pursuit of the truth.

The GOP advisors brought to bear just one relevant skill: data analysis and, arguably, only one aspect of that. The psychologist Ben Wilbrink quips that economists analyze data sets assembled by others, in contrast to the more experimentally inclined psychologists who often manage all aspects of their studies from start to finish, including the design and implementation of the data collection. Consequently, psychologists are more likely to truly understand their data sets' contents.

Moreover, the data analysis techniques of the GOP advisors are taught, understood, and used by many thousands of researchers worldwide. There is nothing special about their analytical methods. So, ultimately, what justifies their extraordinary, exclusionary elitism? It is neither relevant skills nor experience (Levinovitz, 2016).

Information Can Be Hard to Find When One Doesn't Know Where to Look

Starting in the 1970s and continuing into the early 1980s, state after US state developed systemwide testing programs.[9] As many of the era's high school exit exams contained a single passing score set at a low level of achievement—a middle or junior high school level—they came to be known as "minimum competency" exams. Thirty-eight US states had developed minimum competency testing programs by 1983 (Odden, 1983).[10]

The state of Indiana did not develop its own test but, instead, required all school districts to annually administer their choice of a nationally normed achievement test at three grade levels. After a few years, a group of PhD program evaluators in the department studied the program and concluded that student achievement had, indeed, improved, at least partly because of the testing program. The study was not published.

This was typical of much testing program research then and is probably still common today. State and local program evaluation reports, including those conducted by outside consultants, end up on a shelf. So, too, do most test developers' reports. The reports are sometimes considered proprietary and not particularly appealing to the general public given technical language.[11] The US military, too, has conducted a voluminous amount of testing, and evaluations of its testing programs, for over a century.

With its resources, the feds in 2001 could have unearthed many of those unpublished studies. Instead, they relied on their academic economist and

political science advisors who, at best, conducted internet keyword searches or, more often, just "asked around."

Only academics would be so foolish as to assume that academic journals on the internet would contain the universe of policy-relevant research on such an applied topic. Sometimes, a reasonable search for relevant information requires more knowledge and effort than a research assistant can muster for a web keyword search.

On occasion over the past several decades, some of those responsible for evaluating state or local testing programs presented their results at professional meetings. Most of them made little effort beyond that to disseminate their findings. They were not academics, incentivized to get published in scholarly journals. Getting a paper accepted at a conference typically meant their employer would pay for a trip, usually to an interesting location where they could hobnob with old friends and professional colleagues. For them, there existed no further incentive to endure the gauntlet of scholarly journal review.

Occasionally, state and local evaluators might go to the trouble to submit the text of their conference presentation to the US Education Department's Education Resources Information Center (ERIC). In the early 2000s, some of these contributions remained in ERIC, photocopied and available in microforms.

In 2004, the new Institute of Education Sciences (IES) in the US Education Department decided to cut much of ERIC loose. IES would maintain only some material that had been digitized, or link to the journal or organization originally responsible for it. That left a cornucopia of some junky, but also some useful material to die lonely deaths in those library archives that hadn't yet gotten around to discarding old, no-longer supported resources.[12]

Case in Point: Objective and Secure Grade-Span Testing

Current educational testing programs in the United States are anachronistic. Starting with the No Child Left Behind (NCLB) Act in the early 2000s, and continuing today, the federal government requires each state to administer tests at seven grade levels in reading and math, and at three grade levels in science. Students are not held accountable for their test performance, but their schools, and sometimes their teachers, are (Fitzhugh, 2010, 2013).

With two decades of familiarity, this educational testing structure may now seem normal. It is not. We used to do it differently. Most of the world does it differently. "Grade-span testing" is a general term some use to describe a much more common testing system structure.

For decades, all but a couple of the world's industrialized countries have structured their examination systems a certain, familiar way. Tests are

administered at transition points between levels of education—between lower and upper secondary (i.e., middle and high school in the US) and between upper and post-secondary (i.e., high school and college in the US). Moreover, test performance typically bears some consequences for the student, either "high stakes" (e.g., determining whether the student advances to the next level) or "medium stakes" (e.g., determining an award, scholarship, or curriculum track).

This design was not chosen arbitrarily or haphazardly; rather, over the decades it had proven optimal.

Among other reasons, trustworthy examinations require objective and consistent administration by authorities external to the schools, which have their own interests in the results. But secure, external exam administration on a state- or nationwide scale portends enormous effort and expense. It is not something one does easily every year in every grade in every school.[13]

To accommodate annual administration at seven grade levels throughout the fifty states, federally mandated testing in the United States makes compromises. Among them:

- tests bear no consequences for students, who have little incentive to do well
- tests are administered by the students' own teachers and schools who have every incentive to skirt security procedures
- only two or three subject fields are tested, encouraging schools to slight other subjects

Given the ambiguity of test security alone, the current US testing program provides untrustworthy results.

Table 1.1 compares objective and secure grade-span testing to No Child Left Behind (NCLB) Act's annual testing at consecutive grade levels, which remains our current national testing program.

Table 1.1 is introduced here to emphasize the viability of an option that apparently was never considered in the US policy formation process circa 2001, nor over the following two decades. This oversight is equivalent to policy advisors submitting an options memo to their boss with just the options they happened to like.

Grade-span testing seems more valid to the public, which may help explain why public opinion regarded educational testing was more supportive twenty years ago. It makes more sense to them—the testing has a purpose—to make decisions about next steps at the next education level. Moreover, adding consequences, even if relatively small, to student test performance signals a purpose and importance for the test, a reason for its being. To many, annual

Table 1.1. Characteristics of annual and grade-span testing.

Annual (NCLB testing)	Typical Grade-Span Testing
single target (1 scale, 1 cut score)	multiple targets possible
2.5 subject areas	5+ subject areas possible
every student and teacher, every year	test only every 3 or 4 years
no stakes for students	stakes for students possible
more student-hours to take	fewer student-hours to take
more educator-hours to administer	fewer proctor-hours to administer
greater facility requirements	fewer facility requirements
lax security almost guaranteed	tight security possible
more expensive	less expensive
months to return results	days or weeks to return results
privacy threats from longitudinal and SEL data collection	fewer privacy threats
makes value-added measurement (VAM) possible	value-added measurement (VAM) not possible
in theory, better for continuous student monitoring and intervention	tests too infrequent for continuous student monitoring and intervention

testing at consecutive grade levels with no consequences for students seems like a lot of testing for no good reason.

Economists like having such longitudinal data for their own research projects and for calculating value-added measurements (VAM). The rationale offered the public, however, is that annual testing is needed for individual student diagnosis and monitoring. But, as it inevitably turned out, the annual test scores are seldom used for student diagnosis. For one thing, NCLB test results aggregate too highly to pinpoint individual student problems and arrive too late to facilitate timely interventions (Mathews, 2006; Weber, 2014; Phelps 2020b).

Given the overall superiority of the grade-span structure, why has the United States stuck with the NCLB-induced annual testing program for two decades and counting? It seems that, over the course of two decades, relevant policymakers never considered a grade-span system, at least in part because they were never presented the option, or any arguments or evidence in its favor.

In 2014–2015, Senate Committee Chairman Lamar Alexander explicitly requested that comparison (Edwards, H. S., 2015; U.S. Senate, 2015).[14] Even then, however, no testimony included genuine arguments in favor of a grade-span system.[15]

The No Child Left Behind Act could have incorporated a national grade-span testing program instead of the consecutive annual program adopted from Texas. Or the federal government could have left well enough alone, given that most states already ran their own grade-span testing programs.

Between 1982 and 1992, forty-two states increased high school course completion requirements, and forty-seven states had developed competency testing programs by 1992. Passage of the state competency test was required for graduation or promotion in twenty-four states in 1990 (Medrich, Brown, Henke, Ross, and McArthur). By 2002

> little more than 10 years after the idea of standards entered the public arena, 49 of the 50 states have adopted statewide content standards for elementary and secondary schools. Forty-eight states have statewide tests or examinations at one or more grade levels, and more than half have set or plan to implement graduation or promotion requirements based at least partly on test results. (Rothman, Slattery, Vranek, and Resnick, 2002)

No Child Left Behind and Common Core would arrest and reverse that trend, and over time erode state testing programs.

Progs and Trads

In debates over curriculum and instruction, observers commonly distinguish between "progressives" and "traditionalists," or "progs" and "trads" for short. The classification is not perfectly neat, any more than is the practice of casually lumping all citizens into progressive and conservative groups on a presumed unidimensional political spectrum.

Neither do the prog and trad groupings for curriculum and instruction issues perfectly align with their political counterparts. Some political progressives advocate traditional curriculum and instruction, and vice versa. The leftists who managed the Soviet Union and now run the Chinese Communist Party, for example, chose very traditional methods. Meanwhile, some conservative wealthy industrialists send their progeny to chic progressive schools.

Moreover, gross classifications may encourage stereotyping of people and groups. But it does help to clarify the large disparity possible between some tendencies and preferences. For example, there is a rough comparison in Table 1.2.

Certainly, the validity of these "back-of-the-envelope" classifications can be reasonably challenged. But the point here is not to construct the most thorough lists, but to illustrate how distinctive two preference lists can be.

One can find many education school professors and graduates who hold all the preferences on the table's left side. Likewise, one can find others who prefer all those on the right. Each group may consider its preferences to be reasonable. And, indeed, there exists at least some convincing evidence to support most of the preferences listed on either side.

Table 1.2. Comparing curriculum and instruction preferences, progressive and traditional.

Progressive	Traditional
student-directed learning (teacher is "guide on the side")	teacher-directed learning (teacher is "sage on the stage")
read contemporary, socially relevant books	read tried-and-true classics
read practical, informational texts	read compelling literature
project-based learning	explicit instruction
constructivism, inquiry-based learning	direct instruction
process-focused standards	clear, specific content standards
"deeper" learning	"deeper" means slower, more confusing
explain your answer	"rote understanding"
no need to teach facts, they're on the web	knowledge accumulation essential to "automaticity"
should teach "critical thinking," not facts	critical thinking requires knowledge base
lots of group work	only occasional group work
teach to learning styles, multiple intelligences	ignore them, as they do not exist
personalized learning is best	personalized learning is impractical
discipline can stifle self-esteem	students benefit from learning self-control
too much control can stifle creativity	control is necessary for efficiency

Sources: Chaney and Burgdorf, 1997; Darling-Hammond et al., 2013; Driscoll et al., 2003; Garelick, 2016–2021; Hirsch, 2016; Kirshner, 2017; Kirschner and Hendrick, 2020; Kirschner, Sweller, and Clark, 2006; Stone, 1996; Stone and Clements, 1998; Hunt, 2001; Skogstad, 2019.

Twenty years ago, curriculum and instruction traditionalists had trouble even getting a hearing in education media and policy venues.[16] Now we see high-profile discussions among policymakers about the "science of reading," complete with state executive and legislative efforts to reform reading curricula and instruction (Goldstein, 2022).

There is little new about the "science of reading," though. Efforts to raise awareness of the feeble evidence for constructivist approaches and the stronger evidence for phonics date at least as far back as the 1950s and Rudolph Flesch's *Why Johnny Can't Read*.[17]

If, at long last, policy trends seem to favor a reasonable measure of consideration for curriculum and instruction traditionalists, exactly the opposite trend now disfavors testing and accountability traditionalists.

How to categorize two schools of thought on testing and accountability? As with the earlier curriculum and instruction comparison, the same caveats apply. There's a rough sketch of a binary comparison in Table 1.3.

The "Big Bang" at Educational Testing Firms

Shortly after World War II, during a key phase in the history of educational

Table 1.3. Comparing testing and accountability preferences, progressive and traditional.

Progressive	Traditional
validity more important than reliability	there is no validity without reliability
only what is tested is taught, so tests must cover all topics	test what can reasonably be tested, set other requirements for arts, gym, term papers, etc.
the multiple-response format is old and outdated	the open-ended response format is much older, by at least two millennia
"innovative" test formats have improved testing	unfamiliar and complex formats introduce confusion and penalize at-risk students
should be "seamless" transition between classroom testing and large-scale testing	each testing type should be optimized to its best advantage
process-focused standards	clear, specific content standards
should be single target for everyone—more democratic	should be multiple targets, so all students have challenging goals
a single test should do it all—diagnose, monitor, evaluate	using one test for disparate purposes waters down its validity for each purpose
cheating is often justified; test security is immoral	cheating is rarely, if ever, justified; test security is essential to fairness
teachers should proctor tests in their own classrooms and administrators manage test materials in their own schools	tests are neither valid nor reliable if they are not secure; tight test security is reliably attained with external administration
college admission tests should be aligned to high school curriculum	college admission tests should be predictive of desired college outcomes
high school GPA is more predictive than admission test scores, so we should end admission testing	admission test scores are more predictive than most other factors considered in college admissions
aptitude testing is unfair	aptitude is part of life
exit exams should be abolished as they increase dropping out	exit exams increase student achievement overall and signal importance of coursework

Sources: AERA, APA, and NCME, 2014; Amrein-Beardsley, Berliner, and Rideau, 2010; Bennett and Gitomer, 2009; Bridgeman, 1991; Crocker, 2005; Darling-Hammond and Pecheone, 2009; Eckstein and Noah, 1997; Feinberg, 1990; French, 2017; Goodman and Hamilton, 2005; Griffin and Heidorn, 1996; KERA Update, 1999; Ligon, 2007, 2019; Marion et al., 2019; National Research Council, 2003; Phelps, 1999, 2008/2009a, 2011c; Stricherz, 2001; Wiggins, 1994.

testing, College Board joined with the Carnegie Foundation and the American Council on Education (ACE) to create the Educational Testing Service (ETS),

an independent scientific community dedicated to developing and administering standardized tests.

ETS was handed responsibility for several ongoing testing programs, including the national teacher examinations (from ACE), graduate records examinations (from Carnegie), and the SAT (from College Board) (Phelps 2007a, pp. 21–22). Some programs became ETS's to own, others just to manage. All the programs met important public needs, but none were moneymakers at the time.

The current leadership of these organizations created at most a small portion of the value in the products they now own. The programs were developed and improved largely through the efforts and expenditure of the public, either directly through government agencies, or indirectly through the tax relief offered nonprofit foundations.[18]

Some years ago, ETS's Randy E. Bennett penned a guide (2011) to the moral restraints that non-profit educational testing firms should assume for themselves.

In the words of then ETS president Kurt Landgraf (p. i):

> In this paper, Bennett uses ETS as a case study. He begins by reviewing the federal tax code relating to educational nonprofit organizations. He then analyzes the circumstances that led to ETS's founding.

The second section describes at length the angst of mid-twentieth century educational testing leaders, such as Carl Brigham, Henry Chauncey, and James Conant. They worried about how to balance the need for a sustaining return on investment with the public interest, ongoing research, and objective science. Their tentative solution was to incubate educational test development inside nonprofit organizations resembling university research centers, run by applied scientists.

Ironically, the latter, third section of Bennett's report, meant to cover organizational behaviors of the past half-century and the future, comprises only several paragraphs. In it (p. 9), he writes, "The challenges that Brigham, Chauncey, and Conant posed well over 50 years ago remain largely unresolved today."

An understatement. Even a casual observer would recognize little similarity between the well-defined and limited roles of educational testing nonprofits from the mid-twentieth century into the 1990s, and their aggressive market behavior of today.

Arguably, ETS first signaled the new order at the turn of this century when former DuPont Chemical executive Kurt Landgraf was hired, at a corporate CEO's salary, to replace Nancy Cole, the last in a stream of psychometrician CEOs who had run ETS from its origins. As the *New York Times* reported,

E.T.S., the world's largest testing organization, has traditionally paid salaries comparable to those at colleges, universities ... But under the leadership of Kurt Landgraf, a former chief operating officer of the DuPont Company who became president of E.T.S. two years ago, compensation has soared.

Mr. Landgraf himself received nearly $800,000 for his first 10 months on the job—about twice as much as Gaston Caperton, who heads the College Board—and more than all but two college presidents in the nation. (Lewin, 2002)[19]

Mr. Caperton, a former West Virginia senator, would catch up and cash in. By 2009, his total annual remuneration easily cleared $1 million. In his last year at College Board (2012), he received close to two ($1,848,009). Current College Board CEO David Coleman cleared $1 million already by the 2016 tax year ($1,445,613) (Strauss, 2015).

The new order tore the boundaries between organizations that had given each a well-defined role and kept each in its place. ETS, for example, created new corporate entities to compete in the occupational-testing market and the K–12 classroom testing market against national tests developed by for-profit K–12 textbook companies (McGraw-Hill, Harcourt, and Houghton-Mifflin). The firm has since entered other new markets, both here and overseas.

From then on, all testing companies would operate more like competitive businesses, wooing and pleasing customers. This cultural change profoundly affected testing and measurement research.

Previously free to write and publish accurate and objective research studies, psychometricians would now sign gag orders and publish less outside the comfort zones of their employers, and less outside the company, period. Research truth needed to be weighed against potential customer beliefs, preferences, and satisfaction (Baskerville, 2021; Phelps, 2017a; Sachs, 2022; Yoffie, 2021).[20]

As one might suspect, testing experts—psychometricians—who generally support the use of testing tend to work in organizations that develop and administer tests. Psychometricians who are opposed to some of the common uses of tests tend not to work in testing organizations. They can often be found instead working as faculty in schools of education, where they may teach courses in testing and measurement from a skeptic's point of view.

With most pro-testing testing experts locked away as in a Cistercian Abbey, who is left to debate testing policy in public?[21] PR professionals with little background in psychometrics dish saccharine corporate talking points for test development firms, avoiding controversy.

Testing opponents in graduate schools of education, now dominated by constructivists and radical egalitarians, remain free to talk, however (Asher, 2018, 2019; Benbow and Stanley, 1996; Gottfredson, 1994; Kramer, 1991; Levine, 2006, 2007; Phelps, 2021e; Schalin, 2019; Wilson, N., 2019). So,

too, is education journalists' favorite, the misnamed Center for Fair and Open Testing (FairTest), which supports only the least open, most obscure forms of testing, such as matrix sampling.[22]

In hopes of obtaining the "other side" of testing policy issues, journalists may consult the think tanks, which lack testing expertise but may proffer advice on testing policy anyway.

Also circa 2001, the New Standards Project

In the late 1990s and early 2000s, three states tried out some innovative, allegedly "higher-order," more "authentic," performance-based testing programs. In California (CLAS), Maryland (MSPAP), and Kentucky (KIRIS), state leaders tolerated the dysfunction for a while but ultimately canned the unreliable tests tied to fuzzy standards.[23]

Those testing programs failed because of unreliable scores; volatile test score trends; secrecy of items and forms; an absence of individual scores in some cases; individuals being judged on group work in some cases; large expenditures of time; inconsistent (and some improper) test preparation procedures from school to school; inconsistent grading on open-ended response test items; long delays between administration and release of scores; little feedback for students; and no substantial evidence after several years that education had improved.

Resounding public distaste killed those programs. But ten years is a long time in the ever-"innovating" world of US education policy, long enough for those new to education policy to be unaware of the earlier fiascos. The same individuals and organizations responsible for the doomed New Standards Project would resurface in the mid-2000s, with Bill Gates's wallet, to develop and promote the so-called Common Core State Standards.

Also circa 2001, Massachusetts and Virginia built traditional standards/assessment programs like one sees in most of the countries killing the US on international tests. Massachusetts moved from the middle of the pack of states to the top, where it remained until it, too, replaced its demonstrably successful program with the untried Common Core.[24]

Federalism as Learned Helplessness

The state education departments in the latter decades of the twentieth century typically comprised over a dozen divisions. About half managed the ordinary inward-facing functions one would find on any organization chart, such as accounting, operations, data management, and human resources.

The other, outward-facing divisions portrayed the identity and character of the department and conducted real education-related work. They were

organized according to different lines of federal grant funding: migrant education, compensatory education, education for those with disabilities, free and reduced-price lunch, and so on.

The good intentions of the "Great Society" federal social programs, which began in the 1960s, came with some unfortunate side effects, such as a "cargo cult" state and local dependency on federal funding and a deference to federal organizational structures, goals, vocabulary, problem identification, and analytical methods.

Even more profoundly, however, came a loss of initiative and entrepreneurship that had characterized many state and local education agencies in the first half of the twentieth century, when there was no question but that state and local agencies were responsible for education and the federal government was not.

It was states on their own, however, that initiated the statewide testing programs of the late 1970s to early 1980s minimum competency testing era. At first, most states new to statewide testing employed "off-the-shelf" national norm referenced tests (NRTs).

Then came the federal courts' "opportunity to learn" decision in the *Debra P. v. Turlington* (1981) case regarding Florida's high school exit exam. Twelve African American families sued the state superintendent of education, claiming the NRT covered subject matter that differed from what their schools had taught their teenagers. A "content match" alignment study commissioned by the court concurred (Buckendahl and Hunt, 2005).

From then on, US states developed state-specific standards-based tests, typically hiring a test development firm to work with newly organized state testing divisions. First, however, each state needed to develop its own subject-area standards, upon which those tests would be built.

In the process, US states rediscovered initiative and entrepreneurial spirit during the 1980s and 1990s while building their own standards and assessment systems and conducting their own "sunshine law–" or "sunset provision–" required program evaluations (Cuevas, 2021).[25]

Then came the 2000 decade's one-two punch of the No Child Left Behind (NCLB) Act, which imposed a uniform testing and measurement structure, and the Common Core Standards Initiative (CCSI), which imposed uniform content and performance standards on all public schools, including the formerly independent charter schools. Once again, state and local education agencies would defer to the federal government.

NOTES

1. https://dfer.org/.
2. https://en.wikipedia.org/wiki/Matthew_effect.
3. The testing program in Texas circa 2001 that, with some modifications, become our national testing program, was atypical for its time. Despite its flaws, was student achievement higher in Texas in the 1990s because of the testing program than it would have been with no testing program? The evidence suggests that it was, probably because almost any testing program improves student achievement (Grissmer, 1998; Toenjes and Dworkin, 2002). The same goes for No Child Left Behind testing. But better testing programs could have improved student achievement much more, and we have abandoned most of those.
4. https://cresst.org/.
5. https://en.wikipedia.org/wiki/National_Center_for_Research_on_Evaluation,_Standards,_and_Student_Testing.
6. About information suppression, there may be no wiser student of the topic than the Australian Brian Martin. Helpfully, he provides a web page with links to many relevant writings: https://www.bmartin.cc/pubs/supp.html.
7. They await in profusion in the indexes of scholarly journals with names such as *Journal of Experimental Education*, *Journal of Education Research*, *Journal of Research in Science Teaching*, *Journal of Educational Psychology*, *Journal of Experimental Psychology*, and *Psychological Science*.
8. Date of search: January 29, 2022. https://eric.ed.gov/?q=pubyearmax%3A2002+effect+of+testing.
9. Some current observers identify the circa 1980 statewide testing proliferation as a reaction to the famous *Nation at Risk* report. It was not. The US Department of Education published *Nation at Risk* in April 1983, long after many states had already established systemwide testing programs. Rather, both the states and the committee that wrote *Nation at Risk* simultaneously responded to the same widespread belief that US education standards and achievement had deteriorated along with many 1960s- and 1970s-era liberalizations.
10. Ironically, largely socialist Europe, with its smaller socioeconomic (and academic achievement) disparity, acknowledges that children are different and offers them a range of academic options and multiple achievement targets. In the more libertarian United States, with its greater income inequality and larger socioeconomic (and academic achievement) disparities, pressure is brought to bear for all children to take the same curriculum (i.e., what is often called the "college track") and a single academic achievement target is set for all.

When only one academic achievement target is offered, by necessity it must be low. If not, politically unacceptable numbers of students will fail, and the educational system would collapse on itself. When the single target is low, however, responsive school systems focus effort and resources on bringing the lowest-achieving students up to that target. Unfortunately, they also may neglect the average- and higher-achieving students or, in the most perverse cases, deliberately hold them back.

11. Often, state and local program evaluators are granted permission to present some version of their results at professional meetings. Two incentives draw government and contractor evaluators to professional meetings: pride in discussing their work and travel to a typically interesting city paid for by their employer. There is little incentive for government workers to rewrite their work for consideration at scholarly journals and endure the often mean and dispiriting, and always time-consuming, gauntlet of editorial review.

12. According to current ERIC staffers (email conversations, March 2–4, 2022), only digitized resources are available in full text online. There exist two impediments to digitizing what remained on microfiche after some materials were weeded out in 2004. First, some photocopies were in poor condition, and they are working to restore those they can in digital form. Second, they had received legal permissions those many years ago to reproduce documents specifically on microfiche, not in digital format. Thus, even if ERIC undertook the extraordinary effort to find all those who originally submitted documents to ERIC over several decades, they will not be able to obtain new legal permissions from now-deceased authors or from discontinued journals.

To empirically examine the extent of the "natural" attrition of policy-relevant research, I compiled a list of the journals and research organizations cited in the last of the many printings of C. C. Ross's *Measurement in Today's Schools* (Ross and Stanley, 1972). See Appendix 2 online, https://educationpolicy.us/Malfunction/App2.pdf. Ten of the thirty-four journals cited have ceased publication, and three others have changed their names. Seven of the ten cessations occurred long before the internet was created, leaving no one responsible to consider digitizing the archives, even as non-searchable photocopy.

13. It can make sense to conduct short, no-stakes student diagnostic or system monitoring tests more frequently, in part because they are less expensive and complex, but mostly because they can be reliably internally administered.

14. Among those specifically recommending annual testing in consecutive grades in 2001, 2002, 2007, 2013, or 2015: Theodore Hershberg, University of Pennsylvania; Edward B. Rust, Business Coalition for Excellence in Education, CEO, State-Farm; Kurt Landgraf, CEO, ETS; Mark Musick, chair, NAGB; Robert Balfanz, Johns Hopkins University; Ken Bradford, LA assistant super; Michael Vollmer, GA, executive director, Office of Ed Accountability; John Boehner, Ohio congressperson; Rod Paige, US secretary of education; Mary Ann Schmitt, CEO, New American Schools; Grover "Russ" Whitehurst, IES director; John King, NYS commissioner.

15. I hedge with the word "genuine" because, offered only the binary choice, groups that opposed testing in general offered token support for the grade-span option, but only because they assumed that it would portend less testing quantity than the alternative (telephone conversation with Lindsay Fryer, November 2, 2020). They opposed mandated testing requirements, period; they did not appreciate grade-span testing for its own sake by, for example, citing any of the advantages enumerated above in Table 1.1.

16. With dogged persistence, however, they only recently managed to break through the walls of information suppression and at least engage an effective debate (Stone

and Clements 1998, Hunt 2001; Locke 2005; Waterhouse 2006). It took sustained effort by outsiders, principally psychologists to court the publicity necessary to promote their research where it mattered for policy formation (e.g., John E. Stone, Daniel Willingham). Perhaps also pertinent, much of the effort was led by non-Americans, in the United Kingdom, the Netherlands, Australia, and elsewhere (Kirschner, Sweller and Clark, 2006; Kirschner, 2017; Kirschner and Hendrick, 2020; Skogstad, 2019).

17. https://en.wikipedia.org/wiki/Rudolf_Flesch.

18. Common Core critics will notice similarities with the Council of Chief State School Officers (CCSSO) and the National Governor's Association (NGA), two organizations that, despite their official-sounding names, are private, independent, and beholden primarily to their own boards. Though the public and some foundations paid to develop the Common Core standards, the CCSSO and NGA co-own the copyright.

19. A popular narrative has it that Landgraf was hired to right a mismanaged, sinking ship. But Lewin of the *New York Times* reported:

> Through much of the 1990s, E.T.S. lost money. In the fiscal year ended July 1998, it had a deficit of $8.2 million. In 1999, the deficit was reduced to $206,256, and in 2000—the year before Mr. Landgraf arrived—the service had an operating surplus of $29 million, which grew to $34 million last year.

20. As if to emphasize its own transformation from traditional to progressive advocacy, ETS recently hired a long-time CRESST citation cartel member to manage their research centers. She had passed the previous quarter-century largely ignoring, dismissing, or demeaning much ETS research. https://news.ets.org/press-releases/laura-hamilton-named-general-manager-of-research-centers-at-ets/ and https://nonpartisaneducation.org/Review/Resources/LauraHamilton.htm.

21. Articles such as Lawrence Feinberg's "Multiple-choice and Its Critics: Are The 'Alternatives' Any Better?" (1990) and Brent Bridgeman's 1991 "Essays and Multiple-Choice Tests as Predictors of College Freshman GPA" (which found the multiple-choice format clearly superior) emanated from a College Board quite different than today's, which sways in whatever policy direction it perceives to be most popular at any given moment. Or consider ETS reports finding the multiple-choice format superior in just about every way, even for testing deep thinking or creativity (Rudman, 1992; Lukhele, Thissen, and Wainer, 1994; Powers and Kaufman, 2002).

Other pro-traditional testing and accountability articles of the era include Ebel, 1981; Frary, 1982; Traub, 1993; Tuckman, 1994; Griffin and Heidorn, 1996; Chaney and Burgdorf, 1997; Tuckman and Trimble, 1997; McMillan, 2001; Jozefowicz, Koeppen, and Case, 2002; Driscoll et al., 2003; Reville, 2004, and Roediger and Marsh, 2005. I doubt that articles like these would be published in mainstream education publications today.

22. https://www.fairtest.org/search/node/matrix%20sampling.

23. See, for example:

- *For California*: Michael W. Kirst and Christopher Mazzeo, (1997, December). "The Rise, Fall, and Rise of State Assessment in California: 1993–96," *Phi Delta Kappan*, *78*(4); Committee on Education and the Workforce, US House

of Representatives, One Hundred Fifth Congress, Second Session, (1998, January 21). National Testing: Hearing, Granada Hills, CA. Serial No. 105–74; Representative Steven Baldwin, (1997, October). Comparing assessments and tests. *Education Reporter*, 141. See also Klein, David. (2003). "A Brief History Of American K–12 Mathematics Education In the 20th Century," In James M. Royer, (Ed.), *Mathematical Cognition*, (pp. 175–226). Charlotte, NC: Information Age Publishing.
- *For Kentucky*: ACT. (1993). *A Study of Core Course-Taking Patterns. ACT-Tested Graduates Of 1991–1993 And an Investigation Of The Relationship Between Kentucky's Performance-Based Assessment Results And ACT-Tested Kentucky Graduates Of 1992*. Iowa City, IA: Author; Richard Innes. (2003). "Education Research From A Parent's Point Of View." Louisville, KY: Author. https://www.eddatafrominnes.com/index.html; KERA Update. (1999, January). Misinformed, misled, flawed: The legacy of KIRIS, Kentucky's first experiment.
- *For Maryland*: P. H. Hamp, and C. B. Summers. (2002, Fall). "Education." In P. H. Hamp and C. B. Summers (Eds.), *A Guide to the Issues 2002–2003*. Maryland Public Policy Institute, Rockville, MD. http://www.mdpolicy.org/docLib/20051030Education.pdf; Montgomery County Public Schools. (2002, Feb. 11). "Joint Teachers/Principals Letter Questions MSPAP," Public Announcement, Rockville, MD. https://www.montgomeryschoolsmd.org/press/index.aspx?pagetype=showreleaseandid=644; HumRRO. (1998). "Linking Teacher Practice with Statewide Assessment of Education." Alexandria, VA: Author. https://www.humrro.org/corpsite/page/linking-teacher-practice-statewide-assessment-education.

24. Gobs of money and shiny professional appointments would later convince Massachusetts state leaders to abandon the country's best program with one based on unrealistic promises, designed by those responsible for earlier spectacular failures.

25. Examples of current state program evaluation provisions: (California) Cal. Code Regs. Tit. 17, § 56732 - Program Evaluation, https://www.law.cornell.edu/regulations/california/17-CCR-Sec-56732; (North Carolina) Article 7C. Program Evaluation. § 120-36.11. Program Evaluation Division established https://www.ncleg.net/EnactedLegislation/Statutes/PDF/ByArticle/Chapter_120/Article_7C.pdf; (Iowa) Title I - STATE SOVEREIGNTY AND MANAGEMENT; Chapter 2A - LEGISLATIVE SERVICES AGENCY; Section 2A.7 - State government oversight and program evaluation; Universal Citation: IA Code § 2A.7 (2021) https://law.justia.com/codes/iowa/2021/title-i/chapter-2a/section-2a-7/.

Chapter 2

The Triumph of Strategic Scholarship

"It is preoccupation with possession, more than anything else, that prevents men from living freely and nobly."
—Bertrand Russell

How does science progress? The preface introduced Karl Popper's dialectical theory, here summed up neatly by Saul McLeod (2020a):

- Karl Popper believed that scientific knowledge is provisional—the best we can do at the moment.
- The Falsification Principle . . . is a way of demarcating science from non-science. It suggests that for a theory to be considered scientific it must be able to be tested and conceivably proven false.
- For example, the hypothesis that "all swans are white," can be falsified by observing a black swan.

Earlier writings of J. S. Mill (1978) and recent writings of Jonathan Rauch (2021) concur.

If scientific progress requires falsifiability, it follows that new research should specify how it differs from earlier research, which requires:

1. Acknowledgment of that previous research
2. Accurate representation of that research

New research should be falsifiable, too, which requires:

3. A scholarly environment that allows disagreement
4. Engagement by scholars with challenges to their research

US education policy research is sorely lacking in all four corollaries.

Popper argued that scientific progress depends on a tolerant, open market for ideas. That befits the ideal image of scholars as independent, dispassionate, objective truth seekers. As Rauch adds in his *Constitution of Knowledge*, it is not about you, or me, or any other personalities but rather the information itself. Scholars may produce new knowledge, but once produced, that knowledge should glide freely into and around the marketplace of ideas without friction.

In US education research, however, friction seems ubiquitous. Consider the following common behaviors:

- *Valuing credentials over content*: knowledge is judged not by its inherent quality, or the genuine expertise of the scholar, but by the social status of the scholar disseminating it (Bright, 2021; Brooks, 2021; Leef, 2021; Origgi, 2018).
- *Prioritizing quantity over quality*: scholars maximize the amount of their, or their group's, apparent scholarly production (e.g., publications, citations, mentions) and minimize time spent otherwise (e.g., reading previous work) (Barbaro, 2021; Fox, 2016a; Hussein, 2020; Polese, 2019; Teixera de Silva, 2021).
- *Strategic disagreement*: scholars are more likely to criticize the work of those who cannot affect their career advancement, and less likely to criticize the work of those who can (Biagioli and Lippman, 2020; Vial, Muradoglu, Newman, and Cimpian, 2022).
- *Strategic acknowledgement*: scholars are more likely to cite the work of those who can affect their career advancement (i.e., in citation cartels) (Biagioli and Lippman, 2020; Davis, 2012).
- *Suppressing knowledge for reasons unrelated to the knowledge*: a variety of irrelevant excuses are common justifications for suppressing information, such as tone policing, guilt by association, potential hurt feelings, and personal dislike (Graham, 2008; Ratner, 2018; Rohrer, 2019; Vial, Muradoglu, Newman, and Cimpian, 2022).

Over time, some enterprising scholars have developed and perfected methods and rationales for manipulating the knowledge production system for personal or small group gains.

These scholarly incentive structures have been superimposed upon an antiquated honor system lacking any adverse consequences for information suppression, save for plagiarism (Associated Press, 2021a, 2021b, 2022; Biagioli, 2020; *Daily Star,* 2021; Diehl and Trenkamp, 2013; Hamel, 2021; *Retraction Watch,* 2011, 2022).

Where Is Research Integrity?

One detects much more concern about research integrity in the hard sciences than in the social sciences and, among the social sciences, more in psychology than the others (APS, 2021a; Barber, 2021; Biagioli and Lippman, 2020; Fanelli, 2009; Fang, Bowen, and Casadevall, 2016; Gallagher, 2009; Lawrence, P. A., 2007; Oransky and Marcus, 2016, 2017; Ritchie, 2020, 2022; Vazire, Schiavone, and Bottesini, 2022).

Serious, practical, and honest discussions of research integrity and how to improve seem to occur least where they are most needed—in education, public policy, and economics. "Honest" is included here among the adjectives to distinguish genuine research integrity from the empty virtue-signaling one sometimes witnesses from more ethically flexible scholars.

Ultimately, in many academic fields, including education, scholars can say and write whatever they please about others' work, whether accurate and truthful, or not. There are few applicable legal constraints. No fiduciary responsibility. No Hippocratic Oath.

Granted, it is generally not permissible to insult—as in "Professor X is a jerk." Yet it is perfectly permissible to write that Professor X "failed to consider . . ." or "neglected to include . . ." or "seems to have been unaware of . . ." or any one of thousands of other apparently factual statements, even if the statements are false.

All it takes is one editor and one to a few reviewers at a single journal among the thousands available for one's dishonest attacks to enter the scholarly record. And, again, editors rarely care to correct inaccuracies that their reviewers overlooked. In a truth-seeking, knowledge-accumulation culture, corrections would be obligatory; in our CV-thickening culture, it is simply not worth an editor's time (Wager and Kleinert, 2011).

Even advertisers are bound by hard and fast rules of behavior, lest they face criminal penalties (Arens, 2005; Garcia, 2022; ICC, 2018). Not so scholars in education research.

Meanwhile, virtually all scholarly effort focusses on the mad dash to produce more and more publications and mentions in social media. Stopping to consider past publications, or to correct errors they may contain, only impedes that progress. Revisions, rebuttals, and retractions remain rare in US education research.[1] It is not a truth-seeking knowledge accumulation process; it is a career-advancement pyramid scheme.

Celebrity Scholars

> "The celebrity professor is a new phenomenon and not a good one. In celebrity-driven academia, 'getting ahead' means beating other people,

which means establishing a personal reputation and denying it, to the extent possible, to rivals."

—Harry Lewis, as quoted in Russell, 2007

In 2007, then recent Harvard graduate Jacob Hale Russell wrote "A Million Little Writers: Welcome to The World Of Celebrity Academics—And the Behind-The-Scenes Scribes Who Help Make Their Fame and Fortune Possible." Harry Lewis, whom Russell interviewed, then served as dean of Harvard College.

Russell's article focused on what Lewis called the "atelier phenomenon," wherein ambitious academics hire teams of poorly paid graduate students, ghost writers, computer programmers, and even bright high school students to do much of the work they take credit for themselves.

The help is needed to produce enough work quickly enough to attract attention to their personal brand in the public intellectual marketplace. Recognition among the scholarly elite requires an extraordinarily prodigious output of papers, articles, reviews, presentations, and interviews. "Top" scholars' curriculum vitae can exceed a hundred pages, single-spaced.

The tasks assigned to the lumpenproletariat working in the atelier may be considered the "grunt work" of the scholarship process, such as literature searches and reviews, computer programming, reference and citation management, and proofreading. Still, the public is led to believe that the celebrity scholar's knowledge and expertise directed every aspect of production. As Russell wrote,

> The cult of celebrity that Harvard's high-profile professors often cultivate requires a production line of unnamed accomplices who help maintain the professor's prolific output—and status as an intellectual star.

Russell mentions other tricks of the celebrity research trade, too, such as picking the trendiest topics for study, frequenting popular media venues and other public relations efforts, and lowering quality control to produce shoddier work more quickly.

A journalist or policymaker may choose to consult with one scholar rather than another based on superior credentials. Paradoxically, most of the work responsible for celebrity scholars' superior credentials may have been conducted by students and contingent workers.

The situation parallels the teaching assignment paradox, whereby a prestigious college assigns graduate students to teach introductory courses (to free up their celebrity professors' time for writing and research) while a

less prestigious college assigns professors to teach those courses (see also Deresiewicz, 2014).[2]

Whereas Russell's article focused on the "production" side of celebrity scholarship, Lewis's quote above refers to what one might call the "reduction" side—besting scholarly rivals by denying them attention or denigrating their work or reputation—something that celebrity scholars, with their readier access to media outlets, can manage to considerable effect.

The "atelier phenomenon," describes small organizations dedicated to promoting the brand of an individual celebrity scholar. Such promotion can be multiplied many times over through the cooperation of other scholars and other workshops. Harvard itself is a celebrity impact force multiplier.

Also relevant, however, each Harvard school maintains a public relations office, with full-time staff specifically dedicated to getting their professors in the news. Few ordinary universities, much less individual programs at those universities, can afford such dedicated service (Carrigan, 2019; Grout, 2019; Haimson, 2020; Yettick, 2011).

Celebrity impact may be multiplied still more through the support of well-funded *national* groups; think federally or foundation-funded research centers and think tanks.

The Dead Weight of the Literature Review

The film *Shattered Glass* recounts the remarkable story of former *New Republic* reporter Stephen Glass, who fabricated content in twenty-seven of the forty-one articles he wrote for the magazine. As *Vanity Fair* described it:

> At 25, Stephen Glass was the most sought-after young reporter in the nation's capital, producing knockout articles for magazines ranging from *The New Republic* to *Rolling Stone*. Trouble was, he made things up—sources, quotes, whole stories—in a breathtaking web of deception that emerged as the most sustained fraud in modern journalism. (Bissinger, 2007)

The century-old *New Republic* had earned a stellar reputation in the publishing industry in part because of its rigorous fact-checking procedures. But Glass had spotted a loophole in those procedures—reporters' notes were generally accepted as is.

The fraud continued for years and could have continued for more. Those who had suspicions either did not want to mess with proven success; dared not risk a conflict with a popular and successful colleague; or had no incentive to spend the time and resources necessary to build a solid, convincing case against Glass. Ultimately, it was journalists at another publication, *Forbes*, who accidentally uncovered the fraud.

Thorough fact-checking takes time and produces no revenue. *New Republic* staffers had checked Glass's assertions as best they could from their desks, through internet and reference source searches and telephone calls. That wasn't enough, however, to counter the efforts of a determined fabulist.

Many scholars similarly exploit a loophole in scholarly publishing in the introductory section of their manuscripts, where the literature review is typically found. Often, and probably most of the time, they are not checked (*Retraction Watch*, 2018).

One finds literature searching listed among the "grunt work" tasks that celebrity researchers assign to students and contingent workers, according to Russell. Yet, that alleged grunt work is an integral part of the research process. One conducts literature searches and reviews for more than obligatory reasons, to ground oneself in the subject matter, understand the larger contexts, and gain genuine expertise (Herring, 2001; Stevens-Rayburn, 1998).

New research typically forms the bulk of a scholarly article. But any single article is just one among many. In the literature review, the writer attempts to circumscribe the universe of knowledge on the topic. To fit the new research most profitably into that universe—to maximize its social benefit—the literature review requires as much precision as the new study.

Thorough literature reviews may not be analytically taxing, but they can be tedious and enormously time-consuming, challenging one's patience (Gusenbauer and Haddaway, 2018; Haddaway and Gusenbauer, 2020).

Moreover, a thorough literature review requires a familiarity with often obscure vocabulary, a range of academic disciplines, the evolution of terminology over time, variations in terminology across disciplines and across countries, available databases, the mechanics of searching the internet, various intranets, and microfiche, and a willingness to spend some amount of time inside libraries. As the bestselling author Dan Brown quipped, "Google is not a synonym for research."[3]

Ideally, a scholarly article presents the Popperian dialectic in miniature. The literature review summarizes all relevant prior information, from all relevant sources. Either the new confirms the old, or updates it, proposing a new scientific consensus.

In US education research, however, there exist only the slightest hurdles to saying whatever one pleases in the introductory section of an article. Some take advantage of the opportunity to:

- brag;
- misrepresent (i.e., demean) the work of rivals;
- neglect to mention conflicts of interest (Shapiro and Wolfe, 2022);
- evade the task altogether, claiming no previous research on topic;

- showcase the work of friendly colleagues who will return the favor; and
- signal expertise (which they may or may not genuinely possess).

An incoming manuscript may be critiqued by one to a few reviewers selected by a journal's editor. But journals typically pay reviewers nothing. It is difficult enough to find reviewers willing to read the new research presented, much less critique the manuscript's introduction that describes the larger context. If an author claims that no previous research exists, few reviewers will take the time to conduct their own time-consuming literature search to check. (See Fenske, 2021; Wager and Kleinert, 2011.)

Now imagine a reviewer for an economics journal confronting a no-previous-research claim on a topic that psychologists have been studying intensely for decades. As far as the economics reviewer knows, having zero familiarity with the research literature in psychology, the claim is valid.

Of course, there exists the possibility that a reviewer here or there might be familiar with the relevant research literature. But even if one reviewer dings a manuscript for falsely claiming no previous research, there exist other journals one can try . . . many others. The author has already done the work to prepare the manuscript for journal review. It is far less time-consuming to change the name of the journal and submit the same paperwork than it would be to conduct a weeks- or months-long literature review.[4]

Alternatively, they have three choices:

- just mention some of the previous research and hope that satisfies;
- skip the literature review entirely; or
- fake it—pretend to have done a responsible literature search and found nothing.

For many scholars, especially those celebrity scholars with ready access to many publication outlets, simply presenting one's research with no mention of previous work in the field should suffice. Nonetheless, many of those scholars who could just skip the literature review and still get published choose to fake it. Why?

Because the literature review is more than just a review of the literature; it is an *expertise signal*. It tells the reader that one has not only conducted a new study, but one is also familiar with the entire field of study. It signals that one is a subject matter expert. Which is exactly what someone avoiding a literature search is not.

For some topics, even reading an entire research literature does not suffice for genuine expertise. True understanding may require direct experience—skin in the game (Taleb, 2018). This is particularly important for reading education research literatures bloating with misleading, false, and

fraudulent studies. The passive reader without direct experience in a field is susceptible to believing information that experienced readers would know makes no sense.

Regardless, those *perceived* as experts receive calls from journalists and policymakers, get invited to panels at conferences, and more easily win promotions. For any scholar facing the decision to do an honest literature review or not, here's the trade-off in a nutshell:

- Potentially enormous time loss and no benefit for doing it
- No time investment and attractive benefits for falsely claiming to have done it
- No adverse consequences for not doing it and falsely claiming to have done it

As the ethicist Michael Josephson said, "What you allow, you encourage."[5] Life is filled with constant calculations of what the rules are, which of them are strictly enforced, and which are cosmetic or aspirational, but not seriously enforced. Josephson's point is that rules that are never enforced encourage defilement.

Moreover, unlike with plagiarism, against which enforced rules apply, written rules are rare regarding fake literature reviews.[6] Ironically, plagiarism misrepresents just one piece of the research literature. Fake literature reviews can misrepresent hundreds or thousands. Yet, whereas plagiarism may end one's career, only benefits flow from dismissive reviews.

Dismissive reviewing may be selfish, dishonest, and unethical, but substantial rewards await those who do it.

Urge to Purge

With a dismissive literature review, a researcher assures the public that no one has yet studied a topic or that very little has been done on it. Of course, some dismissive reviews can be accurate—for example, with genuinely new scientific discoveries or technical inventions. But, often, and probably usually, they are not.

Ironically, as research studies accumulate so do incentives and opportunities to dismiss them. The time required for conducting an honest, thorough literature review grows larger with each new journal issue. According to Ivan Oransky, "There are about 3 million papers published in peer-reviewed journals every year . . . and that number has been steadily increasing for decades" (Fenske, 2021). In a publish-or-perish environment, a genuine literature review is a time sink that impedes professional progress (Barbaro, 2021; Barber, 2021; Oransky, 2015; Taswell et al., 2020).

Meanwhile, dismissive reviews carry a host of advantages over engaging the wider research literature (Baccini, De Nicolao, and Petrovich, 2019; Bartlett, 2012; Bogazzi, 2017; Martin, B., 1996; Palevitz, 1997; Ribeiro, 2022). A scholar

- saves a ton of time not doing a literature search and review.
- saves time having to explain why some other evidence contradicts one's own.
- avoids messy and time-consuming scholarly debates.
- wins the argument by avoiding debate (and Popperian falsifiability challenges).
- can cover more topics over time, which aids in the appearance that one is broadly informed.
- signals to journalists and policymakers that they need not bother searching for rival evidence because, allegedly, it does not exist.
- adds to his or her citation totals, or those of one's group, while not adding to rivals'.
- establishes (false) *bona fides* as an "expert" on the topic (as experts are expected to know the research literature).
- attracts extra attention by allegedly being "first," "original," "a pioneer."
- increases the likelihood of press coverage for the same reason.
- increases prospects for research grant funding to "fill knowledge gaps."
- puts rivals in the position of appearing petulant if they protest their exclusion or misrepresentation, of having "sour grapes."
- does not seem personal as rival scholars are not even identified. (To protest the misrepresentation, by contrast, an offended rival must identify those who have misrepresented them, which can be interpreted as a personal attack.)

The real beauty of a dismissive review lies in the anonymity (or, alleged nonexistence) of the criticized target. Were a scholar to identify those whose work is being dismissed or denigrated, a responsible journalist or editor might feel compelled to offer them an opportunity to respond. And the dismissive or denigrating review might then be shown to be false. By not naming names, one can pretty much characterize others' research in any manner one pleases (Grant, 2009; Savage, 1989; Wager and Kleinert, 2011).

These numerous benefits accrue to individual scholars or organized groups of scholars. Meanwhile, the costs of dismissive reviews accrue to society as a whole:

- Many people, including other scholars, journalists, and policymakers, believe them, and discontinue searching for the dismissed information.

Indeed, they may convince others that the dismissed information does not exist.
- The dismissed information is not considered in policy discussions.
- Public policies are skewed.
- Foundations and governments may pay again for work that has already been done.
- False expertise and celebrity supersede genuine expertise.

The more prominent and trusted the scholar, the greater the damage. While a widely read scholar can add only one study at a time to the collective working memory, she can dismiss an entire research literature each time. When a scholar subtracts more from the collective working memory than she adds, her net benefit to society's understanding is negative. But her curriculum vitae (CV) reveals only what was added (Duede, 2022).[7]

Moreover, the more prominent the scholar, the more likely they are to get away with a (false) dismissive review, and the more likely journalists will simply repeat their dismissive reviews without checking. Most who could defend their work against its dismissal are non-celebrities who have difficulty getting a hearing. And, even if they can get a hearing, they are easily dismissed as inferior researchers who are simply jealous.

Finally, it is easier to get a research grant if one can convince donors of a "knowledge gap" on a policy-relevant topic (Wallace Foundation, 2022). The funder can then feel satisfied that they are uniquely filling an important societal need. That can be a source of pride, and an accomplishment worthy of mention in an annual report.[8]

How prevalent are dismissive reviews? See for yourself. Web search phrases such as: "this is the first study," "no previous studies," "paucity of research," "little research," or their variations. Granted, the search "counts" in some of the most popular search engines are rough estimates and not actual counts. Still, scrolling through, say, just the first five hundred results can be revealing—dismissive reviews are far more common than they have any right to be.

Here are the search engine counts returned by Google (January 15, 2022) for certain phrases:[9]

"absence of research"	~188,000,000
"absence of studies"	~51,900,000
"this is the first study"	~13,400,000
"little research"	~10,500,000
"paucity of research"	~11,100,000

The situation could be much improved if all followed the meta-analyst's example—specify exactly where one has looked and summarize only what is found there.[10] But, more generally, we should alter the meaning of "contribution" to research. Currently, original works are considered contributions, and quality literature reviews are not.

For other researchers, a dismissive review is a stop sign. It assures that any further searching for previous work is unnecessary because it would be fruitless. Given the large time demands of a thorough literature review, and its nonexistent professional benefits, a stop sign may well elicit a feeling of relief.

Thus, dismissive reviews encourage scholars to conduct research that may have already been done. Given that most scholarly research is either directly (e.g., through grants or research center funding) or indirectly (e.g., as expected parts of public university professors' work schedules) funded by taxpayers, we all end up paying for these redundant expenditures (Blaine, Brunnhuber, and Lund, 2021; Kochen, 1987).

Some argue that we should want redundant studies, as verification checks on the earlier work. Indeed, replication studies are profoundly important to the progress of science. The case of a funded scholar initiating a study while dismissing previous work on the topic, however, raises a few concerns:

- First, the funding is provided under false pretenses; the funders might have chosen to fund something else if they had known of the earlier work on the topic.
- Second, the benefit of replication comes from a comparison of a new study with the old, which requires an acknowledgement of the existence of the prior work.
- Third, new studies can benefit from the background context that earlier studies can provide, even if a new study incorporates different data and methodology.

One might expect journal editors and peer reviewers to protect us from false dismissive reviews. Their profusion, however, suggests that that line of defense was breached long ago in some fields (Balietti, Goldstone, and Helbing, 2016; Phelps, 2021a; Wager and Kleinert, 2011).

Perhaps we err by believing the current journal review system even capable of policing our modern information torrent. The research volume on many topics may be not only too deep and broad for any individual's brain to comprehend. It may also be too large for any single academic discipline to manage (Lamont, 2020; Ledzińska and Czerniawska, 2008; Simon, 1971).

The year 2006 saw 1.35 million scientific journal articles published. The annual total increased to 1.57 million just six years later (2012), for an annual rate of increase of 2.5 percent, or three new papers a minute (Firestein, 2013).

One might have surmised that the voluminous accumulation of research information would produce clear social benefits. "Knowledge gaps" would be filled. Literature review prologues to scholarly journal articles would lengthen. Scholars' expertise would deepen. The public and policymakers would be better informed. A fuller understanding of our world would improve the quality of our lives.

To the contrary, as research information proliferates, so do dismissive literature reviews.

For a single individual, knowing an entire research literature may no longer be possible, especially for topics that cross several academic disciplinary boundaries, where one finds unique vocabulary and research methods. A substantial proportion of the relevant information may not be available in any academic journal but, rather, in the archives of local, state, and national governments, their independent private contractors, or commercial entities. Much may not be indexed. Even some that is indexed exists only in paper form in just one or a few libraries. Some has already been lost.

And, that wonderful dissemination tool, the World Wide Web, provides only information that someone, somewhere was paid to upload.

Much of the old stuff is just photocopied (i.e., it lacks searchable text), if it is available on the internet at all. Some is photocopied with word recognition technology that makes it somewhat searchable, but imperfectly. Anyone familiar with trying to copy and paste from these documents is also familiar with the many misread characters, missing or added spaces, and other anomalies that make them unusable for searching by exact phrases.

Moreover, some pre–World Wide Web information will never be uploaded at all. Think of a single copy master's thesis from the mid-twentieth century, or the issues of a discontinued professional journal (Else, 2021). No one living has either an obligation or incentive to upload those documents to the web, even as simple, non-searchable photocopies.[11]

Lessons from the Dismissive List

The Dismissive List collects and organizes dismissive reviews made by celebrity education policy scholars in citation cartels. It is published online and periodically updated (Phelps, 2016b). To date, it includes over a thousand statements that dismiss or demean research conducted outside the cartels. Most statements are inaccurate; others are misleading. Each entry includes the dismissive statement, the names of the authors and co-authors, title of source, date, and page numbers and hyperlink to the source, when available.

The collection was a lark at first, but then patterns began to emerge.

"Dismissive review" is the general term. In the "type" column of the files, a finer distinction is made among simply "dismissive"—meaning a claim that there is no or little previous research; "denigrating"—meaning a claim that previous research exists but is so inferior it is not worth even citing; and "firstness"—a claim to be the first in the history of the world to ever conduct such a study.

Of the three types, firstness claims carry particular importance (Bartlett, 2012; Cohen, 2017; Eagles, 2012; Elson, Huff, and Utz, 2020; Grant, 2008; Greenspan, 2009; Labaree, 2021; Lawrence, P. A., 2002; Makel and Plucker, 2019; Powers, D., 2015; Träger, 2016; Zwaan, Etz, Lucas, and Donnellan, 2018). According to Bright (2021, p. 121) in "Why Do Scientists Lie?":

> Scientists win credit by establishing priority on new claims . . . to be the first to get such a thing out in one of the field-acknowledged venues for placing interesting work.

Media analyst Devon Powers adds,

> Firstness has become a core value in the system of economic rewards connected to, and reliant upon, cultural circulation. The accolades for being first can and often do outstrip those for being credible, comprehensive, or right. (2015, p. 13)

Ultimately, the "strategic" rule seems to be: one can say one is the first and previous work does not exist so long as one does not neglect to cite someone with power over one's career. That is, if those responsible for the previous work are relatively unknown and powerless—i.e., dismissible—one can and should dismiss their work.

Dismissive reviews are typically raw declarations made without explanation as to how they were derived. No mention is made of where the authors looked for sources, or how (or, even if). Celebrity researchers, whose claim to fame is their allegedly superior research skill, provide no evidence or analysis whatsoever for their claims.[12]

When a group of dismissive reviewers joins to support each other, they form a "citation cartel." Essentially, they cite and reference each other and ignore, dismiss, or denigrate others' research. Citation cartels can advance researchers' careers substantially. Each member of the cartel receives more exposure in general while, at the same time, their professional rivals receive less. Universities consider the numbers of citations as evidence of research productivity and influence and use those numbers in appointment and advancement decisions (Davis, 2012; Oransky and Marcus, 2017; Wilsdon et al., 2015).

One might have suspected that dismissing a real, extant research literature would be observed, noted, and disciplined. Such behavior is obviously unethical and runs counter to the notion that scientific progress requires knowledge accumulation and open debate.

Shockingly, there is little such discipline, and none when those in one academic discipline dismiss a research literature that largely resides in another (Moran 1998). Scholars are free to write and repeat dismissive reviews without fear of any negative consequences. While most ordinary scholars' dismissive reviews probably have little effect, the dismissive reviews of the most celebrated scholars can have enormous effect.

After the Dissmissive List accumulated a few hundred dismissive reviews, one could observe a strong correlation between the research cited and the disciplinary field of the author and the journal. That is, almost all previous research acknowledged to exist fell within the author's subject field. One after another after another author of manuscripts published by Harvard's National Bureau of Economic Research (NBER), for example, claimed a "paucity of research" on education topics.

On those occasions when they did acknowledge prior work, however, it was in economics. Report after NBER report declared "no previous research exists," when, at best, they had only looked for previous research within their single field of economics.

After the list accumulated *several* hundred dismissive reviews two more patterns emerged. First, the two oldest, and most prominent and celebrated, scholars among them had been writing dismissive reviews for several decades across a variety of topics.[13] As Harry Lewis had implied in his 2007 interview,[14] dismissive reviews may be a feature, not a bug, of successful scholarly careers.[15]

Second, the narrowing of the knowledge base among some of the most celebrated researchers was even more extreme than could be explained by subject field myopia. When some "top" scholars cited previous research, it was overwhelmingly that which had been conducted by others within their citation cartel.

Not only were economists not acknowledging all the research on their topic, they were not even acknowledging all the research on their topic within economics. They were only acknowledging the existence of research that had been conducted within their group, their club, their gang—that is, among colleagues they knew would reciprocate the gesture.

Research conducted by anyone outside their tight circle of, at most, a hundred individuals, was implied to be of such little value that they felt justified in declaring it nonexistent. Thus, all research on their chosen topic conducted prior to a couple of decades ago—gone. Almost all research on their chosen topic conducted outside the field of economics (and maybe,

grudgingly, a little from political science)—gone. All research on their chosen topic conducted outside the United States (or, maybe on occasion, a couple of Western European countries)—gone.[16] All research on their chosen topic written in a language other than English—gone (Al-Janabi, 2022; Di Bitetti and Ferreras, 2017).

Most astonishing of all, all relevant education research ever conducted within the disciplines of psychology or program evaluation—gone.

For the most part, the List includes statements made by "serial dismissers," scholars who dismiss repeatedly on a variety of topics. This is done to help counter the argument that they might be innocent, did try to look for previous research, and simply could not find it. In some cases, they dismiss a research literature that is hundreds or thousands of studies deep. And, when they do that repeatedly across a variety of topics, the odds that their dismissive behavior could be innocent fade to miniscule (Markowitz, 2022).

(See also Appendix 3 online for lists of research literatures dismissed by certain scholars and journalists, https://educationpolicy.us/Malfunction/App3.pdf.)

Moreover, the List includes only statements of those whose dismissive reviews can inflict real harm. If a master's student at a middling, not particularly well-known college writes a dismissive review in his or her thesis, the effect on the world may not even be noticeable.

But the people included in the List, as some of them are fond of telling us themselves, are "influential" (e.g., Hess, 2021, 2022). They rank among the most widely quoted and cited researchers in education policy. They advise presidents, international education organizations, federal education secretaries, and legislators. Journalists have their telephone numbers on speed dial. They have been profusely awarded with professional sinecures, prizes, titles, and other manner of prestige. What they say and write matters when it is accurate, but probably even more so when it is not.

Finally, the List is far from a complete compendium. Given the propensity that some celebrity researchers have for dismissive reviews, likely there are thousands more to be found.

Sticks and Stones

Just among the bunch of high-profile researchers featured in the Dismissive List, one finds hundreds of denigrating terms employed to discourage the public, press, and policymakers from searching for work done by others. Some in-context examples:

- "The shortcomings of [earlier] studies make it difficult to determine . . ."
- "What we don't know: what is the net effect on student achievement?

- Weak research designs, weaker data
- Some evidence of inconsistent, modest effects
- Reason: grossly inadequate research and evaluation"
- "Nearly 20 years later, the debate ... remains much the same, consisting primarily of opinion and speculation. ... A lack of solid empirical research has allowed the controversy to continue unchecked by evidence or experience ..."

By way of illustrating the alacrity with which some researchers dismiss others' research as not worth looking for, Table 2.1 offers a compilation of the operative words used in the "denigrating" category of the List (Phelps,

Table 2.1. Terms employed to denigrate research conducted by other, unidentified scholars.

Frequency	"Previous Research ...	Denigrating terms used
43	... is not	"systematic"; "aligned"; "detailed"; "comprehensive"; "large-scale"; "cross-state"; "sustained"; "thorough"
31	... is not	"empirical"; "research-based"; "scholarly"
29	... is	"limited"; "selective"; "oblique"; "mixed"; "unexplored"
19	... is/has	"small"; "scant"; "sparse"; "narrow"; "scarce"; "thin"; "lack of"; "handful"; "little"; "meager"; "small set"; "narrow focus"
15	... is not	"hard"; "solid"; "strong"; "serious"; "definitive"; "explicit"; "precise"
14	... is	"weak"; "weaker"; "challenged"; "crude"; "flawed"; "futile"
9	... is/has	"anecdotal"; "theoretical"; "journalistic"; "assumptions"; "guesswork"; "opinion"; "speculation"; "biased"; "exaggerated"
8	... is not	"rigorous"
8	... is/has not	"credible"; "compelling"; "adequate"; "reliable"; "convincing"; "consensus"; "verified"
7	... is/has	"inadequate"; "poor"; "shortcomings"; "naïve"; "major deficiencies"; "futile"; "minimal standards of evidence"
5	... is not	"careful"; "consistent"; "reliable"; "relevant"; "actual"
4	... is not	"clear"; "direct"
4	... is not	"high quality"; "acceptable quality"; "state of the art"
4	... is/has not	"current"; "recent"; "up to date"; "kept pace"
4	... is/has	"statistical shortcomings"; "methodological deficiencies"; "individual student data, followed school to school"; "distorted"
2	... is not	"independent"; "diverse"

2016b). To consolidate the mass of verbiage somewhat, similar terms are grouped in the same row.

As well as illustrating the facility with which some researchers denigrate the work of rivals, the table also illustrates how easy it is. Hundreds of terms stand ready to dismiss the work of other scholars and entire research literatures.

Sincere and Strategic Scholars

At the risk of some simplification, there exist two types of scholars: sincere and strategic. Karl Popper's scientific progress depends on sincere scholars working in open societies to manage the steady, freely contested, and transparently curated accumulation of knowledge. Each new discovery adds to all of those made before, and those made before are acknowledged and respected. As Isaac Newton famously said, "If I have seen further it is by standing on the shoulders of giants."[17]

Sincere scholars try to do the right thing. They either conduct forthright and thorough literature reviews, or they specify exactly where and how they looked for previous relevant research.[18] They cite all other relevant research regardless of their own personal opinions of the individual scholars involved or their own personal preferences for their research results. They provide full and accurate citations of all that previous work so that readers will have no trouble finding it. They attempt to direct the reader to the location in humanity's body of knowledge where they believe their new work fits. It is, after all, the steady accumulation of knowledge that facilitates progress (*Economist*, 2019b; Garfield, 1996, 1997; Kochen, 1987).

The cooperative world of sincere scholars values independence of thought and action. Independence is necessary for fair consideration of contrary ideas and evidence. Few will challenge established conventions when rejection by established authority is certain.

Thousands of sincere researchers continue to bulk up the shoulders of Newton's giants just by "doing research." Conduct a study, get it published in a reputable journal, and there it is "in the research literature" for all to see and use. They may even write quaint instructions in their article discussion sections like "Our findings suggest that policymakers would be wise to consider . . ." as if there were a positive probability that policymakers read their journal.

Sincere scholars do not allow their personal biases, prejudices, or ambitions to color their research, or their references to others'. Unprompted, they point journalists and policymakers toward the work of rivals so that they may appreciate and consider the full diversity of evidence and viewpoints,

and judge for themselves. That's how one treats people and processes that one respects.

Above all, sincere scholars do not claim to be experts in fields in which they are not. Instead, they admit their lack of expertise to any inquiring journalist or policymaker. If they know of others who may possess the relevant expertise, they may offer a referral.

Were all scholarship sincere, it would justify the predilection of some education journalists and policymakers to source their education truth exclusively from those with the glossiest credentials. Assume that all scholars and all scholarship were completely sincere and objective, and one might reasonably assume that the most competent and knowledgeable would be recognized as such and rise to the pinnacles of their professions. Those most celebrated would be the most trustworthy and informative sources. Level of celebrity would correlate strongly with level of genuine expertise.

Now let's get real. The most sincere, honest, and forthright may not rise to the top. As the late baseball manager Leo Durocher said, "Nice guys finish last" (Keyser, 2015).

In US education research, there exist few incentives for scholars to behave sincerely. Meanwhile, a cornucopia of methods and opportunities present themselves to more ambitious scholars with the "will to power" (Lawrence, P. A., 2002, 2003, 2007, 2008; Lipton and Williams, 2016; Vial, Muradoglu, Newman, and Cimpian, 2022).

The *strategic* scholar optimizes his or her career advancement. In its purest form, strategic scholarship serves to advance one's own career while depressing those of rivals. Those rivals may be alive or long dead. In the latter case dismissal is aided by natural inhibition (Conix, De Block, and Vaesen, 2021; Stroup, 2021).

If I Don't Like You, I Don't Cite You

Sincere scholars work to expand society's knowledge and understanding. They cite all the relevant research, even that produced by those they disagree with or personally dislike. They encourage debate. For the sincere scholar, a citation is a responsibility, and proper and thorough citations demonstrate research quality.

For the strategic researcher, a citation is an asset to be used career-advantageously. As a certain former governor of the state of Illinois once said about his responsibility to fill an open US Senate position, "I've got this thing and it's (expletive) golden. I'm not just giving it up for (expletive) nothing."[19]

Career-strategic scholars do not cite the work of others outside their group, unless they must because that other work is so well known their slight would be widely noticed. Debates are generally avoided with those outside one's

cartel. Citing only that research conducted by one's friends and allies creates an impression that the entire research world agrees with you.

Given the contrasting dynamics, over time the work of career-strategic scholars will attract more attention, produce better scholarly metrics which, in turn, leads to better employment outcomes and higher status. As Nicholas Taleb (2016) put it, "the most intolerant wins." The work of sincere scholars, unreferenced by the career-strategic scholars now leading their professions, drifts into the internet age's vast sea of ignored information (Goldhaber, M. H., 1997; Ribeiro, 2022; Rubin, 2014).

Imagine a society of twenty scholars—ten career-strategic and ten sincere—all researching the same topic. The strategic scholars cite only each other, whereas the sincere scholars cite everyone.

Assume ten publications a year per scholar, each with ten citations. Those ten citations are contained within the group among the strategic scholars but spread across all by the sincere.

After one year, the strategic scholars as a group will have accumulated 1,500 citations, one thousand from themselves and another 500 from sincere scholars. Meanwhile, the sincere scholars as a group will have accumulated only the 500 citations of their own. After two years, the strategic scholars will have accumulated 3,000 citations, whereas the sincere scholars will have accumulated only 1,000.

The ratio after ten years: 15,000 for the strategic and 5,000 for the sincere. After twenty years: 30,000 to 10,000. After thirty years: 45,000 to 15,000. (See Figure 2.1.)

Lopsided ratios in information dissemination can produce large disparities in society's knowledge production and understanding of reality. Status and rewards in academia are based on scholars' perceived production and impact, relative to others. Policymakers and journalists tend to direct their attention toward, and trust, those scholars with the most credentials.

Moreover, when celebrity scholars hold all the microphones, they can debate other scholars when and if they choose. Acting strategically, they are more likely to choose to debate when they feel they can win. Thus, the better the argument made against their work, the less likely a debate will ensue.

When the public, policymakers, or journalists get advice from sincere scholars, they receive a thorough and honest appraisal of the subject. When they get advice from strategic scholars, they receive only the subset of the relevant policy research that benefits those scholars' careers. When government or foundations fund sincere scholars they, again, receive a thorough and honest appraisal of the subject. When they fund strategic scholars, they receive only a skewed subset. Indeed, their funds will likely serve to dismiss more policy-relevant information than is newly produced. Likely, they fund a degradation in public understanding (Secchi, 2022).

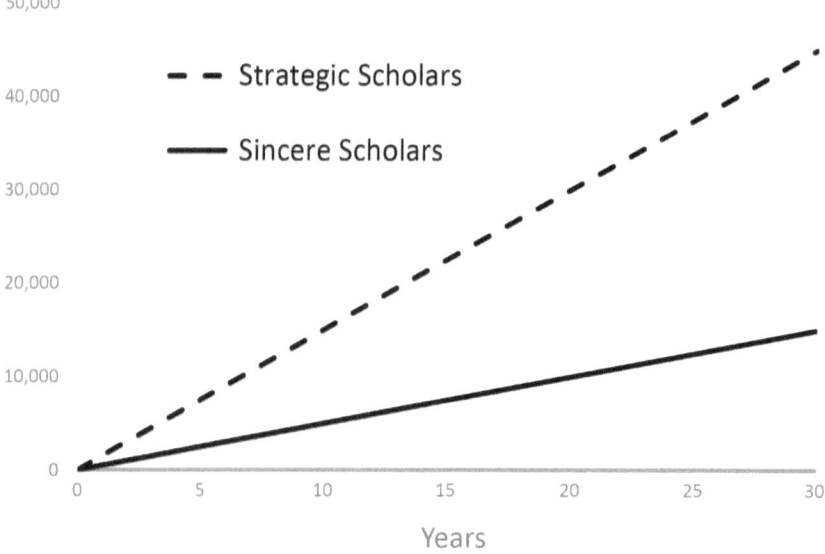

Figure 2.1. Comparing strategic and sincere scholarship citation accumulation over thirty years.
Source: Author created.

The "Celebrity Threshold"

A rule of thumb for celebrity scholars: scholars who criticize or disagree may need to be confronted if they are well known—i.e., they exist above the "celebrity threshold." One's critics from above the celebrity threshold can manage just as much public attention and could win the argument if one doesn't respond. As for the vast multitude of scholars who lie below the threshold and can attract no substantial amount of public attention on their own—they may simply be ignored or dismissed. Ignoring them avoids a time-consuming debate that one might lose and carries the added advantage of not drawing attention to them, while also suggesting that their opinions are unimportant because they are unimportant. One's celebrity juxtaposed against one's critics' lack thereof is offered as proof enough that one must be right, and one's critics must be wrong. (See also Vazire, 2017.)

Some journalists pay no attention to information sources below the celebrity threshold.

Scholarly journals proliferate. Scholarly articles proliferate. The proliferation expands the thicknesses of scholars' curriculum vitae. Scholarly

incentives stimulate more and more and more and more. Meanwhile, claims of oddly nonexistent research literatures on long familiar topics and "first-ever" studies proliferate in tandem.

Discussions of the research literature transpire within scholarly journals that are entirely different than those that occur among policy-influential celebrity researchers. The proportion of research even considered in policy discussions amounts to a small fraction of what could be made available to policymakers. We risk losing the benefit of a massive quantity of knowledge accumulated prior to the mid-1990s, when the World Wide Web appeared. We risk losing the benefit of most post-1990s knowledge accumulated by most researchers—those who operate below the celebrity threshold (Holmquist, 2016).

Whereas other ethical affronts, such as plagiarism or data fabrication, can attract much public attention, the far more consequential bad behavior of "citation cartels" receives little.

Citation cartels in US education research have been tolerated for so long—and with so little negative consequence—they have become endemic. Veteran cartel members now train new members (e.g., their graduate students and research assistants) in the same information suppression techniques—i.e., cite and praise those in one's group, ignore or dismiss others. New cartel members who have never known any other way may simply accept the behavior as standard operating procedure.

Many believe dismissive-reviewing strategic scholars without understanding the underlying technical issues or the analytical methods. They believe them because they are well known. As Davide Secchi offers, however, "the question is whether they became influential because of [their] cartel or because of the science they publish."[20]

Credentials *Über Allis*

In the final chapter of his final book, *The Educational Morass*, the late Myron Lieberman (2007) argued that few in the US understand education's more arcane or technical issues, such as collective-bargaining regulations—his specialty—or testing and measurement. They trust the judgments of others, to whom they give credence.

This is no less true for well-known economists and political scientists than it is for anyone else. How does one know whom to believe? The standard signals in academia relate to honors and prestige—a Harvard professor is presumed to know better than your community college professor; an awarded, tenured professor is presumed to know better than an itinerant adjunct; and so on (Bauer, 2021; Brooks, 2021; Leef, 2021; Rauch, 2021; Vazire, 2017).

When a journalist or policymaker under deadline needs information, whom should they trust? In that hurried moment, credentials loom more important

than expertise, because genuine expertise takes too long to evaluate. As Gloria Origgi (2018) put it:

> There is an underappreciated paradox of knowledge that plays a pivotal role in our advanced hyper-connected liberal democracies: the greater the amount of information that circulates, the more we rely on so-called reputational devices to evaluate it. What makes this paradoxical is that the vastly increased access to information and knowledge we have today does not empower us or make us more cognitively autonomous. Rather, it renders us more dependent on other people's judgments and evaluations of the information with which we are faced.

Many assume that the research and dissemination process works to cull the good from the bad, the true from the false, the worthy from the unworthy. It may sometimes. But, often it does not, and in the much-maligned field of education research the process works least well.

These days, most quantitative analysis is so technical and obscure that only a small proportion of the population can understand it. Even then, it can take weeks to reverse-engineer a quantitative analysis published in an economics or psychology journal article (Piereson and Riley, 2013). Yet, each article still contains hundreds of nooks and crannies that might hide errors, innocent or deliberate. Who has the time to investigate all the many possible ways one of these articles could be wrong? Other scholars in the same citation cartel will not sacrifice that much time, especially when they are not inclined to publicly criticize the work of a fellow cartel member, anyway.

When the author of an article withholds essential information, it becomes impossible to evaluate their work. (See, for example, *Nonpartisan Education Review*, 2012.)

Retraction Watch[21] is an effort by two science journalists to summarize retraction activity in scholarly journals. One may notice far more retraction activity in the "hard" sciences (e.g., biology, physics, chemistry) than in the social sciences (e.g., psychology, sociology, economics), however, and the least of all in journals publishing education research.

Does this mean that what is published in education journals is of such higher quality that retractions are never called for? Or, the opposite, that the journal editors are less willing to retract?

Scientific progress depends, according to Popper, on an "open society" and an operational Hegelian dialectic: thesis—antithesis—synthesis.

For US education's celebrity scholars, there is no antithesis. None, that is, besides what the in-groups themselves contrive: staged debates conducted entirely within the confines of the group (e.g., Petrilli and Greene, 2016, Pondiscio and Forster, 2021). Not allowed: any challenges that might cast doubt on the group's anointed positions and their facade of expertise.

What resources subsidize the impregnable position of celebrity scholars?

- Blind trust of powerful politicians
- Government grants and subsidies, most importantly those for dedicated topical research centers (e.g., CRESST, CALDER)
- Pack funding from private foundations, including some of the world's wealthiest
- Cooperation from pay-to-play media outlets and journalists attracted to celebrity

As political pundit Charley Sykes (2019) opines,

> there is a pattern here that seems distinctive to our time: the panting after celebrity, the sheer brazenness of the flim-flammery, the dominance of star-bleeping over substance, and the embrace of charlatans by the rich and powerful.

Darkness Descends

In the 1999 sci-fi flick *Dark City*,[22] trench-coated ghouls manipulate humans through memory control. Each night—the humans experience no daytime in Dark City—each human's memory is reworked a bit to satisfy the manipulators' curiosity. One night a couple might enjoy a loving relationship. The next, one might murder the other. A third night could find each with entirely different memories and different partners. There seemed to be little point to the constant experimentation other than the ghouls' salacious voyeurism.

Dark City represents an apt metaphor for US education policy research. Why? Because so little effort goes toward preserving its past accumulation, while strong incentives work to dismiss and denigrate.

NOTES

1. See http://retractiondatabase.org/RetractionSearch.aspx.
2. See also https://econospeak.blogspot.com/2007/12/ethics-of-elite-professors.html.
3. https://www.goodreads.com/quotes/193166-google-is-not-a-synonym-for-research.
4. Just how much work is a forthright, thorough literature review? I have some idea. I have over the years in my "spare time" collected and reviewed thousands of documents on the effect of testing on student achievement. Compressing all the time spent—mostly evenings and weekends—into one chunk, I estimate over one working year (Phelps, 2012b, 2019e).
5. https://www.goodreads.com/quotes/488339-what-you-allow-you-encourage.

6. I have found one. In the *Journal of Pediatric Dermatology* authors guide, under "4. Preparing the submission: General style points": "Firstness: Claims of being the first case report of its kind should be avoided unless a detailed search methodology is included. Please include rationale for claim and search methodology in the letter to the editor." https://onlinelibrary.wiley.com/page/journal/15251470/homepage/forauthors.html#preparing.

7. Selective referencing and dismissive reviewing suffice to suppress most valid, but unwanted information produced from the vast research proletariat. But occasionally, a conflicting voice can be heard above the background noise, rising above the threshold where celebrity researchers debate—where it might even be heard and reported by journalists—and must be directly confronted. On such occasions, the preferred method of information suppression seems to be character assassination. It is virtually impossible for an ordinary scholar lacking a publicity platform or group network to defend himself or herself against personal attacks from well-funded government research centers or think tanks supplied with their own information dissemination bureaus.

8. See, for example, "The Wallace Approach" at https://www.wallacefoundation.org/how-we-work/pages/default.aspx.

9. These are not actual counts but, rather, very rough estimates calculated by algorithms. On the one hand, they probably overestimate by including double counts. On the other hand, not all relevant text is searchable on the internet, thus the estimates undercount.

10. In a comment on *Retraction Watch* (March 29, 2021), C. C. Yoing suggested institutionally and professionally separating new research and literature reviews. An interesting idea. They do require different skills. Moreover, literature reviews might be valued (and scrutinized) more if they were reviewed by other specialists in literature reviewing.

11. See Appendix 2 online for an example of such information attrition, https://educationpolicy.us/Malfunction/App2.pdf. The sources cited in C. C. Ross's *Measurement in Today's Schools* (1941, 1972) are classified by their temporal continuation or end date.

12. By contrast, meta-analysts, researchers who specialize in research literature summaries, provide thorough descriptions of where and how they look for source material, identifying in detail the bibliographic data bases and search engines used, the search algorithms, keywords, time periods, and geographic coverage. Meta-analyst claims are easily verified because another researcher can trace the steps taken. Celebrity researchers' dismissive reviews must be accepted on faith.

13. https://nonpartisaneducation.org/Review/Resources/EricHanushek.htm and https://nonpartisaneducation.org/Review/Resources/DanielKoretz.htm.

14. See Russell, J. H. (December 12, 2007). "A Million Little Writers: Welcome to The World Of Celebrity Academics—And the Behind-the-Scenes Scribes Who Help Make Their Fame and Fortune Possible." *Views from the Occident*. [blog] https://occident.blogspot.com/2007/12/million-little-writers.html.

15. Some scholars responding to *The Scientist*'s survey regarding "citation amnesia" (Grant, 2009), speculated that citation amnesia was more prevalent among more celebrated scientists.

16. See, for example, Glenn and de Groot, 2002.

17. Written in a 1676 letter to Robert Hooke according to *Wikiquote*, which attributes a similar phrase made earlier to Bernard of Chartres. http://en.wikiquote.org/wiki/Isaac_Newton.

18. For example, they might specify the keywords, indexes, databases, and date ranges used in a literature search.

19. https://www.chicagotribune.com/news/ct-xpm-2010–06–29-ct-met-blagojevich-trial-0630–20100629-story.html.

20. Email message from Davide Secchi, June 8, 2022.

21. https://retractionwatch.com/.

22. https://www.imdb.com/title/tt0118929/.

Chapter 3

The Education Establishment Cartel

"Half the truth is often a great lie."

—Benjamin Franklin

Some years ago, one of the nation's largest test development firms hired a new senior vice president for research and development. Given that the firm's primary business was selling standardized tests, most of the hundreds of R&D employees were of the testing craft—psychometricians, statisticians, standards and test item writers, and the like. The new guy, however, had no such training or experience. His expertise: strategic partnerships

Why did the company need expertise in strategic partnerships? The theory was that organizations in education research and policy needed allies to win the favor of those institutions tossing around billions in funding, particularly the US federal government and the Bill and Melinda Gates Foundation. The amounts of money in play had become so large that winning pieces of the prize could stake one's organization for a generation and place it in the center of the action. Conversely, losing out could relegate one's organization to irrelevance.

The firm's strategic partners included at times the Education Trust, Mark Tucker's National Center on Education and the Economy (NCEE), and, always, the Gates Foundation. The firm's research reports would be skewed to include those strategic partners' talking points and filled with trendy and superficial ideas *du jour* and citations limited to widely known celebrity researchers' or the strategic partners' works, with popular inaccuracies included.

In return, strategic partners would promote the firm's products or grant it funds.[1]

A good strategic partner is one who can help boost one's own profile. Whether they are correct in anything they say is beside the point. What matters is getting attention. Do they have the public platforms, PR operation, relationships with journalists, or the money to buy them?

Influence is important. Indeed, the relative influence of the various actors in policy debates is essential to fully understanding current events. It is simply not very important for understanding practical solutions to public policy problems. Strategic partnerships prioritize influence, and influence values money and power. A constant striving for attention has no necessary correlation with effective public policies, public understanding, or fact finding.

Citation cartels are a type of strategic partnership. Some big foundations belong to strategic partnerships, too. A popular belief among them is that each one alone cannot effect the big changes they wish to see in society, but together they can (Barnum, 2021; Face Value, 2006; Huang and Seldon 2014; Samali, Laidler-Kylander, Simonin, and Zohdy, 2016). So, the Gates Foundation goes in one direction and a flock of other foundations follows.

Call it "pack funding." They repeat each other's talking points and collectively recruit and fund "opinion leaders" to promote their goals (and, in turn, to hound, suppress, ridicule, shun, and ostracize those who disagree) (Delborne, 2015). When new foundations arrive with massive fortunes (e.g., from Buffet, Jobs, Zuckerberg) they jump on the same pile.

(See also Appendix 4 online, "Pack Funders and Strategic Partners: Some Examples," https://educationpolicy.us/Malfunction/App4.pdf.)

Government and pack foundation funding for the Common Core Initiative pretty much bought every national group or opinion leader with influence and cleared the field of any possible consideration of feasible alternatives.[2] Those purchased became invested in their claims and owe each other favors.

For education journalists who limit their sourcing of expertise to those with power, celebrity, and influence, stories on Common Core during its first decade meant promoting Common Core.

These days, if one wishes to be an education policy celebrity, one must access a good deal of money, which probably comes with strings. One must join a citation cartel. As with membership in a street gang, there are rules: group loyalty is rewarded, and disloyalty punished. Independent, disruptive voices are dismissed or silenced.

Holding one's tongue facilitates compromise, compromise facilitates partnerships, and partnerships get things done. And, by golly, don't we need to get things done in education?

Well . . . no. We have gotten lots done in US education over the years, and it has taken us from fad to fad to fad, with little real progress to show for all the extra effort and expense (Stone and Clements, 1998).

What we need is better information for making policy decisions. Better information comes from encouraging free and open discussion from a wide variety of knowledgeable and interested parties. Ultimately, strategic partnerships stifle discussion.

Gaslighting[3]

The Center for Research on Evaluation, Standards, and Student Testing (CRESST) is an assemblage of education school professors and think tank researchers working on the topics identified in its name. Since around 1980, it has usually bid successfully for federal funding as well as conducted work for other clients on contract.

Though the exact composition of its membership has changed over time, certain institutions and personnel have almost always been involved over the course of its four decades: the Rand Corporation and the education schools at UCLA and the universities of Colorado, Pittsburgh, and Southern California. Some other institutions involved for long stretches of time have included: Boston College, Stanford and Arizona State universities, and the University of California, Santa Barbara.

The primary, and very successful, tactical innovation of CRESST in education policy was an affectation of openness toward any research result, while declaring the relevant knowledge base insufficient. For example: "There is simply too much that we currently do not know about how to design testing policies that promote desirable outcomes and prevent undesirable ones" (Hamilton, 2003, p. 57).

That is, they do not directly confront or attack the people and evidence they oppose; they publicly express an openness to all . . . all that they acknowledge exists, that is. They steadfastly avoid debate or direct confrontation with opponents or opposing evidence.

Instead of directly opposing new testing proposals or programs, they demure that we do not know enough about what works to implement them with any assurance, particularly so with the types of tests most disliked by US education professors—externally administered high-stakes tests—tests with consequences that education insiders do not themselves control. Any testing proposal is characterized as something new, not tried before, and for which we do not know enough to implement properly. More research is needed . . . and always will be (Herman, 1997).

No matter that such a program may have been well studied in the past; CRESST declares relevant past research nonexistent or no good, without referencing any of it (as referencing it would help people to find it and judge for themselves). No matter that such a program may have been in use in hundreds of other countries, CRESST still declares it to be new.

They then busy themselves writing inconclusive research reports that largely recycle what they had written previously. Read thirty years of CRESST grandee Daniel Koretz's publications, for example, and one may be struck by their sameness. For each new wave of outsider political or business education reformer reading his work, however, it is new.

Years go by, CRESST's research programs drag on producing more doubts, promoting ambiguity, and offering no clear policy direction, and eventually the testing program would fizzle out and policymakers would tire from the lack of any clear progress. The policymakers who proposed the "new" testing program move on, but CRESST is still there, ready to go another round (Phelps, 2018a).

CRESST's alleged research gaps in 1980 were still present in 1985, and in 1990, and in 2000, despite millions in taxpayer funds granted to them over the years to close those gaps. But all along CRESST principals remained well funded, highly visible, and persistently engaged in diverting attention away from other research that contradicted their claims.

Here is a capsule summary of the CRESST method for dealing with policymakers:

- We are not opposed to testing, standards, or accountability.
- We just don't know enough yet to endorse this [*current proposal*].
- Little research has been conducted on this [*current proposal*].
- So, we need to do more research first [*and we can do it, pay us*].

CRESST members have been successful in suppressing most of the evidence relevant to educational testing policy because:

- Most education professors oppose externally controlled high-stakes tests, and many are willing to support dismissing the evidence of benefits and encouraging doubts.
- They managed to co-opt the group of education policy advisors to the Republican Party that most nominally conservative education policy groups trust.
- With the alliance, CRESST members and affiliates attracted conviction and support from the group of large education reform funders allied with the Bill and Melinda Gates Foundation, such as the Hewlett, Walton, and Broad Foundations.
- Few scholars were willing to oppose them because they controlled so much funding, so many contracts and appointments, and so many information dissemination channels.

For CRESST, each proposed testing program was characterized like a new medication that requires years of clinical trials before one could have any confidence in its widespread use. According to them, politicians can be in too much of a hurry:

> Education consumers also like to have things sooner rather than later. For example, performance assessment was a rage in the early 1990s because it was something new and flashy, and looked to have great promise. Before almost any research was done, a number of states dropped their multiple-choice accountability systems, replacing them with performance assessments. The research, much of it carried out by CRESST partners, highlighted a number of substantial problems including reliability, efficiency, and costs. Most states, recognizing the issues themselves, quickly returned to multiple-choice accountability systems, even when researchers like Lee Cronbach were asking for more time to help make performance assessment work. (Baker, Linn, and Herman, 2006)

In fact, the alleged "new and flashy" performance assessments had been in widespread use for millennia and studied experimentally for over a century.

Stealth Cartel

The National School Boards Association published an article in their popular magazine in 2005, after the US Congress had passed the No Child Left Behind Act, but just before state and local educators would implement the act's accountability requirements. A CRESST co-director and assistant director wrote "From standards to assessment to results—what school leaders need to know in the NCLB era" (Herman and Dietel, 2005).

Nine other scholars and practitioners are cited throughout, their apparent diversity and collective representation of all relevant thought and experience seeming to verify a professional consensus on the topic of educational accountability.

CRESST is mentioned just once. Near the article's beginning, a Rochester, New Hampshire, superintendent is quoted in reference to a CRESST research study apparently being conducted in his school district. That notifies the reader that CRESST services are available for hire by local educators.

Apart from that one aside, however, the article reads like news reportage on a wide sampling of current, relevant research on the topic. There are descriptions of six different, mostly ongoing applied research projects in California, Washington State, Kentucky (2), Massachusetts, and a dozen states. A short paragraph describes the work of another education research organization, Achieve. The observations of several different scholars are noted or quoted; they are identified as "Harvard professor," the "coauthor of the Iowa Test of

Basic Skills," and four others each simply as "researcher," including those from the various projects—one from California, one from Washington State, and three from Kentucky.

Such variety! Projects from coast to coast. Researchers in the field, local educators, a professor at a prestigious university, the director of a major testing program.

The first six individuals, however, all happened to be longtime principals at CRESST; the last three individuals worked directly on CRESST projects. Except for a single historical reference, the article included no reference to anyone or any work outside of CRESST.

The article was a CRESST advertisement. It is telling, however, that the authors went to such lengths to hide the fact. It betrays both their guilt and their complicity in research behavior they knew was wrong.

The article pretends to be an objective and broad overview of a current situation—what they know they should be providing the reader, and what the taxpayers had been paying them millions of dollars to provide. Yet, they cannot seem to help themselves. With over a quarter century of taxpayer largesse, they mastered the techniques of *citation stacking* (citing only those in their group—their citation cartel) and *citation amnesia* (not citing anyone else, especially professional rivals) (Grant, 2008, 2009).

CRESST's taxpayer funding was not intended to be used exclusively for their own self-aggrandizement. Yet, CRESST principals learned that they could get away with exactly that. Steadily over time, they cited others' research less, and their own more, until they cited only their own. Rival research was ignored, dismissed, or misrepresented.

The Successful Degradation of Research on Educational Testing

The "scientific" study of school testing—that is, the statistical analysis of test use and its effects—dates to the 1890s. By the early 1920s, commercially produced standardized educational tests were still relatively new, but had already proliferated widely. By the early 1940s, many testing programs had been evaluated and dozens of experimental studies conducted. C. C. Ross, a former student of the testing and measurement pioneer Edward Lee Thorndike, referenced some of those studies in his 1941 tome *Measurement in Today's Schools*.

In just under six hundred pages, Ross wrote both a how-to guide for developing tests and testing programs and a systematic review of the abundant research literature on test use from the first four decades of the twentieth century. In addition to more than a thousand footnotes and citations, most of Ross's several dozen chapters end with a section entitled "Selected

References for Further Reading," in which the author provides bibliographic detail to help the reader find other books relevant to educational testing research—hundreds in all.

Most of Ross's exhaustive coverage of the subject remains relevant today. To be sure, today's testing and testing research differ; there were no computer-delivered tests in 1941, for example. But, in most essential aspects, the use of tests, and how students and teachers relate to them, remain the same.

That doesn't mean that all in his mother lode of research studies on the effects of educational testing would be easy to find later. The time goes by, more gets lost. Less than half of the scholarly journals Ross referenced, for example, still exist under the same name today (see Appendix 2 online, https://educationpolicy.us/Malfunction/App2.pdf).

Fast forward to 1971, and much had changed. By then, for example, most of the old teacher apprenticeship "normal" schools had evolved into graduate schools of education, producing their own research and researchers.

In that year, the profession's flagship review journal *Review of Educational Research* published a literature review by one Marjorie C. Kirkland (1971), then working at a military base branch campus of Alabama's Troy State University. "The Effects of Tests on Students and Schools" contains 234 references, many of which lead one to sources in counseling and guidance or intelligence tests. Fewer lead to genuine research studies of the more quotidian "effects of tests on students and schools" as promised by the article's title.

Instead, one finds within Kirkland's forty-seven-page article numerous cautions for and criticisms of educational test use, plus several bold declarations that little empirical research existed. For example:

> Since these issues affect the lives of so many, and since so much has been written about tests, one would expect to find a great deal of empirical research in this area. However, a review of the literature revealed only a few small-scale and somewhat peripheral empirical studies. (p. 306)

Of the over six hundred authors mentioned in C. C. Ross's 1941 tome, Kirkland cited only sixteen.

Fast-forward another decade, to 1980, and another testing effects literature review, this one by researchers at the UCLA Center for the Study of Evaluation (CSE) (Lazar-Morrison, Polin, Moy, and Burry, 1980), the forerunner to CRESST.

The Center's 1980 "Review of the Literature on Test Use," however, cited only fifty-five sources, of which six were their own. Moreover, only ten predated 1970. Apparently, the Center authors saw no need to review the pre-1970 literature because someone else had already done that—that someone

being Marjorie Kirkland—and her effort allegedly "revealed only a few small-scale and somewhat peripheral empirical studies."

Center authors did not include even the small number of empirical studies that Kirkland had cited. Instead, they chose to emphasize Kirkland's assertions of a lack of research, and added dozens of their own, for example (emphases added):

- "Almost ten years ago, Kirkland (1971) reviewed the literature on test impact on students and schools and found that while much had been written about tests, *few empirical studies were evident*" (p. 3).
- "What is significant about [Kirkland's] exclusions is the correct observation that these issues are 'implications,' often *not founded on empirical research*" (p. 3).
- "Kirkland's review of the literature is concentrated mainly upon the social and psychological issues in testing, more than upon instructional issues. Also, then as now, *little empirical research had accumulated on the latter*" (p. 3).
- "*There is little research-based information* about current testing practice" (p. 3).
- "*Only recently has the testing dialogue begun to* move away from social and psychological issues . . . to *focus on the instructional issues of testing*" (p. 3).
- ". . . *little is known about the amount of other testing* that takes place" (p. 6).
- "Although much has been written about minimum competency issues, *there has yet to be any report of the actual uses or extent of the use of competency-based tests*" (p. 7).
- "The kinds of *contextual factors* which influence testing *and the use of test results are just beginning to be appreciated*" (p. 9).
- "As of yet, *there is no evidence* about how teacher attitudes toward other types of tests affect the use of those assessments" (p. 19).
- "These factors have been considered in research on teachers' instructional decision-making or in studies of the social or organizational qualities of the classroom. *The investigation of these variables* as factors affecting teachers' use of tests and test data *is minimal*" (p. 20).
- "The question of whether test scores affect a student's self-concept has also been raised. . . . As indicated previously, *information on any of the aforementioned issues is scant*" (p. 24).
- "The impact of other testing must also be considered. In-class assessments made by individual teachers *have yet to be examined in depth*" (p. 24).

Raw declarations all: the authors provide no description of where or how (or even if) they looked for evidence. The reader is expected to assume that they did. Of the over six hundred authors mentioned in C. C. Ross's 1941 book, the UCLA authors cited none.

With one more decade, came one more literature review from CRESST (Herman and Golan, 1991). "Effects of Standardized Testing on Teachers and Learning—Another Look" contains thirty-nine citations. Twenty-nine lead to CRESST work and another seven to the work of close allies and frequent collaborators. Of the over six hundred authors mentioned in C. C. Ross's 1942 book, the CRESST 1991 literature review cited none.

Jump ahead another decade, to the earliest years of the new millennium. Texas governor George W. Bush was the Republican candidate in the presidential election of 2000, and for the first time in American history, standardized testing in the schools emerged as a major national campaign issue. Education professors gang-tackled it with hundreds of anti-testing books, op-eds, panel discussions, and interviews (Phelps, 2003).

In response to this mugging, Republican Party education policy wonks had little to say. For whatever reason, the GOP had long relied on economists for its more academic education policy information, and economists had paid little attention to education program evaluation, academic standards, or testing and measurement. These GOP policy-advisor economists—along with a few political scientists—knew little of the rich research literature on educational test use and its effects in schools.

Yet, a national testing program was coming, and the new Republican administration needed policy advice. If the advisors admitted to how little they knew, they risked forfeiting their places in the power elite at the moment their side had taken over and was setting national policy. After all, genuine experts know the research literature in their field.

CRESST presented an attractive alternative: assert that no previous research exists, and one could claim expert status with just a single new study (Phelps, 2012a). The party's in-house education policy advisors would "fake it until they could make it."

Literature reviews are like jury duty. Responsible citizens with time on their hands may find it interesting and like the idea of participating in government. Ambitious careerists with their own priorities may welcome any excuse to avoid it.

To really know a research literature typically requires years of patient study. By pretending there to be no previous work to study, one can get right to work. Moreover, any work one does in a barren, blank-slate research field is "new," "first," and "pioneering" (Grant, 2009). "First" research work is more prestigious, more likely to attract the public's attention, and more likely

to be considered newsworthy by journalists (Nichols, Kendall, and Boomer, 2019; Powers, 2015).

In early 2003, shortly after the passage of the No Child Left Behind Act, with its educational testing mandate, the US House Education and Workforce Committee would publish the following from a Brookings Institution–based GOP advisor in a press release: "It is important to keep in mind the limited body of data on the subject. . . . We are just getting started in terms of solid research on standards, testing and accountability."

With that, the acknowledged quantity of a century's worth of research on educational testing declined to zero. (See Figure 3.1.)

When our country most needed to consult the research literature, policymakers' most trusted advisors told them there was nothing to find. The president and Congress would fly blind, and US citizens got the No Child Left Behind (NCLB) Act.

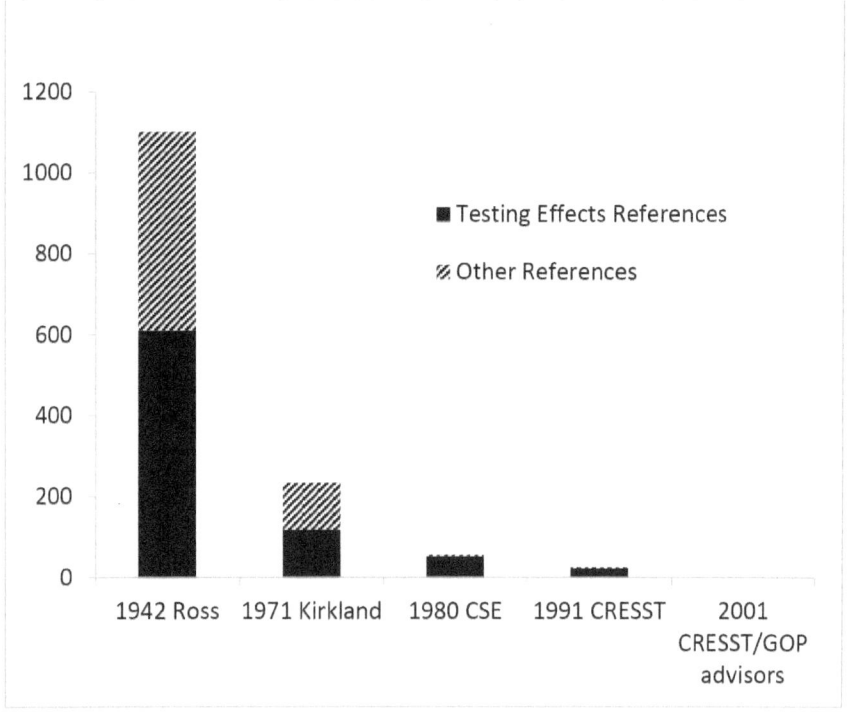

Figure 3.1. Number of studies on testing and testing effects, as reported by researcher or research organization.
Source: Author created.

The world had experienced "test-based accountability systems" for over two millennia. Yet, for their part, in 2002, CRESST's leaders wrote (Baker, Linn, Herman, and Koretz):

> Because experience with accountability systems is still developing. . . . It is not possible at this stage in the development of accountability systems to know in advance how every element of an accountability system will actually operate in practice or what effects it will produce.

And, they were available to conduct studies—for a fee.

Anatomy of a "Sincere" Dismissive Review

Most dismissive reviews in US education policy research are likely insincere. That is, scholars imply that they are familiar with an entire research literature when, in fact, they are not, and haven't seriously bothered to look.

There was one contemporary case, however, of a sincere search and review of the literature on educational testing effects. It may also have had a substantial influence on US policy formation, given both its timing and wide dissemination.

"Sincere" means the author demonstrated some effort at searching and summarizing the literature. The author apparently genuinely believed that he had conducted a literature search sufficiently thorough to justify making global claims about the character of that literature.

Yet the scholar underestimated the size of the relevant research literature by many orders of magnitude, with perhaps profound results for US public policy. How could that happen?

Affirming both the scholar's stature and the popularity of his results, his study was realized, with only slight variations, in several high-profile venues from 1998 to 2002: as a featured address at a large professional conference and in at least three publications with wide circulation (Mehrens, 1997, 1998a, 1998b, 2002). The theme of his article: there was little research on the consequences of educational testing, either good or bad.

His article's circulation coincided with the 2000 presidential campaign and election. Moreover, it served as background to the discussions among scholars and policymakers that would eventually produce the assessment program of the No Child Left Behind (NCLB) Act, a program whose basic structure remains federal law over two decades later.

In the scholar's own words, he searched for "several types of effects."[4] In total, the author, William Mehrens, referenced fifty-six sources, only thirty of which were studies of the effects of testing. The remaining twenty-six provided background information or others' dismissive reviews.

In 2012, the International Test Commission's *International Journal of Testing* (*IJT*) published the results of a meta-analysis of the research literature on the effect of educational testing on student achievement (Phelps, 2012b). The database analyzed would include 668 sources (and over a thousand effects, as most experimental studies include more than one), 434 of which had been published in 2002 or earlier.[5] Moreover, the *IJT* article concerned only one of Mehrens's five categories of testing effects: "Improvement in student learning."[6, 7] Had it included all five of his types, the haul of past studies would have been larger.

Table 3.1 and Figure 3.2 compare counts of testing effect studies captured by the two literature reviews, Mehrens's and the *IJT*'s, broken out by categories of sources.

The two reviews of the literature share but three sources in common.

The number of null categories for Mehrens's literature review may be the table's most eye-catching feature. He looked only at K–12 education publications, and only certain types among them—mostly recent (i.e., 1990s) studies of large-scale US state testing programs. There is nothing inherently wrong with such a focus. But the title of his article and his concluding summary statements skew more globally, implying confidence about the entirety of the research literature on educational testing effects.[8]

Studies of testing effects, however, exist outside the worlds of testing and measurement experts, education professors, the United States, and the K–12 level of education.[9, 10] The field of psychology presents perhaps the starkest example; they comprised 18 percent of the sources retrieved for the *IJT*

Table 3.1. Number of testing effect studies 2002 and earlier, by category.

Source type	Mehrens's 1998–2002 articles	IJT meta-analysis
Education journal	6	109
Psychology journal	0	78
Research/advocacy organization	11	44
Education association	5	42
Dissertation or thesis	0	30
Book	0	29
Governmental agency	5	26
Education magazine	3	21
Higher education journal/publication	0	15
Non-education association	0	13
Language testing journal	0	12
Testing in the professions journal	0	11
Program evaluation journal	0	4
TOTAL	30	434
. . . of which, International	0	57

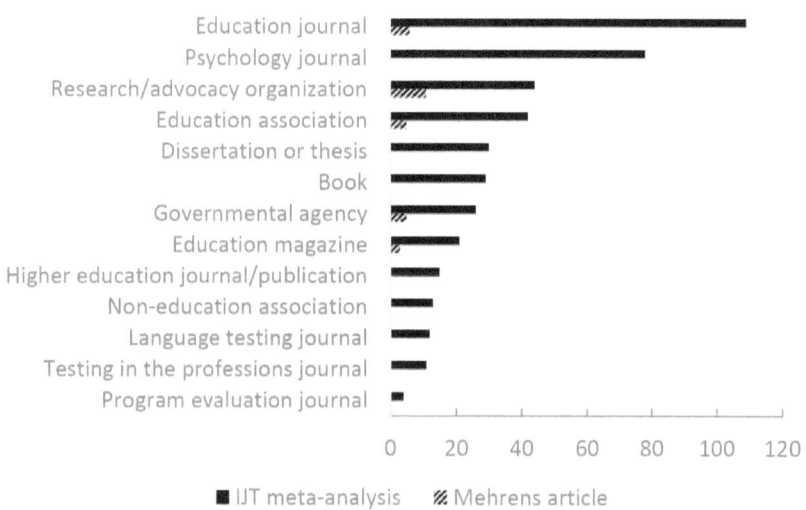

Figure 3.2. Number of testing effect studies, 2002 and earlier, by category.
Source: Author created.

article.[11] (Appendix 5 online breaks out the source categories in even more detail, https://educationpolicy.us/Malfunction/App5.pdf.)

Other fields of inquiry which have studied educational testing's effects include language teaching (from whence the concept of "washback" emanates), education subject areas (e.g., science, technology, math, or reading education), program evaluation, the professions (e.g., medical, nursing, or legal education), personnel (i.e., industrial-organizational) psychology, and the military.

Mehrens apparently thought that any substantial testing effects literature would show up among the sources he consulted. Such an assumption might be valid if the incidence of any given research topic were evenly spread across all journals or journal types. The *IJT* article's search, however, revealed that the testing effects literature is not spread evenly across all types of journals; rather, it is "lumpy."[12] Themes in research can be lumpy over time, as well, with a flurry of research on popular topic for several years, until scholars tire of it or answer all the relevant questions and move on to different topics.

Mehrens devoted much of his article's space to citing and quoting others' dismissive reviews. Apparently, he regarded that as evidence. But the other dismissive reviews he cited were "insincere"—simple declarative statements made without any supporting evidence or record of a search process. Citing an insincere dismissive review is akin to citing hearsay in a court of law—it

should not be admissible evidence. Citing many dismissive reviews simply multiplies by zero (Alexander, 2021).[13,14]

Literature Review Blind Spots

What one might call Mehrens's literature review "blind spots" are hardly unique to him. The following are recognizable "blind spots" underlying many literature reviews:

- A belief that a forthright, thorough literature review is much easier than it is[15] (i.e., "my research assistant, or Google, can do it") (Gusenbauer and Haddaway, 2018; Haddaway and Gusenbauer, 2020; Nuzzo, 2015; Wong, 2004)
- A romantic notion that each of our individual, size-constrained brains can keep up with an ever-expanding universe of knowledge (i.e., "if there was research on this, I would know about it") (Hills, 2019; Kornell, 2014; Kornell and Bjork, 2009; Nuzzo, 2015)[16]
- The eyewitness fallacy: what we see and hear in our own social circles, or the first pages of our internet searches is all there is to see, or at least representative of all (Baccini, De Nicolao, and Petrovich, 2019; Dunning, 2011)
- Earlier dismissive reviews are trustworthy and reliable and multiple dismissive reviews even more so[17] (Backus and Little, 2020; Rekdal, 2014; Wood, 2020)
- All research of equal quality has an equal chance of being published, cited, and accessed (Backus and Little, 2020; Bartlett, 2012; Brock, 2019; Hills, 2019; Larivière, Shu, and Sugimoto, 2020; Lose and Klarskov, 2017; Merton, 1968; Vazire, 2017), regardless of its popularity, its marketing, etc.
- Confirmation bias (Nichols and Williams, 2008; Resnick, 2017)[18]

Mehrens's conclusions were influential. For example, according to the National Research Council (NRC) (Heubert and Hauser, 1999, p. 36): "A recent review of the available research evidence by Mehrens (1998) reaches several interim conclusions. Drawing on eight studies . . ."

That NRC report, in turn, was referenced frequently by the first director of the Institute for Education Sciences in the George W. Bush administration (Whitehurst, 2011):

- "in 1999 the National Academies of Science came to the conclusion that: 'One striking fact is that the complex world of education—unlike

defense, health care, or industrial production—does not rest on a strong research base.'
- "In no other field are personal experience and ideology so frequently relied on to make policy choices, and in no other field is the research base so inadequate and little used."

Dismissive Reviews Are Not Harmless

Obviously, policymakers' belief in an absence of research on testing effects did not stop the US Congress at the end of 2001 from passing the No Child Left Behind Act,[19] which required annual testing at several grade levels in all US public schools. It did, however, forestall consideration of the extant research literature that could have guided them in considering and structuring a much better system, or in leaving well enough alone.[20]

As a result, a Texas testing program was adopted wholesale as NCLB's. The debate over the character of the testing program ventured little beyond the most rudimentary considerations, such as: is testing good or bad?

NOTES

1. I attended a presentation by Mark Tucker around this time (at the Gates Foundation's DC launch of the Common Core Initiative) and he did, indeed, spend an incongruous amount of time recommending that firm's products without any mention that he was, essentially, being paid in barter to promote them.

2. See https://www.gatesfoundation.org/our-work/programs/us-program/k-12-education and https://www.gatesfoundation.org/about/committed-grants.

3. https://www.imdb.com/title/tt0036855/.

4. "A. Curricular and instructional reform: Good, bad, or nonexistent?
"B. Motivation/morale/stress/ethical behavior of teachers: Increase of decrease?
"C. Motivation and self-concepts of students: Up or down?
"D. True improvement in student learning, or just higher test scores?
"E. Restore public confidence or provide data for critics?"

5. See The Effect of Testing on Achievement: Meta-Analyses and Research Summary, 1910–2010: Source List, Effect Sizes, and References for Quantitative Studies; The Effect of Testing on Achievement: Meta-Analyses and Research Summary, 1910–2010: Source List, Effect Sizes, and References for Survey Studies; The Effect of Testing on Achievement: Meta-Analyses and Research Summary, 1910–2010: Source List, Effect Sizes, and References for Qualitative Studies.

6. My meta-analysis includes quantitative, survey, and qualitative studies. All quantitative and survey studies calculated only one type of testing effect—that on student achievement (i.e., student learning). A small number of the qualitative studies

finding motivation gains were classified as "indirectly" supportive of achievement gains.

7. I have yet to read thousands more collected documents, some of which may contain relevant testing effect study results. Nor have I yet collected some older documents only to be found in paper form in certain libraries, non-English language studies, most studies requiring a fee to obtain, or, indeed, most studies unavailable in published form in journals or standard indexes (e.g., most state or district internal testing reports).

8. For example:

- "I . . . investigate what the research evidence says about assessment consequences." (abstract)
- "I . . . present some tentative conclusions about the whole issue of the consequences of assessment and the amount of evidence available and needed." (abstract)
- "Because the evidence is insufficient, my tentative conclusions about the consequences of assessment will, at times, obviously and necessarily be based on less than adequate evidence" (p. 3 of 30).

9. A purist might argue that, for example, higher education and higher education students differ in essential ways from K–12 education and its students. A valid argument, to be sure, but the two types of students also share much in common, including most basic human nature and the classroom format. To conclude that the many testing effect studies conducted in higher education include nothing whatsoever that might usefully inform K–12 education policies seems extreme.

10. Generally, Mehrens looked for evidence of testing effects within his familiar everyday professional world. He looked at the writings of his colleagues, read the types of reports one would typically read in his line of work, reviewed the academic journals most central to his subfield, and included presentations from the professional conferences he regularly attended. For example, he cited five presentations from the joint annual meetings of the National Council on Measurement in Education (NCME) and the American Educational Research Association (AERA), and eleven articles from their journals. Indeed, his article was a presidential address to a division of AERA.

But, as erudite and refined as his familiar professional world may have been, it did not represent the universe of human knowledge on the topic. Not even close.

Furthermore, he looked where he was least likely to find what he was looking for. Of fifty-six references, a single popular magazine for educators, the *Phi Delta Kappan*, accounts for seven. Thirteen more references lead to publications of CRESST and its captured Board on Testing and Assessment at the National Research Council. Thus, about half of his sources were die-hard opponents of educational testing with consequences.

11. Of course, even if dismissive reviewers were to admit that the sources that I have uncovered do, indeed, exist, they could still dismiss them as inferior or not relevant in some way (e.g., by claiming that any testing effect study conducted

among college students, or non-US students, or more than [x] years ago, or . . . is not applicable to current US K–12 classrooms. That would reduce the number of relevant sources; yet a still large number would remain.

12. Twenty-six pre-1999 testing effect studies were found in the *Journal of Educational Psychology*, twenty-three in *Teaching in Psychology*, eighteen in the *Journal of Educational Research*, fifteen in the *Journal of Experimental Psychology*, eight in *Memory and Cognition*, and seven in the *Journal of Experimental Education*. Meanwhile, other education, assessment, or psychology research journals published no testing effect studies at all over the course of several decades.

13. Bill Mehrens was a well-regarded psychometrician—a professional trained in testing and measurement—who had mastered several doctoral-level statistics courses in his training. Nor was he "anti-testing." Indeed, Bill Mehrens sometimes served as a psychometric expert in legal teams defending the use of consequential testing in court cases (Mehrens, 2000).

14. He had applied deep statistical knowledge throughout his career. He knew that summary statements about whole populations require either measures of every unit in the population (i.e., a census) or a sufficiently large and representative sample. One might surmise, then, that he believed:

- his search was a census—i.e., he reviewed the entire research literature on educational testing effects;
- his sources comprised a representative sample of that research literature; or
- basic statistical sampling rules do not apply to literature reviews.

15. We may be seduced by technological advances, by the ease and quickness of internet search engines, for example. But, as the author Dan Brown wrote, "Google is not a synonym for research." An internet search quickly delivers *some* results—neither all results nor even a representative sample of all—just some. Moreover, delivered results can skew heavily toward the popular (for any reason) and the deliberately promoted and well financed.

This seduction may have worsened research. Scholars no longer visit libraries, reference librarians have retired and not been replaced, and librarians remain underpaid and underappreciated. Examples: What Works Clearinghouse and OECD systematic reviews appear to be conducted entirely from the web yet imply comprehensiveness (Phelps, 2014b, 2017g).

Some time ago, Academia.edu told me that 5,702 search terms were used to find the papers that I had posted on their site. I cannot verify their numbers. But I can say that in my own meta-analysis efforts I would have missed most sources I eventually found had I been content with a search just on the most obvious keywords or in the most obvious indexes.

16. Antiquated overconfidence in the mental osmosis theory of information acquisition assumes that if one is simply open to knowing about a topic one will become aware of the breadth of its research literature without a deliberate, persistent, expensive, or focused effort. This is the "I would know" or "someone would have told me" explanation for limiting literature searches. That one can read elite scholars still using

phrases like "no previous research that I am familiar with" or "I know of no previous studies" suggests that they regard a lack of information acquisition by mental osmosis a legitimate excuse for not searching the research literature. If previous studies had been done, they would know about them, or someone would have mentioned them. Such is a remarkably passive excuse, as if to say, "I was open to knowing about previous studies, but none were made known to me, ergo I am justified in declaring that none in fact exist."

17. Keep in mind that (an insincere) dismissive review can be written in a few seconds, whereas a single quality literature review can take months or years. Reviews dismissive of the testing effects research may also be popular among many in education simply because testing is unpopular with many of them.

18. Regarding confirmation bias, Mehrens may have thought that his search through his familiar neighborhood of publications and colleagues' work would suffice as a literature review, in part, because he felt confident that he knew the answer before he posed the question. Consider, for example, these passages in his article:

> I actually chose this topic at last year's (1997) convention when I attended a symposium on consequential validity. . . . I left that session believing that not enough evidence was available but that it would be worthwhile to review the evidence more thoroughly. Then, last summer . . . I again was left . . . unsatisfied with respect to the evidence on consequences. (pp. 1–2)

> I would conclude . . . that "a better research base is needed to evaluate the degree to which newly developed assessments fulfill expectations." (p. 5)

> The definition of a consequence implies a cause-and-effect relationship, but most of the evidence has not been gathered in a manner that permits a scholar (or anyone else with common sense) to draw a causative inference. (pp. 5–6)

> Problems in doing research on the consequences of assessment. Among them are that few school systems will welcome reports of unanticipated negative consequences, so cooperation may be hard to obtain. (p. 6)

19. US Department of Education. (2008). No Child Left Behind Act of 2001, Public Law print of PL 107–110. Retrieved from http://www.ed.gov/policy/elsec/leg/esea02/107-110.pdf.

20. Moreover, Mehrens had convinced a former student and influential psychometrician, who repeated his mentor's dismissal of the research literature on testing effects. That former student and professor just happened to be the only psychometrician consistently engaged with the small group of scholars advising the George W. Bush administration and Republican members of the US Congress on education policy during the design of the testing program component of the No Child Left Behind Act (Cizek, 2001). For example:

> From a public policy perspective, however, perhaps the most troubling aspect of the current debates is the almost total omission of any serious articulation or consideration of the positive consequences of high-stakes testing. (p. 22)

As with all of the previously-mentioned consequences, the evidence bearing on this outcome is just beginning to come in. Because all research on the consequences of high stakes tests is comparatively recent, the evidence on positive and negative consequences is necessarily skimpy (see Mehrens, 1998). (p. 31)

Chapter 4

Linchpin of the Cartel Alliance

Koretz, Cannell, and the Ghost of Test Security

"Men will not cease to be dishonest, merely because their dishonesties have been revealed or because they have discovered their own deceptions. Wherever men hold unequal power in society, they will strive to maintain it."

—Reinhold Niebuhr[1]

He has been one of the most influential scholars in US education research and policy over the past quarter century. More than any other single individual, he facilitated the grand merger between the Education Establishment Citation Cartel and the Education Reform Citation Cartel.

Ironically, he is also arguably the single US education researcher most responsible for undermining trust in educational testing. He says, essentially, that the results of any tests with "stakes" (i.e., consequences) cannot be trusted. Yet, somehow, even before the turn of the millennium, he managed to win the trust of some allegedly pro-testing high-profile education reformers, such as Eric Hanushek, apparently convincing them that he was an objective researcher and, at least some of the time, on their side.[2]

When newly elected president George W. Bush turned to his retainer of education policy advisors for advice on designing a testing and accountability program—a very technical topic about which they knew next to nothing—they, in turn, consulted Daniel Koretz. He had no experience in designing such a program either, but he was widely regarded to be a testing expert, even *the* testing expert, and was magnificently credentialed. He and his colleagues at the Center for Research on Education Standards and Student Testing (CRESST) deftly steered the Republican advisors away from the cornucopia

of research and information that could have helped their Republican clients make informed decisions, arguing that it did not exist (or couldn't be any good even if it did exist). This suggested to the GOP advisors that they could be pioneers by building a brand new, or newly "rigorous" research literature from scratch.

Unknown to the Reform Cartel then and perhaps still, Daniel Koretz played the leading role in covering up US educational testing's largest-ever, existentially threatening scandal, Dr. John J. Cannell's (1987, 1989) "Lake Wobegon Effect" exposé (CBS News, 1990).

Lake Wobegon

> "Where all the women are strong, all the men are good-looking, and all the children are above average."
>
> —Garrison Keillor

Starting in the mid 1970s, a conviction spread widely across the United States that the loosening of educational standards in the 1960s and early 1970s may have gone too far. Some educators and policymakers advocated toughening academic requirements and adding tests to measure progress.

Some states adopted familiar, widely available, commercially sold, norm-referenced tests as systemwide measures of student learning. Moreover, some states attached "stakes" to these tests, the most common being a graduation requirement—no high school diploma without passing the test. Because most passing scores (or "cut scores") for graduating were set at a middle or junior high school level, these tests came to be known as "minimum competency exams."

The norm-referenced tests (NRTs) employed, however, were not based on most states' curricula or content standards, where such existed. Rather, each NRT assumed its own a highly generalized national curriculum.

A few years into Florida's statewide testing adventure, a group of African American students who were denied high school diplomas based on their test scores sued and, eventually, won in federal court. They employed an "opportunity to learn" argument: the content of the test did not match the content of the courses they were required to take. The court ordered a content match study that confirmed the students' argument (Buckendahl and Hunt, 2005).

By the mid-1980s, many states had already undertaken efforts to develop state content standards and unique state tests aligned to them. Meanwhile, many were still administering NRTs statewide, but now without any stakes. With no consequences, students faced less incentive to perform well, and educators saw little reason to maintain tight security.

Enterprising state and local educators learned to take advantage. They could control (i.e., relax) most aspects of the tests' administration, such as time allowed and the security of test materials. They could even repeat use of the same test forms over time. Finally, they could choose their own "norms."

A "norm" is the test performance profile of a group of students who took the test previously. A norm group could be nationally representative, or it could represent a particular subgroup, such as "inner-city" students.

About this time, a general practitioner in rural West Virginia by the name of John J. Cannell heard state and local education officials claiming their students scored above the national average on standardized tests. On his own time, and with mostly his own resources, he investigated (Cannell, 1987, 1989).

Long story short, he discovered that across much of the United States, and particularly in poorer states, NRT test security was virtually nonexistent. Moreover, by pretending to be a school district official interested in ways to obtain higher test scores, he learned from test company salespersons that educators could choose their norm group.

So, in addition to relaxing any test security protocols, educators could choose to whom their students would be compared. Thusly, all states and school districts in the United States could score "above the national average." This phenomenon was tagged, by Chester A. "Checker" Finn, the 'Lake Wobegon Effect,'" after the mythical radio comedy community where "all the children are above average."

Some of the most insightful education policy studies are conducted by outsiders—those free from the implicit prohibition against criticism inside the profession.

Cannell's work received a flash of attention. He appeared on episodes of television's *60 Minutes* and other network news programs that also featured interviews with educators, lawyers, and public officials testifying to pervasive cheating among educators amid almost comically lax test security (CBS News, 1990).

Testing and measurement experts would reluctantly acknowledge the reality of "test score inflation." Test developers promised to improve their norming procedures and, according to some who tracked the changes, they did make meaningful improvements (Chatterji, 2003, p. 25). Some scholars promised to look more deeply into the matter.

No group took to the task more enthusiastically than those working at the only federally funded research center devoted to the study of educational testing, the Center for Research in Educational Standards and Student Testing (CRESST). Meanwhile, Dr. Cannell had a life to live and moved on.

Initially, CRESST officials praised Dr. Cannell for his intrepid efforts, but their tone changed once he had moved beyond earshot. Dr. Cannell had

"emphasized" "sinister" reasons for test score inflation, they wrote, and they would do "more sophisticated" research on the topic.

Three of their publications expressed that allegedly more sophisticated research. The first displayed a table purporting to list all the possible causes of test score inflation for them to consider. Cannell's primary suspect of lax security was absent (Shepard, 1989, 1990). CRESST would argue for the next three decades that score inflation occurs uniquely with high stakes tests and is caused by "teaching to the test." In other words, score inflation: (1) does not happen with low-stakes tests; and (2) lax security does not cause score inflation. Moreover, they said that score inflation was unpredictable, highly volatile, and sometimes massive.

The second and third CRESST studies examined certain patterns in the pre- and post-test scores from the first decade (i.e., late 1970s and early 1980s) of the federal government's compensatory education program (Linn, 2000) and the "preliminary findings" from the early 1990s of a test "perceived to be high stakes" in an unidentified school district (Koretz, Linn, Dunbar, and Shepard, 1991).

The Source of Lake Wobegon

> "Simply throw away the results you don't want and publish widely those you do."
>
> —Darrell Huff, *How to Lie with Statistics*

In the 1980s, Dr. Cannell found test company salespersons in cahoots with education administrators to produce positive trends in their test results by whatever means possible. He found forty-eight US states with testing programs bragging that their students' average scores were "above the national average," a mathematical impossibility.

Cannell exposed systemic corruption and grossly lax security across the country in the administration of nationally norm-referenced tests, at both state and school district levels.

The counternarrative managed by Koretz and his CRESST colleagues claimed their more "sophisticated" analysis found the pressure of "high stakes tests" leading educators to "teach to the test" and that caused score inflation (Baker, 2000; Linn, 2000; Shepard, 2000; Koretz, 2008).[3] This was quite a tall tale given that, with a single state exception, none of the Lake Wobegon tests bore any stakes for students. At most, some states incorporated what one might call positive "medium stakes," such as awards or cash bonuses for *educators* based on student test score gains (Cannell, 1989, p. 10; CBS News, 1990).

CRESST's take on test-score inflation established a stable, decades-long political equilibrium within US education. The wider community of education school professors, state and local administrators, and testing firm officials welcomed the CRESST narrative. They were all off the hook. Stakes—something they didn't like anyway—were the culprit. They had done nothing wrong.[4]

Koretz's and CRESST's successful cover-up of the Lake Wobegon Effect scandal continues to profoundly affect US education and research. Cannell's exposé should have induced a nationwide reckoning over test security. Instead, the stark revelation of a serious, deeply embedded problem evaporated like a bad dream on a sunny spring morning (Phelps, 2005f, 2008/2009b, 2011c, 2016d, 2017b, 2017d).

Consequently, test security is still regularly compromised in the United States (Campbell, 2013; Martel, 2011; Martin, 2013; Matthews, 2013a, 2013b; Maxwell, 2013; Merrow, 2013a, 2013b, 2013c; US GAO, 2013). Liberties are taken with test security in our schools that would not be tolerated in other countries, nor by US occupational licensing test administrators.

Moreover, the successful CRESST coverup set a precedent for the design of research studies on testing effects for years to come. Even the "top" researchers of the Reform Cartel would follow their lead. Neither level of security nor most other aspects of test administration are included as variables or moderators in their research studies, as if they couldn't matter.

It shouldn't even need to be studied. In experiments conducted by researchers outside the Cartel Alliance, when only the level of security is varied, and all other factors controlled, students in the laxer security group score higher (Ryan et al., 2015; Steger, Schroeders and Gnambs, 2018; Bradshaw, 2019; Zhao et al., 2021).[5]

Test score inflation is real. But a full review of the evidence does not point to high stakes as its *cause* (see Table 4.1).

Other falsehoods Koretz would promote include:[6]

- There has been no past research on dozens of different topics, or none that is any good, anyway.
- Trends in no- or low-stakes tests are consistent and reliable, supposedly "because there is no incentive to increase scores."[7]
- No-stakes tests can be used in parallel with high-stakes tests to "audit" the latter to detect evidence of test score inflation.

(See also Appendix 3 online for lists research literatures dismissed, by certain scholars and journalists, https://educationpolicy.us/Malfunction/App3.pdf.)

Table 4.1. Spot the causal factor.

	Level of Security in Testing Program	
	High Security (external administration)	Lax Security (internal administration)
Level Of Stakes in Testing Program		
High Stakes	NO test score inflation e.g., occupational licensure exams	YES inflation possible e.g., NCLB, Common Core tests
Low/No Stakes	NO test score inflation e.g., US National Assessment (NAEP)	YES inflation possible e.g., Cannell's "Lake Wobegon" tests

The Black Hole of Test Security

> "If you can't prove what you want to prove, demonstrate something else and pretend that they are the same thing."
>
> —Darrell Huff, *How to Lie with Statistics*

In the 2000s, an aggressively competitive manager at ACT, Inc., where the ACT college admission exam is developed, convinced some state governments to administer the ACT statewide for free to all their high school juniors. By more than doubling the number of high school students sitting for the exam, some students who would not otherwise have considered going to college now would, after receiving high test scores and the resulting attention from college recruiters. That was generally described as a benefit, though, in some cases, those same students might end up among the Unites States' too-large number of highly indebted college dropouts (ACT, 2009; Phelps, 2009). That same manager would later work for the College Board, and the SAT, too, would also be offered statewide.

The dramatic change in college admission test security seems scarcely to have been noticed. Previously, ACT and SAT tests had been administered in highly controlled environments under the watchful eyes of proctors trained and paid by ACT or SAT. With statewide administration, ACT and College Board could relieve themselves of the cost and burden of test security by outsourcing it to students' own teachers. The students' own teachers, of course, operate under a quite different set of incentives than do paid proctors. Who's to know if a teacher here or there gives his or her students an extra minute or two on paper and pencil tests? Future computer-based administrations can relieve some of the security concerns, but not all. Other factors held equal; students tend to score higher when their test proctor is someone familiar to them (Fuchs, 1985).

Likewise with the testing regime mandated by the No Child Left Behind (NCLB) Act, which continues today. Comb through all the testimonies related to NCLB delivered before the US Congress in 2001–2004. Or read what the Republican education policy advisors had to say at the same time. One will not detect any concern about test security, even though, given annual administration at several grade levels, NCLB tests could only be administered by school-level educators themselves. With fifty states, tens of thousands of school districts, hundreds of thousands of schools, and several different test suppliers, test security protocols were bound to vary, along with their adherence.

Toward the end of the 2000s decade, US testing and measurement professionals busied themselves with updating their most important set of professional standards, the *Standards for Educational and Psychological Testing* (AERA, APA, and NCME, 1999, 2014). *The Standards* are to psychometricians what state and local building codes are to construction workers. Indeed, judges commonly cited them in legal decisions that involved standardized testing (Buckendahl and Hunt, 2005; Camara, 2007; Mehrens, 2000).

Later in the updating process, in 2011, the National Council on Measurement in Education (NCME) hosted a session at its annual meeting at which members were invited to comment on the final draft version, which important insiders had been working on for several years.

Oddly, even though *The Standards* had been in existence for decades, they contained few standards for test security. There was a "placeholder" for an entire section devoted to the subject, in that one chapter contained "test security" in its title, but that chapter contained no such text. The 2011 draft had added nothing at all. Over two hundred pages. Hundreds of standards. Nothing on test security, that is, nothing beyond the "cop-out" of foisting any responsibility for test security on state and local educators who administered tests (Phelps, 2011b).

Such evasions form black holes of responsibility (Nichols and Williams, 2008).

Blind Eye Turned

"We must be careful not to believe things simply because we want them to be true. No one can fool you as easily as you can fool yourself."

—Richard Feynman

That those in the Reform Cartel chose to believe CRESST's and Koretz's error-filled myths is surprising, given both their falsehood and their conflict with the Republican Party's expressed interests. Nonetheless they did and,

apparently, still do. The Reform Cartel's self-proclaimed "top researchers" believe the myths despite a surfeit of "red flags" (Nichols, Kendall, and Boomer, 2019; Phelps, 2005f; 2017d).

Koretz et al.'s foundational study . . .

- was conducted in an unnamed school district with unidentified tests and content. Given the secrecy, the study is neither replicable nor falsifiable (Milgram, 2012; Funk and Smith, 2022). Koretz maintains the secrecy necessary to protect the school district.
- was never published in a peer-reviewed journal, suggesting that it was rejected wherever it was submitted. The authors presented the paper at an education research conference in 1991 (Koretz, Linn, Dunbar, and Shepard, 1991).
- in fact, proved just the opposite of what they claim. Koretz et al. administered a parallel form of the same test with no stakes to a sample of students—a form that could not have been "taught to"—and found no difference in results.[8] This result was acknowledged in the paper presentation peripherally but explained away (Koretz, Linn, Dunbar, and Shepard, 1991, pp. 14–15).[9]
- then administered an (also unidentified) "competing" test to a sample of the same students. This time, the students scored worse on the competing test. Koretz et al. claim that the students should have done just as well; a claim that could only be valid if the competing test covered the same content. At the time, the most popular norm-referenced tests did not.[10]
- in fact, was conducted with a no-, not high-, stakes test, as Koretz would admit years later (2013a, p. 166). The "high-stakes" label was rationalized with an archaic 1970s definition of the term disavowed later by the same scholar who had coined the definition (Popham, 1987, 2004).[11] The Koretz et al. test was not high stakes by any commonly understood or meaningful definition of the term.
- has been mischaracterized by Koretz for thirty years as an "experiment" (2015, p. 7). It was not. There were no controls for any aspect of test administration, such as level of test security, test content, nor for most factors that have been shown to influence student test performance. (Meanwhile, most of the test coaching studies Koretz had declared nonexistent were genuine experiments with controls.)

The Koretz et al. study checks most of the boxes for poor research design that produces untrustworthy results.[12]

Yet, over the past three decades, members of both Citation Cartels and the press have consistently regarded the Koretz et al. study as valid, reliable, and accurate—essentially as fact. Some from the Reform Cartel initiated their

own studies based on their belief in the veracity of Koretz's claims. (See, for example, Greene, Winters, and Forster, 2003, 2004; Jacob, 2005; Jennings and Lauen, 2016).

For the US education press, Koretz has served for the past quarter century as the ultimate authority on educational testing and measurement. Thus, they have blithely passed Koretz's myths on to an innocent public.[13] Koretz was not just some journalist's "go-to" source for stories on certain educational testing topics, he was every elite education journalist's go-to source.

How did Koretz et al. manage to "pull the wool over the eyes" of so many?

- He worked at prestigious and trusted organizations: first, at the Rand Corporation, a longtime CRESST affiliate, then the Urban Institute, and, later, received a named, tenured appointment on the faculty at Harvard's Graduate School of Education (HGSE) (Pipes, 2021). He also served on virtually every top-level prestigious educational testing research panel assembled in the past few decades.
- Reform Cartel members and journalists knew so little about testing and measurement that they could not recognize the obvious flaws in the story.
- Leading scholars in testing and measurement either supported him or kept silent.
- Despite an abundance of contrary research, Koretz persistently repeated that no such research existed (or was any good). Gullible people accepted his word on the matter over others' who lacked access to so many information dissemination platforms.[14]
- Koretz enjoyed numerous opportunities over the decades on many prestigious platforms—including virtually every prestigious information dissemination channel in US education—to repeat his theory, with no counterpoint ever presented alongside.
- The Koretz et al. study—the written version of the paper presentation—is not an easy read. Its logical flow is convoluted, its syntax muddled. It contains both technical terms and confusing, but scientifically sounding, terms (e.g., "test B," "test C"). It is doubtful that many have taken the time to understand its details.
- Opposing voices within the psychometric community were ignored or silenced (see, for example, Delborne, 2015; Phelps, 2019b).

One will find a remarkably similar list of causes explaining several decades of delusion among the scientific elite for the Piltdown Man hoax in Richard Harter's (1996–1997) reconstruction of the story. There exists no shortage of other examples of popular scholarly falsehoods persisting for decades in the face of mountains of conflicting evidence (e.g., constructivist

pedagogy, multiple intelligences, facilitated communication) (Auerbach, 2015; Hendrick, 2015; Hunt, 2001; Skogstad, 2019; Oreskes, 2021).[15]

Researchers have studied the test coaching issue at least since the 1920s. Indeed, such studies were numerous enough as far back as the 1970s to populate meta-analyses.[16] They have found that test coaching has a consistent, moderate positive effect, but not the volatile, unpredictable, and "sometimes absolutely massive" effect claimed by Koretz (Barnum, 2018a).

NOTES

1. Reinhold Niebuhr, "Moral Man and Immoral Society" (1932).

2. See, for example, Hanushek and Jorgenson, 1996. Koretz has long shared with some education reformers an antipathy toward "fuzzy" assessment, such as portfolios and low-reliability performance tests.

3. It remains a popular notion among US education professors and both Citation Cartels that scores on standardized tests can be increased by coaching students on test-taking skills entirely unrelated to the subject matter—"teaching to the test" (Phelps, 2016d, 2016f, 2017b). Indeed, a profitable test preparation industry exists to prepare students for high-profile standardized tests, such as the ACT or SAT college admission tests. Some of the preparation offered is subject matter instruction and format familiarization. But some is instruction in gaming multiple-choice test items allegedly to find correct answers even in the absence of any subject-matter knowledge. Indeed, the Princeton Review test preparation firm was admonished by the Better Business Bureau (2010) for fraudulently promising exactly that—increased scores even without subject matter knowledge.

Familiarity with a test's format, instructions, and administration conditions prior to test day can be very helpful (Crocker, 2005). For example, imagine a student homeschooled through high school who then encounters a timed, secure, multiple-choice test for the first time when applying to college. Some prior familiarity with what is expected should help reduce poor performance that is unrelated to subject matter mastery.

4. Most agreed that another cause of the Lake Wobegon Effect was outdated norms. Nationally normed tests are first administered to a norming group to set its scales. Ideally, the norming group should be representative of a student population of interest, typically US students nationally at a particular grade level. If the norms are not continuously updated, however, they may become less representative over time. Moreover, test publishers employed other norming samples, too. Cannell and his team found test salespersons offering state and local administrators their choice of "national norms." For example, wealthy suburban school districts could choose a test publishers' national "inner-city norms" for comparison with their own students' scores, then brag about how high their students scored "above the national norm."

In response to the Lake Wobegon Effect scandal, test publishers admitted to no cheating, but did agree to update their norms.

5. A researcher can obtain the outcome predicted by Koretz and CRESST—with high stakes causing test score inflation only by ignoring the effect of test security. Vary the stakes between two groups, without controlling for levels of test security, et voila! The group with stakes performs better on the test with rewards or punishments attached . . . after they cheat (e.g., Jacob, 2005). So, the high stakes *caused* the differential test score gains? What about the cheating?

6. Perhaps Koretz's (and CRESST's) greatest accomplishment has been to convince large numbers of people, including some of the most influential, of many falsehoods. Among them:

- There is no, or almost no, research finding benefits to high-stakes testing.
- Standardized educational testing, particularly when it has stakes, is enormously costly in monetary terms.
- All types of high-stakes testing are prone to "test-score inflation" due to "teaching to the test."
- High stakes, not lax security, cause test score inflation.
- No- or low-stakes tests, by contrast, are not susceptible to test-score inflation because there are no incentives to manipulate scores.
- As score trends for high-stakes tests are unreliable and those for no- or low-stakes tests are reliable, no- or low-stakes tests may be used validly as shadow tests to audit the reliability of high-stakes tests' score trends.
- The primary cause of educator cheating in testing administrations is high-stakes; without high-stakes, educators do not cheat.
- State NAEP is a bad idea and will cause test-score inflation.
- Very little research has been conducted on the benefits of personnel testing.
- Very little research has been conducted on testing's achievement effects.
- Very little research has been conducted on test-score inflation.
- Very little research has been conducted on test coaching, or teaching to the test.
- Test "stakes" are much higher now than they were thirty years ago.
- A single test cannot cover an entire content domain, say, for a semester course.

None of the above is a small falsehood, either. Each one is a whopper. In Koretz's care, thousands of studies in personnel testing disappear. Thousands of studies on tests' educational achievement effects are wiped out. Dozens of studies on the effects of test coaching and test score inflation go poof!

See, for example, Phelps, 2005f, 2008/2009b, 2016d, 2017b, 2017d.

7. A cornucopia of research exists contradicting Koretz's and CRESST's faith in the reliability of low- and no-stakes test scores and their trends. No matter, CRESST researchers simply ignore it. See, for example, Abdelfattah, 2010; Barry, Horst, Finney, Brown, and Kopp, 2010; Brown and Walberg, 1993; Eklof, 2007; Finn, 2015; Liu, Rios, and Borden, 2015; Mathers, Finney, and Myers, 2016; Rios, Guo, Mao, and Liu, 2016; Sessoms and Finney, 2015; Smith, Given, Julien, Ouellette, and DeLong, 2015; Steedle, 2014; Wainer, 2011; Wise and DeMars, 2005; Wise and DeMars, 2010; Zilberberg, Anderson, Finney, and Marsh, 2013.

8. "The ideal result from our perspective was to obtain reasonably similar results from the parallel form and the district's administration of Test B. This is what we found. All of our parallel-form comparisons were within a range of one academic month or two percentile points" (pp. 14–15).

9. The comparison was explained away as "included . . . more for methodological than for substantive reasons" (p. 14) ostensibly as a test for "motivation" effects.

10. Koretz et al. asserted that the public is not interested in students' performing well on a particular mathematics test but, rather, in all of mathematics (1991, p. 20). That is doubtful. Most everyone knows that the quantity of subject matter is boundless. No one can learn all the mathematics there is to learn, or even what is considered by various parties throughout the globe to represent all that might be considered third-grade level mathematics. Likewise, no one can learn all the mathematics that is covered in all the various third-grade mathematics textbooks, standards documents, curriculum guides, and so on.

More likely, what the public wants their third graders to learn is some coherent and integrated mathematics curriculum. I would wager that most Americans would not be picky about which of the many possible mathematics curricula their third graders had learned, if only they could feel assured that their third graders had learned one of them.

Contemporaneously, other scholars had conducted content comparison studies among the several national norm-referenced tests and found that they were not comparable. Each contained content different enough—not only topically but also in the sequencing of topics—to be useless as proxies for each other. The most straightforward conclusion of the Koretz et al. study, then, is that the students scored worse on the competing test because it was based on different content (i.e., it contained content to which they had not been exposed).

In their chapter of the book, *Designing Coherent Education Policy* (1993, p. 53), David Cohen and James Spillane argued (see also Floden et al. 1978; Freeman et al. 1979):

> Standardized tests often have been seen as interchangeable, but one of the few careful studies of topical agreement among tests raised doubts about that view. Focusing on several leading fourth grade mathematics tests, the authors observed that "our findings challenge . . . th[e] assumption . . . that standardized achievement tests may be used interchangeably" (Freeman and others, 1983). The authors maintain that these tests are topically inconsistent and thus differentially sensitive to content coverage.

More recently, Bhola, Impara, and Buckendahl (2003) studied the curricular alignment of five different widely available national norm-referenced tests for grades four and eight, and for high school, to Nebraska's state reading/language arts standards for grades four and eight, and for high school (p. 28).

> It was concluded that there are variable levels of alignment both across grades and across tests. No single test battery demonstrated a clear superiority in matching Nebraska's reading/language arts standards across all standards and grade levels. No test battery provided a comprehensive assessment of all of Nebraska's reading/language arts content standards.

The use of any of these tests to satisfy NCLB requirements would require using additional assessment instruments to ensure that all content standards at any particular grade level are appropriately assessed. . . .

Our findings are consistent with those of La Marca et al. (2000) who summarize the results of five alignment studies that used different models to determine degree of alignment. In general, all these alignment studies found that alignments between assessments and content standards tended to be poor.

Summarizing, studies finding non-comparability across competing tests:

- Among norm-referenced tests (NRTs): Cohen and Spillane, 1993; *Debra P. v. Turlington*, 1981; Floden, Porter, Schmidt, and Freeman, 1978; Freeman, Kuhs, Knappen, and Porter, 1979; Freeman, Kuhs, Porter, Floden, Schmidt, and Schwille, 1983; La Marca, Redfield, Winter, Bailey, and Despriet, 2000; Wainer, 2011.
- Among content standards: Archbald, 1994; Bhola, Impara, and Buckendahl, 2003; Buckendahl, Plake, Impara, and Irwin, 2000; Impara, 2001; Plake, Buckendahl, and Impara, 2000; Phelps, 2005f.
- Among criterion-referenced tests (CRTs): Massell, Kirst and Hoppe, 1997; Wiley, Hembry, Buckendahl, Forte, Towles, and Nebelsick-Gullett, 2015.

11. CRESST researchers (Shepard, 1989, 1990, p. 17) cited a definition they attributed to James Popham from 1987 ascribing "high stakes" to any test whose aggregate results were reported publicly, or which received media coverage. With the widespread passage of "truth in testing" and other open records laws, starting with California and New York State in the late 1970s, the aggregate results of all large-scale tests became public record. By their out-of-date definition, *all* large-scale tests are "high stakes." For his part, Popham (2004) recommended eliminating the phrase "teaching to the test."

12. For example, it matches at least ten out the twelve characteristics in "A Rough Guide to Spotting Bad Science," by Compound Interest (2014) https://www.compoundchem.com/2014/04/02/a-rough-guide-to-spotting-bad-science/.

13. For example, Barnum, 2018a; Barshay, 2020; Cech, 2008; Strauss, 2006; Viadero, 1998.

14. Typically, the only research that he acknowledges to exist on any given topic is that which supports his point of view. On some topics, thousands of studies that do, in fact, exist are declared by Koretz to not exist. Conversely, even if only a handful of studies conducted by him and his close colleagues support his views on a topic, then they are the only studies that exist on that topic.

15. See also https://www.facilitatedcommunication.org/.

16. It doesn't require much searching to find a cornucopia of test coaching studies, many of them randomized experiments. They date at least as far back as 1927. At least seventy-nine relevant studies were published between 1927 and 2019. In chronological order, Gilmore (1927); DeWeerdt (1927); French (1959); French and Dear (1959); Ortar (1960); Marron (1965); ETS (1965); Messick and Jungeblut (1981); Ellis, Konoske, Wulfeck, and Montague (1982); DerSimonian and Laird

(1983); Kulik, Bangert-Drowns, and Kulik (1984); Powers (1985); Jones (1986); Fraker (1986/1987); Halpin (1987); Whitla (1988); Snedecor (1989); Bond (1989); Baydar (1990); Becker (1990); Smyth (1990); Moore (1991); Alderson and Wall (1992); Powers (1993); Oren (1993); Powers and Rock (1994); Scholes, Lane (1997); Allalouf and Ben Shakhar (1998); Robb and Ercanbrack (1999); McClain (1999); Camara (1999, 2001, 2008); Stone and Lane (2000, 2003); Din and Soldan (2001); Briggs (2001); Palmer (2002); Briggs and Hansen (2004); Cankoy and Ali Tut (2005); Crocker (2005); Allensworth, Correa, and Ponisciak (2008); Domingue and Briggs (2009); Koljatic and Silva (2014); Early (2019).

Meta-analyses or research summaries of test coaching studies were published in 1981, 1983, 1983, 1983, 1984, 1990, 1993, 2005, 2005, 2006, and 2017. There's even a US Department of Education summary of some college admission test prep studies available on the internet, though it only dates back to the mid-1990s.

To be sure, some of the studies were conducted by or for test development organizations that, some might say, had a vested interest in a particular result. But most were not.

Chapter 5

The Education Reform Cartel

"Contemporary public intellectuals are mainly academics and think tank staff who do not risk their jobs or reputations by errors of prediction or assessment. Absent any risk when they are mistaken, they have become irresponsible in their analyses, predictions, and assessments of social policy."

—Richard Posner

When Harvard University enters a field, it does so in a big way (Bradley, 2005; Lewis, 2006). In the 1970s, its leaders decided to build a new graduate school in an already-crowded field of study—public administration and policy—the Kennedy School of Government.[1] When it opened, it was already larger than similar programs at other universities. Within several years, its size more than doubled. Harvard is blessed with a relative surfeit of steady donations and, for over a decade, those from donors with some flexibilities were steered toward the new school. Soon, the new school was ranked among the top in the United States despite its recent origins.

Similarly, in the 1990s, the university decided to enter the world of education reform. The established Harvard Graduate School of Education was afflicted with intellectual sclerosis like most US education schools, assuming the governance structure of the US public school system—their system—inviolate, and willing to consider reforms only at the margins. The primary challenge as always for Harvard was how to build a new program from scratch and, almost immediately thereafter, have it regarded as the country's best.

Harvard appointed political scientist Paul Peterson head of the new Program on Education Policy and Governance (PEPG), which then entered the aforementioned pact with the Thomas B. Fordham Foundation in Washington, DC, Stanford's Hoover Institution, and the University of Washington's Center on Reinventing Public Education (CRPE).[2] The Harvard and Stanford folk brought the scholarly prestige, Fordham chipped in cash and the DC and

Republican Party contacts, and the CRPE . . . well, the CRPE was located near the headquarters of the Bill and Melinda Gates Foundation. PEPG and Hoover soon launched *Education Next*, their joint publication platform, but just one of many to which group members have ready access.[3]

Education Next staff and Koret Task Force members comprised just the core of the hegemonic ingroup. Former students and workmates of Harvard and Stanford professors would soon occupy lead education policy posts at nationally focused think tanks (e.g., Brookings, AEI, Manhattan); the Fordham Foundation founder's favorite former assistants would run the Fordham Institute (and edit *Education Next*); the spouse of the Hoover Institution's chief education economist ran another think tank at Stanford.

This newly formed Education Reform Citation Cartel would overpopulate research programs funded by the wealthiest foundations, the US federal government, and the international Organization for Economic Co-operation and Development (OECD). Other favorite former students or office workers would eventually operate new, lushly funded research centers at Brown and Johns Hopkins universities and the Department of Education Reform at the University of Arkansas, located near the Walton Foundation's Bentonville headquarters.

How the Reform Cartel gatekeeps what the public gets to hear is simple: those who honor their presumed eminence may be acknowledged by them as worthy—invited to participate in panels, cited and referenced in group publications, and mentioned to journalists as good sources for stories. Those who expose (i.e., embarrass) them when they pontificate on topics for which they lack expertise may be shunned or ridiculed.

Witness, for example, how they mocked and insulted the late Myron Lieberman, one of our country's foremost experts on school governance and labor relations, after he criticized one of them for making policy proclamations on a topic that they had made little effort to learn (Phelps, 2014a). Sandra Stotsky, hero of the Massachusetts Education Miracle, was ignored by the Cartel for a while, then later unfairly demeaned (Phelps, 2021c).

Cartel leader Chester A. "Checker" Finn waxed nostalgic about the early days of his Thomas B. Fordham Foundation's predecessor, the Education Excellence Network, and Diane Ravitch's key, co-leading role in both (Finn, 1996). But, now that she disagrees with the Cartel on some issues, current Fordham President Michael Petrilli insults her as a "kook," (Education Gadfly, 2011), her longstanding relationship with the Brookings Institution was revoked on an absurd technicality (Ravitch, 2012), and an *Education Next* essay insults her personally and generally ridicules her as an allegedly inferior intellect (Greene, 2014).

The self-proclaimed experts in educational accountability steadfastly evade accountability. And, when they can't avoid reacting to criticism, they

can lash out with personal and condescending attacks (see also, for example, Hess, 2010; Pondiscio, 2017a, Shuls, 2019)

According to Karl Popper and others, acknowledgement and consideration of criticism is essential to scientific progress (APS, 2017; Kudesia, 2021; Leslie, 2021; Stephens, 2017; Williams, J., 2011). For the Reform Cartel, the response is cancelation (Olson, 2017; Rauch, 2020; Vogels et al., 2021; Wood, 2020).

Furthermore, the Reform Cartel mimics one of the Establishment Cartel's most effective and unethical tactics: they pretend that most research does not exist, even on topics with voluminous research literatures.

Certainly, the Cartel retains expertise. It does not, however, extend to all education topics. They and the other policy wonks they would acknowledge as worthy of attention had trained as academic political scientists and economists, and some had worked as congressional staff. Thus, they tended to know about education governance, political processes, education finance, and labor economics (Fukuyama, 2018).

They knew much less about curriculum, instruction, standards, or assessment, which just happen to have been the topic areas in which expertise would have been most useful in this millennium's first two decades (Burnett, 2016; Castel, McCabe, Roediger and Heitman, 2007; Clabaugh and Rozycki, 2011; Cuban, 2010; Feltman, 2015; Kenyon, 2016; McClay, 2009; Schmerier, 2016). Moreover, most Cartel scholars retained little familiarity with day-to-day work inside the education industry as administrators, analysts, data managers, program evaluators, or test developers. They lacked "skin in the game" (Taleb, 2018).

Professor Peterson could have surveyed the research literatures in curriculum, instruction, standards, and assessment. But that would have taken quite a lot of time. Or, he could have frankly admitted to his political and foundation sponsors that he and his colleagues knew little about the topics and they should find genuine expertise elsewhere. But that would have done him and his colleagues no good professionally and wasted a golden opportunity for power and influence in the thick of things.

It did benefit him professionally to promote his and other Harvard PhD graduates as experts, despite their lack of expertise. After getting "his people" in positions of power and influence, those appointees would owe him for their places in the penumbra of policymaking and provide him access to the latest and greatest issues, datasets, and research contracts.

A lack of relevant training and experience did not discourage Peterson's progeny from offering wide-ranging policy prescriptions, however. (See Fox, 2016; Makel and Plucker, 2014; Powers, D., 2015.) Nor did it discourage policymakers and journalists from asking for them.

The Millennium Turns

Most Republican and conservative groups defer to the Reform Cartel under the mistaken assumption that its members can be trusted to serve them sincerely and forthrightly. The past two decades have demonstrated that that trust is misplaced.

The 2000 presidential election was probably the first in US history in which educational testing emerged as a prominent campaign issue. As was to be expected, attacks on candidate George W. Bush's educational testing proposals from the education establishment were frequent, and many were unfair and inaccurate. How did the newly formed Reform Cartel react? They didn't at first, probably because they didn't know what to say.

Then they decided to wing it; "fake it until you make it," as they say. For most policy wonks, a place in the pantheon where policies affecting millions would be crafted comes along only once in a lifetime. But how would they reconcile the hopelessly conflicted scholarly opinions on educational testing and the contradictory suggestions for the proper structure of testing systems? In a hurry, whom should one trust?

Like many, they chose to trust those with more credentials—even though they were education establishment, education school credentials. They relied on prominent, celebrated scholars, such as Daniel Koretz, who pointed them toward his preferred echo chamber, where they found his research and that of his colleagues affiliated with CRESST.

It was CRESST-affiliated researchers who had launched the tawdry October surprise a few weeks before the 2000 election that nearly did in the GOP presidential campaign (Phelps, 2003, Chapter 5). Nonetheless, in 2005, CRESST had its contract with the federal government renewed for another several years by the Republican-run US Department of Education.[4]

Indeed, George W. Bush's appointee to oversee research at the US Education Department, Grover "Russ" Whitehurst, hired longtime partners in CRESST information suppression activities—the Rand Corporation's education standards and testing group—to provide him education research literature reviews and help him set a research agenda (Whitehurst, 2002, p. 11). They, in turn, tunneled his gaze further down their long narrow tube.

Perhaps because the Reform Cartel members are all of a type, the entire group forms beliefs as a whole—their "groupthink" strong and adamant (Janis and Mann, 1977; Janis, 1989; 't Hart, 1991; Bai, Fiske and Griffiths, 2022). At this point, after twenty years, they have repeated CRESST orthodoxies so often that they have staked their reputations to them. And even though they have had twenty years to discover that they were misled, they still have not (see, for example, Hanushek, 2019).

Though Koretz may have proffered the introductions, the courtship was lush. CRESST had gifts to give. For example, they had long ago assumed effective control of the Board on Testing and Assessment (BOTA) at the US National Research Council (NRC). They could offer the Ed Reform Cartel honoraria, seats at head tables, trips around the country, status, and prestige. The offers were accepted.[5]

The GOP-affiliated research and policy folk faced an historic opportunity with enormous implications to benefit their GOP clients and US education in general. They had the resources to blast open the seal of information suppression the Establishment Cartel had used to hide a huge research literature. Instead, they chose to *reinforce* the suppression.

The Reform Cartel canceled a huge mass of policy-relevant information one could find outside their circle—thousands of scholars, tens of thousands of studies, millions of data points. Nonexistent. Not rigorous. Not new. Not done by us.

Like Kids in a Candy Store

"Real knowledge is to know the extent of one's ignorance."

—Confucius

In a hurry to make an impact, Reform Cartel leaders anointed a gaggle of young researchers less than a few years out of graduate school with virtually no professional experience and let them loose on the body politic. They put dozens of microphones in front of them, gave them franking privileges with mailing lists of thousands, and promoted their output with few questions asked. Soon, the kids were better known than a large population of erudite scholars who had spent lifetimes accumulating specific knowledge and skills. The kids were overnight experts—in any fields or subfields they fancied (Juyal, Thawani, and Dhawan, 2020; Juyal, Thawani, Sayana, and Pal, 2019; Little and Backus, 2020).

They could have conducted thorough literature searches and read a range of other scholars' works in each topic, but that would have taken a lot of time and, besides, whatever they wrote would be published regardless. The little background reading they did, when they did any, tended to be that which could be done most conveniently, predominantly the publications of other celebrity researchers and research groups.

Understandably, some of their work was naïve and ill-informed. Nonetheless, it was generously funded by governments, foundations, or allied advocacy organizations. For all its resources, power, and wealth, the Reform Cartel was and remains a small group of people, with a narrow range of skills

and expertise—generally what they picked up in graduate school classes and from each other. Likely, one or two other members of the Cartel, with similarly narrow backgrounds, looked at the youngsters' work before it was posted or published. Apparently, that was not sufficient to the task, because some dreadfully poor work got out, and was disseminated as widely as yesterday's ball scores (e.g., Dee and Wyckoff, 2017; Harris, Taylor, Levine, Ingle, and McDonald, 2008; Nichols-Barrer, Place, Dillon, and Gill, 2015).

How to "Drop Out" of School Without Ever Leaving

The Ed Reform Cartel thrust recent Harvard PhD Jay P. Greene into the limelight early in the George W. Bush administration. Greene had read Walter Haney's Summer 2000 beatdown of Texas education, "The Myth of the Texas Miracle in Education." Being new to the topic of educational testing and apparently unaware of Haney's tendency to embellish data and analyses (Haney, Madaus, and Lyons, 1993; Phelps, 1994, 1998, 2003, pp. 127–144), Greene may have accepted what Haney wrote at face value.

Haney had employed several statistical tricks to disparage Texas education during Governor Bush's tenure. To support his contention that state testing programs increased dropouts and reduced graduation numbers, Haney implied that Texas had deliberately deceived the public with misleading statistics for both. So, Haney calculated his own "graduation rate." His was an "on-time" ratio: the number of first-year high school students who graduated in May three school years later. Any not graduating "on time"—and not a day "late"—Haney classified as "dropouts."

Thus, any student who delayed their graduation by so much as a week was defined as a dropout, even if they were awarded their diploma soon after. Students who graduated "late" due to absences for illness or other personal reasons, or to make up credits for previously failed courses, were classified as dropouts even if they had never actually dropped out of school.

Haney's method was less valid or reliable than the high school completion ratio for Texas that any US citizen could retrieve from the US Census Bureau.

Whether he remembered Haney's statistical trick consciously, subconsciously, or genuinely thought of it on his own as he claimed, Jay P. Greene would the following year begin a several-years-long advocacy for an "on time" graduation rate. He called it "The Greene Method" (Greene and Winters, 2002a, 2002b, 2002c, 2005, 2006).

He would also assert several falsehoods: (1) that "The Greene Method" was new and original; (2) that statisticians in the US Education Department and the US Census Bureau were unaware of on-time graduation rates; (3) that they used only a single graduation rate statistic, which was flawed; (4) that his on-time rate was better: less flawed and more forthright. (See, for

example, Clements, 2007; Entwisle, Alexander, and Olson, 2004; George-Ezzelle, Zhang, and Douglas, 2006; Hoffman, 2002; Hudson, Kienzl, and Diehl, 2007; Ingels, Curtin, Kaufman, Alt, and Chen, 2002; Seastrom et al., 2005; Seastrom, Hoffman, Chapman, and Stillwell, 2007.)

With little apparent notice in the media, the Haney-Greene method of calculating high school completion statistics was roundly criticized by statisticians, practitioners, and other experts in the field (Adelman, 2006; Chavez, 2006; Clements, 2007; Mishel and Roy, 2006; Phelps, 2005e, 2009; Reynolds, 2006; Sebring, 2007; Solomon, 2008a, 2008b; Warren, 2005).[6] Oblivious, *Education Week* adopted the Haney-Greene measure as their official graduation rate measure, replacing any on offer from the USED or Census Bureau (Solomon, 2008b).

The education press chose to promote the flawed and erroneous claims of a celebrity over those of several dozen less celebrated, but more expert scholars (Carrigan, 2019; Fox, 2016a, 2016b; Goldhaber, M. H., 1997; Grout, 2019; Hanson, 2021; Pinker, 2018; Stegenga, 2014).

Some journalists accused education statisticians of ignorance and fraud. *Time* magazine featured Greene's "discovery" of this allegedly new method of calculating graduation rates in a front-page story, largely based, it seems, on Gates Foundation promotion (Bill and Melinda Gates Foundation, 2008; Schwab, 2020). According to *Time*:

> In 2001, Jay Greene, a senior fellow at the Manhattan Institute, published a study that peeled back the layers of statistical legerdemain. Poring over raw education data, he asked himself a basic question: What percentage of kids who start at a high school finish? The answers led Greene and subsequent researchers around the country to place the national graduation rate at anywhere from 64% to 71%. (Thornburgh, 2006, p. 33)

Gobs of money oozed from ed reform groups to finance more studies employing his allegedly "widely respected method to calculate public high school graduation rates."

Apparently, none thought to get a second opinion from any of dozens of genuine experts on the topic—some with graduate degrees in statistics who had spent their careers working with the data. The genuine experts working at ED's National Center for Education Statistics (NCES) or the US Census Bureau may have thought that Greene's braggadocio was foolish. But, as civil servants, they could not get involved in public debates.

A direct line formed, then, from Greene's naïve dalliance in the arcane world of education statistics to . . .

- high schools that enforced standards—keeping students in school until they genuinely fulfilled all course requirements and validly earned their diplomas—being labeled "dropout factories" because their students were not graduating "on time" (Chavez, 2006; Clements, 2007; Reynolds, 2006; Sebring, 2007; Shackleford, 2007).
- our current situation in which high schools now graduate anyone, often through phony "credit recovery" schemes, even those who have genuinely and voluntarily dropped out (Blum, 2002; *The Economist,* 2019a; Hinojosa, 2013; Isenberg, 2018; Malkus, 2018; Martel, 2017a, 2017b, 2017c, 2017d, 2018; Muñiz, 2018; Smith, M., 2014; Solomon, 2008a, 2008b; Stein, 2018).

Greene and, later, Robert Balfanz (2008) of "dropout factories" fame, spent a lot of other people's money and took up a lot of other people's time. Statisticians who had better things to do were forced to divert time to explain ed statistics to people who wouldn't have otherwise inquired, and to defend their methods and collections against unfair accusations. But Greene and Balfanz were invited to speak to congressional committees; genuine experts on graduation statistics were not (Phelps, 2005e, 2009).[7]

Ultimately, we are all worse off. Graduation stats in 2001 had some issues; current graduation rates are meaningless, and now so are academic course completion requirements (Chaney and Burgdorf, 1997; Meyer, 2021; Nelson, 2017).

Also in the early 2000s, Jay P. Greene would produce a similarly naïve report allegedly supporting the use of high-stakes tests. He believed Daniel Koretz's false assertion that test score trends for no-stakes tests are stable (in fact, they tend to be more volatile than trends for high-stakes tests). So, Greene, et al., compared no- to high-stakes test score trends in a few jurisdictions (Greene, Winters, and Forster, 2003, 2004; Braams, 2003). Their study was promoted at various Reform Cartel venues (Bourge, 2003).

Several years later Jeb Bush's "Chiefs for Change" organization would promote the use of high-stakes testing. For scholarly support, they cited but one piece of "evidence": that Greene, Winters, and Forster study. Scholars had been studying the effects of testing, and high stakes, for over a century. Hundreds of experimental studies were available to reference (Larsen and Butler, 2013; Phelps, 2012b; Roediger and Karpicke, 2006). Regardless, Chiefs for Change cited only the one paltry and invalid study emanating from their resident advisors' echo chamber.

That Greene commanded two massively expensive and consequential fiascos rendered him no negative repercussions, however. He remained superbly credentialed, well-appointed to prestigious panels and commissions, and a

favorite with the Permanent Education Press for several more years (Kovacs and Boyles, 2005, pp. 13–19).

As the late Myron Lieberman (2007) observed in *Educational Morass*:

> There is no accountability for even the most egregious mistakes coming from the most prestigious sources of educational information and policy leadership. On this issue, both the supporters of public education and its critics are often unreliable and will continue to be so as long as there is no accountability for major mistakes. (p. 247)

> Public intellectuals on educational issues . . . should be regarded cautiously. They are not always mistaken, but they are mistaken often enough on critical issues to warrant much higher standards for assessing what they have to say. As long as no negative consequences follow . . . better educational policies are improbable. (p. 292)

Jay P. Greene is hardly the only Reform Cartel member to pay no price for producing highly impactful and erroneous work. (See, for example, Kovacs and Boyles, 2005; Martel, 2017a; Phelps, 2014b, 2015b, 2015c, 2015e, 2015i, 2016a, 2019b, 2020a, 2020b, 2021b; Dupre 2017; Stotsky, 2017, 2018, 2019a; Tampio, 2018; Tough, 2019; Wiley et al., 2015; Wilson, J. K., 2021; Wood, 2015.) His story provides just one example of what can happen under the following common conditions:

- A scholar claims expertise in a field without bothering know the field (e.g., conducting a thorough literature review, talking to those working in the field, or working in the field for some years), yet has access to multiple high-profile information dissemination platforms.
- A population of donors, advocates, and journalists consider the scholar an expert despite an absence of experience in the field or any substantial study of it.
- No one in that population seeks (or, perhaps, would even consider) any counterpoint.
- Other, knowledgeable scholars do not publicly challenge, because challenges are considered traitorous and countered with personal shunning and derision.

Lieberman (2007) had something to say on the latter condition, too.

> Most think tanks must constantly raise funds. In this context, criticism is perceived as a threat to organizational and personal survival. The result is much less criticism of think tank products by analysts in think tanks of the same or similar broad policy orientation. . . . Thus, without any formal treaty or agreement,

there is a striking absence of criticism among think tanks that appeal to the same funders. (p. 292)

Thusly forms the citation cartel information dissemination paradox:

- One cannot publicly challenge the expertise or competence of other cartel members without being expelled from the cartel.
- The cartel ignores or dismisses any criticism emanating from outside the cartel.
- Ergo, cartel members' work cannot effectively be challenged, regardless of quality (or lack thereof).

Obsessive Influencia

"The 'appetite for applause' counts amongst the lowest of human character traits."

—Jan-Willem van der Rijt

Also in *The Educational Morass* (2007, pp. 295–96), Lieberman relates the story of the Thomas B. Fordham Foundation's purchase of a service from Editorial Projects in Education (EPE), the enterprise that publishes *Education Week*. Fordham's director at the time, Chester "Checker" Finn, paid EPE to produce a report on the "most influential" persons and organizations in US education policy. Finn served on a panel that EPE assembled to judge who was most influential. Finn was ranked among the top ten most influential in the ensuing report (Swanson and Barlage, 2006).

Keeping track of their success in, as Harvard Dean Harry Lewis put it, "beating other people . . . establishing a personal reputation and denying it, to the extent possible, to rivals" (Russell, 2007), appears to occupy a substantial amount of Reform Cartel members' time and resources (Eveleth, 2014). Frederick M. "Rick" Hess of the American Enterprise Institute, who enjoys ready access to many Cartel information dissemination platforms, has also proselytized for two decades from a regular column *Education Week* grants him. There, he provides yet more exposure to the work of fellow Cartel members, while suppressing the work of rivals (Hess, 2011; Kovacs and Boyles, 2005, pp. 20–24).

Since 2010, Hess has also paid to produce "Edu-Scholar Public Influence Rankings," which he publishes annually, also with the help of a celebrity panel (see, for example, Hess 2021, 2022a, 2022b). Of course, genuinely measuring "influence" is impossible without access to brain waves across the

entire target population. Instead, Finn and Hess have measured what are now commonly referred to as "mentions" in public media.

Why the obsession with counts and rankings of media mentions? "Obsession" is not an unfair choice of words here. After all, production of the rankings is neither effortless nor cheap (Hess, 2022a). Assuming rankings are compiled validly, the process requires quite a lot of time and care just to delete the many false positives that derive from searches through indexes on persons' names.

Why go to all the trouble? Assume that Finn's and Hess's motives go beyond bragging about how successful they have been in promoting their group and suppressing others. Likely, they wish to imply that attention is highly correlated with merit (and never mind about their aggressive strategic behavior) (Haselby and Stoller, 2021; Labaree, 2021; Leef, 2021; Pinker, 2018; Rosenberg, 2021).

As if all that breast-beating were insufficient, Finn's successor as head of the Thomas B. Fordham Institute, Michael Petrilli (2017), assembles another measure of "who is dominating Twitter and other forms of social media in the education policy world." He ranks people by their number of Twitter followers and mention-measure "Klout score." Fordham Institute funders pay for this, apparently, and he advertises it in the Cartel's magazine *Education Next*.

Yet another Cartel member has devised yet another influence measure that incorporates Petrilli's twitter follower counts. Jay P. Greene (2013) calls his ratio of the number of one's tweets to number of followers a "Narcissus Index." This group naval-gazing topic stimulated at least four blog posts and received several dozen responses from Cartel colleagues.

How to Be "Influential"

These days, any merchandizer trying to sell product online knows about search engine optimization (SEO), the grab bag of methods for maximizing one's exposure on social media (or minimizing others'). Anyone can employ SEO techniques, if they have the time and are willing to learn the tricks. But those who can pay for it can employ far more. In social media, popularity can be purchased.

The Education Reform Citation Cartel, or the staff they hire to manage their marketing and promotion, know SEO, to be sure. Nonetheless, the Cartel leaves no member name unmentioned in its full-frontal assault to, borrowing Petrilli's term, "dominate" information dissemination in education policy. According to Laurie Spivak (2005), "William Baroody of the American Enterprise Institute . . . said, 'I make no bones about marketing. We pay as much attention to the dissemination of product as to the content.'"

Not only do they cite each other, and not cite others. Not only do they mention each other's names whenever it might seem remotely appropriate, and not mention others' names even when obviously called for. They also create phony opportunities to proliferate mentions. Some of their puff pieces are so vapid as to suggest that their only purpose is SEO, to add still more mentions of Cartel member names in cyberspace.

The Cartel's principals also proliferate mentions via staged events. Here's an example of how it works. One member of the group posts an essay. Another member of the group posts another essay that comments on the first essay. Then, yet another member of the group posts an essay that comments on the first and second essays. All in-group writers mention each other's names and refer to each other as good friends and admirable colleagues.[8]

It's a Mutual Admiration Society. Sure, they disagree with each other; if they didn't there would be no excuse for the succeeding, follow-up essays. But all disagreements are manageable among superlatively complimented, highly esteemed colleagues.[9]

Cartel members steadfastly avoid real debates—with real opponents, that is. They do, however, frequently fluff up pillow fights among themselves (e.g., Petrilli and Greene, 2016; Pondiscio, 2017b; Pondiscio and Forster, 2021) and proffer them to journalists as "news events." As Carl Sagan (1987) reminded us:

> [John Stuart] Mill argues . . . that alternative opinions must be heard from persons who actually believe them, who defend them in earnest, who do their very utmost for them. We must know them in their most plausible and persuasive form, and not by the propagandists for each side talking to its own citizenry.

Their closed loop is further reinforced by constant chatter—many mentions—which, in turn, assures consistent placement of their names on page one of search engine results. In the old library-dependent days, many points of view were represented roughly equally; librarians saw to that as part of their professional responsibility. Getting attention in the internet era requires links that pop on page one.

Any individual human's attention is limited (Hari, 2022; Illing, 2022; Simon, 1971; Wikipedia, 2022b). Members of the public, policymakers, and education journalists have only so much time to absorb information (Baddeley, 1992). So long as the citation cartels saturate their attention with their prolific output and leave them no time to investigate elsewhere, they will continue to succeed in "dominating" education policy discourse. (See also Ledzińska and Czerniawska 2008; Levitt 2014; Phelps 2016c; Resnick 2016.)

So long as journalists and policymakers narrowly source their information from those with the most microphones or shiniest credentials (with no regard

for the relevance of those credentials to the subject matter at hand), or whose skill at promotion exceeds their knowledge of a subject, they will not source it from genuinely knowledgeable experts. (See also Kendzior 2015; Kolowich 2016; Selingo 2016; Wellmon, Vinarov, Manasché, and Piper 2015.)

Credential Hoarding

We live in an age of information profusion and scholarly specialization. To keep up with a field of study—its research literature, terminology, history, legal context, etc.—to be a genuine expert—requires an enormous commitment of time and focus. Genuine experts know the research literature in their subfield, and many of those research literatures are massive. Finding it requires visits to multiple libraries, reading microfiche, talking to people, and requesting unadvertised and un-disseminated reports from government agencies and private companies.

It is all any serious scholar can do to keep up with the volume of information in just one chosen subfield.

Yet the alleged experts of the Reform Cartel flit from one dense subject field to another month by month. Here, for example, is a list of topics over which just one alleged expert in anything and everything has claimed mastery over two decades, gleaned from his C.V. (* designates topics for which he claimed no previous research existed [source: Phelps, 2016b].):

*Student achievement testing; *Non-cognitive skills and tests; *Effects of class size; *Student retention in grade; Developing and implementing surveys; *Measurement of non-cognitive and social-emotional traits; Brain organization and working memory; *Public perceptions of public service quality; Neuroanatomical correlates of the achievement gap; *Teacher choices of defined contribution plans; Charter school performance; Neural connectivity and language exposure; Stratification in randomized experiments; Children's brain function and conversational exposure; The judiciary's role in education; *International comparisons of school accountability, autonomy, and choice; *Pursuing educational adequacy in the courts; Effect of the No Child Left Behind Act on accountability politics and practice; *Public opinion on US schools; Public opinion on school spending; Impact of home-based childcare unionization; Performance indicators of Strategic Data Project; *Effect of alternative grade configurations on student outcomes; Effect of urban teacher residency; Teacher earning outside of education; *School responses to teacher effectiveness; International comparisons of the history of religious school resistance to public schooling; *School consolidation and school outcomes; *Which school systems sort weaker students into smaller classes; *Effect of school choice threats on public school accountability systems; *International

comparisons of class size effects; *Participation in a national voucher program; *Reforming teacher collective bargaining; *College costs and parental preferences

His apparent productivity is extraordinary. Consider also that he must teach classes, fulfill administrative responsibilities, and show up for meetings of the many boards and commissions he's been appointed to.

He has used his celebrity status and ready access to multiple information dissemination platforms, however, to dismiss or denigrate more policy-useful information than he has newly provided. Despite all his considerable effort, he is, on balance, a subtractive scholar—his net impact on society's working memory strongly negative. But his CV lists only what he has added, and not what he has subtracted. His career has blossomed spectacularly.

Similar apparently prodigious bounty emanates from other members of the Cartel. For example,

- "[He] has written or edited, to date, somewhere in the neighborhood of 40 books. He's also a regular op-ed contributor to *Forbes*, the *National Review*, and *Education Week*, where he writes [a] popular blog. He's a resident scholar at the American Enterprise Institute in Washington, D.C. and also an executive editor of (and regular contributor to) the Harvard-based *Education Next* magazine" (Hough, 2022).
- "Along with two assistants, [he] runs the Manhattan Institute's Education Resource Center, produced 13 'studies' in two years. And last year alone, according to a recent article in *Education Week*, [his] team 'published 43 newspaper opinion pieces and was cited on radio, on television, or in print more than 500 times'" (Cavanaugh, 2004; Kovacs and Boyles, 2005, p. 7).

One may wonder about the quality of such quantity. One may also be reminded of Steve Bannon's famous political media tactic: "Flood the zone with (expletive)" (Stelter, 2021). As many a propagandist before Bannon recognized, if one side dominates more than 95 percent of the dialogue, it likely wins the debate, regardless of what's true (Brunton and Nissenbaum, 2017). There's even experimental evidence for this (Bai, Fiske, and Griffiths, 2022; Brewer, 1979, 2002; Fazio, Brashier, Payne, and Marsh, 2015; Lipton and Williams, 2016; Rai, 2022).

The Reform Cartel also floods the education policy domain with hundreds of allegedly "grassroots" organizations, all of which owe their existence, and their loyalty, to the Cartel. Such phony grassroots organizations have earned the sobriquet: "astroturf organizations" (Connellan, 2020; O'Connell, 2020; Schneider, 2021).[10]

For two decades, the Reform Cartel has largely ignored the psychology and program evaluation research literatures. Indeed, they seem to be working toward wholesale replacement. That's unfortunate because they could have learned a thing or two from psychologists. For example, regarding genuine expertise from Kirschner and Hendrick:

> John Sweller's article [on cognitive load theory, 1988] forms the basis for why domain-specific knowledge is so necessary for solving problems and why domain-independent skills . . . don't exist. If only researchers . . . educational policy makers, and politicians had read and applied the content of this article, then we could have saved a lot of wasted time, money, and energy spent chasing those elusive domain-independent skills. (2020, p. 15)

Such as public policy analysis, for example?

Race to the Top

Though few in number, Reform Cartel members produce hundreds of edited books, conferences, and research reports every year, saturating the education policy space. Look through many of them, however, and one may be struck by their sameness—the same people, the same references, the same ideas—repeated over and over.

The implication is, as always, that these scholars are the best, the top, the smartest, and the most informed. But, if they only talk to each other, and they read only each other's' work, how informed can they be (Nguyen, 2018; Pariser, 2012; Phelps, 2016b)?

Cartelists argue that they cite those who do "rigorous" research and dismiss those who do not.[11] It would be pure coincidence then that the small group of scholars exclusively conducting that rigorous research just happens to comprise a single group of frequent collaborators who attended the same graduate programs at the same few universities, working under the same few faculty.[12]

Cartel members not only limit their citations and references to each other, they also package stories for journalists such that the entire history of a line of research is portrayed as beginning and ending with them. "Early" research is the first research on the topic conducted within their group, even if what is early for them occurred a century later than others.'[13] Journalists receive names of "objective, rigorous" scholars to contact at distant universities (who just happen to be former graduate school chums) for "independent" critiques of the featured "first" studies (see, for example, Barnum, 2017a, 2017b, 2018b, 2018c, 2019).[14]

The Harvard Kennedy School now boasts a foundation-funded bureau called "The Journalist's Resource" that gives journalists advice, suggestions,

and leads.[15] The Resource frequently publishes at the web site of a professional association of education journalists, the Education Writers Association (EWA).[16] Indeed, a Resource staffer sits on the EWA board.[17]

Recently, the Journalist's Resource suggested that education journalists prioritize newer research over older.[18] Note that virtually all Harvard Kennedy School's education research is recent; its Program on Education Policy and Governance (PEPG) only formed in 1996.[19] Thus, the Journalist's Resource also appears to favor the "single study syndrome," so long as the single study is one of theirs (Beresini, 2015; Nichols, Kendall, and Boomer, 2019; Oransky, 2015; Wagenmakers, Sarafoglou, and Aczel, 2022).

In a truth-seeking, knowledge-accumulation research culture, the Popperian dialectic would assure that newer was indeed better. In Cartel Alliance culture, with its pervasive information suppression, the opposite is often true.

Harvard's Resource also recommends the "high-quality working papers" of Harvard's National Bureau of Economic Research (NBER), despite elsewhere recommending that journalists stick with peer-reviewed articles.[20]

Only We Can Fix It

In late 2011, the US House of Representatives Subcommittee on Early Childhood, Elementary and Secondary Education hosted a hearing, "Education Research: Identifying Effective Programs to Support Students and Teachers." The continued existence of the Institute of Education Sciences (IES), a key component of the Education Sciences Reform Act (ESRA) of 2002, focused attendees' attention. Formed several years earlier during a Republican administration, its mandate was now due for renewal under a Democratic administration.[21]

Invited to testify were several of those who had benefitted from IES largess and who likely hoped to continue to benefit. Not surprisingly, their evaluations of IES ranged from superlative to magnificent. Among some testifiers, generous condemnation of others' prior work accompanied the praise for their own.

One speaker worked as an economics professor at Stanford University, had formerly taught at Harvard, and had also managed the education portfolio at the National Bureau of Economic Research (NBER) for several years (during which time, dismissive reviews in NBER working papers proliferated[22]). Here's some of what she said to the subcommittee:

> There is a common theme in my research and the research of the many PhDs I have trained: we attempt to answer questions in education by applying the most reliable, most advanced, most scientific methods to the best available data.

> The Education Sciences Reform Act (ESRA) of 2002 greatly transformed education research. . . . ESRA stated unequivocally that the Institute for Education Sciences (IES) should facilitate research that met high, scientific standards in order that it produce reliable results.
>
> Prior to ESRA, Department of Education–funded research routinely provided misinformation to American families and schools. (Hoxby, 2011)

Many would agree with her characterizations of some, perhaps even most, previous education research. (See, for example, Asher, 2018, 2019; Innes, 2003; Kaestle, 1993; Kramer, 1991; Labaree, 1996; Levine, 2007; Schalin, 2019.) But, the blanket, all-or-nothing portrait she paints oversimplifies.

First, US education research—at least since the mid-twentieth-century formation of graduate schools of education—has suffered more from ideological and self-interest biases than it has from methodological incompetence. Some of what may appear to be poor methodology may represent deliberate effort to reach predetermined conclusions. By contrast, some of what may appear to be good methodology may hide deliberate obfuscation, such as fudged or falsified data, surreptitiously altered definitions of terms, selective references, and so on.

More "rigor" does not fix bias.

Second, how could education economists' recent research be universally superior to one hundred years' worth of psychology and evaluation research? According to the same speaker before the US House committee in 2011:

> Since its creation, IES has consistently promoted scientific methods by favoring studies that employ experimental and quasi-experimental methods such as randomized controlled trials, randomization built into pilot programs, and regression discontinuity.

Unlike economics, psychology had long been an experimental science. Many, if not most, research studies in psychology are randomized experiments and have been since the early 1900s. The speaker and other (mostly economist) scholars privileged to have been included within IES's circle of funding sometimes speak as if experimentation in education research first began with them, in their post-1995 "early" studies.

Besides, they've punched holes in their own blanket condemnation of education research. One might reasonably surmise that if an entire profession is corrupted, or incompetent, or intolerantly biased, the characterization would hold true throughout and up and down the status ladder. Indeed, one might assume the top dogs *most* responsible for the bias or corruption.

Yet, the Harvard and Stanford economists and political scientists cut out an exemption for their own two institutions and, in turn, their associated

colleagues at a few others. All education school research is awful, except for that conducted in *our* education schools?

With Friends Like These . . .

In the pivotal period of the early 2000s, Republican policy advisors advocated traditional Republican policies on a wide variety of issues, with two glaring exceptions: (1) testing and measurement and (2) curriculum and instruction. On those issues, the Republican advisors adopted Democratic Party, progressive education talking points.

It is difficult to believe that genuinely conservative Republican lawmakers would have approved either the nationalizing No Child Left Behind (NCLB) Act or the fuzzy Common Core standards had they been forthrightly and broadly informed on the relevant issues.

The "anchoring effect" endures from the Reform Cartel's early 2000s decision to eschew any study of relevant research literatures and instead trust the research dismissals of CRESST and the CRESST-captured Board on Testing and Assessment at the National Research Council.

For example, Reform Cartel members continue to ignore the reality of the "opportunity to learn" principle in federal case law. Commercial "off-the-shelf" nationally norm-referenced tests (NRTs) are not tenable as K–12 accountability devices, per *Debra P. v. Turlington* (1981). Nonetheless, Cartelians wax nostalgic about NRTs, untied to any specific curriculum, advocating their use as consequential, summative assessments (Greene, 2015; Jacob, 2005; Shuls, 2018).[23]

The notion that "standards don't matter" also appeals (Greene, 2015; Loveless, 2021; Mahnken, 2021). Yet, standards-based tests cannot exist without standards. Standards are more than "aspirational" documents, to borrow one Cartelian's phrasing. For standards-based tests, each item is written precisely to a standard, and all standards are covered with their respective items, often using some of the same wording (AERA, APA, and NCME, 2014, chapters I.1, III.4).

It might have helped if any members of the Reform Cartel had had any experience in writing standards, developing tests, or designing curriculum.

A recent taxpayer-funded publication is all too typical of Cartel work (Goldhaber and Özek, 2018, Kaufman, 2021). "How Much Should We Rely On Student Test Achievement as a Measure of Success?" was published by the federally funded National Center for Analysis of Longitudinal Data in Education Research (CALDER), which is run by Reform Cartel members. The publication attempts to answer its question by summarizing dozens of scholars' writings on the topic. Not one of the dozens of scholars cited had

any training or experience in developing, administering, or processing tests. All of them belonged to the Reform Cartel.

NOTES

1. The school's name has since been changed to the "Harvard Kennedy School."
2. The CRPE has since moved its office to Arizona State University in Phoenix.
3. Other platforms include, for example, the newsletters and blogs of the Hoover Institution, Brookings Institution, Manhattan Institute, Fordham Foundation and Institute, American Enterprise Institute, Harvard University, Stanford University, University of Washington, University of Arkansas, Koret Task Force, George W. Bush Center, the National Bureau for Economic Research, and regular columns in the publications *Education Week*, *National Affairs*, and *US News and World Report*.
4. Grover "Russ" Whitehurst, George W. Bush's appointee to oversee research at the US Education Department apparently knew little about CRESST or the National Research Council and accepted what they said and wrote at face value—including their information suppression claims. For example, this was said before a US congressional committee in February 2002, in regard to federally funded research centers (Whitehurst, 2002a):

> Ms. Woolsey: Well, a problem maybe that you could address that these centers are working towards a solution. I would like to know what your opinion is on how well they are doing on the question of assuring that all kids are fairly tested.
>
> Mr. Whitehurst: CREST [*sic*] the center at UCLA, is a stellar center, in my view, and is doing very important work on testing and assessment. It has the characteristics that I just mentioned. It has their leading experts in this area, and they are pursuing not only scientific problems, but problems that lead to solutions. . . . So I think that the center mechanism is working very well there.

5. For example, David Figlio was appointed to the NRC's Committee on Test Design for K–12 Science Assessment, https://www.nap.edu/read/11312/chapter/1#v. Julian Betts and Susanna Loeb were appointed to the NRC's Committee on Evaluation of Teacher Certification by the National Board for Professional Teaching Standards, https://www.nap.edu/read/12224/chapter/1#v. Paul Hill, Susanna Loeb and Tom Kane were appointed to the Committee on Incentives and Test-Based Accountability in Public Education, https://www.nap.edu/read/12521/chapter/1#v. Julian Betts was appointed to the Committee on Highly Successful Schools or Programs for K–12 STEM Education, https://www.nap.edu/read/13158/chapter/1#iv. David Figlio and Susanna Loeb were appointed to the Committee for the Five-Year Summative Evaluation of the District of Columbia Public Schools, https://www.nap.edu/read/21743/chapter/1#v. Elaine Allensworth, James Kemple, Morgan Polikoff, and Sean Reardon were appointed to the Committee on Developing Indicators of Educational Equity, https://www.nap.edu/read/25389/chapter/1#v.

6. The well-known Larry Mishel and Joydeep Roy (2006), Linda Chavez (2006), and Clifford Adelman (2006) wrote scathing takedowns of Greene's work. As his article never identified Greene by name, however, Adelman's critique may have had no effect beyond the world of education statistics insiders.

7. Greene, J. P. (September 21, 2011). Testimony before the United States House of Representatives Education and Workforce Committee Subcommittee on Early Childhood, Elementary, and Secondary Education; Balfanz, R. (February 3, 2015). Testimony for Senate HELP Committee Roundtable on "Fixing No Child Left Behind: Innovation to Better Meet the Needs of Students."

8. In *The Common Good* (1998), Noam Chomsky suggested, "The smart way to keep people passive and obedient is to strictly limit the spectrum of acceptable opinion but allow very lively debate within that spectrum—even encourage the more critical and dissident views. That gives people the sense that there's free thinking going on, while all the time the presuppositions of the system are being reinforced by the limits put on the range of the debate."

9. Cartel members are paid well for their internet chatter. Writing is part of their salaried employment. Perhaps no one will notice when they say nothing new, nothing important, and nothing that hasn't been said a thousand times elsewhere. Perhaps no one will notice that "the news" is nothing more than a conversation among friends.

10. https://www.merriamwebster.com/dictionary/astroturfing.

11. Also common is dismissal of entire research literatures based on methodology. Economists' preferred analytical methodology (multiple regression) is acceptable. What doesn't count, even minimally: any qualitative or survey study. They may not even be aware of some quantitative methodologies popular among psychologists, such as structural equation modeling and factor analysis.

12. Ed Reform Cartel members cited my work for several years until it became obvious that I would continue to criticize them for prescribing policy on topics they barely understood and for declaring nonexistent research literatures they hadn't bothered to find. For a while, my work was worthy of attention, then suddenly it was not. The "rigor" of the work didn't change; their personal opinions of me did. The same holds for others blacklisted, such as Sandra Stotsky, Myron Lieberman, John Merrifield, Diane Ravitch, and Erich Martel.

13. For the Reform Cartel, "early research" in most subfields of education commenced in the mid-1990s, about the same time they got involved and Netscape Navigator first made the World Wide Web searchable.

14. 2017a: "Anna Egalite, a researcher at North Carolina State University who has also found benefits of teacher diversity in her own research, reviewed the study at *The 74*'s request. She praised the paper—which has not gone through formal peer review—as 'interesting' and said she did not 'see any obvious biases or glaring issues with the research design.' As it turns out, Ms. Egalite is hardly independent. She works for [the Ed Reform Cartel] *Education Next*, and "Anna J. Egalite holds a Ph.D. in Education Policy from the [ed reform cartel] University of Arkansas; she completed her postdoctoral fellowship in the [Ed Reform Cartel] Program on Education Policy and Governance at Harvard University."

2017b: Research from 1999 to 2014 is called "early research." Reporter accepts self-interested researcher's word that their work is "rigorous" and "more sophisticated" and everything done earlier was crummy. A "void" in the research is determined by a search with two keywords in a single web-based index that, nonetheless, found 157 studies—though less than a couple dozen are referenced, and none pre-date 2002.

2018b: The journalist simply declares no previous research, without offering any evidence.

2018c: As evidence that little previous research exists, reporter simply cites another author, in an *Education Next* article, who makes the claim *ex cathedra*.

2019: Authors of the profiled study claimed that theirs was "one of the first"; journalist Barnum claims it to be "the first." Barnum cites a 2016 literature review, which itself: refers to several other randomized controlled trials of the topic funded at the same time by the same source (US DOJ) (https://nij.gov/funding/awards/pages/awards-list.aspx?solicitationid=3878#), admits its literature review is not exhaustive (see footnote 14); and, apparently, performed only a web search. Of the literature review's 69 references, one emanates from 1993, another from 1998, and all the rest from after the year 2000, with half from after 2009.

15. https://journalistsresource.org/.

16. https://www.ewa.org/find/results/Journalist%2526%2523039%3Bs%20Resource.

17. https://www.ewa.org/board-directors.

18. https://www.ewa.org/education-research; https://www.ewa.org/highlight/questions-ask-about-research-reviews.

19. https://www.hks.harvard.edu/centers/taubman/programs-research/pepg.

20. https://www.ewa.org/education-research.

21. For a different, more critical take on the IES's performance, see the GAO review (Scott, 2013).

22. See, for example, http://nonpartisaneducation.org/Review/Resources/NBER.htm.

23. Incidentally, I sent comments explaining the legal issue to two of the publications just cited. While one printed others' comments, neither printed mine.

Chapter 6

A Dense Web of Common Core Confederates

"One of the saddest lessons of history is this: If we've been bamboozled long enough, we tend to reject any evidence of the bamboozle. We're no longer interested in finding out the truth. The bamboozle has captured us. It's simply too painful to acknowledge, even to ourselves, that we've been taken. Once you give a charlatan power over you, you almost never get it back."

—Carl Sagan, *The Demon-Haunted World*

The so-called Common Core State Standards were built on promises. But, from the start, most made little sense. The consortia tests, PARCC and SBAC, were promised to measure student mastery of the K–12 curriculum, predict success in college, and predict success in careers—three separate purposes that separate tests would optimally measure.

As for their promise to "close" the achievement gap with progressive pedagogy, students who enter school with smaller vocabularies and little background knowledge do not benefit from learning each new lesson several different ways or by discovery learning that must extrapolate from their more meager knowledge base. They benefit from instruction that is clear, logical, sequential, and direct. Similarly for assessments—best for them are familiar, straightforward, and unadorned formats; they test mastery of subject matter directly, and not the ability to navigate convoluted "next generation" formats (Garelick, 2010, 2021; Milgram and Stotsky, 2013; Phelps and Milgram, 2014, 2015; McQuillan, Phelps, and Stotsky, 2015; Wood, 2015).

Bellwether of the New Education Journalism

Education news aggregation at the *RealClearEducation* (*RCE*) website purports to be journalistic, independent, thorough, and somewhat representative of the whole.[1] During a period from 2014 to 2016, however, it was run directly by leaders of the DC consulting group Bellwether Education Partners (BEP). During that period, *RCE*'s selection of source material was lopsidedly skewed toward those issues and perspectives favored by BEP and financed by the Gates Foundation and allies (Phelps, 2018b).

RealClearEducation of this period was about as biased a news source as is humanly possible to devise. Its coverage of the Common Core Standards Initiative (CCSI) ranged from blatant promotion to a variety of disingenuously framed news and opinion pieces featuring individuals and organizations receiving funds from Common Core's donor groups, without revealing their conflicts of interest.

Bellwether's behavior in managing a news outlet raises larger questions about the trustworthiness of information provided by education policy funders and recipients, the incestuous nature of the interlocking interests at both ends of the funding, and the near total absence of representation of most of the US population from education policy discussions.

In *RCE*'s own words at the time:

> *RealClearEducation* is a joint project between *RealClearPolitics* and Bellwether Education . . . *RealClearEducation* operates independently, and no content should be considered to be the viewpoint of Bellwether . . . or any of its funders or clients.[2]

In Bellwether's words,

> Bellwether works with a broad array of organizations, including districts, states, charters, foundations, nonprofits, associations, and mission-driven for-profit organizations across the nation.[3]

The links to the "broad array of organizations" led one to, essentially, a list of organizations whose staff, documents, and reports were also linked and cited daily by Bellwether in *RCE*[4]—overwhelmingly, the paid Common Core proponents of the Cartel Alliance.

Bellwether's *RealClearEducation* made barely any effort at balance on coverage of the Common Core Initiative (CCI).[5] Some individual and organizational Common Core opponents were occasionally linked[6] . . . on other topics. But most Common Core critics, as well as many excellent blogs,[7] were never linked in Bellwether's *RealClearEducation*, on any topic.[8]

So, did Bellwether stonewall Common Core criticism completely? No, that would have made their bias too easy to attack. Bellwether tokened fourteen individuals and one group.[9]

Meanwhile, over the same period, Bellwether linked to 160 pro–Common Core articles, reports, essays, and outright PR promotions. (See Figure 6.1.)

A deeper reading in *RCE* archives also reveals some interesting anecdotes:[10]

- Common Core supporter Jay Mathews of the *Washington Post* was referenced by *RealClearEducation* twenty-one times. Bellwether never referenced Valerie Strauss, the *Post*'s other K–12 education columnist and an outspoken opponent of Common Core.
- In January 2015, *RealClearEducation* referenced an op-ed column in the US military newspaper *Stars and Stripes* promoting Common Core. But *Stars and Stripes* had published the piece as half of a point-counterpoint pair. Bellwether did not reference the companion column opposing Common Core.
- Bellwether linked to an anti–Common Core op-ed written by Louisiana governor Bobby Jindal in the *Wall Street Journal* (February 10, 2015) but smothered it with eight critical editorials from the pro–Common Core *New Orleans Times-Picayune*.[11] Several links were also provided to Louisiana Common Core sympathizers John White (state superintendent), Public Impact, *The Advocate*, and New Schools for New Orleans.

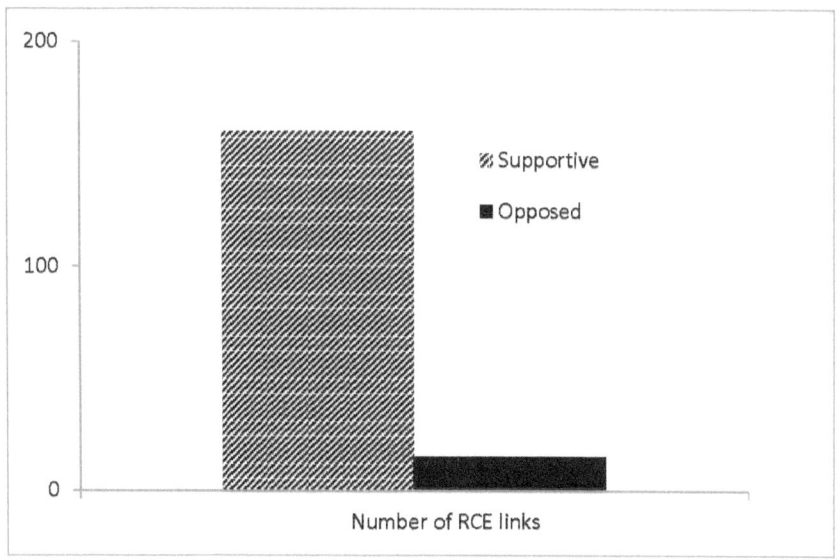

Figure 6.1. Number of links to articles supportive or opposed to Common Core Initiative.
Source: Author created.

- Some regional newspapers were referenced, but only when they published editorials or op-eds supporting Common Core.[12]
- Bellwether gave lots of favorable coverage to Common Core proponent Jeb Bush, and little coverage to other presidential candidates.

Finally, one observes loose bounds of propriety in Bellwether's linking when criticizing Common Core critics. Substantial amounts of nasty, condescending, speculative innuendo made their way into the lists.[13] In general, one would get this impression from Bellwether: Common Core advocates are knowledgeable, altruistic, and pure of heart; opponents are either ignorant locals, educators opposed to standards and accountability because they're incompetent, or hypocritical and self-serving politicians, pandering to the basest instincts of the uninformed masses and entrenched vested interests.[14]

"Social Entrepreneurs" . . . by the Thousands

While biased towards Bellwether's policy preferences and partner organizations, Bellwether's *RCE* at least tried not to appear completely elitist. Every several days or so, Bellwether linked to relatively unknown organizations. These links were not, however, randomly selected: (1) they aligned well with Bellwether's policy preferences and work projects and (2) they received funding from the Gates and other familiar foundations (e.g., Hewlett, Broad, Lumina, Joyce, Walton) that frequently pooled their resources to fund Bellwether Education Partners and allied organizations.

(See also Appendix 6 online for lists of linked organizations, donors, and board members, https://educationpolicy.us/Malfunction/App6.pdf.)

These obscure organizations, run by "social entrepreneurs," may do some admirable work. But, in many cases, their work had little to do with curriculum, instruction, assessment, or Common Core. Nonetheless, many of them went out of their way to publicly express support for the Common Core and its related assessments, causes supported by their own funders (Piereson and Riley 2013).[15]

Bellwether also appeared to showcase individual school staff. Seemingly ordinary, could-be-your-child's teachers just happened to be writing op-eds for major publications asserting their support for Common Core. But each op-ed read like ones appearing elsewhere: professionally written, polished, and with familiar talking points. Digging deeper into writers' backgrounds one discovered that, ultimately, they benefited from Common Core funders, too.[16, 17, 18, 19]

Bellwether's Tax Returns

"Nonprofit" organizations can still make money. In the United States, public "charities" with annual revenues over $50,000 must file a Form 990, "Return of Organization Exempt from Income Tax," with the Internal Revenue Service. A perusal of those from Bellwether Education Partners, Inc. is quite revealing. Tens of millions of dollars flowed through Bellwether's books. Most of it filled staffers' pockets.[20] Bellwether promoted itself as a champion of the less privileged, but their own salaries hardly resembled those of social workers.[21]

The IRS did not require nonprofits to itemize their funding sources, so Bellwether did not list its donors on its Form 990s, and its website confusingly mixed donors and clients together—all 330 of them.[22] So, for details on Bellwether's donors, one must consult donor documents.

Between 2010 and 2022 Bellwether accepted $10,321,227 from the Gates Foundation[23] and, between 2012 and 2020, $6,067,781 from the Walton Family Foundation.[24] One may wonder how strongly such funding streams would have continued to flow if Bellwether had sought more balance in its *RCE* coverage of the issues these foundations coveted.

Interlocking Directorates and Washington's Staff for Life

In his 1960s classic, *Who Rules America?* (1967), sociologist G. William Domhoff describes the concept and power of interlocking directorates—powerful individuals sitting on each other's corporate boards reinforcing group norms and protecting each other's interests.[25]

With the single exception of their nonprofit status, the interlocking directorates of the Cartel Alliance resemble those of Domhoff's corporate power elite. Directors of one education organization can be found sitting on the boards of others, facilitating interorganizational strategic partnerships.[26] Foundations and other donors collaborate extensively, "pack funding" one nonprofit after another (Vogel, 2016).

Some complain about lifetime professional politicians—those who stay in Washington, DC, long after their peak years, typically to work as lobbyists. Bellwether introduces us to another group—lifetime political staff. Unlike Cincinnatus, the legendary Roman leader who returned to his farm when he felt he had accomplished what he had been invited to Rome to do, some Beltway staffers choose not to return home when their bosses retire, change jobs, or lose an election. Rather, they form or join a think tank, making use of their contacts and experience. Political lifers form the core of Bellwether Education Partners and some of its allied groups.[27]

Many of the rest arrive through several familiar channels. Read the short bios of the writers of linked articles, and one often learns that the author worked for Teach for America, did a Broad Residency, worked at the Gates Foundation, or completed a public policy degree. It's a club, an inbred, insular, exclusive club. (See Lofgren, 2015; Savage, G. C., 2016; Waldman, 2019). As with any club, membership has privileges and rules.

Bellwether Education's preferred network of education policy organizations, for example, are so thoroughly interlocked they're immovable. And so many individuals and groups are involved that no one can be held accountable. Consider an announcement from the Center for American Progress (2015) introducing yet another small new nonprofit. The organization having just been born, was already allied with at least forty other nonprofit "organizational partners."[28]

Is this degree of cooperation good? How is their cherished social innovation even possible when countless organizations run by committees must agree on the same plan? When a hundred funders all fund the same thing? When all the social entrepreneurs come from the same background? It's the collaboration of a summer picnic sack race. (See also Chapman, 2018; educationrealist, 2013; Lubienski, Brewer, and La Londe, 2016; Petersen and Poulson, 2016.)

After reading through page after page of reports, essays, and blogs from many of these "astroturf" groups, two aspects stand out: impressive style and deficient substance (Connellan, 2020; O'Connell, 2020; Schneider, 2014, 2021).[29] Their work—their websites and their publications, for example—look very professional. Masses of donor funds bestow upon even the smallest, newest, and most narrowly focused of these nonprofits the aura of established institutions.

Contrasting the appearance of quality professionalism is pervasive superficiality of content. Missions are launched based on the findings of one or a few reports from in-group think tanks or advocacy organizations. Reference lists in one group's reports mirror the reference lists in others'. Vast research literatures, easily accessible from the local library, remain ignored, in favor of policy solutions recommended by a familiar small group of well-funded celebrities.

Thomas B. Fordham Institute: Influence for Hire

Bellwether Education Partners' aggressive support for the Common Core at least aligns with their principals' long-held convictions. Had one interviewed the group's leaders long before Common Core's creation, one would probably have discerned similar policy preferences.

Not so with the Thomas B. Fordham Institute, another organization key to the Common Core's success. Fordham flipped 180 degrees from previous positions on curriculum, assessment, and standards (*Nonpartisan Education Review,* 2013; Phelps, 2015i, 2016a, 2018c; Ravitch, 2016; Schneider, 2013).

In return, it absorbed $11,091,462 from the Gates Foundation between 2003 and 2021,[30] and $7,977,780 from the Walton Family Foundation between 2002 and 2020.[31]

The Fordham Institute claimed on its website "humility, and . . . willingness to change our minds—and admit when we are wrong." Also common, however, has been a proclivity to suppress dissent, shun or ridicule those who disagree, and promote their ingroup as the only legitimate spokespersons for the "conservative" side along a wide range of policy issues.

Robert Pondiscio is their senior fellow and vice president for external affairs. His *Education Next* essay, "Lessons on Common Core: Critical Books Offer More Folly Than Wisdom," typifies Fordham's "humble" approach (2017a). Pondiscio reviewed six books written in opposition. Throughout, he portrays himself as a cool, measured, reasonable fellow, with the public—"parents and taxpayers alike who simply want a decent education for their kids"—on his side. The Common Core–critical book authors, meanwhile, are "carping," "spleen venting," "fear mongering," and "conspiratorially minded" "excitable enemies."

Short on substance and long on selective and colorful prejudicial quotations, adjectives, and adverbs,[32] he characterizes Mercedes Schneider's exhaustively researched *Common Core Dilemma* (2015), for example, as "riddled with scare quotes and sarcasm." Other descriptors employed for the authors: "bombast," "overreach," "dark mutterings," "hyperbole," "obsession," "paranoia," "folly," "frets," "paranoid conspiracy theories," and "overreach."

Individuals Pondiscio agreed with, however, were "thoughtful," "serious," "sober," and "principled."

"Lessons on Common Core" effortlessly contradicts, too (see also Gass 2014a, 2014b). For example, Pondiscio supports the Common Core Standards for the "desperately needed" direction they provide teachers, "at a time when the nation's 3.7 million teachers desperately needed help, when 'What should we teach?' was at long last being asked in earnest."

At the same time, he argues that standards really don't matter much and good teachers ignore them completely:

> Far more compelling arguments can be made not about how much Common Core matters, but how little. . . . To be upset by academic standards is to invest them with a power they neither have nor deserve. In my five years of teaching fifth graders, I never—not even once—reached for English language arts

standards when deciding what to teach. . . . First things first: What is it you want to teach?

Early on in his *Education Next* essay, Pondiscio prominently brandishes his classroom teaching experience to establish his bona fides as a front-line educator.

But teachers wrote five books Pondiscio reviewed, and he ridicules them mercilessly as ignorant rubes lacking the understanding that might qualify them to engage in a debate he believes to be beyond their intellectual reach.

On its website, the Fordham Institute proclaims:

> We see much wisdom in "subsidiarity"—the doctrine that important matters ought to be handled by the competent authority that's closest to the action, which in education usually means parents, teachers, and schools.

Yet, Fordham enthusiastically supported, first, the No Child Left Behind Act's nationalization of testing and accountability regimes and, second, the Common Core's nationalization of standards, assessment design, and instructional recommendations.

Cronyism, Corruption, and Conflicts of Interest

Also unfortunately typical of Fordham essays on causes it is richly paid to promote: never once did Pondiscio mention his or their conflicts of interest. As Joy Pullman (2015) wrote,

> Common Core's supporters are typically rich elites using their excess money to manipulate public opinion.
>
> First, we have an obvious conflict of interest problem here. People deserve to know when a prominent official or self-proclaimed "expert" who is testifying before state legislatures or writing op-eds is making money from their persuasive efforts. It means their judgment is not entirely independent, even if they feel it so. Basic ethics requires someone with a financial or personal stake in the outcome of a public decision to recuse himself from participating in that decision. That has not been happening.
>
> Second, it indicates rampant cronyism, which is a form of political and social corruption. We see that Common Core is infested with essentially the same set of people rewarding each other with taxpayer dollars and huge private grants, decades before there can be any proof that all this money laundering produced a genuine public good. Common Core is a giant experiment, remember. Bill Gates says he won't know if his 'education stuff' worked for "probably a decade."[33]
>
> Former public officials (or semi-public officials, which is what I label the Common Core coauthors, because while we did not elect them we all must live

with their decisions) are amply rewarded for doing what the rich and powerful wanted with sweet compensation packages following their "public service."

Arguably, the Fordham Institute is the country's most influential in education reform. Moreover, it has spun (or, purchased, depending on your point of view) a large, elaborate web of institutional and individual partnerships. A "common core" of people moves in, out, and across the groups. People inside the web know each other well, they share friends and enemies, and they owe each other favors. They are less likely to criticize others inside the network and more likely to criticize (or ignore) those outside the network.

Moreover, the network replicates itself through such training vehicles as Fordham's Emerging Education Policy Scholars Program.[34] If the graduates of these programs turn out to be just as censorial and clannish as those training them, our country may look forward to more narrow-mindedly conceived and hugely expensive white elephants like the Common Core.

Many citizens abhor the influence of money on US politicians. But look at the influence of money in the Common Core era on supposedly independently minded education reformers. Rich donors have demonstrated that most education policy wonks can be bought.[35]

That should frighten us all. It may be an obvious point, but it may also bear repeating, as Au and Ferrare (2015, p. 10) put it regarding Gates in particular (see also Grek, 2013; Giridharadas, 2018):

> If the Gates and Gates Foundation funded reforms don't work, and there is not much evidence, if any, that they do work, what can the public do about it? What is the mechanism for holding Gates and his foundation accountable for any damage done. . . . The answer is that there is no such mechanism.

NOTES

1. https://www.realcleareducation.com/about.html, December 2016.
2. https://www.realcleareducation.com/sponsors_and_funders.html, December 2016.
3. https://bellwethereducation.org/about-us, December 2016.
4. https://bellwethereducation.org/who-we-work, December 2016.
5. Indeed, the only substantial critical presence comprised the few straddlers who took money from the Bill and Melinda Gates Foundation and then, when it became clear that Common Core was not the fait accompli that had been promised, orchestrated the "good idea; poor implementation" pretense, which is not opposition (e.g., American Enterprise Institute, American Federation of Teachers).

See, for example, an interesting essay by Peter Cunningham in the *Education Post* (September 28, 2015) comparing the "old" and "new" Rick Hess, Hess being of the

American Enterprise Institute, which accepted Gates Foundation money early on to promote Common Core. Also on point is Sam Dillon's (2011) column in the *New York Times*.

6. E.g., George F. Will, Quin Hillyer, Peggy Noonan, Pedro Noguera, Ben Wildavsky, Lance Izumi, Jay P. Greene, and David J. Armor were each linked once. Bellwether linked to Common Core critics Diane Ravitch, Stanley Kurtz (*National Review*), and AFT member Peter Goodman twice each, but not about Common Core. Bellwether linked to Common Core critics Aaron Pallas (Columbia University), Neal McCluskey (Cato Institute), and Jason Bedrick (Cato Institute) each three times, but not on Common Core.

7. E.g., CCSSI Mathematics, LifeZette, Pioneer Institute, Heartland Institute, Heritage Foundation, Truth in American Education, Caffeinated Thoughts, Missouri Education Watchdog, Bluegrass Institute, Nonpartisan Education Group, and countless state and local "Stop Common Core" grassroots citizens' groups across the country.

8. The eighteen months of *RCE* contain over two thousand links. Just some of the many knowledgeable public Common Core opponents not referenced over that long span of time: Peter Wood, R. James Milgram, Michelle Malkin, John Stone, Alan Singer, Carol Burris, Mercedes Schneider, Duke Pesta, Marina Ratner, Barry Garelick, Ted Rebarber, Lisa Jones, Joye Walker, Scott Garrett, Richard Innes, David Randall, Charles Grassley, Robert Eitel, Kent Talbert, Ralph Ketcham, Teresa Mull, Alan Caruba, Heather Kays, Anthony Esolen, Brad McQueen, Nancy Thorner, Donna Hearne, Terrence Moore, Donna Garner, David Anderson, Wayne Bishop, Anthony Cody, Lindsay Graham, Ted Cruz, Phyllis Schlafly, Mary Grabar, Rand Paul, Joy Pullmann, Lennie Jarratt, Steven Rasmussen, Craig Sower, Thomas Newkirk, Mark McQuillan, Jason Becker, Will Fitzhugh, Emmet McGroarty, Jane Robbins, and Shane Vander Hart.

9. They are teachers Michael Godsey, Mia Hood, and Brian Zorn; the Heritage Foundation; Nicholas Tampio, a Fordham University professor writing for Al Jazeera (twice); Jim Stergios (Pioneer Institute); Louisiana governor Bobby Jindal; Robert Holland (Heartland Institute); Jason L. Riley (Manhattan Institute); Alveda King (Alabama Eagle Forum); and Williamson Evers (Stanford University). Also linked is a short newspaper debate between critic Sandra Stotsky and a Common Core supporter. Incidentally, four of the fifteen links direct one to writings of Stanford's Williamson Evers—the one member of the *Education Next*/Koret Task Force group opposed to Common Core.

10. From February through July 2015, the education-focused *Hechinger Report* hosted a debate between Carol Burris, a New York State school district superintendent and Common Core opponent, and Jayne Ellspermann, a Florida high school principal, National Association of Secondary School Principals Principal of the Year, and Common Core supporter. Over the course of six months, each wrote six essays. Three of Ms. Ellspermann's Common Core-supportive essays were described and linked in RealClearEducation; none of Ms. Burris's essays were ever mentioned. See https://hechingerreport.org/category/columnists/core-debate/.

11. Those pieces featured titles such as "Jindal Plan to Ditch 'Core' Would Take Louisiana Backward" (March 19, 2015) and "Jindal Abused His Power on Common

Core" (June 19, 2015). Other pro–Common Core, critical-of-Jindal editorials were published in the *New Orleans Times-Picayune* (and linked by *RealClearEducation*) Dec. 3, 2014; February 9, 2015, and March 6, 2015.

12. E.g., *Catalyst Chicago*; *Charlotte Observer*; *Columbus Dispatch*; *Oklahoman*; *Portland Press Herald*; *Scholastic*; *St. Louis Post-Dispatch*; *Stars and Stripes*; *The State* (South Carolina); *Toledo Blade*; *The Phoenix Business Journal*.

13. See, for example, Campbell Brown, March 2, 2015, in the *Washington Post*; the *New York Times* editorial board, June 8, 2015; the *St. Louis Post-Dispatch*'s editorial on the same day; Paul Peterson's August 20, 2015, declaration in *Education Next*; Jennifer Rubin's excoriation of Scott Walker (June 11, 2015) in the *Washington Post*; Bruce Taylor's insistence in *Catalyst Chicago* that Common Core is a fait accompli (November 13, 2014); Emmaline Zhao describing Common Core opponents, "Haters gonna hate?" in *RCE* (March 27, 2015); a Farleigh Dickenson University "Public Mind" poll, sponsored by the pro–Common Core education school finds Common Core opposition riddled with "false beliefs" on Feb. 23, 2015; Laura Waters's or David Weigel's criticism of Chris Christie's and Andrew Cuomo's allegedly self-serving "flip flops" in *Newsworks* (December 5, 2013) and *Bloomberg View* (October 20, 2014), respectively; or the stereotyping humiliation of Common Core critics by Jennifer Hanno in the May 1, 2015, *McSweeneys*.

14. As lopsided as RCE's Bellwether-era Common Core coverage was, other issues have perhaps been even more so. Consider the short-lived debate on federal testing mandates during deliberations for the new federal ESSA law. If you relied on *RealClearEducation* then as your only source of news and expertise, you would have been well exposed to those arguments favoring federally required annual testing and a continued federal role in local schools. But you would have had little or no exposure to arguments on the other side, say, for less onerous, but more subject matter inclusive "grade-span" testing (the kind most countries use), with fewer federal requirements. Bellwether frequently linked to essays arguing for increased federal control, more student-data-gathering, and preservation of the national Common Core aligned tests in any test-reduction scheme (i.e., dump the allegedly inferior state and local tests instead).

15. E.g., November 24, 2014, and March 20, 2015, to Stand for Children; December 5, 2014, to Teach Plus; December 12, 2014, to iNACOL; November 10, 2014, to the Alliance for College-Ready Charter Schools and Achievement First; February 5, 2015, to Cartier Winning Images.

16. Colorado's Tyler Lawrence (May 4, 2015, op-ed in the *Colorado Springs Gazette*), upstate New York's Meaghan Freeman (February 4, 2015, op-ed in *The Atlantic*), and Michigan's Danielle Alexander (February 16, 2015, op-ed in the *Detroit News*) were "Teaching Fellows" with America Achieves when they wrote their pro–Common Core essays. America Achieves received funding from the "Laura and John Arnold Foundation, Bloomberg Philanthropies, Charles Butt, the Heckscher Foundation for Children, the Leona M. and Harry B. Helmsley Charitable Trust, the William and Flora Hewlett Foundation, the George Kaiser Family Foundation, the Kern Family Foundation, the Edna McConnell Clark Foundation and others," https://americaachieves.org/our-funders/.

Denver fourth-grade teacher Kyle Schwartz was working with Teach Strong when she published pieces in the *Chicago Tribune* and *Washington Post* (March 24, 2015, in the *Chicago Tribune*; March 25, 2015, in the *Washington Post*). "The organizational partners in TeachStrong" are listed here: https://www.americanprogress.org/press/release/2015/11/10/125052/release-40-education-organizations-unite-tolaunch-teachstrong-a-campaign-to-modernize-and-elevate-the-teaching-profession/.

Oakland, California's, Robbie Torney and New Iberia, Louisiana's Lauren Trahan were "part of Student Achievement Partners' Core Advocate program" when they wrote their commentary for *RealClearEducation* (Oct. 9, 2014). In "Student Achievement Partners' Core Advocate program . . . educators from across the country work closely with Student Achievement Partners to develop, curate, and review Common Core resources for teachers." David Coleman, Susan Pimentel, and Jason Zimba, lead writers of the Common Core State Standards, founded Student Achievement Partners. https://www.realcleareducation.com/articles/2014/10/09/common_core_classroom_perspectives_teachers_carol_burris_1114.html.

Memphis's Karen Vogelsang was a Hope Street Group Fellow when she wrote her pro-Common Core two-bits for the *Nashville Tennessean* (January 8, 2015). Hope Street Group funders included the "Bill and Melinda Gates Foundation; Blue Shield of California Foundation; City Bridge; Cancer Treatment Centers of America; Foundation for Excellence in Education; Harold K. L. Castle Foundation; Hawaii Community Foundation; The William and Flora Hewlett Foundation; The Henry J. Kaiser Family Foundation; LinkedIn; McInerny Foundation; NewVentureFund; Omidyar Network; OPTUM; Peter G. Peterson Foundation; Rodel Foundation of Delaware; Robert Wood Johnson Foundation; VOYA Financial; Walmart Foundation; ALCOA Foundation; The Joyce Foundation." https://hopestreetgroup.org/whowe-work-with/funders/.

Boston's Emily Griggs was a Teach Plus Policy Fellow and a teacher in the UP Education Network (https://www.upeducationnetwork.org/about) when she wrote a pro–Common Core commentary for *RealClearEducation*. Funding Teach Plus were the "Barr Foundation; Bill and Melinda Gates Foundation; the Boston Foundation; Charles and Lynn Schusterman Family Foundation; Eli and Edythe Broad Foundation; Eli Lilly and Company Foundation; Harold Whitworth Pierce Charitable Trust; The Indianapolis Foundation, a CICF Affiliate; The Joyce Foundation; The Leona M. and Harry B. Helmsley Charitable Trust; The Mind Trust; Moriah Fund; Noyce Foundation; Reeder Foundation; SheGives; Shippy Foundation; W. Clement and Jessie V. Stone Foundation; The Walton Family Foundation; Wasserman Foundation" https://www.teachplus.org/donate.

17. Many former state teachers of the year wrote Common Core initiative affirmations linked by Bellwether: Josh Parker, Hechinger Report, January 5, 2016; Karen Vogelsang, Nashville Tennessean, January 8, 2015; Alison Grizzle, Amanda McAdams, Kristie Martorelli, Beth Maloney, John-David Bowman, Ouida Newton, Elizabeth Miner, Jemelleh Coes, Jeff Baxter, Melody Arabo, Angie Miller, Jeff Hinton, James Ford, Lori Michalec, Mike Funkhouser, Terry Kaldhusdal, Amy Traynor, Jane McMahon, Diana Callope, and Mick Wiest, Education Week, May 19, 2015.

18. Indeed, there exists an organization entitled National Network of State Teachers of the Year (NNSTOY), funded by the Bill and Melinda Gates Foundation, Pearson and ETS, the PARCC test developers and administrators, College Board, the National Education Association, and several other Common Core backers. https://www.nnstoy.org/about-us/our-sponsors/.

19. Several senior administrators from the Educational Testing Service, the Council of Chief State School Officers (CCSSO) (the co-owner of the Common Core standards copyright), and the NEA serve on NNSTOY's Board of Trustees. https://www.nnstoy.org/about-us/board-members/.

20. Bellwether Form 990s may be found here:

- 2013: https://nonpartisaneducation.org/Review/Articles/BWForm990_2013.pdf
- 2014: https://nonpartisaneducation.org/Review/Articles/BWForm990_2014.pdf
- 2015: https://nonpartisaneducation.org/Review/Articles/BWForm990_2015.pdf

21. The IRS required that Form 990s list all staff receiving over $150,000 in compensation. Bellwether listed ten such staffers for the 2014 tax year, eight for 2013, and six for 2012. Two or three staff members—Kimberly Smith, Mary K. Wells, and Andy Rotherham—pulled in more than $250,000 a year. And remember, all travel and lodging—of which Bellwether staffers partook plenty—was expensed elsewhere in the budget. All the most highly remunerated staff worked in "thought leadership," "strategic advising," or "talent services." Annual bonuses ranged from $15,000 to $55,000. See https://bellwethereducation.org/about-us.

22. https://bellwethereducation.org/who-we-work.

23. https://www.gatesfoundation.org/about/committed-grants?q=Bellwether #committed grants.

24. https://www.waltonfamilyfoundation.org/grants-database?q=Bellwetherands =1andp=1.

25. Though created to protect the assets, plans, privileges, and culture of those inside them, the separation from the outside world created by the walls and moats surrounding interlocking directorates isolates powerful insiders. New, useful and enlightening—but perhaps disruptive—information and resources do not find their way inside the walls. Those inside the walls learn only from each other, from those they know and trust, those they already agreed with before they set themselves apart inside the castle.

26. Some nonprofits maintain two or three boards [e.g., "advisors," "trustees," "editorial"].

27. Given Washington, DC's, magnetic pull on members of this group, it should come as no surprise to hear them so often suggest federal solutions for education problems. The Tenth Amendment to the US Constitution, which grants "unenumerated" powers, such as any related to education, to the states, seems of little interest or concern. When faced with the choice, these people chose to remain in DC rather than return home. Federal involvement in education means more work for them there, debating, lobbying, researching, and writing talking points.

28. "The organizational partners in TeachStrong are: Alliance for Excellent Education, America Achieves, American Association of Colleges for Teacher Education, American Federation of Teachers, ASCD, Center for American Progress, Council of Chief State School Officers, Deans for Impact, Digital Promise, Education Post, The Education Trust, the Education Policy Program at New America, Educators 4 Excellence, Educators Rising, Emerson Collective, Hope Street Group, Knowledge Alliance, Leading Educators, Learning Forward, National Board for Professional Teaching Standards, National Center for Learning Disabilities, National Center for Teacher Residencies, National Center on Time and Learning, National Commission on Teaching and America's Future, National Council on Teacher Quality, National Education Association, National Institute for Excellence in Teaching, National Network of State Teachers of the Year, National Women's Law Center, New Leaders, New Teacher Center, Public Impact, Relay Graduate School of Education, Stand for Children, Teach For America, Teach Plus, Third Way, TNTP, Urban Teachers, and The VIVA Project."

29. https://www.merriamwebster.com/dictionary/astroturfing.

30. https://www.gatesfoundation.org/about/committed-grants?q=Fordham#committed_grants.

31. https://www.waltonfamilyfoundation.org/grants-database?q=fordhamands=1.

32. See also, Phelps, 2015g.

33. http://www.washingtonpost.com/blogs/answersheet/wp/2013/09/27/bill-gates-it-would-be-great-if-our-education-stuffworked-but/.

34. https://edexcellence.net/about-us/emerging-education-policy-scholars-eeps.html.

35. Common Core money even corrupted the profession of psychometrics—the technicians who develop and analyze standardized tests. Some violated their own "bible" of good practice, the *Standards for Educational and Psychological Testing*, by working for and promoting the not-yet-validated Common Core tests.

Chapter 7

The Permanent Education Press
A Breed Apart

"The fact that modern journalism has transformed itself to an upper-class profession is blindingly obvious to outsiders, but not well understood within the profession itself. The belief that it's up to journalists to lead public opinion in particular directions and lead them away from inconvenient facts is nothing less than a disaster for democracy."

—Greg Lukianoff, FIRE[1]

At the risk of some simplification, there exist two types of journalists: those who report the news and those who filter it for us (Metcalf, 2020). Most journalists probably do some of both, but some lean strongly one way or the other. When covering research and policy, members of the US Permanent Education Press skew sharply away from reporting and toward filtering.

Problems arise when an "explainer journalist"—in filtering and interpreting the news for us—abandons their reporter role completely because they believe they know what is true and good, and so ignores rival sources and evidence. Once they halt efforts to diversify sources and evidence, their reporting becomes more a verification of settled beliefs among a chosen elite than any approximation of reality. Their curiosity dissipated; they have ceased to learn. They have become more spokespersons for interest groups than reporters. Their work is more public relations and advocacy than journalism.

Explainer journalists wish to be the ones who tell us what to do and how to think, rather than the ones who give us a thorough, unadulterated list of options from which we can decide for ourselves.

Yet, in covering policy research, journalists typically possess neither training nor experience in the issues they proselytize. (See also Appendix 7 online, "Career Paths of the Permanent Education Press," https://educationpolicy.us

/Malfunction/App7.pdf .) So, how do they decide—why do they think they know—what is true and good and best for us?

They believe certain sources over others, apparently based on credentials and personal relationships. Top priority goes to academic credentials from universities and think tanks; actual work experience in a field seems to count for little. The more celebrated and prestigious the institution the better. A professor at Harvard or Stanford trumps one from San Diego State or the University of Northern Iowa. A scholar at internationally known think tanks, such as the Brookings or Hoover Institutions, trumps one at the Pioneer Institute or the Education Consumers Foundation (ECF).

Furthermore, pretty much any scholar at Harvard, Stanford, Brookings, or Hoover trumps any source anywhere else, regardless of relevant expertise. That is, a scholar from one of the more prestigious institutions tends to be considered a better source on a topic even if he or she is unfamiliar with the topic and lacks any relevant experience. Few readers will notice.

Talking to those with the flashiest credentials (even if irrelevant to the topic at hand) at the most prestigious universities and think tanks lends stories more prestige and legitimacy and creates opportunities to rub elbows with celebrities.

Moreover, typically the choice preferences are not just proportional, but verge on total. A member of the US Permanent Education Press does not, say, consult sources at Brookings or Hoover more often than at Pioneer or ECF. Typically, they consult sources at Brookings or Hoover always—day after day, week after week, month after month, year after year, decade after decade—and never at Pioneer or ECF (Feldon, 2007; Mazar and Wood, 2022).

Sourcing bias became particularly noticeable when the "pack" of Common Core funders led by the Gates Foundation endeavored to buy anyone and everything in the top credentials layer—the entire celebrity class of education scholars. They largely succeeded, much as the Council for Tobacco Research prevailed in scholarly circles from the 1940s to the 1980s when "Twenty-seven Nobel laureates took money from Big Tobacco, and every major university was showered with cash" (O'Dwyer, 2021, Lawrence, F., 2022).

This left the few, brave holdouts against Common Core, no matter how knowledgeable and principled, to publish their opposing evidence and opinion at Breitbart, the *Federalist*, Diane Ravitch's blog, the *Nonpartisan Education Review*, the Pioneer Institute, and other non-mainstream outlets that lay beneath the celebrity threshold, where elite journalists dread to tread.

The confident working class beat reporters of yesteryear may well have seen through the braggadocio and bluster of today's know-it-all Harvard, Stanford, and Brookings scholars, or even just doubted them on principle. But today's Ivy-educated Permanent Education Press seems to gulp the pretense

whole. Perhaps they feel the common tie of a familiar social circle (McGill 2016; Ungar-Sargon, 2021; Wai and Perina, 2018).

As defined in this book's Introduction, members of the "Permanent Education Press" have large regional or national audiences and remain on the education beat for life. That loyalty to education topics should have advantages: they should get to know topics more deeply and, by following them over time, can compare with evolving backgrounds and changing contexts. But they also get stuck in ruts . . . deeply (Feldon 2007; Mazar and Wood 2022).

It is common for Permanent Education Press members to rely exclusively on "go-to" sources, thus skewing their coverage toward those sources' particular knowledge base, incentives, and biases.

Moreover, their own community is tight and self-reinforcing; one journalist's "go-to" source may be others' as well. Permanent Education Press groupthink is pervasive (Bai, Fiske, and Griffiths, 2022; Janis and Mann, 1977; Janis, 1989; 't Hart, 1991; Turley 2021).[2]

(See also Appendix 8 online, "Media Expertise Source Counts," https://educationpolicy.us/Malfunction/App8.pdf.)

An earlier chapter featured a section on the early 2000s celebrity of Reform Cartel star Jay P. Greene. Perhaps because there are now so many other Reform Cartel members available, the education press pays less attention to Greene than it used to.

Meanwhile, Greene may have matured as a scholar in his middle age. He's one of the few Cartel members willing to openly criticize Common Core or press coverage. Behold his lament for a lack of quality education journalism, written in his personal blog (Greene, 2018):

> First . . . Education is mostly a local story and local newspapers and their ranks of education reporters have been decimated by the rise of internet news over the last two decades. Second, the national and often foundation-subsidized outlets we have left are often focused on advancing various agendas . . .
>
> Third, and perhaps most alarming . . . there is a new type of education journalist who imagines him or herself as a mini-social scientist who adjudicates for us what "the research says." Despite having no social science training or experience conducting research, this new breed of education journalist holds forth on what the correct interpretation of the social science evidence is.
>
> But the truth is that there is usually no simple narrative about what social science has to say and reporters are very poorly positioned to adjudicate the truth about social science. In the past, reporters understood this and used to leave claims about what the evidence says to researchers. Reporters who covered research saw their role as quoting competing researchers so audiences could get some understanding of the issues in dispute.

Not any more. Now this new breed of *faux* social scientist/reporter regularly holds forth on what the evidence tells us. And not surprisingly, the cool kid club of social scientists whose research is affirmed by this new breed of reporter has plenty of praise to heap upon the reporter for being so smart and wise as to say that the researcher is correct. These reporters and researchers have formed a mutual admiration society. Any criticism of either reporters or researchers in this tight circle is met with considerable outrage and re-iteration of praise for each other, typically on Twitter.

Jay P. Greene may be hypocritical in criticizing others for faking expertise. But he is also correct in what he wrote here, with one exception. Explainer journalism among members of the Permanent Education Press is not new, though it may now be more pervasive.[3]

Biopic Vision

One unfortunate side product of America's political duopoly—its two-party system—may be a tendency for journalists, as well as the rest of us, to view political issues binarily even when they are multi-sided. If a journalist interviews a Democratic-leaning expert on an issue, it naturally follows that they should then interview a Republican-leaning expert on the issue. "Both sides" of the issue are then covered, even if other sides may not be.

Are there issues for which the education press ignored or suppressed relevant, important points of view? Emphatically, yes! Educational testing and Common Core. Which happened to be two issues on which both the Establishment and Reform Citation Cartels largely agreed.

With Common Core, talking points of paid promoters, both Democratic and Republican, were often repeated verbatim in news stories. Paid promoters were rarely identified as such, however. Worst of all, some reporters consulted Common Core promoters to explain the motivations of their opponents (see, for example, Associated Press, 2021a; Bidwell, 2014; Pondiscio, 2015). The result? Common Core opponents were sometimes characterized as parents of children who couldn't handle "higher" or "rigorous" standards or, more generally, as tinfoil-helmeted, latter-day Luddites opposed to progress.

The Test: Why Our Schools Are Obsessed with Standardized Testing—but You Don't Have to Be

In 2015, a National Public Radio reporter published a book by the above title (Kamenetz, 2015). One can safely characterize the book as totally biased in favor of the progressive and against the traditionalist view of testing. It

would be easy to believe that she had held an anti-testing bias before writing it (Camara and Shaw 2012; Phelps, 2015d).

She did, however, try to get *two* sides to the story; so, maybe she didn't start out so biased. That is, she spoke with members of both the Establishment and Reform Cartels. Granting her the benefit of the doubt, she may have presumed that the Reform Cartel would validly represent the "other" side of the story.

Ultimately, the journalist-author interviewed no testing experts to argue for traditional, objective testing. None. Hundreds of pages, and only those on one side of the issue were consulted. All progressive testing; no traditional testing.

A huge, unfortunate side effect of the Cartel Alliance has been to muddle many education debates and hide traditionalists from view.

Many education journalists don't see a problem, though. After surveying their members nationwide, the Education Writers Association (EWA) (2016) declared this a "golden age for education reporting." EWA revealed that 95 percent of its member-respondents think "My journalism makes a positive impact on education." (See also Walsh, 2016.)

The EWA also asked its members for their "most frequently cited sources of story ideas." Sources number one and number two were, respectively, "news release, news conference, or public relations professional" and "news coverage." The first source type requires money and organization, something common among Cartel insiders and nonexistent among independent outsiders. The second source type—also known as pack journalism—simply multiplies the effect of the first.

Zero Degrees of Freedom

Over the past few decades, when Jay Mathews of the *Washington Post* sought an expert comment on education policy, odds are overwhelming that he called someone in the Reform Cartel, usually at Fordham or Brookings.[4] Similarly for Lauren Camera and Allie Bidwell at *U.S. News and World Report*[5] or Greg Toppo and Erin Richards at *USA Today*.

The British magazine *The Economist* runs stories on US education research and policy several times a year. (They have twice as many readers in the United States as they do in their United Kingdom home base.) Almost always when they have consulted an expert, they have contacted someone in the Reform Cartel, typically someone in or closely tied to the Fordham Institute. Over the span of a quarter-century, stories and story reporters have come and gone, but the information source has remained the same, at *The Economist*, at *USA Today*, at *Bloomberg View*, at *U.S. News and World Report* . . . (see also Appendix 8 online, https://educationpolicy.us/Malfunction/App8.pdf).[6]

With a large, variant, and verdant information landscape waiting to be explored, the Permanent Education Press prefers to stay in a small, familiar space, like six-year-olds learning to play soccer (i.e., football), pushing the ball around a field all together in a crowd.

"Degrees of Freedom" is a foundational concept in statistics. Statisticians analyze patterns of variation in sets of numbers. Those patterns are most revealing when the numbers are collected independently of one another. That is why we so often see an emphasis on random sampling of populations. Randomly collected data more likely fairly represent their population than those from a cluster of related data from a particular section of a population.

So, it is with information and evidence. The more independent sources a journalist consults, the more robust the news story. Strategic partnerships, citation cartels, and pack funding reduce journalists' degrees of freedom (Resnick, 2016; Phelps, 2019a). A journalist relying on a "go-to" source limits their degrees of freedom to zero.

When a *Washington Post* columnist repeatedly sources his information and evidence from those working with the Thomas B. Fordham Institute and the Brookings Institution, he may tell himself that he has diversified his sources because he talks to more than just one individual at each place, and they sometimes disagree among themselves. But his degrees of freedom are still zero. Those who work directly or indirectly for Fordham are not independent of each other. They depend on each other for their livelihood, for attention, for favors, and for career opportunities. There is information they cannot or will not reveal, for risk of endangering their position in the group, and there is information they will propose in the interest of mutual benefit that they might not if they were truly independent.

How about a reporter for a conservative media outlet who rotates sourcing among a variety of nationally focused think tanks, say, Brookings, American Enterprise, Hoover, Manhattan, the National Bureau of Economic Research (NBER) to name just several. Even then, the degrees of freedom add to zero.

That is because all these think tanks hire their education expertise from the same small, inbred group of education reform luminaries, heavily dominated by economists, political scientists, Harvard, Stanford, Gates, Walton, and the Fordham Institute. Membership in that group has rules. It promotes its own and ignores, dismisses, ostracizes, or demonizes those who question the group's presumed expertise and authority (Moran, 1998; Neville-Hadley, 2019).

The fabulist, Stephen Glass, sometimes covered his tracks from the fact checkers at the *New Republic* by posting fake websites (at internet addresses he provided) or having family members pose as individuals named in his stories (at telephone numbers he provided). Whenever Glass could determine

the direction of the fact checkers' gaze in advance, he could arrange a ruse where he knew they would look (Bissinger, 2007).

As with the CRESST magazine article for the National School Boards Association mentioned earlier, articles can easily be arranged to appear to source information broadly even when they do not. A faculty member commenting "independently" on another scholar's research may be working on the other side of the continent but dig deeper, and one may find they are close colleagues who went to school together, worked on an earlier project together, or studied under the same celebrity professor.

Worse than journalists' passive sourcing of expertise, it has become common for US education journalists to print stories that are completely scripted for them (Alba and Nicas, 2020). Too often, these stories contain assertions that the research is "the first of its kind" or "more sophisticated" or "more rigorous." When a journalist passes those claims along, they are complicit in pushing promotional advertising for a particular research brand.

Credentials *Übër Allis*, but Which Ones?

> "There is a principle which is a bar against all information, which is proof against all arguments, and which cannot fail to keep a man in everlasting ignorance. That principle is contempt prior to investigation."
>
> —Herbert Spencer

Many of the world's most distinguished, most expert specialists in testing and measurement and curriculum and instruction work in the United States, as professors, consultants, and practitioners. Few have made the effort to become celebrity scholars. Most would talk to the Permanent Education Press if they were contacted. Few are.

In juxtaposition, one of the more prolific press panderers, Michael Petrilli of the Thomas B. Fordham Institute, is also, by some measures, the Permanent Education Press's single most frequently consulted and quoted expert source on education research and policy, despite an absence of relevant scholarly training or work experience.[7] (See also Appendix 9 online, "Michael Petrilli's Expertise," https://educationpolicy.us/Malfunction/App9.pdf.)

As explained by Robin Hanson (2021),

> Are elites nicer than other people? No, but they are better at being nice contingently, in the right situations where niceness is rewarded. . . .
>
> Consider a case where two parties to a dispute are of very unequal status, and where the topic is one where there's a perception that elite consensus agrees with the high status party. In this case, the higher status party only needs to offer

the slim appearance of argument quality. Just blathering a few related words is often completely sufficient.

Thus, the crucial importance of the Cartel Alliance's successful degradation of a century's worth of psychology, evaluation, statistical, military, and international research, even on topics psychologists invented, such as testing and measurement and curriculum and instruction. The Cartel Alliance has convinced the Permanent Education Press to classify as low status the most genuine experts.

As a result, members of the Permanent Education Press do not even bother to read or listen to counterarguments against the Cartel Alliance. Those who disagree with the Cartels are more likely to be treated by journalists with disdain, derision, and contempt. Hanson continues,

> Thus in our world today the quality of arguments only matters for positions "within the Overton window." That is, positions that many elites are seen to take seriously. Which is why contrarian positions are so often unfairly dismissed.[8]

Once a faction has convinced journalists as a group that its opponents live outside the Overton window (and below the celebrity threshold)—beyond where points of view are considered acceptable or important—they have it made. There remains no need to defend, to debate, to convince. Instead, the faction is essentially granted a license to embellish at will and define their rivals as imbeciles, that opposition having been banished to the hinterlands, to the outlying islands, to the Gulag, where journalists do not seek them out.

If I Don't Like You, I Won't Source You

ResearchED is "a grass-roots, teacher led organisation" founded in the United Kingdom whose mission is to "raise research literacy, bring people together, promote collaboration, increase awareness, promote research, and explore what works."[9] ResearchED has also organized in Australia, Canada, the Netherlands, New Zealand, Norway, and the United States.

In 2017, US ResearchED hosted a panel discussion on media coverage of education research.[10] The panel comprised a journalist, the head of the Education Writers Association (EWA), a media critic, and a moderator.[11]

The main points expressed by the critic: the two dominant citation cartels—establishment and reform—aggressively suppress other education research, information, and points of view through selective referencing, dismissive reviews, citation cartels, tone policing, condescension, and character assassination. (See, for example, Bechtoldt, Beersma, and Dijkstra, 2020; Garelick, 2015; Phelps, 2015e, 2016b, 2019b, 2021d; Rohrer, 2019; Schafer, 2021).

In response, the EWA head insisted that they:

- accept donations from a wide variety of sources; and
- are open to receiving story tips from anyone.

Those two points seem to represent the only sourcing standards the EWA has or has ever had, judging from a search through two decades of EWA documents. There's nothing about diversifying sources or representing all points of view and evidence.[12]

And those two points are remarkably passive. Note EWA donors have money to hire fulltime PR staff and donate to media outlets. What about those who cannot afford to "pay to play" (Alba and Nicas, 2020)?

In sharp contrast, the Society of Professional Journalists (SPJ) seems far more respectful of traditional journalistic norms. In the "Act Independently," section of their *Code of Ethics* (2022), SPJ asserts that journalists should:

- "avoid conflicts of interest, real or perceived. Disclose unavoidable conflicts."
- "refuse gifts, favors, fees, free travel and special treatment, and avoid ... activities that may compromise integrity or impartiality or may damage credibility."
- "be wary of sources offering information for favors or money; do not pay for access to news. Identify content provided by outside sources, whether paid or not."
- "deny favored treatment to advertisers, donors or any other special interests, and resist internal and external pressure to influence coverage."
- "distinguish news from advertising and shun hybrids that blur the lines between the two."
- "expose unethical conduct in journalism, including within their organizations."

The EWA and the US Permanent Education Press habitually ignore all the above. The EWA website, for example, posts contrived research and policy articles promoted, presented, and written in the same manner as any EWA news story, with a single exception: small, italicized print below the article's end reveals that it is paid for.[13]

In some cases, their biased sources received six-figure annual salaries and enough additional funds from the Gates and allied foundations to hire large staffs. Yet, at best, EWA identifies them as "a Common Core proponent," "a strong supporter of the controversial standards," or "a think tank supportive of the common core" (Carroll, A. E., 2018; Haimson, 2020; Shapiro and Wolfe, 2022).

When the ResearchED media panel critic suggested that journalists should "stop taking the money," one in the audience responded, "we have to," apparently alluding to the slow disintegration of the traditional news business model (Belmonte and Kelley, 2022; Gottfried, Mitchell, Jurkowitz and Liedke, 2022). The critic responded, likely to no effect whatsoever, "You would do less, but you would be independent."

Contrast the US Permanent Education Press with US business journalism. Some business news broadcasts host a dizzying array of expert sources to interpret events. One day, a spokesperson at company X will appear to comment on an inflation story. The next, a spokesperson from company Y might comment on a supply chain story. The third day, a spokesperson from company Z may offer their analysis of the latest employment figures.

There seems to be a common, sustained effort to widely diversify sources in business journalism. Everybody gets a turn.[14]

Furthermore, in business journalism, it is standard practice to identify an analyst's financial holdings if they might relate to the story at hand. It isn't a perfect check against bias, but such disclosure is better than nothing.

In the "Seek Truth and Report It," section of their Code (2022), the Society for Professional Journalists (SPJ) asserts that journalists should:

- be vigilant and courageous about holding those with power accountable.
- give voice to the voiceless.
- support the open and civil exchange of views, even views they find repugnant.
- seek sources whose voices we seldom hear.

Rather something closer to the opposite holds for the US Permanent Education Press, which seems content to let public relations flaks and donors set their agenda. It is not the journalism of war correspondents or investigative reporters but, instead, more passive and entitled (Haimson, 2020; Lofgren, 2015; Yettick, 2011).

Aggressive career-focused researchers—strategic scholars—are more likely to feel that promoting their research with the media is professionally appropriate. By contrast, many sincere scholars feel that research discussions belong more properly in scholarly journals, and journalists should not be arbitrarily picking single studies from the research literature, or studies from a single organized group, and recommending policy based on them (Carrigan, 2019; Schmidt and Oh, 2016; Wagenmakers, Sarafoglou, and Aczel, 2022).

When informed that economists were featured in media coverage of education far more often than psychologists, the late Frank Schmidt offered that media promotion was generally frowned upon among psychologists. In part, he was alluding to what some call the "Carl Sagan Effect," the stigma that

scientists who popularize science are not serious enough about their craft (Martinez-Conde, 2016). (See also Bazerman and Malhotra, 2006.)

If You're Not the Lead Dog ...

Of course, the topic—racial disparities in career-technical education (CTE) enrollments—deserves readers' attention. Yet perhaps the *Hechinger Report* writer thought her article needed some more oomph to appeal. So, a firstness claim gets equal billing in the article's title, "First nationwide look at racial breakdown of career education confirms deep divides." It continues in the article's subtitle ("first identified") and in the caption below the lead photo ("advocates have long called for data that breaks down enrollment by race and ethnicity. ... Those statistics, released for the first time") (Butrymowicz, 2021).

A remarkable claim. Along with at least several professional associations and advocacy groups, many researchers would have had an interest in the topic for several decades' past. The federal government's National Center for Education Statistics (NCES) generally collects the type of data to which the *Hechinger Report* refers. It would have been odd, and uncharacteristic, of NCES not to have collected CTE enrollment by racial/ethnic group all these years.

Take a quick trip to nces.ed.gov, and search for "career technical education" (choose "any words," "subject," and "before September 2021"). An early 2022 search returned 102 results. Alternatively, go directly to nces.ed.gov/surveys/ctes/ and one may retrieve links to several dozen publications going back to the early 1990s, contemporary to the birth of the World Wide Web. Those links take one to NCES publications that have been digitized; one must consult microfiche or paper copies for earlier reports.

Did none of the surveys associated with these many publications collect CTE enrollment data by racial/ethnic group? As a matter of fact, they did, as even some of the earliest digitized publications report.[15]

Perhaps there remains some genuinely "first" aspect or detail of the *Hechinger Report* study and article. But the journalist asserted, "the first nationwide look at racial breakdown," which it was not, and "previously, the Department of Education only reported enrollment in CTE career areas by gender," which also is not accurate. The firstness claim was, apparently, meant to imply that a story on race and CTE the journalist wrote the previous year had prompted a "new" US Department of Education data collection.

That previous article, by the way, was republished by other news outlets, testimony to the multiplicative influence of the *Hechinger Report*, which provides its articles gratis to other publications.

As when scholars make (false) firstness claims or dismissive reviews, the effect when journalists do it is to elevate the status of the one claiming to be first, and to discourage readers from looking for other, previous evidence.

Another journalist asserted that in addition to what he was told by his sources, his "sense" of a research literature told him that no previous research existed (Kornell and Bjork, 2009). The topic in question was the effect of curriculum choice on student learning gains. In this case, dismissive reviews were written not only by the usual think tank and elite university scholars, but also by the former head of the Institute of Education Sciences (IES), arguably the single person most responsible for managing and preserving the country's education research literature (Chingos and Whitehurst 2012).

A simple search for academic journals with the word "curriculum" in their title unearths more than a dozen journals with around six thousand articles dating back to 1968.[16] All that represents just a proportion of research articles on curriculum that one would find if one searched all of the hundreds of education-related journals dating back a century, as well as the "gray literature" of graduate student theses, program evaluations, and governmental reports. A search on "curriculum" in the IES's own ERIC[17] database generates 215,139 hits, in Google Scholar, 3,440,000 hits. To believe the dismissive review, one must believe that none among these millions of sources was a curriculum evaluation or comparison.

This journalist—the one whose "sense" of the research literature told him no previous research existed on the topic—encouraged critics to send him any relevant references. In other words, he felt justified in declaring as a fact a nonexistence of previous research based on nothing more than some scholar's self-interested claim and his own "sense." It was critics' responsibility to spend the time searching the research literature to prove him wrong.

Research Journalists: Barnum and Barshay

"It is impossible for a man to learn what he thinks he already knows."

—Epictetus

Covering education research used to be only a part-time job for journalists, just one type of education story they wrote, alongside other stories about education, politics, crime, personalities, and what have you (Ungar-Sargon, 2021).

In the past decade some publications have accumulated enough funding (from the usual sources) to employ journalists full time on the education research beat. Such should have been good for both policymaking and public understanding. Alas . . .

The *Hechinger Report* is an online publication devoted exclusively to education. It gets around, cooperating with dozens of other publication outlets to co-publish articles.[18]

Its "About" web page tells us:

Education is one of the most important issues of our time. Our reporters and editors push education reporting to new levels of quality, clarity, depth and breadth, to explain why education policy matters and how it's affecting young people.

Excerpts from its "Our Mission" web page list the following:

- "Independent: Our journalists ask tough questions and report on facts that contradict the status quo and threaten powerful interests."
- "We offer sources the right to respond. If a story includes criticism of a person, school, agency or company, we give the criticized party a chance to respond."
- "We seek balance. Balance does not mean acting as if every side has an equal number of voices, but we acknowledge conflicts or disagreements."
- "At *Hechinger*, we strive to hear from multiple perspectives."
- "We are not advocates. Our journalism provides information to the public, based on the facts our reporters collect. While we may present conclusions or analysis of those facts, and explore programs or ideas that could solve a problem, we do not advocate for particular policies, programs or educational models."

Scanning to the bottom of the page: "The *Hechinger Report* also adheres to the values and ethics of the Society for Professional Journalists." Not only does *Hechinger Report* research coverage not adhere to SPJ values, it does not adhere to its own.

Jill Barshay has worked fulltime on *Hechinger*'s education research and policy beat since at least 2015. At least that's how far back one can retrieve her columns at the *Hechinger* website. One can search through them for names: names of sources, expert or otherwise, names of institutions, such as universities or think tanks, and names of publications. From the period 2015 to 2022, the list includes about 225 different named entities, mentioned about six hundred times.

(See also Appendix 10 online, "Expertise Sources of Barnum and Barshay," https://educationpolicy.us/Malfunction/App10.pdf.)

Most of the nation's thousands of universities, think tanks, and research publication outlets were never mentioned in Barshay's articles. There are far too many for any one journalist to include, even over several years. Seventy-five percent of her named entities were mentioned just once or twice.

Most of the remainder were mentioned three to six times between the years 2015 and 2022.

That leaves just 11 percent of the entities to account for half (over three hundred out of about six hundred) of the mentions. The composition of the 11 percent corresponds strongly with that of the Reform Cartel: certain researchers at Harvard, Stanford, Brown, Johns Hopkins, Northwestern, Brookings, the Urban Institute, and, of course, the Thomas B. Fordham Institute. Harvard and Stanford alone crown the top with sixty-nine mentions of their people or studies.

Any speculation, passing thoughts, opinions, or unreviewed working papers from the Cartel Alliance are newsworthy. Thousands of peer-reviewed papers in other fields, such as psychology and evaluation, and hundreds of meta-analyses are not.

One discerns little evidence of the "balance," "multiple perspectives," or non-advocacy promised in Hechinger's mission statement, much less any "tough questions and report[ing] on facts that contradict the *status quo* and threaten powerful interests." Rather, Barshay's stories read like promotional press releases for the powerful vested interests (Brewer,1979, 2002).

Most of her individual and institutional sources may be classified into four groups. Of course, people are complex, and pigeonholing them into mutually exclusive categories cannot be precise. But the results are so lopsided, the skew is obvious. See for yourself in Table 7.1.

Obviously, Jill Barshay sees nothing wrong with narrow and repetitive sourcing, or uncritical boosterism of their work. An illustration of her rationale may be found in a rather odd article she wrote shortly after the death of renowned Johns Hopkins University professor, Robert Slavin (Barshay, 2021).

Barshay obviously liked Slavin and talked to him often. His work was featured in at least eight of her articles. Yet, of all the possible quotations from her collection that she could have featured in memorial, she chose just this one: "'John Hattie is wrong,' Slavin wrote. 'Hattie and others who uncritically accept all studies, good and bad, are undermining the value of evidence.'"

She explained,

Table 7.1. Jill Barshay's expert sources on research and policy, 2015–2021.

	Individuals		*Institutions*	
Group	Number	Percent	Number	Percent
Reform Cartel	74	76	184	69
Establishment Cartel	19	20	83	31
Independent Traditionalists	4	4	1	0
Common Core Opponents	0	0	0	0

Slavin's views are diametrically opposed to those of John Hattie, the bestselling author of *Visible Learning*, who has written several books about what works in education by factoring in all studies.

Some views of the two men differ; "diametrically opposed" unfairly describes those differences. Moreover, in *Visible Learning* (2008), Hattie did not "factor in all studies." He meta-analyzed others' meta-analyses, to produce a meta-meta-analysis. The authors of the original meta-analyses had employed their own inclusion standards.[19]

A search for evidence that Barshay attempted to solicit a response from Hattie to Slavin's accusations found nothing. Yet, the *Hechinger Report* claims, "If a story includes criticism of a person, school, agency or company, we give the criticized party a chance to respond."

The incident suggests that Jill Barshay long ago took a side. She decided that she knows who and what are right and who and what are wrong, and her job is to give her readers the benefit of her superior wisdom. Why waste her readers' time with evidence and perspectives she knows are wrong?

Except that she lacks both the training and the experience that would qualify her to pick and choose among researchers and research studies. Ergo, she must rely on proxy selection criteria and, apparently, hers are academic institutional prestige and personal preference. Economists, the Harvards, Stanfords, and Johns Hopkinses are "top" and, so, must be at all times and in all matters correct. Therefore, it is right and just that they should be granted a platform unopposed, from which they may dismiss and denigrate everyone else's research.

Even more accommodating to the Cartel Alliance is her colleague, Matt Barnum. From 2015 to 2017, he wrote regularly for *The 74*, a news outlet founded by and dedicated to the Reform Cartel. It is managed by some of their principals (e.g., Andy Rotherham, Romy Drucker) and funded by the usual suspects (e.g., Gates, Walton, Chan Zuckerberg, Joyce, Carnegie). It is unashamedly pro-Common Core and not only typically employs Reform Cartel members as sources, but also frequently as authors.[20] *The 74* claims: "Our stories are backed by investigation, expertise, and experience. *The 74's* reporting aims to challenge the status quo, expose corruption . . . ."

Except that, they *are* the status quo, and they're not about to expose their own corruption.

Since 2017, Barnum has written for the national chain of education news outlets, *Chalkbeat*.[21] He glided smoothly from one news outlet openly run by advocates to another that claims independence and objectivity. The tenor of his work did not change.

The Permanent Education Press has erased the line that once separated journalism and public relations. Vested interests now frequently and openly

purchase the services of both journals and journalists, as if it were the most natural thing in the world. Journalists hired to work at commercial and advocacy organizations full time obtain higher-paying, steadier jobs; the special interests gain their persuasive skills and access to their accumulated, extensive networks of movers, shakers, and media buddies.[22] (See also Appendix 7 online, https://educationpolicy.us/Malfunction/App7.pdf.)

Whether in *The 74* or *Chalkbeat*, Matt Barnum's articles bloat with such phrases as: "the first-of-its-kind study," "a thin research base," "there are no firm data," "documenting for perhaps the first time," and "the research is among the first national, rigorous attempts."[23]

It's a chummy little world. They have money and status (Harvard, Stanford, Brookings, etc.) and invite him to their conferences. They compliment his cleverness as he promotes their work. He returns the favor by promoting their research as the only worth mentioning. (See Bechtoldt, Beersma, and Dijkstra, 2020; Prooijen J-Wv, 2022; Schafer, 2021.)

Counting and categorizing Matt Barnum's sourcing produces a table like Jill Barshay's, only even more skewed toward the Reform Cartel (see Table 7.2).

The 74 Media, Inc. received $3,115,344 from the Bill and Melinda Gates Foundation between 2014 and 2020, and $5,694,800 from the Walton Family Foundation between 2016 and 2020.[24]

Chalkbeat accepted $3,022,491 from the Bill and Melinda Gates Foundation between 2014 and 2022, and $1,788,000 from the Walton Family Foundation between 2015 and 2020.[25]

The 74's and *Chalkbeat*'s own long donor lists are reproduced in Appendix 4 online, "Pack Funders and Strategic Partners," https://educationpolicy.us/Malfunction/App4.pdf.

When Barnum and Barshay mention a source publication, it is most often an economics journal or think tank publication, sometimes an education journal. Only once in their combined fourteen years of coverage has either of them ever mentioned a psychology journal. Neither of them has ever referenced a program evaluation or statistics journal.

Table 7.2. Matt Barnum's expert sources on research and policy, 2015–2021.

	Individuals		Institutions	
Group	Number	Percent	Number	Percent
Reform Cartel	310	83	491	77
Establishment Cartel	55	15	144	23
Independent Traditionalists	3	1	0	0
Common Core Opponents	4	1	1	0

Who else could Barshay and Barnum source for education research and policy expertise?

- The American Psychological Association (APA) comprises 133,000 members, of which 1,800 belong to its Educational Psychology division. An unpublished number also belong to its School Psychology and Teaching of Psychology divisions.[26]
- The Association of Psychological Science (APS) comprises 25,000 members, of which 186 and 983 list their "primary major field" as "educational" or "cognitive."[27]
- The American Sociological Association (ASA) contains 579 and 695 members in its Teaching and Learning in Sociology and Sociology of Education divisions.[28]
- The American Evaluation Association (AEA) includes over 6,000 members.[29]
- The National Council on Measurement in Education (NCME) included over 1,400 members as of 2019.[30]
- The Association for Institutional Research (AIR) claimed over 3,000 members in its 2020–2021 annual report.[31]
- The National College Testing Association boasts more than 2,300 members.[32]
- The European Federation of Psychologists' Associations comprises over 350,000 members.[33]
- The International Association for Educational Assessment (IAEA) and the International Test Commission (ITC) register over 160 and 700 members, respectively.[34]

This list could continue for several pages to include state- and regional-level academic organizations; international-, national-, regional-, and state-level practitioner associations, international-, national-, regional-, and state-level government research bureaus; corporate research divisions; and so on. And it still would not cover the universe of relevant, but journalistically neglected sources of expertise.

In 2009, the American Psychological Association published *Correcting Fallacies about Educational and Psychological Testing*. Authors included some of the world's most distinguished experts in testing and measurement. Lists of resources were provided where journalists or policymakers could find thorough answers to most common questions about test use and testing policies.

No matter. No journalist ever reviewed *Correcting*; likely none ever read it. Meanwhile, the ill-informed, one-sided book mentioned earlier, *The Test*, written by a journalist, was reviewed by several other journalists.

Centripetal Force: The Education Writers Association

> "Journalism, at its best, provides a necessary check against powerful interests. But what happens when journalists themselves become part of a powerful, elite class?"
>
> —Josh Kraushaar, *National Journal*[35]

If there was any education organization that one might suppose would promote high journalistic standards and model virtuous behavior, the Education Writers Association (EWA) would be it. It claims over three thousand members, presumably mostly education journalists. It organizes an annual conference, hosts webinars, posts articles, and advocates emphatically in favor of explainer journalism.

The EWA also rather transparently takes sides on research issues. They grant easy access and close to total support for those they have decided are right (or they personally like), and close to the opposite for those they have decided are wrong (or they personally dislike).

(See also Appendix 11 online, "EWA Sourcing over the Years," https://educationpolicy.us/Malfunction/App11.pdf.)

The EWA functions to concentrate expertise sourcing nationwide. If there were no EWA, their many members would initiate expertise sourcing on their own. The result, in the absence of EWA's suggestions, would be a greater variety of expertise sourced. The US public and policymakers would then be more broadly informed.

Through efforts such as EWA Seminars, radio broadcasts, and annual conferences, the elitist, national group imposes its bias toward power and celebrity onto its thousands of members. As a result, it represents not the stereotypical muckraker or spokesperson for the less powerful, but exactly the opposite. EWA vigorously supports the public relations push of US education's wealthy, vested interests.

Recently, EWA's board of directors added more managers from the research brands it likes to showcase.[36] They include two editors of Gates-funded "Education Labs" (at the *Seattle Times* and *Dallas Morning News*) and six public relations staff from vested interest organizations.[37] The twelve-member board also includes two, count 'em, *two* practicing journalists who might possibly not be paid by the Gates Foundation.

Then, there is Denise-Marie Ordway, managing editor of the Journalist's Resource at the Harvard Kennedy School, a foundation funded effort to, allegedly, help journalists write better stories about education research.[38] The Resource strongly recommends that journalists continue to attempt the impossible: to judge for themselves which research is right, which is wrong, which is good, and which is bad.

The Resource does not advise journalists to get all sides of a story, search out differing evidence and points of view, and let the various sources tell their own stories.³⁹ Instead, Harvard's Journalist's Resource emphatically promotes explainer journalism and, by implication, demeans traditional objective reportage as passé.

As smart and talented as they may be, journalists are unlikely to build sufficient analytical expertise by reading Ordway's EWA website advice columns. Such expertise takes PhD students several years of full-time study to master. Journalists under deadline are more likely to fall back on academic status rankings as a proxy for research quality or follow Ordway's specific suggestions for where to look for right and good information.

Between 2003 and 2021, the Education Writers Association accepted $5,949,475 from the Bill and Melinda Gates Foundation; from 2012 to 2020, EWA collected $2,513,050 from the Walton Family Foundation.⁴⁰

Despite those and many more millions in direct donations from other funders with agendas, EWA offers most of what it does for sale (Chapman, 2019).⁴¹ Most anything they do can be "sponsored," for a price. EWA will also disseminate others' articles, press releases, and broadcast messages (via their website, newsletters, print, or email) if one pays them enough.

NOTES

1. Editorial Review of Batya Ungar-Sargon's *Bad News*, at its Target web page: https://www.target.com/p/bad-news-by-batya-ungar-sargon/-/A-86682596.

2. See, for example, https://hechingerreport.org/partners/.

3. For example, in the late 1990s and early 2000s, the highly prescriptive, I-have-the-solutions journalism of Craig Jerald, Lynn Olson, Robert Rothman, and Thomas Toch.

4. A search through Jay Mathews's *Washington Post* columns from May 2016 through April 2019 revealed the following mention counts, overwhelmingly from the Ed Reform Citation Cartel: Fordham Institute/Foundation, 17; Trevor Packer (AP guru at College Board), 12; Brookings Institution, 10; Tom Loveless, 9; Michael Petrilli, 5; Diane Ravitch, 5; Robert Pondiscio, 4; Checker Finn, 4; E. D. Hirsch, 4; Hoover Institution, 4; Jal Mehta, 3; Sarah Fine, 3; American Enterprise Institute, 3; Richard Kahlenberg, 3; Phil Daro, 2; Yong Zhao, 2; Paul Hill, 2; Seth Gershenson, 2; many others with 1; and many more with 0. Traditionalists in testing and measurement or curriculum and instruction? There's only E. D. Hirsh (4), unless one also classifies Diane Ravitch that way, then 9.

5. Camera and Bidwell source mostly from the Reform Cartel, and sometimes from the Establishment Cartel or Traditionalists. Checking several dozen names via *U.S. News*'s own search engine: number of mentions: Reform Cartel, >54 (e.g., Caroline Hoxby, 15, Eric Hanushek, 13, Matthew Chingos, 10, Robin Lake, 4, Andy

Smarick, 3, Mike Petrilli, 3); Establishment Cartel, >10 (e.g., Martin Carnoy, 5, Linda Darling-Hammond, 4); Traditionalists, >13 (e.g., Mark Bauerlein, 9, Wayne Camara, 2). Mark Bauerlein wrote a regular column, almost always focused on higher education issues.

6. Ironically, *The Economist* led a story (2013) on a related topic (of scientific censorship) like this: "Blunt criticism is an essential part of science, for it is how bad ideas are winnowed from good ones." Yet its "go-to" source on US education research and policy stories for the past quarter century emphatically censors and avoids criticism.

7. Petrilli has been the most popular expert source at the Education Writers Association (EWA) website, with 57 mentions, and at *USA Today*, with 22 mentions.

8. According to Wikipedia (2022a), the term "Overton Window"

is named after American policy analyst Joseph P. Overton, who stated that an idea's political viability depends mainly on whether it falls within this range, rather than on politicians' individual preferences. According to Overton, the window frames the range of policies that a politician can recommend without appearing too extreme to gain or keep public office given the climate of public opinion at that time.

The Overton window is an approach to identifying the ideas that define the spectrum of acceptability of governmental policies. Politicians can only act within the acceptable range. Shifting the Overton window involves proponents of policies outside the window persuading the public to expand the window. Proponents of current policies, or similar ones within the window, seek to convince people that policies outside it should be deemed unacceptable. (See also Mackinac Center for Policy Research 2022.)

9. https://researched.org.uk/about/our-story/ and https://researched.org.uk/about/our-mission/.

10. ResearchED_US. (October 7, 2017). "Media coverage of education," ResearchED—New York City. https://researched.org.uk/event/researched-new-york-2017/.

11. https://www.ewa.org/.

12. Meanwhile, the Society of Professional Journalists publishes the 307-page *Media Ethics: A Guide for Professional Conduct*. https://www.spj.org/ethicsbook.asp.

13. See, for example: https://www.ewa.org/press-release/ncw-white-paper-fev-tutor-shows-how-districts-can-accelerate-student-growth-data.

14. To be complete, when business journalists source a story from an academic scholar, they may favor celebrity academics from the more prestigious universities, just as US education journalists do.

15. See, for example: https://nces.ed.gov/pubsearch/pubsinfo.asp?pubid=2008035 (see, for example, Table 2.20) or https://nces.ed.gov/pubsearch/pubsinfo.asp?pubid=92669 (see Tables 37+) or https://nces.ed.gov/pubsearch/pubsinfo.asp?pubid=97391 or https://nces.ed.gov/pubsearch/pubsinfo.asp?pubid=95024 or https://link.springer.com/chapter/10.1007/1-4020-3034-7_8 or https://nces.ed.gov/pubs/web/96004ch2.asp.

16. *Curriculum Inquiry*, from 1968, >2,500 articles; *Journal of Curriculum Studies*, from 1968, >1,500 articles; *Language, Culture, and Curriculum*, from 1988, >450

articles; *Curriculum Journal*, from 1990, >700 articles; *Curriculum and Teaching*, from 1995, ~500 articles; *Teachers and Curriculum*, from 1997, >200 articles; *Curriculum and Teaching Dialogue*, from 1998, >500 articles; *Journal of Curriculum and Pedagogy*, from 2004, >300 articles; *Curriculum Matters*, from 2005, ~100 articles; *Journal of Curriculum and Instruction*, 2007–2014, >50 articles; *International Journal of Curriculum and Instruction*, from 2008, >150 articles; and *Journal of Curriculum and Teaching*, from 2013, >300 articles.

All that represents just a portion of research articles on curriculum that one would find if one searched the many thousands of education journals dating back a century, as well as the "gray literature" of graduate student theses, program evaluations, and governmental reports. A search on "curriculum" in ERIC gets 215,139 hits, in Google Scholar, 3,440,000 hits. To believe the dismissive review, one must believe that none among these many thousands of sources conducted a curricular evaluation or comparison.

17. "ERIC" stands for the "Education Resources Information Center."

18. https://hechingerreport.org/partners/.

19. Slavin and Barshay may well have wanted Hattie to pick his way through each and every one of the many studies included in each and every one of the hundreds of meta-analyses he summarized. Had Hattie tried, he would never have finished the project. Moreover, he would have been accused of second-guessing others' inclusion criteria decisions and "cherry-picking" his data to achieve preferred results.

20. https://www.the74million.org/about/.

21. https://www.chalkbeat.org/.

22. Some examples: From *Education Week*: Craig Jerald later worked for the Education Trust and College Board; Michelle McNeil for College Board; Lynn Olson for the Gates Foundation and Aspen Institute; Robert Rothman for CRESST and the Alliance for Excellent Education; Linda Perlstein moved on from the *Washington Post* to work at the Education Writers Association, Bill and Melinda Gates Foundation; Center on Reinventing Public Education (University of Washington); Edunomics Lab (Georgetown University); and Aspen Institute. For more, see Appendix 7 online, "Career Paths of the Permanent Education Press," https://educationpolicy.us/Malfunction/App7.pdf.

23. See, for example: https://nonpartisaneducation.org/Review/Resources/Journalists.htm.

24. https://www.gatesfoundation.org/about/committed-grants?q=The%2074%20Media%2C%20Inc; https://www.waltonfamilyfoundation.org/grants-database?grantee=00000169-91e6-d2a9-a7eb-bffe6b460000.

25. https://www.gatesfoundation.org/about/committed-grants?q=Chalkbeat and https://www.waltonfamilyfoundation.org/grants-database?q=Chalkbeatands=1.

26. See https://en.wikipedia.org/wiki/American_Psychological_Association; https://apadiv15.org/.

27. See https://www.psychologicalscience.org/about; https://member.psychologicalscience.org/directories/member-directory.

28. See https://www.asanet.org/file/20862.

29. As of 2022. See https://www.eval.org/About/About-AEA.

30. https://www.zoominfo.com/c/national%20council%20on%20measurement%20in%20education/27001149.

31. See https://www.airweb.org/docs/default-source/documents-for-pages/governance/annual-reports/2020–2021_air-annual-report.pdf.

32. See https://www.ncta-testing.org/about.

33. See https://www.efpa.eu/who-we-are.

34. https://iaea.info/about-us/ and https://www.intestcom.org/page/25.

35. Editorial Review of Batya Ungar-Sargon's *Bad News*, at its Amazon web page: https://www.amazon.com/Bad-News-Media-Undermining-Democracy/dp/1641772069.

36. https://www.ewa.org/board-directors.

37. For Linda Darling-Hammond's Learning Policy Institute, the University of Southern California, the American Association of State Colleges and Universities, the Alliance of Public Charter Schools, DC's Widmeyer Communications, and one independent flak.

38. https://journalistsresource.org/.

39. See, for example: https://www.ewa.org/reporter-guide/making-sense-research-literature-reviews-and-meta-analyses; https://www.ewa.org/tip-sheet/ewa-tip-sheet-writing-about-colleges-finances-amid-coronavirus; https://www.ewa.org/profile/denise-marie-ordway; https://www.ewa.org/blog-educated-reporter/education-research-where-find-it-and-how-evaluate-it.

40. https://www.gatesfoundation.org/about/committed-grants?q=Education%20Writers%20Association; https://www.waltonfamilyfoundation.org/grants-database?q=Education+Writers+Associationands=1.

41. See, for example, https://www.ewa.org/sponsorship-opportunities.

Chapter 8

The View from 2023

Is US education research and policy better now than in 2001? Scholars, organizations, and pundits who have benefitted most from the generosity of the federal government and wealthy foundations in the interregnum say so.

Let's take stock. Overall, US education research and policy is now massively more centralized, censorial, and strategic. The result is a semantic facade (Paige, Smith, and Sizemore, 2015; Phelps, 2015g; Moscowitz, 2022; Wen and Lei, 2022):

- a national education structure federally run, but with a "state-led" label;
- lower content and performance standards, but with "higher" labels;
- narrow and naïve education policy research, but with a "more rigorous" label;
- less useful, informative, or reliable testing, but with a "higher-quality" label;
- less accountability where it is most needed (with students); and
- more accountability, with invalid measures, where it is inappropriate.

Current trends point toward still lower standards and weaker accountability to come.

Federalism

Despite the Tenth Amendment to the US Constitution, which defers "un-enumerated" responsibilities, such as education, to the states, the federal government now determines testing and accountability (via the No Child Left Behind Act) and curriculum and instruction (via Common Core, which remains fully present, despite some cosmetic renaming) nationwide. States have reverted to dependency roles.

Those who supported the concentration of education research, evaluation, and measurement in the federal government may well have believed their

own rhetoric—that they would do a better job than their counterparts in fifty US states had done before them. But even those nationalizers would have to admit that they were drastically reducing the range and variety of education knowledge.

Not only does the federal government continue to fund topical education research centers (e.g., CRESST, CALDER), ideal environments for incubating citation cartels. It now funds the direct establishment of citation cartels through its "Research Networks Focused on Critical Problems of Education Policy and Practice Grant Program."[1]

Philanthropy

More and more funding has gone to fewer and fewer *independent* recipients, narrowing the pool of expertise and reducing the amount of information available to the public and policymakers (Face Value, 2006; Huang and Seldon, 2014; Levin, 2018; Lubienski, Brewer, and La Londe, 2016; Samali, Laidler-Kylander, Simonin, and Zohdy, 2016; Scutari, M. 2018; Tompkins-Stange, 2016). Ironically, the more the big funders spend in the centralizing fashion of the past two decades, the less we know. Giving more resources to strategic scholars and citation cartels reduces the amount of independent information available, while supercharging strategic scholars' electric careers.

Big funders could drain the educational morass tomorrow if they really wanted to; according to Lieberman,

> There are dozens of philanthropic foundations that have the resources to bring about a higher level of accountability among the media, universities, and think tanks, even if their personnel are opposed to independent evaluation of their own projects or publications. Such evaluation might foster safer, more conservative philanthropy, but the results in the absence of any accountability are not impressive. (2007, p. 293)

Organizations

A host of (indeed, most) influential national advocacy, membership, and media organizations have voluntarily surrendered their former independence and intellectual diversity. In exchange, they have grown bigger, richer, more like each other, and more comfortable as their finances have stabilized. There, they shall remain so long as their funders continue to like them, fundamentally transformed and dependent.[2]

The Council of Chief State School Officers (CCSSO), for example, was the primary professional membership association of state superintendents of

education. Twenty years ago, it subsisted largely on membership dues. Its work was more independent, representing the diversity of its members.

In the most recent financial audit posted to its website—for the year 2017—CCSSO's income from "contracts, grants and sponsorships" overwhelmed its income from "membership dues" and "registration fees" by a factor greater than ten to one.[3] The CCSSO accepted $138,728,703 from the Gates Foundation between 2002 and 2022,[4] and $3,178,315 from the Walton Family Foundation between 2018 and 2020.[5]

And Gates and Walton are just two among many possible funders. In its 2021 annual report, CCSSO lists other corporate and foundation funders, along with a slew of education industry organizations apparently "paying to play."[6]

Suppose a state superintendent proposed today that CCSSO decline all funding from sources with agendas in the interest of CCSSO's independence. Such a change would necessitate laying off most of its staff. It would also portend a diminution of the programmatic revenue sharing each member state now receives that is funneled through and divvied up by CCSSO.

In other words, it won't happen. CCSSO will never again be what it once was. The same goes for a multitude of other once independent professional organizations.

Journalism

The line between independent journalism and public relations advocacy has disappeared, as journalists, too, have become comfortably dependent on pack funders.

In research and policy, the only sources that seem to matter to the Permanent Education Press are those with the resources to promote themselves. Many journalists have gotten comfortable with stories coming to them. Expert sources' conflicts of interest are rarely mentioned, perhaps because the Permanent Education Press has so many of its own.

Their Overton Window has narrowed to frame members of the Cartel Alliance and others who pay to play. Most remarkably, most genuine expertise in testing and measurement and curriculum and instruction now lies *outside* the Permanent Education Press' Overton Windows on those topics, among the multitude of media-ignored psychologists, program evaluators, and practitioners.

Standards

Twenty years ago, the demonstrable success of Massachusetts' and Virginia's clear, specific, objective, and incremental standards served as models for

other jurisdictions (Mass Insight Education, 2002, 2003; Driscoll et al., 2003; Reville, 2004).

Twenty years later we have Common Core standards, which are "state" in name only. Most of the state-developed standards and assessment systems of the 1990s are gone.

With the backing of pack foundation funding and an enormous recession-era windfall from the federal government, leading politicians of both major parties chose to overrule proven state successes in favor of Common Core's empty promises (educationrealist, 2020; Pioneer Institute, 2022; Stotsky, 2013, 2014a, 2014b, 2017). Moreover, they then hired those responsible for proven earlier failures of fuzzy, subjective process standards and performance testing in three states (California, Kentucky, and Maryland) to write the Common Core standards.

Whether "laboratories of democracy" is an apt description of the US states or not, their sheer number assures a diversity of action by comparison with a single, national monopoly (Wikipedia, 2022d).

When the most important decisions are made in Washington, local and state groups and individuals have little access and little influence. Real influence tends to coalesce around large, well-funded, national groups, which both promote their interests and suppress others' (Phelps, 2017c, 2017e; Stotsky, 2019; Stotsky and Holzman, 2015; Tampio, 2018).

Ultimately, Common Core "raised" standards in grades K–2 with age-inappropriate curricula while lowering standards above grade three and into high school (Bauerlein and Stotsky, 2012; McQuillan, Phelps, and Stotsky, 2015; McRae, 2013; Milgram and Stotsky, 2013; Phelps, 2018e; Phelps and Milgram, 2014, 2015).

Nationalizing Testing

The No Child Left Behind (NCLB) Act abandoned accountability measures for the primary actors in the educational process—the students—in favor of often unfair accountability measures for schools and teachers. (Fitzhugh, 2013a; Phelps, 2020a, 2020b; Price, 2020)

In 2001, most US states managed their own testing programs, which focused on student accountability.[7] An array of US testing firms serving state clients existed with long histories, expertise, large item banks, and time-series data. Soon after, that industry was upended, and it remains in flux (Bauman and Hoover, 2021). Some firms left the industry entirely (Cavanagh, 2019). Psychometric personnel now move with each contract turnover.

We were on our way to establishing a sensible, popular accountability system from the late 1980s up to the early 2000s—state-led, full battery,

objective, grade-span testing, just like most developed countries have (Phelps, 2006). A rise in NAEP scores followed.[8]

Since the implementation of NCLB requirements (around 2006–2007) and Common Core requirements (around 2014), most states have abandoned their previous testing programs, and public trust of testing has declined (Wachen, 2017). We are now down to just seven states requiring state high school exit exams for all students (USED, 2022).[9] Common Core promoters have openly encouraged states to drop those tests, to focus on the allegedly "more rigorous" Common Core tests, which have no stakes for students (Council of Great City Schools, 2016; Doorey and Polikoff, 2016; Fitzhugh, 2013b; Kamemetz, 2015b; Phelps, 2016a; Stotsky, 2019b).

By 2018, NAEP scores plateaued in reading and math, despite the extra sustained focus just on reading and math, and the huge infusion of cash.[10]

Degrading Tests

Tests are not all the same. One wouldn't administer medical or law board exams to kindergartners. One wouldn't administer an in-the-cockpit pilot's exam to enter the accounting profession. One wouldn't administer an IQ test for certification from an HVAC repair program.

A test is most valid and efficient when optimized for a particular purpose (AERA, APA, and NCME, 2014, pp. 11–26). The content of a high school exit exam, for example, should be directly determined by that covered in students' previous coursework. Exit exams retrospectively measure how well a student mastered that material. They are standards-based achievement tests.

By contrast, the best college admission exams are those most predictive of desired college outcomes, such as good college grades, persistence in college, or college program completion (Kuncel and Hezlett, 2007, 2010). Two outstanding features encouraged colleges to include them among the array of factors they consider in admission decisions. The first is the consistent nationwide standard of comparison in contrast to highly variable high school measures, such as high school GPA, class rank, recommendations, essays, and extracurricular activities (Clinedinst 2019, chapter 3).

The second outstanding feature was the aptitude component, which isolates abilities of individual applicants that are highly correlated with college success but are not measured by the other admission factors considered. Especially in the United States, college differs from high school, and different skills, aptitudes, habits, and preferences emerge more important (Lohman, 2005; Phelps, 2018f; Sandham, 1998; Smith, Given, Julien, Ouellette, and DeLong, 2013).[11]

College Board, the organization responsible for the SAT, had chipped away at its aptitude features for years, as if they were shameful. Then, a decade

ago, it hired the "architect" of the Common Core standards, David Coleman, despite his lack of training or experience in testing or managing large organizations (Hoover, 2012; Meltzer, 2018; Phelps, 2015f).

Coleman promised to align the SAT directly to the K–10 Common Core standards, thus making the SAT a retrospective achievement test, highly correlated with other admission factors, such as class rank and grade-point average (Clark and Burd, 2019). Some of the several percentage points of "incremental predictive validity" the old SAT had provided would disappear.

Meanwhile, ACT Inc. (2016) declined Common Core alignment in order to preserve its predictive validity. While preserving its test's usefulness for its higher education customers, however, ACT may have lost some state contracts as a result. Journalists reported that College Board's promise of a tighter Common Core alignment may have tipped the scales in its favor for statewide college admission testing contracts in Michigan and Illinois (Higgins, 2015; LaFond, 2016; Michigan Department of Education, 2015; Phelps, 2018d; Rado, 2016).

K–12 educators in those two states may have assumed that their students would perform better on a Common-Core aligned test. But it's a min-max game. The more valid a test's scores are retrospectively, the less valid they can be predictively (*District Administration*, 2010; Phelps, 2015h, 2018f; Phelps and Milgram, 2014, 2015). What may have seemed advantageous to high school educators should have seemed less so to college admission officers, but they were less involved in the contract decisions.

Most US states now administer a single test in high school to both retrospectively measure achievement and prospectively predict college success, thus reducing its validity for one or both purposes. Those tests are the SAT or ACT, or variations on the original Common Core PARCC and SBAC tests.

Test Security

As Dr. Cannell showed, many state and district educators played with commercially produced national norm-referenced tests (NRTs) in the 1980s, deliberately administering them insecurely so they could goose positive average score trends over time and brag about their alleged managerial prowess. They could do this, in part, because NRTs had become less meaningful after the *Debra P. v. Turlington* (1981) federal court decision and had no stakes.

At the same time, however, also because of *Debra P.*, most states were developing their own standards-based, full-subject-battery testing programs, most of which had some stakes and were, at least in some jurisdictions, administered more securely. When states manage their own testing programs, they are more likely to take them seriously.

By 2021, most of those testing programs had been discontinued, as states focused on the federally mandated NCLB testing requirements, reading and math, with no stakes for the students, and no external test security (Lannan, 2022). Schools now handle the test materials themselves and teachers administer the tests in their own classrooms to their own students.

College admissions tests also relaxed test security. In 2001, SATs and ACTs were administered with tight security in testing centers proctored by SAT and ACT employees. Now, many states administer college admission tests to all high school juniors, whether they intend to go to college or not. Test security is left to the schools themselves, which have only the weakest incentives to be vigilant.

In sum, large-scale education tests in the United States have become more subjective, less consequential, slower in returning results, less useful, more expensive, more disadvantageous to underprivileged children, more ambiguous in purpose, and less efficient (Binkley, 2021).

The High School Diploma

It was far easier for high schools in 2001 to maintain standards for student performance. When a student stopped coming to school, they received no diploma. The chaos of the early 2000s "on time" graduation rate fiasco aside, we are worse off now because graduation has become meaningless as a standard of academic achievement. High schools are now judged by their graduation rate, so are incentivized to pass students along with lax "credit recovery" programs, or even no program.

Some high schools change teachers' grades so students can "pass" courses; some grant diplomas to absentee students, thus lowering the school's dropout rate and raising its graduation rate.

Some of these unprepared students then enter college, where they may accumulate massive debt before dropping out. Dropping out of high school is not good but can be remedied later with inexpensive (usually free) adult education courses. Dropping out of college is far more problematic (Martel, 2017; Muñiz, 2018; Simpson, 2021).

Privacy

Longitudinal data systems and socio-emotional learning surveys may help satisfy economists' hunger for more "micro data" (i.e., data on individual students), but they seriously threaten student and family privacy. The public is expected to believe that school data systems can provide ironclad protection. Would that be before or after they pay off all the school data system

ransomware attacks (Byrne, M., 2021; Kiesecker, 2018; Germain, 2020; Hanna, 2022)?

How We Got Here

In the early 2000s, the US federal government's executive and legislative branches crafted a policy that for decades to come would directly and substantially affect over sixty million students a year, millions of teachers, hundreds of thousands of schools, tens of thousands of school districts, and tens of millions of parents. Everyone says that education is hugely important to our country's population and its future, and that our education policies should respect that importance.

Given its abundant resources, the federal politicians involved could have conducted history's widest, deepest, most thoroughly informative review of policy relevant information pertaining to educational testing and accountability.

Instead, they asked a small group of familiar faces, who asked the first group of alleged experts they heard about, who told them that no policy-relevant information existed. The familiar faces then stopped looking, and the policymakers said fine.

Lawmakers typically vouch for the value of competitive markets and eschew the harms of monopolies. Unregulated monopolies, they might tell you, lower quality; raise prices; abuse power; reduce output, efficiency, innovation, and consumer choice; raise barriers to entry from potential competitors; and divert resources to lobbying, politicking, and personal benefit.

Yet, the education policy advisors of the Cartel Alliance exhibit all these classic monopoly behaviors, not only poorly serving the American public, but poorly serving their politician clients. Like good monopolists, they restrict access to policy discussions to their group of colleagues who can be reliably trusted to reference each other and dismiss rival research or researchers (Bauer, 2004).

The social costs to such behavior can be huge. Citizens and policymakers remain unaware of most of the information from which to draw policy options. The vast bulk of past research, much of it paid for by the public directly or indirectly, is suppressed. Sometimes, the policy advisors hoodwink policymakers, foundations, and the public into paying them to fill fabricated holes in the research literature. As a result, taxpayers end up paying again for research that had already been done (Blaine, Brunnhuber, and Lund, 2021).

NOTES

1. See, for example: https://www.federalregister.gov/documents/2022/08/19/2022-17847/applications-for-new-awards-lead-of-a-career-and-technical-education-cte-network-research-networks; https://www.federalregister.gov/documents/2022/08/19/2022-17850/applications-for-new-awards-research-networks-focused-on-critical-problems-of-education-policy-and.

2. Organizations now dependent on pack funding are too numerous to list here. Some of the larger ones include: CCSSO, National Governors Association Center for Best Practices, Achieve, Thomas B. Fordham Institute, Bellwether Education Partners, Center on Reinventing Public Education, Deans for Impact, Council of the Great City Schools, ExcelinEd, Alliance for Excellent Education, Education First, *The 74*, Education Writers Association, *Chalkbeat*, *Education Next*, National Association of State Boards of Education, Association for Supervision and Curriculum Development, American Association of School Administrators, American Association of College Registrars and Admissions Officers, Education Commission of the States, American Association of State Colleges and Universities, Association of College and University Educators, and the National Association of Student Personnel Administrators.

3. $35,486,370 to $3,404,105. https://ccsso.org/resource-library/ccsso-audit-report-2017.

4. https://www.gatesfoundation.org/about/committed-grants.

5. https://www.waltonfamilyfoundation.org/grants-database.

6. For example, Cognia, ETS, Pearson, Curriculum Associates, NWEA, Data Recognition Corporation, Instructure, Metametrics, Smarter Balanced, Cambium Assessment, Renaissance Learning, ACT, AIR, Amplify, McGraw Hill, Microsoft, New Meridian, SAS, Google, and Voya. See https://753a0706.flowpaper.com/CCSSO2021AnnualReport/#page=13.

7. The stakes could be high in that successful passage of a test was required for grade promotion or graduation. But those stakes were typically counterbalanced by low performance thresholds (e.g., middle-school level content in a high school graduation exam), several to an unlimited number of opportunities to pass, and an abundance of free remediation programs, such as tutoring and extra classes.

8. See https://www.nationsreportcard.gov/highlights/mathematics/2019/; https://www.nationsreportcard.gov/highlights/reading/2019/.

9. Six other states require attainment of a threshold score on the ACT or SAT.

10. See https://www.nationsreportcard.gov/highlights/mathematics/2019/; https://www.nationsreportcard.gov/highlights/reading/2019/.

11. One may recall that an original purpose of the Scholastic Aptitude Test was to find the "diamonds in the rough," the bright students with college potential who may have been stuck in poor schools, or in too-slow-moving academic tracks, but had acquired some relevant knowledge and skills on their own (Marx, 2002; Wikipedia, 2022c). The aptitude test was designed to help capable but poor students compete in the admissions process against wealthy students advantaged by better-resourced schools and home environments.

Conclusion

When What Is Left Out Is More Important

"There is a remarkable asymmetry between the ways our mind treats information that is currently available and information we do not have. . . . Information that is not retrieved . . . from memory might as well not exist. [The human mind] excels at constructing the best possible story that incorporates ideas currently activated, but it does not (cannot) allow for information it does not have."

—Daniel Kahneman

A cooperative truth-seeking culture honors the steady, deliberate accumulation of knowledge. By contrast, CV-thickening culture encourages the continuous destruction of the historical record to showcase every shiny new trifle from the most ambitious strategic scholars.

The Campbell Collaboration[1] represents a sincere and worthy effort to alleviate some negative anomalies of current research culture. For example, it provides a "repository" where scholars record in considerable detail their plans for a new research project, including their purpose and the hypotheses they intend to test. This "registration" of new studies serves as a check on an unfortunate tendency among some scholars to "make things up as they go along" (e.g., letting results determine the hypothesis; "p-hacking").

Some regard the Campbell Collaboration's effort as the most powerful check available against research bias.[2]

In 2018,[3] and then again in 2022,[4] the Collaboration posted a "Title Registration for a Systematic Review: Testing Frequency and Student Achievement." The "protocol" offered two justifications for a new review: first, absence-of-research claims (i.e., dismissive reviews) made by several

prominent scholars and organizations;[5] and second, a typical "scorched earth" review of some small amount of previous work (i.e., criticize previous research as poorly done or inadequate in order to justify a new project).[6]

In a century of scholarly research on the effect of testing on student achievement—thousands of studies—testing frequency has been the most common experimental factor (Phelps, 2011a).[7] Yet, the authors of the title registration mention just one earlier meta-analysis, "Bangert-Drowns and Kulik (1991), which is 27 years old," while neglecting to mention a substantial number of studies conducted after 1991, including at least four meta-analyses.[8,9]

Paraphrasing an old maxim: often, the devil is in the details . . . that are left out.

One of the Campbell Collaboration's key principles reads: "Avoiding duplication, by good management and co-ordination to ensure economy of effort." This title registration will test that principle.

Claims that previous research does not exist when, in fact, it does, or that it is of poor quality when, in fact, it is not, do not aid humanity's understanding. Instead, they diminish it. The authors of the title registration clearly wish to conduct the study they propose. So much so that they are willing to ignore, dismiss, hide, or demean far more research than they can possibly themselves provide.

Report registration does not eliminate the threats to human understanding posed by strategic scholarship. As with most research reforms tried to date, it still relies on the no-longer-realistic expectations and persistently ignored norms of the honor system. The huge career successes of strategic scholars have proven the honor system inadequate to manage research and policy fairly and beneficially. Remember, resources given to sincere scholars increase the public welfare; resources given to strategic scholars tend to reduce it.

Campbell Collaboration registration, for all its merits, does nothing to address the largest gaping loophole in the honor system: authors of publications (and peer reviewers) are free to write whatever they please about others' work. Indeed, they are free to write whatever they please about entire research literatures.[10] Strategic scholars with the most resources and greatest access to communication outlets enjoy the most such opportunities and do the most damage.

Noble efforts at promoting viewpoint diversity, such as the Heterodox Academy[11] and ResearchED[12] also fall short. While they may disseminate information that is otherwise neglected or suppressed, they also do not discriminate against strategic scholars, citation cartels, and dismissive reviews. Indeed, in welcoming all, they provide strategic scholars additional platforms from which to promote their work and dismiss or demean others' (Berner, 2021; Petrilli, Davidson, and Carroll 2022; Phelps, 2017f; Pondiscio and

Forster, 2021).[13] (See also Appendix 1 online, "The Enablers," https://educationpolicy.us/Malfunction/App1.pdf.)

Therein lies a dilemma. Standard considerations for free speech and an open marketplace for ideas favors welcoming all, which would include those who misrepresent others' work.

Karl Popper (1945, p. 581), however, disagreed. In his "Paradox of Tolerance," he argued science requires a tolerance for others and cannot progress if certain categories of information (or people) can be successfully suppressed (see also Wikipedia 2022d):

> Unlimited tolerance must lead to the disappearance of tolerance. If we extend unlimited tolerance even to those who are intolerant, if we are not prepared to defend a tolerant society against the onslaught of the intolerant, then the tolerant will be destroyed, and tolerance with them.
>
> We should therefore claim, in the name of tolerance, the right not to tolerate the intolerant. We should claim that any movement preaching intolerance places itself outside the law, and we should consider incitement to intolerance and persecution as criminal, in the same way as we should consider incitement to murder, or to kidnapping, or to the revival of the slave trade, as criminal.

So long as strategic scholars continue to be rewarded for dismissing and demeaning the work of others, more and more research will be dismissed and demeaned, in an extinction vortex that only the best financed can survive (Edwards and Roy, 2016; Taswell et al., 2020).

Some have proposed a new regime of "post-publication review," whereby a submitted manuscript that meets basic standards for publication (e.g., readable, understandable, relevant), is posted online as a temporary preprint and then critiques are welcomed via a broadcast invitation to a wider circle of potential reviewers.

Post-publication review should reduce the currently superabundant number of opportunities for passive-aggressive distortions of the scholarly record: peer reviewers write unfair reviews under cover of anonymity; and authors misrepresent others' work in their literature reviews knowing that those misrepresented have no recourse.[14]

The already up-and-running PubPeer offers this to some extent and has altered the fate of some articles.[15] Comments on published articles must pass through a PubPeer review, which is independent of the subscribing journals. But, once passed, comments may address an article's alleged errors of fact, or counter perceived unfair criticisms.

With PubPeer, suddenly scholars whose research is unfairly maligned have an opportunity to defend their work. And once strategic scholars realize that those they criticize unfairly can respond, they may be less prone to criticize

unfairly (though, granted, the many misrepresented and deceased scholars shall remain silent) (Chan, Jones, Jamieson, and Albarracin, 2017).

PubPeer is voluntary, however, and more widely adopted in the "hard" than the social sciences. Characteristically among the social sciences, psychology stands out for its widespread adoption. That includes psychology journals focused on education.[16] Two US educational testing and measurement journals also use PubPeer.[17]

One will not find PubPeer in use, however, among scores of other US education research journals. It is also pervasively absent among economics journals and publications of think tanks and government-funded research centers.

As least as far back as 1977 some critics of scientific research culture proposed an even more substantial solution to strategic scholarship's opportunism and passive aggressiveness: research courts with a dedicated population of professionally trained judges permanently independent of journals, cartels, and professional associations.[18] The courts could air scholarly disputes and perhaps even settle them (Bauer, 2004, 2017, 2021; Kantrowitz, 1977; Pamuk, 2021, 2022; Siegerink, Pet, and Rosendaal, 2022; Szafrański, 2022).

Who would pay for such a system? Some obvious candidates are those entities who have fueled the wreckage wrought by strategic scholarship thus far: the US federal government, the captured education research groups within larger research agencies (e.g., National Research Council, National Science Foundation, World Bank), and wealthy foundation pack funders.

Awareness of strategic scholarship's harms to the public welfare grows in the hard sciences and in psychology, the "hardest" of the social sciences, along with cumulating efforts to confront them. By contrast, elites in US education research and policy refuse even to acknowledge or consider the harms. Meanwhile, many take advantage of lax research standards and ethical loopholes to thicken their CVs, boost their celebrity profiles, and suppress more useful information than they provide.

NOTES

1. https://www.campbellcollaboration.org/.

2. In its mission statement, the Collaboration outlines its principles: collaboration, enthusiasm, avoiding duplication, minimizing bias, keeping up to date, relevance, access, quality, continuity, and wide participation. https://www.campbellcollaboration.org/about-campbell/vision-mission-and-principle.html.

3. https://campbellcollaboration.org/media/k2/attachments/ECG_Dietrichson_Title.pdf.

4. https://onlinelibrary.wiley.com/doi/full/10.1002/cl2.1212.

5. Eric Hanushek and the US National Research Council among them.

6. For example, the authors criticized previous studies based only on what appeared in the printed publications. For example, here is one of their criticisms of one work: "the effect size of interventions in primary schools are not reported."

Typically, an enormous amount of information is left out of scholarly journal articles. A published journal article is a product of many compromises made between authors, reviewers, editors, and publisher, and subject to space constraints. Not all information that could be included ever is.

If the primary motivation of these authors had been to add to humanity's knowledge base by learning, say, the "effect size of interventions in primary schools," they faced two paths to understanding. The first path, which they followed, was to propose a large, expensive, and completely new study, and expend financial or in-kind support on the order of tens of thousands of dollars (or, in their case, krone) in doing it. A new study, once completed and published, might also help to embellish their curriculum vitae, and support their academic careers.

The second path, which they did not follow, was to simply ask the authors of the article they criticized to calculate the "effect size of interventions in primary schools" from their already accumulated and digitized database. Those authors could have produced such a number in a matter of minutes.

7. Typically, a study compares learning gains of two groups of students over a period during which one group is tested more frequently than the other.

8. Four meta-analyses not mentioned:

- Basol, G., and Johanson, G. (2009). Effectiveness of frequent testing over achievement: A meta-analysis study. *International Journal of Human Sciences* [Online], 6(2).
- Gocman, G. B. (2003). Effectiveness of frequent testing over academic achievement: A meta-analysis study. Dissertation presented to the faculty of the College of Education Ohio University in partial fulfillment of the requirements for the degree Doctor of Philosophy. UMI #3099579.
- Larsen, D. P., and Butler, A. C. (2013). Test-enhanced learning. In K. Walsh (Ed.), *Oxford textbook of medical education* (pp. 443–52). Oxford, UK: Oxford University Press.
- Ramshe, M. H. (November 2014). A review of the studies on the frequent administrations of English tests. *Journal of Language Teaching and Research*, 5(6). 1412–16. DOI:10.4304/jltr.5.6.1412–16.

9. The protocol also promises to focus on "test anxiety" as a factor. Study after previous study is dinged by the title registrants for not incorporating a test anxiety component.

It may be true that the studies they criticize for not including a test anxiety factor did, in fact, not include a test anxiety factor. There exist, however, at least forty-two other testing effect studies, which they do not mention, that did include a test anxiety component, and literature reviews and meta-analyses on the topic that they also ignored:

- Burcas, S., and Cretu, R. Z. (June 3, 2020). Multidimensional Perfectionism and Test Anxiety: a Meta-analytic Review of Two Decades of Research, *Educational Psychology Review*, *33*, 249–73.
- Ergene, T. (2003, August 1). Effective Interventions on Test Anxiety Reduction: A Meta-Analysis, *School Psychology International*. https://doi.org/10.1177/01430343030243004.
- McDonald, A. S. (2001). The prevalence and effects of test anxiety in school children. *Educational Psychology*, *21*, 89–101. doi:10.1080/01443410020019867.
- Roos, A-L., Goetz, T., Voracek, M., Krannich, M., Bieg, M, Jarrell, A., Pekrun, R. (2020, August 16). Test Anxiety and Physiological Arousal: A Systematic Review and Meta-Analysis, *Educational Psychology Review*, *33*, 579–618.
- von der Embse, N., Jester, D., Roy, D., and Post, J. (2018, February). Test anxiety effects, predictors, and correlates: A 30-year meta-analytic review, *Journal of Affective Disorders*, *227*, 483–93.

10. Usual caveats apply. One cannot insult other researchers, call them names, etc. But, so long as what one writes sounds factual, even if it is not, one can characterize other researchers' work any way one wishes to.

11. https://heterodoxacademy.org/.

12. https://researched.org.uk/.

13. In *The Common Good* (1998), Noam Chomsky suggested,

The smart way to keep people passive and obedient is to strictly limit the spectrum of acceptable opinion, but allow very lively debate within that spectrum—even encourage the more critical and dissident views. That gives people the sense that there's free thinking going on, while all the time the presuppositions of the system are being reinforced by the limits put on the range of the debate.

14. Advantages of post-publication review include:

- Increasing the size of the pool of intrinsically motivated potential reviewers manyfold
- Reducing the reliance on overworked junior faculty or, at least, reallocating their time to reviewing articles of more interest
- Reducing the time and expense of the back-and-forth searching for and corresponding with potential reviewers, and its serial repetition with initially rejected manuscripts
- Getting new research findings out into the world more quickly
- Increasing process transparency
- Reducing opportunities for corruption between authors, editors, and reviewers
- Reducing opportunities for dismissive literature reviews (as those knowledgeable of prior relevant studies are provided the opportunity to contradict them publicly)

15. https://pubpeer.com/static/about.
16. E.g., *Journal of Educational Psychology*, *School Psychology Quarterly*, *Journal of Applied Psychology*.
17. https://pubpeer.com/journals.
18. Bauer (2004) wrote:

Actions to curb the power of the (research) monopolies and cartels can be conceived: mandatory funding of contrarian research, mandatory presence of contrarian opinion on advisory panels, a Science Court to adjudicate technical controversies, ombudsman offices at a variety of organizations. Most sorely needed is vigorously investigative science journalism.

References can be found online at
https://educationpolicy.us/Malfunction/References.pdf

About the Author

Richard P. Phelps grew up in St. Louis, Missouri, within a few blocks of Route 66 and the Frisco Route mainline. He taught secondary school mathematics and science at Séminaire St. Agustin in the village of Baskouré, Burkina Faso. Also a Fulbright Scholar, fellow of the Psychophysics Laboratory, founder of the Nonpartisan Education Review, and vice president of the Institute for Objective Policy Assessment, Phelps edited and co-authored *Correcting Fallacies about Educational and Psychological Testing* and *Defending Standardized Testing*.

www.ingramcontent.com/pod-product-compliance
Lightning Source LLC
Chambersburg PA
CBHW021858230426
43671CB00006B/436

www.ingramcontent.com/pod-product-compliance
Lightning Source LLC
Chambersburg PA
CBHW021858230426
43671CB00006B/439

WHEN TEXTS ARE CANONIZED

Program in Judaic Studies
Brown University
Box 1826
Providence, RI 02912

BROWN JUDAIC STUDIES

Edited by

Mary Gluck
David C. Jacobson
Maud Mandel
Saul M. Olyan
Rachel Rojanski
Michael L. Satlow
Adam Teller
Nelson Vieira

Number 359
WHEN TEXTS ARE CANONIZED

edited by
Timothy H. Lim
with
Kengo Akiyama

WHEN TEXTS ARE CANONIZED

Edited by
Timothy H. Lim
with
Kengo Akiyama

Brown Judaic Studies
Providence, Rhode Island

© 2017 Brown University. All rights reserved.

No part of this work may be reproduced or transmitted in any form or by any means, electronic or mechanical, including photocopying and recording, or by means of any information storage or retrieval system, except as may be expressly permitted by the 1976 Copyright Act or in writing from the publisher. Requests for permission should be addressed in writing to the Rights and Permissions Office, Program in Judaic Studies, Brown University, Box 1826, Providence, RI 02912, USA.

Library of Congress Cataloging-in-Publication Data

Names: Lim, Timothy H., editor.
Title: When texts are canonized / edited by Timothy H. Lim.
Description: Providence, RI : Brown Judaic Studies, [2017] | Series: Brown Judaic studies ; number 359 | Includes bibliographical references and index.
Identifiers: LCCN 2017002484 (print) | LCCN 2017006529 (ebook) | ISBN 9781946527004 (pbk. : alk. paper) | ISBN 9781930675957 (hardcover : alk. paper) | ISBN 9781930675995 (ebook)
Subjects: LCSH: Bible—Canon. | Canonization.
Classification: LCC BS465 .W44 2017 (print) | LCC BS465 (ebook) | DDC 220.1/2—dc23
LC record available at https://lccn.loc.gov/2017002484

Printed on acid-free paper.

To Sarah,
whose courage is inspiring

Contents

Abbreviations ix

Contributors xiii

Preface
   Timothy H. Lim xv

An Indicative Definition of the Canon
   Timothy H. Lim 1

The Way of God: Early Canonicity and the
"Nondeviation Formula"
   Manfred Oeming 25

Uses of Torah in the Second Temple Period
   John J. Collins 44

Bad Prophecies: Canon and the Case of the Book of Daniel
   Michael L. Satlow 63

Canon and Content
   John Barton 82

Jesus and the Beginnings of the Christian Canon 95
   Craig A. Evans

Canon and Religious Truth: An Appraisal of
A New New Testament
   R. W. L. Moberly 108

Bibliography 137

Index of Passages 157

Index of Subjects and Authors 162

Abbreviations

ABS	Archaeology and Biblical Studies
ArBib	The Aramaic Bible
AYBRL	Anchor Yale Bible Refrence Library
BASOR	*Bulletin of the American Schools of Oriental Research*
BBB	Bonner biblische Beiträge
BEvT	Beiträge zur evangelischen Theologie
BHT	Beiträge zur historischen Theologie
BibInt	*Biblical Interpretation*
BibInt	Biblical Interpretation Series
BJS	Brown Judaic Studies
BThSt	Biblisch-theologische Studien
BZAW	Beihefte zur Zeitschrift für die alttestamentliche Wissenschaft
CBET	Contributions to Biblical Exegesis and Theology
CBQ	*Catholic Biblical Quarterly*
CBQMS	Catholic Biblical Quarterly Monograph Series
CurBR	*Currents in Biblical Research*
DJD	Discoveries in the Judaean Desert
DMOA	Documenta et Monumenta Orientis Antiqui
DSD	*Dead Sea Discoveries*
EANEC	Explorations in Ancient Near Eastern Civilizations
EdF	Erträge der Forschung
ETL	Ephemerides Theologicae Lovanienses
ExpTim	*Expository Times*
FAT	Forschungen zum Alten Testament
FRLANT	Forschungen zur Religion und Literatur des Alten und Neuen Testaments
GBS.OT	Guides to Biblical Scholarship, Old Testament
GNS	Good News Studies
HBS	Herders biblische Studien
HSS	Harvard Semitic Studies
HTR	*Harvard Theological Review*
HTS	Harvard Theological Studies
JAJ	*Journal of Ancient Judaism*
JAJSup	Journal of Ancient Judaism Supplements
JAL	Jewish Apocryphal Literature Series
JBL	*Journal of Biblical Literature*

x   *Abbreviations*

JJS	*Journal of Jewish Studies*
JSJ	*Journal for the Study of Judaism in the Persian, Hellenistic, and Roman Period*
JSJSup	Journal for the Study of Judaism in the Persian, Hellenistic, and Roman Period Supplements
JSNTSup	Journal for the Study of the New Testament Supplement Series
JSOT	*Journal for the Study of the Old Testament*
JSOTSup	Journal for the Study of the Old Testament Supplement Series
JSS	*Journal of Semitic Studies*
JTS	*Journal of Theological Studies*
KAT	Kommentar zum Alten Testament
LAI	Library of Ancient Israel
LD	Lectio Divina
LHBOTS	Library of Hebrew Bible/Old Testament Studies
LSTS	Library of Second Temple Studies
MdB	Le Monde de la Bible
NICNT	New International Commentary on the New Testament
NIGTC	New International Greek Testament Commentary
NovTSup	Supplements to Novum Testamentum
NSKAT	Neuer Stuttgarter Kommentar, Altes Testament
NTS	*New Testament Studies*
OBO	Orbis Biblicus et Orientalis
ÖBS	Österreichische Biblische Studien
OLA	Orientalia Lovaniensia Analecta
OTL	Old Testament Library
OTP	James H. Charlesworth, ed. *The Old Testament Pseudepigrapha*. 2 vols. Garden City, NY: Doubleday, 1983–1985
OTR	Old Testament Readings
OTS	*Oudtestamentische Studiën*
QD	Questiones Disputatae
RevQ	*Revue de Qumran*
RlA	Erich Ebeling et al., eds., *Reallexikon der Assyriologie*. Berlin: de Gruyter, 1928–2014
SBAB	Stuttgarter biblische Aufsatzbände
SBLDS	Society of Biblical Literature Dissertation Series
SC	Sources chrétiennes
SDSSRL	Studies in the Dead Sea Scrolls and Related Literature
SSN	Studia Semitica Neerlandica
STDJ	Studies on the Texts of the Desert of Judah
StPB	Studia Post-biblica
SVTP	Studia in Veteris Testamenti Pseudepigraphica
SymS	Symposium Series
TA	*Tel Aviv*

Abbreviations   xi

THKNT	Theologischer Handkommentar zum Neuen Testament
ThWAT	G. Johannes Botterweck, Helmer Ringgren, and H.-J. Fabry, eds. *Theologisches Wörterbuch zum Alten Testament.* Stuttgart: Kohlhammer, 1973–2000.
TRE	Gerhard Krause and Gerhard Müller, eds. *Theologische Real-enzyklopädie.* Berlin: de Gruyter, 1977–
UF	*Ugarit-Forschungen*
VC	*Vigiliae Christianae*
VCSup	Supplements to Vigiliae Christianae
VT	*Vetus Testamentum*
VTSup	Supplements to Vetus Testamentum
WBC	Word Biblical Commentry
ZBK.AT	Zürcher Bibelkommentare. Altes Testament
ZNW	*Zeitschrift für die neutestamentliche Wissenschaft und die Kunde der älteren Kirche*

Contributors

Kengo Akiyama (Independent scholar)
John Barton (University of Oxford)
John J. Collins (Yale University)
Craig A. Evans (Houston Baptist University)
Timothy H. Lim (University of Edinburgh)
R. W. L. Moberly (University of Durham)
Manfred Oeming (University of Heidelberg)
Michael L. Satlow (Brown University)

Preface

TIMOTHY H. LIM

If the number of scholarly publications is any indication of importance, then the subject of canon should rank high among the foremost topics in biblical studies. Numerous studies have investigated the formation of authoritative scriptures. Others have shone light on the importance of the scribe in copying and adapting the transmitted text. Still others have illustrated how the rewriting process began in the biblical texts themselves.

In this volume, the contributors were asked to address issues of canonization and canonicity, encapsulated in the title of the volume *When Texts Are Canonized*. How did canonization take place and what difference does it make to a text once it is canonized? On the one hand, we are interested in probing the canonical process: Why were certain books, but not others, included in the canon? What criteria were used to select the books of the canon? Was canonization a divine fiat or a human act? What was the nature of the authority of the laws and narratives of the Torah? How did prophecy come to be included in the canon? On the other side, we want to reflect on the consequences of canonization: What are the effects in elevating certain writings to the status of "Holy Scriptures"? What happens when a text is included in an official list? What theological and hermeneutical questions are at stake in the fact of the canon? Should the canon be unsealed or reopened to include other writings?

The essays of this volume fill a gap in canon research. They bridge the span between biblical criticism and biblical theology by focusing on the nexus between canonical process and canonicity. They address issues that are at the heart of the hermeneutics of canon. These meta-questions are not necessarily separate from historical research, but they include issues that are central to our understanding of the authority of the Bible today.

The issues at stake can be illustrated by two examples important for contemporary society, the divine warrant for violence in the Hebrew Bible/ Old Testament and Paul's teachings about the role of women in his letters. It has become increasingly recognized that divinely sanctioned violence is found in the Bible. This has led to a reexamination of key biblical passages and how they should be understood. One of these biblical passages is Deut

xvi   *Preface*

7:1–2 and Yahweh's command to exterminate the Hittites, the Girgashites, the Amorites, the Canaanites, the Perizzites, and the Jebusites. The divine command to destroy them is a moral problem that is not resolved by the argument that it is theoretical, since the divine intention remains and commands the Israelites to commit what is tantamount to ethnic cleansing.

The divine command is problematic precisely because it is found in the canonical book of Deuteronomy. Suppose that one reads the divine command in a noncanonical book. Would this passage raise ethical problems for moderns? I have yet to read a discussion of the morally ambiguous position posed by *ḥērem* in the Temple Scroll (11Q19ᵃ LXII, 13–16). To be sure, this Dead Sea Scroll rewrites portions of the book of Deuteronomy, but the point remains. It occurs in a noncanonical text and, as such, poses little or no difficulty for moderns. The canonization of the book of Deuteronomy elevates its authority to the status of "Holy Scripture" in a way that is not matched by the esteem accorded to the Temple Scroll.

A second example comes from the New Testament and the contemporary debate over the status and role of women. Several churches today have been discussing and arguing over the ordination of women as ministers, priests, and bishops. In this debate, several passages from Paul's letters have been discussed, one of which is 1 Cor 14:33–34, in which the apostle admonishes that women should keep silent and not be permitted to speak, because they are subordinate according to the law. Paul's letters are occasional missives that address specific issues in the churches that he planted in Asia Minor, Greece, and Rome. The effect of canonizing the letter to the Corinthians is to raise this occasional letter to the status of "Holy Scripture" and, in so doing, to make a specific advice for one community normative for all churches and for all time.

The present volume begins with a discussion of constituent factors that contributed to the canonical process. I suggest that the selection of the books of the canon cannot be explained by criterial logic. One cannot explain why one book is included in the canon and not another, according to a set of criteria or norms. Rather, the definition of the canon is indicative and based on the analogy of family resemblances. I first examine what is often regarded as an absolute criterion of canonization, the divine inspiration of scripture. I suggest that divine inspiration of scripture is not a criterion at all because it is a thoroughly human construct. A text's claim to divine inspiration is just that: a claim. As such, it requires the validation of a community. There were several factors, internal and external, that contributed to the canonical process, and I suggest that most of the books of the canon resemble one another in memorializing the story of Israel.

Manfred Oeming investigates early notions of canonicity as physical measures of length, volume, and weight before discussing how these concepts were adopted in ethical guidance for proper conduct. He observes, in particular, that the formula that prohibits someone from deviating to

Preface   xvii

the left and right was a means of fixing the way of God. This "nondeviation formula" was imported into royal ideology, used by the Deuteronomistic redaction of the Pentateuch and former prophets, and adopted by
the wisdom literature; it also appeared in the prophetic texts. In the late
Second Temple period, the formula was used by Mattathias in his resistance against the decrees of Antiochus, as well as by the volunteers who
joined the community at Qumran.

John J. Collins examines the issue of the authority of the Torah in the
Second Temple period by discussing two case studies. First, he investigates
the nature of Torah and its enforcement in the books of Ezra-Nehemiah.
He argues that the legal enforcement of the Torah of Moses centered on
cultic and Sabbath observance and identity issues related to mixed marriages and the language of worship and communication. The authority of
the Torah was largely symbolic, but it also had some prescriptive force.

Second, he discusses a diverse group of texts previously categorized
as belonging to the genre of "Rewritten Bible." Collins prefers the alternate designation of "rewritten scriptures" to describe the use and reuse of
the text of the Torah before canonization. For Collins, the authority of the
narrative parts of the Torah is evidenced in their rewriting in the so-called
4QReworked Pentateuch, Josephus's *Antiquities*, the Genesis Apocryphon,
the Aramaic Levi Document, and the fragments of Hellenistic Jewish literature. In these works, the narrative parts of the Torah provide the literary frame, scope, and authorial voice from which these texts depart. The
rewriting is literary in the sense that it makes the stories of the Torah more
interesting for a later audience, including a hellenized one.

It is not, however, just the narrative parts of the Torah that were sub-
jected to rewriting. Collins discusses the nature of the authority of the
Torah of Moses and the testimony and the heavenly tablets of the book of
Jubilees, arguing that the author claimed for his own work an equal status
to "the first torah." For the Temple Scroll, the authority claimed is none
other than divine discourse itself. This rewritten text implicitly recognizes
the authority of the traditional Torah, but it also claims that, on the legal
matters that it addresses, its understanding of the law is decisive.

Michael Satlow discusses the canonical process by proposing a new
model to explain how the bad prophecies of the book of Daniel came to be
textualized before being canonized. By "bad prophecies" Satlow means
the predictions in the book that were patently wrong, such as the oracles
about the final battle between the Ptolemies and Seleucids and the death
of Antiochus in the land of Israel. Daniel's written prophecies originated
from a small, scholastic circle associated with the *maśkîlîm*; they were
shelved because they were "bad." When the Romans took control over
Judea, however, the prophecies were rejuvenated by scribes who gave
them new meaning. Satlow's essay shows the canonical process at work
in the adoption of the oracles of one book for subsequent generations.

xviii   *When Texts Are Canonized*

John Barton reflects on the implications of canonicity by showing how different are the modern and ancient understandings of the form and content of scriptural texts and how the interplay between these is affected by the status of the text as canonical. First, Barton discusses the issue of form versus content of a scriptural text by pointing out that it is the book of Jeremiah—or, more precisely, its scroll—not a certain version of the prophecy, that is accepted as authoritative. Most laypeople in antiquity could not compare the proto-Masoretic Text with the shorter Septuagintal text. What mattered to them was the book of Jeremiah in whatever version they had inherited it. He sees the same disjunction between the modern and ancient understandings of the order of the psalms.

The relationship between form and content is raised a second time in the rabbinic concept of Holy Scriptures as physical objects. Barton argues that the disputes in Mishnah Yadayim are not concerned with the content of the books of Song of Songs and Qohelet, since "defilement of the hands" is discussed also in relation to blank spaces and scroll fixings. Rather, the issue concerns the technical and physical question of whether these two texts contained the Tetragrammaton.

Finally, Barton reflects on the effects of canonizing a text. A text that is canonized is read in accordance with the beliefs of the canonizing community. Thus, for instance, the Gospel of John is read in a way that makes it compatible with the Synoptics precisely because the early Christian church canonized all four Gospels. By its nature, the Gospel of the Beloved Disciple is much nearer to Gnosticism. The act of canonization implies a rereading of the Gospel with the emerging Christian orthodoxy and the harmonizing of discrepancies between the accounts.

In the ancient period, therefore, Barton identifies two tendencies that pulled in opposite directions with regard to the form and content of the biblical texts. In one direction, there is a tendency, evidenced in rabbinic literature, to require the exact form of a biblical scroll as a divine physical object. Biblical scrolls are considered "transcripts of divine communication" and should be "flawless." In the other direction, there is little concern over the original form of a biblical book over against different instantiations. What mattered was the version of the book that was accepted by the community.

In Craig Evans's paper, the importance of the model of Jesus for the canonization of the Old Testament in the churches is advanced. He argues that Jesus's tolerance for the Hebrew, Aramaic, and Greek versions of Jewish Scriptures set the pattern for the reception of different canons by churches in the West and East. Assuming that the historical Jesus can be confidently reconstructed from the Gospels, Evans discusses the scriptural passages alluded to, referenced, and implied in various themes related to the kingdom of God, the seating on the throne of glory, resurrection on the third day, the parable of the vineyard, and the identification of the rejected

Preface   xix

stone as the rightful king. Evans's Jesus not only knew Jewish Scriptures in Hebrew; he also made use of exegetical traditions found in the targumim and in the Septuagint. This "versional openness" allowed the Christian churches to pursue a Greek-canon, a Hebrew-Aramaic canon, or a combination of the two.

Lastly, Walter Moberly raises issues of canonicity and canonization by reviewing a recent attempt to reopen the New Testament by the addition of various documents left out of the traditional canon. The publication of *A New New Testament: A Bible for the 21st Century Combining Traditional and Newly Discovered Texts* in 2013 forms the foreground to Moberly's defense of the traditional New Testament canon. The book review begins with a careful contextualization of the self-appointed "New Orleans Council" and its spokesperson, Hal Taussig, who also edited the volume. While not sympathetic with the aims of the book, Moberly describes the book thoroughly before turning to several criticisms. He finds the added material inferior and obscure in comparison to the canonical books. He questions the scholarship (e.g., dating of the texts) implied in the collection as it relates to mainstream New Testament study. He wonders why the Hebrew Bible/Old Testament was not included in this enlarged canon, and he bemoans the absence of a critique of the traditional New Testament canon, given that this *New New Testament* intended an enlargement and reimagination of the Christian self-understanding. Moberly ends his review by offering what he regards as the vision of the traditional New Testament as found in both the life-affirming teachings of Jesus and the sinfulness of humans.

The revised papers included in this volume were originally delivered at a one-day, international conference entitled "Power, Authority & Canon" held at New College, University of Edinburgh, Scotland, on 6 May 2015. Sixty-five delegates attended the conference from various places in the United Kingdom—Aberdeen, St Andrews, Edinburgh, Durham, Cambridge, London, and Oxford—and from abroad, Germany, Lithuania, the United States, and Canada.

The conference opened with a Gunning Lecture on the Hebrew Bible and the Mishnah by Shaye J. D. Cohen of Harvard University, who also provided some reflections on the various papers in a concluding session. Unfortunately, due to the pressures of work Shaye has been unable to contribute to this volume.

The invited participants were asked to discuss the historical, theological, and ethical ramifications of canonization. The papers do not have one answer to the questions. There is open disagreement on some issues, and there has been no attempt to smooth over the opinions. These essays stand collectively to mark the different ways of thinking about the hermeneutics of the canon.

xx   *When Texts Are Canonized*

I would like to thank all the colleagues who welcomed the delegates and presenters and chaired the sessions: Helen Bond, Paul Foster, Hannah Holtschneider, Larry Hurtado, Matthew Novenson, Lena Tiemeyer, Philippa Townsend, and David Reimer. A special word of gratitude to the student helpers, Kengo Akiyama and Chris Lee, for making sure that the program ran smoothly. Our school secretary, Jean Reynolds, expertly organized the event. Funds for the lecture and conference were provided by the Gunning Trust, and Kathy Christie, the Director of Professional Services, was vital in setting up the financial accounts in a way that made the lecture and conference possible. The conference was held under the joint auspices of two Edinburgh research units, the Centre for Christian Origins and the Jewish Studies Network. My former student, now Dr. Kengo Akiyama, worked tirelessly to copyedit the book and compile the bibliography. His contribution to the volume is far more than the mechanical presentation of the manuscript. Finally, thanks to the two anonymous reviewers who provided useful comments on the draft of the volume, and to Saul Olyan for accepting the volume for publication in the Brown Judaic Studies series.

An Indicative Definition of the Canon

TIMOTHY H. LIM

The canon of the Hebrew Bible was defined, if not yet finally closed, by the end of the first century CE. The Pharisaic canon became the canon of Rabbinic Judaism, because the majority of those who refounded the Jewish religion after the destruction of the Temple by the Romans were Pharisees.[1] The process that led to this canonization needs to be explored. How should we think about the books that were eventually included in the canon? Unlike the early church, ancient Jewish communities did not have a central authority that defined the books of the canon. The formation of the Jewish canon was not prescribed by the priests of the Temple of Jerusalem; it emerged from the bottom up, with each community holding to its own collection of authoritative texts.[2]

I suggest that the books of the canon were not selected according to a set of criteria. One cannot explain by a set of standards or norms why one book is chosen over another book. I avoid the terminology of "criteria" and its connotation of an external standard. The canonical process was multifaceted and complex, both in the way that each community formulated its own understanding of authoritative scriptures and in the rationale implied in the selection. We need to apply a different kind of logic to understand how the process worked in defining the canon by drawing on the conceptual resources of analytical philosophy on blurred definitions. The result of this process, the definition of the canon, is explained by indicative logic. I begin by examining the criterial definition of the canon.

Ex Post Facto Rationalization

Sometime around 232 Origen wrote in his *Commentary on the Psalms* that the Old Testament consisted of twenty-two canonical books, the same number as the letters of the Hebrew alphabet, "according to the Hebrew

---

1. See my *The Formation of the Jewish Canon*, AYBRL (New Haven: Yale University Press, 2013).
2. Ibid.

1

2   *When Texts Are Canonized*

tradition." The great text critic of the early church then listed the books in Greek and in Greek transliteration of the Hebrew titles. The list, as preserved in Eusebius's history, is ostensibly faulty, as it includes only twenty-one books (*Hist. eccl.* 6.25). The twelve Minor Prophets, counted as one book, were accidentally left out of his enumeration. The attribution of the canonical list to the Hebrew tradition is typical of the way that the early church fathers deferred to Jewish tradition on the books that make up the canon of the Old Testament. But Origen was not simply following Jewish tradition; he was trying to harmonize the Greek Bible, adopted by the church from Jewish Greek Scriptures, with the Hebrew Bible. He combined the prophecy of Jeremiah, Lamentations, and the Letter of Jeremiah "in one Jeremia," and he designated "the Maccabees," entitled "Sar beth sabanel," as "outside." It seems clear that Origen's criteria for the definition of the canon constitute an ex post facto rationalization. Origen was discussing the criteria of the canon in relation to both the Hebrew and Greek Bibles, the Septuagint having become the preferred version of the Bible in the early church.

Recently, Edmon Gallagher has argued that the use of Hebrew as the original language of a work was an important criterion in the canonization of the Old Testament. He began by criticizing Sid Leiman's four criteria enumerated in Rabbinic Judaism that determined a book's inclusion or exclusion from the canon before discussing the patristic view of the canonization of the Old Testament.[3] Focusing on the correspondence between Origen and Africanus on the status of the book of Susanna, Gallagher suggested that there were three kinds of arguments that were used: (1) that the books of the Old Testament should be restricted to the books of the Jewish canon ("the synagogal criterion"); (2) that the canon should be expanded to include those books that were in the church but were not part of the Jewish canon ("the ecclesiastical criterion"); and, most importantly, (3) that the books of the canon had to have been originally written in the Hebrew language ("the Hebrew criterion").[4] Gallagher wants to suggest that this Hebrew criterion was already evident in pre-Rabbinic Judaism and that it was important for the formation of the Jewish canon.

But Origen and Africanus were clearly discussing the criteria of the canon as understood in the third century CE. This was the canon of the Old Testament. There is no evidence to support the view that the Hebrew language was a criterion in the formation of the Jewish canon. Philo and cer-

---

3. Sid Z. Leiman, "Inspiration and Canonicity: Reflections on the Formation of the Biblical Canon," in *Aspects of Judaism in the Graeco-Roman Period*, vol. 2 of *Jewish and Christian Self-Definition*, ed. E. P. Sanders, A. I. Baumgarten and A. Mendelson (London: SCM, 1981), 57.

4. Gallagher's dissertation has been published as *Hebrew Scripture in Patristic Biblical Theory: Canon, Language, Text*, VCSup 114 (Leiden: Brill, 2012).

An Indicative Definition of the Canon   3

tain unknown scribes may have valued the Hebrew original text, despite using the Greek translation, but that does not mean that they understood Hebrew as a criterion of canonization. The canonical process began much earlier than the Hellenistic Roman period and was not restricted to the Pentateuch and the Greek-speaking Jews. A fragmentary Dead Sea Scroll (4Q464 [Exposition on the Patriarchs]) preserves the earliest mention of "the holy tongue" (לשון הקודש) and associates it with the reversal of the linguistic fracturing at Babel in the eschaton rather than with a collection of authoritative scriptures. It is unlikely that the later criterion of Hebrew language was used in the canonical process, since books that were originally composed in Hebrew (e.g., Ben Sira, Jubilees, and the Temple Scroll) were left out of the rabbinic canon. Other books (Ezekiel, Qohelet, Song of Songs, Proverbs, Esther, and Ruth) were disputed by rabbis despite being written in Hebrew.

Divine Inspiration Examined

There is one criterion that is often claimed to be essential to canon formation: the divine inspiration of the Holy Scriptures.[5] Belief in divine origin is frequently thought to be an important citerion by which a book is included in the canon of the Hebrew Bible. Leiman believes that books authored after the cessation of prophecy in the late Persian period or early Maccabean period have been left out because the canon was already closed and these books were not inspired.[6]

This criterion is based on the Tosefta's statement that the Holy Spirit ceased with the death of the last prophets, Haggai, Zechariah, and Malachi (Tosefta Sotah 13:2; cf. 1 Macc 9:27, 4:26, 14:41; and Josephus, *Ag. Ap.* 1.38–41). Leiman had built a theory of canonization around this statement, arguing that authoritative texts can be divided according to whether they are inspired and canonical or canonical but not inspired.[7] The biblical books are inspired and canonical, but the rabbinic texts (e.g., Megillat ta'anit) are canonical but not inspired. This distinction, however, is difficult to maintain, as rabbinic literature was finally considered not just

---

5. The enigmatic concept of *ṭum'at yādayim* ("defilement of the hands") was used as to define "Holy Scriptures" in rabbinic literature, but this was constructed by priestly theology and is a consequence more than a criterion (see my "The Defilement of the Hands as a Principle Determining the Holiness of Scriptures," *JTS* 61 [2010]: 501–15).

6. Leiman, "Inspiration and Canonicity," 57.

7. Sid Z. Leiman, *The Canonization of Hebrew Scripture: The Talmudic and Midrashic Evidence*, Connecticut Academy of Arts and Sciences Transactions 47 (New Haven: Connecticut Academy of Arts and Sciences, 1976).

4   *When Texts Are Canonized*

canonical but also inspired.[8] Leiman also argued that the tripartite canon of the Hebrew Bible was closed at the time of Judas Maccabeus, but this second-century date of the closing of the canon is untenable.[9]

Underlying Leiman's criterion of the cessation of prophecy is the assumption of the sufficiency of divine inspiration. This principle is not a rabbinic invention, nor is it specific to Leiman's theory. The divine inspiration of scripture was central to the doctrine of the early church, to different church traditions in the nineteenth century, and to the various evangelical churches today.[10] It is evident in pre-rabbinic Jewish and Christian sources. What is the principle of divine inspiration and how does it apply to the canonical process?

The criterion of divine inspiration is often stated, but seldom explained. It is taken as self-evident. The criterion is believed to be so obvious that its invocation in a debate often silences awkward questions about the canonical process altogether. In fact, some feel that it is positively irreverent to be asking just how belief in a book's divine origin explains its inclusion in the list of authoritative writings, for how could a divinely inspired text be anything other than canonical? Also absent is the reasoning for the exclusion of other books that likewise claim that God had revealed the content, if not the very words, of the book to the author.

The confidence in the divine origin of scripture is based on the interpretation of ancient sources, but the explanation of the concept is inferred rather than explicitly stated in the texts. Second Timothy 3:16–17 is one of the passages often cited in support of divine inspiration: "All scripture is inspired by God [πᾶσα γραφὴ θεόπνευστος] and is useful for teaching, for reproof, for correction, and for training in righteousness, so that everyone who belongs to God may be proficient, equipped for every good work" (NRSV). This deutero-Pauline letter is understood to mean that the nature

---

8. See David Kraemer, "The Formation of Rabbinic Canon: Authority and Boundaries," *JBL* 110 (1991): 616. Vered Noam argues that the concept of the *bat qôl* is a secondary rabbinic development of the priestly *dābār*-revelation from the Holy of Holies, familiar from several Second Temple priestly legends ("Why Did the Heavenly Voice Speak Aramaic? Ancient Layers in Rabbinic Literature," in *From Text to Context in Ancient Judaism: Studies in Honor of Steven Fraade*, ed. Michal Bar-Asher Siegal, Christine Hayes, and Tzvi Novick (Leiden: Brill, forthcoming).

9. See my *Formation of the Jewish Canon*, 117. In the eighteenth century, Johann Semler criticized the view that the canon closed with the cessation of the prophetic inspiration (*Abhandlung von freier Untersuchung des Canon*, 4 vols [Halle: Carl Hermann Hemmerde, 1771–1776]). He showed that this was a dogmatic claim rather than a historical explanation (cf. Brevard S. Childs, *Introduction to the Old Testament as Scripture* [Philadelphia: Fortress, 1979], 44, 50).

10. See, among many others, William J. Abraham, *The Divine Inspiration of Holy Scripture* (Oxford: Oxford University Press, 1981); J. N. D. Kelly, *Early Christian Doctrines*, 2nd ed. (New York: HarperOne, 1960), 60-64; and D. A. Carson and John D. Woodbridge, eds., *Hermeneutics, Authority, and Canon* (Leicester: Inter-Varsity Press, 1981).

An Indicative Definition of the Canon   5

of scripture is characterized at its source by divine inspiration, taking θεόπνευστος (lit., "God-breathed") as a reference to the origin rather than the means of inspiration. The anarthrous phrase in the singular, however, πᾶσα γραφή, probably means "every passage of scripture" rather than a reference to the whole Bible, as Anthony T. Hanson has rightly argued.[11] Divine inspiration is not self-evidently valid. After all, it is one matter for someone to claim the divine inspiration of a text and quite another for someone else to believe it. Moreover, 2 Timothy states that "every passage of scripture is inspired by God"; it does not say that all inspired writings are "scripture."[12]

Rabbinic sources have also been adduced to support the criterion of divine inspiration. According to Tosefta Yadayim 2:14, R. Simeon b. Menasia argued that the Song of Songs defiles the hands—the rabbinic litmus test for the inclusion of a book as "Holy Scriptures"—because it was said through the agency of the holy spirit (מפני שנאמרה ברוח הקדש).[13] By contrast, Qohelet or Ecclesiastes does not defile the hands because it is only the wisdom of Solomon. Here, as elsewhere, divine inspiration is stated as a principle, but its rationale is not explained.

Moshe Halbertal offers the following:

> According to rabbinic tradition, the criterion for inclusion in Scripture depends upon whether or not the book was divinely inspired. (From a rabbinic perspective this is a necessary but not sufficient condition. Thus not every prophecy was included in the Bible, only those that were relevant to future generations.).[14]

Halbertal, then, refers to the rabbinic belief in the cessation of prophecy in the Persian period but questions whether that is a likely reason for the exclusion of the Apocrypha from the canon. He suggests that perhaps it is the perceived need to exclude other books from the sealed canon that gave rise to the belief in the cessation of prophecy and not the other way around. He offers no explanation, however, of how divine inspiration leads to canonization.

---

11. Anthony Tyrrell Hanson, *Studies in the Pastoral Epistles* (London: SPCK, 1968), 44.

12. The "sacred writings" (ἱερὰ γράμματα) of 3:15 were likewise written without the article, but later manuscripts added τά. At the end of the letter, Paul reminds Timothy to bring the books and especially the parchments (4:13: τὰ βιβλία μάλιστα τὰς μεμβράνας).

13. The paradoxical principle that a scriptural scroll is considered holy only if it defiles the hands has been variously explained. I have suggested that it is part of a priestly theology that views *kitbê haqqōdeš* as sacred objects that were considered sources of contamination ("Defilement of the Hands"). See now Albert Baumgarten, "Sacred Scriptures Defile the Hands," *JJS* 62 (2016): 46–67, who argued that it was the Pharisees who took the sacred object of the Torah out of its Temple precinct, thus causing an anomaly of the sacred in the profane. The principle of defiling the hands was a way of addressing this anomaly.

14. Moshe Halbertal, *People of the Book: Canon, Meaning, and Authority* (Cambridge: Harvard University Press, 1997), 17.

6   *When Texts Are Canonized*

In the Talmud, Rab Judah (250–290) reported that Samuel did not believe that the Scroll of Esther defiled the hands (b. Meg. 7a). An explanation was sought, since the same Samuel had previously said that the Scroll of Esther was composed under divine inspiration. The seemingly contradictory opinion of Samuel is explained away by the different legal requirements needed for reading and writing. Apparently, there are different degrees of divine inspiration and holiness for the recitation or reading aloud of a text and for the copying of a scroll. But the principle and its degrees of divine inspiration and holiness are left unexplained.

Probably the most explicit association of divine inspiration of Holy Scriptures to canonization is to be found in the final chapter of 4 Ezra. After the law had been burned and the record of God's past works and future plans had been destroyed, the pseudonymous author, known as "Ezra," asked the Lord to send the holy spirit into him so that he could write everything in the divine law from the beginning. This Ezra received the holy spirit by drinking a full cup of something that looked like water mixed with fire. Then, in the course of forty days with the help of five scribes, Ezra dictated the content of the public books and of the books of the wise, a ninety-four-book canon The divine origin of the canon is underscored by the miraculous recording of Ezra's dictation to the scribes, who were themselves unfamiliar with the characters of the words.

Here, it would seem, is the proof that the canon—whether it is the public, twenty-four book collection or the larger, seventy-book compendium of the wise—requires that its books be divinely inspired. Fourth Ezra's final vision, however, is not about canonization as such but the reinstatement of the books of the canon that had been destroyed. Ezra did not give a new public canon; he dictated the content of the books of the received canon, so that the people will again have a copy (see 14:21). Whether 4 Ezra considered itself part of the larger ninety-four-book canon is moot.[15] Its claim to divine inspiration, in any case, was insufficient for it to be included in the canon of Rabbinic Judaism. It is considered a book of the Apocrypha or deuterocanonical writings.

Other Inspired Writings

The exclusion of 4 Ezra from the rabbinic canon raises questions about the criterion of divine inspiration. As Shaye Cohen quipped, "Why these and not those? Why Ecclesiastes but not Ben Sira? Why Ruth but not Tobit?

---

15. Julius Steinberg and Timothy J. Stone argue that the author of 4 Ezra "uses the same language with which he described the 70 books to portray his own work (4 Ezra 12:36–38)" ("The Historical Formation of the Writings in Antiquity," in *The Shape of the Writings*, ed. Julius Steinberg and Timothy J. Stone, Siphrut 16 [Winona Lake, IN: Eisenbrauns, 2015], 34).

An Indicative Definition of the Canon   7

Why Esther but not Judith? Why Daniel and not Enoch? Why Chronicles and not the Temple Scroll?"[16] Or, as James Barr puts it, "No doctrine of inspiration can prove which books were inspired.... it cannot tell us which writings are the ones within and which are the ones without."[17]

Books that claim divine inspiration include the book of Jubilees, which presents itself as a direct revelation of God to Moses on Mount Sinai. The angel of the Presence speaks to Moses in the second person throughout the book. The whole account has been described as a "haggadic commentary to Scripture" that retells the biblical account from Genesis to Exod 24. It is also at the forefront of the current scholarly debate about the genre of rewritten scripture.[18] The prologue states:

> This is The Account of the Division of Days of the Law and the Testimony for Annual Observance according to their Weeks (of years) and their Jubilees throughout all the Years of the World just as the Lord told it to Moses on Mount Sinai when he went up to receive the tablets of the Law and the commandment by the word of the Lord, as he said to him, "Come up to the top of the mountain" [Exod 24:12].[19]

Didymus Alexandrinus, Epiphanius, and Jerome also cited the book of Jubilees. Among the sectarian communities reflected in the Dead Sea Scrolls, the book was considered an authoritative *perush,* or explanation of the Pentateuch. CD XVI, 1–3 states, "Therefore, let a man bind himself to an oath to return to the Torah of Moses, indeed in it everything is specified. The explanation of their times when Israel is blind to all these, it is

---

16. Shaye J. D. Cohen, *From the Maccabees to the Mishnah,* 3rd ed. (Louisville: Westminster John Knox, 2014), 188–89.

17. James Barr, review of *The Divine Inspiration of Holy Scripture,* by William J. Abraham, *JTS* 38 (1983): 375.

18. Emil Schürer, *The History of the Jewish People in the Age of Jesus Christ (175 B.C.–A.D. 135),* rev. and ed. Geza Vermes, Fergus Millar, and Martin Goodman, 3 vols. in 4 pts. (Edinburgh: T&T Clark, 1973–87), 3.1:308–17. The category was first suggested by Geza Vermes to describe Genesis Apocryphon, Jubilees, Liber Antiquitatum Biblicarum, and Josephus's *Jewish Antiquities* (see Vermes, "Bible and Midrash: Early Old Testament Exegesis," in *Scripture and Tradition in Judaism: Haggadic Studies,* 2nd rev. ed., StPB 4 [Leiden: Brill, 1961], 9–10; József Zsengellér, ed., *Rewritten Bible after Fifty Years: Texts, Terms, or Techniques? A Last Dialogue with Geza Vermes,* JSJSup 166 [Leiden: Brill, 2014]). Vermes, following Renée Bloch, believed that the canon was closed in the third century BCE (see my "Origins and Emergence of Midrash in Relation to the Hebrew Scriptures," in *Encyclopaedia of Midrash: Biblical Interpretation in Formative Judaism,* ed. Jacob Neusner and Alan J. Avery-Peck, 2 vols. [Leiden: Brill, 2005], 2:598–99). Recent objections against the terminology center on this assumption. Those who hold that the canon was closed much later argue that the terminology should be adapted to "rewritten scriptures."

19. Translation by O. S. Wintermute, "Jubilees (Second Century BC)," in *OTP* 2:35–142, here 52.

8   *When Texts Are Canonized*

detailed according to the Book of the Divisions of the Times by Jubilees and weeks."[20]

The book of Enoch likewise claims divine inspiration:

> The blessing of Enoch: with which he blessed the elect and the righteous who would be present on the day of tribulation at (the time of) the removal of all the ungodly ones. 2 And Enoch, the blessed and righteous man of the Lord, took up (his parable) while his eyes were open and he saw, and said, "(This is) a holy vision from the heavens which the angels showed me: and I heard from them everything and I understood. I look not for this generation but for the distant one that is coming. I speak about the elect ones and concerning them." (1 En. 1:1–2)[21]

The superscription of the Book of Watchers attributes the blessing of the elect and righteous, and the subsequent judgment on the wicked to the heavenly vision that the angels showed him. Its claim to divine revelation is repeated in all five books and two appendixes that make up the composite work known as 1 Enoch.

Many of the church fathers made use of the book and believed that the divine origin of 1 Enoch was authentic. Similarly, it would seem, did the Epistle of Jude when it cited Enoch in a way no different from scripture. The communities reflected in the Dead Sea Scrolls considered the book of Enoch authoritative. Quite apart from its inclusion in the canon of the Ethiopian Church, however, the book of Enoch was not officially recognized by other ecclesiastical denominations or by Rabbinic Judaism.[22]

Divine inspiration can also occur in unexpected places, such as in a commentary on scripture or in a letter. In Pesher Habakkuk, divine inspiration is claimed for both the biblical text that is cited and the sectarian comment.

> and God told Habakkuk to write down the things that are to come 2 upon the present generation, but the completion of the period He did not make known to him. 3 [space] And concerning what the passage says: in order that the one reading it will run. [Hab 2:2d] 4 Its interpretation concerns

---

20. Translation by Timothy H. Lim, published in *The Formation of the Jewish Canon* (New Haven: Yale University Press, 2013), 131.

21. English translation by E. Isaacs, "1 (Ethiopic Apocalypse of) Enoch," in *OTP* 1:5.

22. According Leslie Baynes, the book of Jubilees was accepted as authoritative in the Ethiopian Church earlier and more decisively than 1 Enoch ("*Enoch* and *Jubilees* in the Canon of the Ethiopian Orthodox Church," in *A Teacher for All Generations: Essays in Honor of James C. VanderKam*, ed. Eric Mason et al., 2 vols., JSJSup 153 (Leiden: Brill, 2012), 2:799–818. Recently, Eugen J. Pentiuc has observed that the Eastern Orthodox Church has never canonized a particular text and has continued to vacillate between the larger canonical corpus of the Catholics and the narrow collection of the Protestants (*The Old Testament in Eastern Orthodox Tradition* [Oxford: Oxford University Press, 2014], 25–26).

the Teacher of Righteousness to whom God had made known 5 all the mysteries of the words of his servants, the prophets. (1QpHab VII, 1–5)[23]

The pesherist states that Habakkuk received a divine revelation and wrote down what he was told, but the sectarian interpreter also claims that God continued to reveal his mysteries beyond the time of the prophets to the Teacher of Righteousness.[24]

In his letter to the Galatians, Paul asserts that his "gospel" is not according to human standards but according to scripture (Gal 3:1–4:13) and is verified by the Holy Spirit (Gal 5:1–15).

> For I want you to know, brothers and sisters, that the gospel that was proclaimed by me is not of human origin; 12 for I did not receive it from a human source, nor was I taught it, but I received it through a revelation of Jesus Christ [δι' ἀποκαλύψεως Ἰησοῦ Χριστοῦ]. (Gal 1:11–12 NRSV)

Other Pharisees did not accept Paul's claim, and his letters were not included in the rabbinic canon.

The examples of texts that claimed divine inspiration could be multiplied. Why were they not included in the canon? What distinguishes one claim from another? Conversely, the Song of Songs, Qohelet, Esther, Ruth, and Proverbs did not claim divine inspiration but were eventually included in the canon.[25]

Divine Inspiration Constructed

Divine inspiration in a text is not a criterion of canonization. It is a claim that the text's source of inspiration comes from God, an angel, or a prophet. It is a human construct, and as such it requires the validation of others. The Temple Scroll (11Q19) LXI, 2–4 addresses the issue in the context of discerning true and false prophecy: "How shall we recognize that which the Lord has not spoken? When a prophet speaks in the name of the Lord but the prophecy is not fulfilled and does not come to pass, that is a prophecy I have not spoken."[26] This is based on Deut 18:20–22: "If a prophet speaks in the name of the Lord but the thing does not take place or prove true, it is a word that the Lord has not spoken" (v. 22 NRSV).

---

23. Translation from Timothy H. Lim, *The Earliest Commentary on the Prophecy of Habakkuk* (Oxford: Oxford University Press, forthcoming).

24. See ibid.

25. Cohen states that the books of Joshua to Kings and virtually all the Writings except Daniel did not claim to be inspired by God (*From the Maccabees to the Mishnah*, 180).

26. Michael Wise, Martin Abegg Jr., and Edward Cook, *The Dead Sea Scrolls: A New Translation* (New York: HarperSanFrancisco, 1996), 488.

10   *When Texts Are Canonized*

Discerning predictive prophecy is a relatively straightforward matter. If the prediction does not come to pass, then the prophecy was clearly wrong. Most prophetic material, however, is not predictive in nature. It does not have an outcome that could be tested and verified. It includes criticisms of the sacrificial cult, the priesthood, the king, and other prophets and consists of admonitions and proclamations of judgment.[27] False prophecy in the biblical texts is determined by the source of the prophets' authority, their message of peace and security over against the impending judgment, and their punishment by God.

But how did the ancients distinguish one kind of prophecy from another? True prophecy is whatever the community determines it to be. The subjectivity implicit in the concept of divine inspiration is raised by the author of 2 Peter in the context of its polemic against "the false teachers." Second Peter purports to be a letter written by Peter to the churches just before his death (1:14). It is often described as a "catholic" letter. It is better understood as a fictionalized testament written by a hellenized Jew who was among Peter's associates in Rome, the letter dating to anywhere between 60 and 120 CE. [28] It is a polemical document that responds to teachers and their disciples who were skeptical about the return of Jesus Christ while the apostles were still alive (3:4). These opponents argued that the parousia remained unfulfilled and that the apostles who preached the return of Jesus had devised myths to support their claim. The prophetic prooftexts adduced to support this claim, so the opponents argued, were not divinely inspired. Rather, they derive from misguided attempts by men who believed that they were the recipients of divine revelation.

To this charge, 2 Peter argues, "no prophecy of scripture is a matter of one's own interpretation [πᾶσα προφητεία γραφῆς ἰδίας ἐπιλύσεως οὐ γίνεται], because no prophecy ever came by human will, but men moved by the Holy Spirit spoke from God" (1:20–21). This passage has been variously interpreted, either as a sentiment regarding contemporary prophecy (cf. 3:16) or as a statement about the origin of biblical prophecy. Does ἴδιος refer to "one's own" or to the biblical prophet's interpretation? Is ἐπίλυσις ever used to refer to the interpretation of scripture, or is it always used for an interpretation of visions and oracles? Both explanations are possible. Second Peter expresses a sentiment found elsewhere about biblical prophecy, namely, that it comes from the prompting of the divine. In my view, it is this similarity that tips the balance in favor of the explanation that the divine origin of biblical prophecy is being discussed.

Philo says the same thing in several places; the closest parallel to

---

27. See now Stéphanie Anthonioz, *Le prophétisme biblique: De l'idéal à la réalité*, LD 261 (Paris: Cerf, 2013).

28. See most recently Jörg Frey, *Der Brief des Judas und der Zweite Brief des Petrus*, THKNT 15.2 (Leipzig: Evangelische Verlagsanstalt, 2015).

An Indicative Definition of the Canon   11

2 Peter occurs in his comment on Gen 20:7 and the prophetic status of Abraham: "For a prophet utters [ἀποφθέγγεται] nothing that is his own [ἴδιον οὐδέν], but everything he utters belongs to another [ἀλλότρια], since another is prompting him [ὑπηχοῦντος ἑτέρου]" (*Her.* 259; my translation).

Both Philo and 2 Peter express the view found in the biblical prophecies that the true prophet, in contrast to the false prophet, does not speak by his own compulsion but is prompted to utter his words by God. As the prophet Amos said, אריה שאג מי לא יירא אדני יהוה דבר מי לא ינבא ("The Lion has roared who will not fear? The LORD has spoken, who can but prophesy?" Amos 3:8).

Second Peter 1:20–21 concerns the divine origin of biblical prophetic writings, not the interpretation of true or false prophecy that is current in the church of the first century. "They [i.e. the opponents] rejected the authority of OT prophecy," stated Richard Bauckham, "by denying its divine origin."[29] Those disparaged as "false teachers" by the author of 2 Peter were skeptical about the claim of the return of Jesus. Their argument is based not on the interpretation of the biblical prooftexts that were adduced but on the authenticity of the biblical prophecy itself. According to the false teachers, the prophecies were of human, not divine, origin and therefore could not be trusted to testify to the return of Jesus.

Second Peter's polemic against its opponents does not so much resolve the subjectivity inherent in the perception of authentic biblical prophecy as highlight it. One might be tempted to adopt the perspective of 2 Peter and its accusation that the opponents are indeed "false teachers" whose views are to be rejected. But to do so would be to privilege the canonical viewpoint as a historical explanation.

Validation of the Community

The determination of authentic prophecy is a subjective judgment that does not admit objective evaluation.[30] The authentication of divine inspiration is determined by a group of people, a church, a synagogue, and a community. This pattern of divine inspiration and validation is evident in the giving of the law on Mount Sinai and is subsequently repeated in the process that eventually led to the canonization of the biblical texts. On Mount Sinai, Moses conveyed all that Yahweh had said to him and wrote it down in a document (ספר) and read it out loud in the hearing of the people (Exod 24:3–7). The people affirmed the truth of the divine words and

---

29. Richard Bauckham, *Jude, 2 Peter*, WBC 50 (Dallas: Word, 1983), 235.

30. Cohen states, "Whether or not this belief [i.e., that the books of the Tanak were revealed or inspired by God] is correct is a question that a historian cannot answer" (*From the Maccabees to the Mishnah*, 178).

12   *When Texts Are Canonized*

declared that they will be obeyed. This same pattern was repeated in the postexilic period when Ezra read out to all the assembled people before the Water Gate the book of the *tôrâ* of Moses. The people stood up and affirmed all that they heard with "Amen, Amen" (Neh 8:1–6). In the second century, the Alexandrian Jewish community accepted the translation of the Hebrew rolls into Greek by reenacting "the Sinai pattern." Then, using the so-called canonical formula *non addetis, neque auferetis* ("do not add, nor take away"), the community pronounced a curse against anyone who would change what has been written down.[31]

Divine inspiration has the semblance of an absolute criterion. That which has been transmitted by divine inspiration carries with it the explicit authority of God. If God revealed it, then surely it must be authoritative. Yet, as we have seen, divine inspiration is constructed both by the text or its author and by the community that affirms its authenticity. The power of constructing this authority lies squarely with the community. Inspiration does not necessarily lead to a place in the canon, since the claim of divine inspiration by someone requires the affirmation by another. Both the claim and validation of divine inspiration are human constructs. They are subjective and define that which is authoritative and canonical for each community. This is why not all writings considered inspired are canonical.

Family Resemblances

The definition of the canon is better explained by indicative rather than criterial logic. Indicative logic points to the fact that a group of texts (such as the Pentateuch and books of the prophets), authoritative in various ways, eventually came to be included in the canon. It does not require that this group of texts meet certain external criteria that other texts do not meet. The features of this group of texts are not sufficient and necessary; their characteristics can also be found in other texts (e.g., Jubilees, 1 Enoch, the Temple Scroll), and their distinctive attributes are not constitutive of the definition of the canon.

A good way of thinking about these factors is to appeal to the biological analogy of the genetic makeup (DNA code) that manifests itself in the physical attributes of a family. Individual characteristics or traits are not all the same in a family, but the genetic information for eye, hair, and skin color; the shape of the nose, face, and head; and height and body type are passed on and contribute to family resemblances. Each familial characteristic (e.g., blue eye color) could also be found in others who are

---

31. For the ecclesiastical use of the formula, see Willem C. van Unnik, "De la regle μήτε προσθεῖναι μήτε ἀφελεῖν dans l'histoire du canon," *VC* 3 (1949): 1–36.

An Indicative Definition of the Canon   13

not biologically related to the family. Similar combinations of physical characteristics, usually among the same ethnic group, could result in coincidental family resemblances.

The concept of family resemblances was used by the analytic philosopher Ludwig Wittgenstein as an analogy for the unbound concept of language, which he compares to a game (*Sprachspiel*).[32] Wittgenstein argues that language as such cannot be defined but is used in narrowly circumscribed contexts that nonetheless make sense. He uses numerous examples from daily life to illustrate his nonessentialist and indicative logic. For instance, if someone were to say, "Playing a game consists in moving objects about on a surface according to certain rules," one could infer that the person is thinking of board games in particular, not all games in general (§3). Other examples include describing an object by its appearance or measurement, making up a story, telling a joke, or translating from one language into another. These are conventional human activities more than they are strict and definite systems of communication. They do not admit an essentialist definition of *game*.

Wittgenstein rejects definitions based on sufficient and necessary conditions. There is no need to look for an essential meaning of a word.

> For someone might object against me: "You make things easy for yourself! You talk about all sorts of language-games, but have nowhere said what is essential to a language-game, and so to language [*was denn das Wesentliche des Sprachspiels, und also der Sprache, ist*]: what is common to all these activities, and makes them into language or parts of language.... Instead of pointing out something common to all that we call language, I'm saying that these phenomena have no one thing in common in virtue of which we use the same word for all—but there are many different kinds of *affinity* [*verwandt*] between them. (§65)

One should follow the word's various and complex uses. Wittgenstein advocates the concept of family resemblances as an alternative to describing these regular language games: "I can think of no better expression to characterize these similarities than 'family resemblances' [*Familienähnlichkeiten*]; for the various resemblances between members of a family: build, features, colour of eyes, gait, temperament, etc. etc. overlap and criss-cross in the same way." (§67)

Wittgenstein does not use criterial logic. His reasoning is based on "showing" or "pointing to" particular samples as indicative of the "schema." He discusses the procedure in the naming of colors and leaves:

---

32. Ludwig Wittgenstein, *Philosophical Investigations: The German Text, with a Revised English Translation*, ed. and trans. Gertrude E. M. Anscombe; rev. 4th ed. by P. M. S. Hacker and Joachim Schulte (Oxford: Wiley-Blackwell, 2009), §23. All English translations cited in the following are from this edition.

14   *When Texts Are Canonized*

When someone explains the names of colours to me by pointing at samples [*zeigt auf Muster*] and saying, "This colour is called 'blue', this 'green' ... ," this case can be compared in many respects to handing me a chart with the words written under the colour samples. — Though this comparison may mislead in many ways. — One is now inclined to extend the comparison: to have understood the explanation means to have in one's mind an idea of the thing explained, and that is a sample or picture. So if I'm shown various leaves and told "This is called a 'leaf,'" I get an idea of the shape of a leaf, a picture of it in my mind. — But what does the picture of a leaf look like when it does not show us any particular shape, but rather "what is common to all shapes of leaf"? What shade is the "sample in my mind" of the colour green — the sample of what is common to all shades of green?

"But might there not be such 'general' samples? Say a schematic leaf, or a sample of *pure* green?" — Certainly! But for such a schema to be understood as a *schema*, and not as the shape of a particular leaf, and for a snippet of pure green to be understood as a sample of all that is greenish, and not as a sample of pure green — this in turn resides in the way the samples are applied. (§73)

Wittgenstein discusses the cognitive link between a sample of a color and part of a plant with the "schema" or general form of green and leaf, a concept he derived from Plato, but he was no Platonist. To understand the universal depends on how the particular is applied. The schema of a leaf or the color green depends on how a particular leaf or color of green is understood.

Wittgenstein's logic is indicative, "showing" or "pointing to" (*zeigen*) particular samples. This procedure is applied to the explanation of a game.

Consider this further case: I am explaining chess to someone; and I begin by pointing to a chess piece and saying [*ich auf eine Figur zeige und sage*], "This is the king; it can move in this-and-this way," and so on. — In this case we shall say: the words "This is is the king" (or "This is called 'the king'") are an explanation of a word only if the learner already "knows what a piece in a game is." That is, if, for example, he has already played other games, or has watched "with understanding" how other people play — *and similar things.* Only then will he, while learning the game, be able to ask relevantly, "What is this called?" — that is, this chess piece. (§31)

Indicative logic is, then, applied to the definition of a game.

What does it mean to know what a game is? What does it mean to know it and not be able to say it? Is this knowledge somehow equivalent to an unformulated definition? So that if it were formulated, I'd be able to recognize it as the expression of my knowledge? Isn't my knowledge, my concept of a game, completely expressed in the explanations that I could give? That is, in my describing the examples of various kinds of game,

showing [*zeige*] how all sorts of other games can be constructed on the analogy of these, saying that I would hardly call this or that a game, and so on. (§75)

An indicative definition points to the family resemblances that are shared among the books that were eventually included in the canon. The features of this family of texts are not unique but may be found elsewhere among other noncanonical texts. The fact that this rather than another group of authoritative texts was eventually canonized is neither a necessary nor a sufficient condition. It was not inevitable, yet it is meaningful and significant.

Indicative Logic and the Canon in the First Century

Indicative logic is the reasoning that points to a phenomenon as a form of definition. The combination of affinities in a phenomenon is deemed to be significant. Indicative logic can be used to analyze the canonical list of the twenty-two-book canon in the first century.[33] As is well known, Josephus articulates a set of books, properly described as "canonical," that is distinguished from other books by the criterion of prophetic succession. He does not define the canon but is following the tradition of the Pharisees.[34] The distinction that he draws is formal, since he uses biblical and nonbiblical sources in the same way in writing his history of the Jewish people. He recognizes that the books of the canon are distinctive, but he does not probe the nature of the prophetic criterion that he uses to distinguish them from other books. I suggest that indicative logic can explain both the books of the canon and the other sources that he uses in writing his *Antiquities of the Jews*.

In *Against Apion* 1.38–41, Josephus writes:

[A]mong us there are not thousands of books in disagreement and conflict with each other, but only twenty-two books, containing the record of all time, which are rightly trusted. Five of these are the books of Moses, which contain both the laws and the tradition from the birth of humanity up to his death; this is a period of a little less than 3,000 years. From the death of Moses until Artaxerxes, king of the Persians after Xerxes, the prophets after Moses wrote the history of what took place in their own times in thirteen books; the remaining four books contain hymns to God and instructions for people on life. From Artaxerxes up to our own time

---

33. It is generally agreed that 4 Ezra has a public canon of twenty-four books that is the same as Josephus's twenty-two-book canon, except for the slightly different counting of some of the constituent books (see my *Formation of the Jewish Canon*, ch. 3).

34. See my "A Theory of the Majority Canon," *ExpTim* 124.8 (2013): 365–73.

16   *When Texts Are Canonized*

every event has been recorded, but this is not judged worthy of the same trust, since the exact line of succession of the prophets did not continue.[35]

Josephus states polemically against his detractors that, unlike the multitude of conflicting Greek histories, there are only twenty-two trustworthy books of the Jews that contain the record of "all time," divided into five books of Moses, thirteen books of the prophets, and four books of hymns and instructions. This history of a little less than three thousand years spans the period from the death of Moses to the reign of the king Artaxerxes. From the Persian period to Josephus's own time, every event has been recorded, but the books were not included on the list because they were not judged to have been "worthy of the same trust, since the exact line of succession of the prophets did not continue."

In practice, however, the canonical and noncanonical books are not treated differently by Josephus in his recounting of the narrative of the Jewish people. In his *Antiquities of the Jews*, Josephus uses the biblical texts but also the Letter of Aristeas, Esdras, and 1 Maccabees to complete the narrative. In his history (*A.J.*), he paraphrases new sources as well as his own earlier work, *Bellum judaicum* (*B.J.*).[36]

Josephus draws a distinction between the books by pointing to the inexact prophetic succession of the noncanonical books. The reason that he gives is debated. Some understand it as a criterion of canonization.[37] Others interpret it as an idealization of the greater authenticity of ancient prophets rather than a belief that prophecy had ended. This nostalgia evokes a sentiment that prophecy continued, but it was just not the same as before.[38]

In fact, there is no need to choose between the two options. Given what Josephus says about prophecy and the so-called sign prophets elsewhere in his writings, his statement to some extent must have been an expression of the wistful affection for a bygone age.[39] Josephus himself reports that prophecy did continue, but he must have considered these

---

35. Josephus, *Against Apion*, translation and commentary by John M. G. Barclay, Flavius Josephus, Translation and Commentary 10 (Leiden: Brill, 2007), 29–30.

36. See Shaye J. D. Cohen, *Josephus in Galilee and Rome: His Vita and Development as a Historian* (Leiden: Brill, 2002), 24–48.

37. See. e.g., Dominique Barthélemy, who holds that the belief in the cessation or interruption of prophecy can be traced back to the second century BCE ("L'état de la Bible juive depuis le début de notre ère jusqu'à la deuxième révolte contre Rome (131–135)," in *Le Canon de l'Ancien Testament: Sa formation et son histoire*, ed. Jean-Daniel Kaestli and Otto Wermelinger, MdB 10 [Geneva: Labor et Fides, 1984], 22–23).

38. In highlighting the importance of the prophetic succession, Josephus is expressing a belief that the prophets of old were somehow closer to God and therefore more trustworthy (so Rebecca Gray, *Prophetic Figures in Late Second Temple Jewish Palestine: The Evidence from Josephus* [Oxford: Oxford University Press, 1993], 12).

39. Most were unnamed, but each of them was clearly a prophet who attempted a sign

An Indicative Definition of the Canon   17

prophets inferior since they are without an exact line of succession (διὰ τὸ μὴ γενέσθαι τὴν τῶν προφητῶν ἀκριβῆ διαδοχήν).

He also uses inexact prophetic succession as a criterion to distinguish the canonical from the noncanonical books, but in practice he treats them no differently. Josephus uses the Greek term ἡ ἀναγραφή forty-two times in his writings to mean "the record." In *Ag. Ap.* 1.38, he states that only the twenty-two books provide "a record of all time" and are rightly trusted (δύο δὲ μόνα πρὸς τοῖς εἴκοσι βιβλία τοῦ παντὸς ἔχοντα χρόνου τὴν ἀναγραφήν, τὰ δικαίως πεπιστευμένα). From Artaxerxes to his own day, Josephus notes that every event has been recorded, "but this is not judged worthy of the same trust as those before them" (πίστεως δ' οὐχ ὁμοίας ἠξίωται τοῖς πρὸ αὐτῶν). And yet he uses them in completing his history. They too provide a record of the history of the Jewish people, just as the biblical texts did for the earlier period. These extrabiblical sources are no different in kind from the biblical texts, except that Josephus judges them not to be worthy of "the same trust." The sense in which they are less trustworthy is not explained.

Josephus tried to account for the distinctiveness of the twenty-two-book canon by pointing to supposed qualitative differences of trustworthiness between the biblical and extrabiblical texts. But this form of prophetic authentication is not a criterion at all, as we have discussed. It is subjective and constructed by the community. Josephus follows Greek historical practices and uses the sources without discriminating between biblical and nonbiblical material for trustworthiness. He received the twenty-two books as a canonical corpus, but he could not successfully account for their distinctiveness.

Indicative logic explains both the canonical books and the noncanonical books that Josephus uses. There are family resemblances in the laws and traditions that are found in the five books of Moses that provide a connected history from "the birth of humanity" to the lawgiver's death. According to Josephus, the prophets likewise wrote the history of their own times in thirteen books. He does not enumerate which books they are.[40] The second category of prophets could apply to the books of Joshua to Kings in the traditional order of the Jewish canon, but it is less clear how the oracles of the prophets of Isaiah, Jeremiah, Ezekiel, and twelve prophets constitute history. To be sure, each of these prophecies was written at a particular time and place, and some include historical elements; but they are not "history" in the way that the books of Joshua to Kings narrate the conquest, the period of the judges, the rise and fall of the united monarchy, and the period of the divided kingdoms. These books are neverthe-

---

in the presence of the masses and at a particular place. See Paul Barnett, "Jewish Sign Prophets—A.D. 40–70," *NTS* 27 (1981): 679–97.

40. Various suggestions have been made about which books make up the twenty-two-book canon (see, my *Formation of the Jewish Canon*, 44–45).

18   *When Texts Are Canonized*

less grouped together. The four remaining books in the third category do not provide any history; they contain hymns and ethical teachings. Yet Josephus includes them under the rubric of "history."

Josephus used criterial logic with mixed success to distinguish between canonical and noncanonical books. He might have been better able to account for them by conceiving of biblical and nonbiblical books according to family resemblances. Biblical texts have affinities one with another as a family of texts, and they coincidentally resemble books that were not included in the canon.

Indicative Logic and the Canonical Process

Indicative logic is also implied in the study of authoritative texts that evidence the formation of the canon, although I am unaware of anyone who has explicitly discussed this in relation to the concept of blurred definitions and family resemblances.[41] The concept of family resemblances is assumed in much of the work on orality and scripturalization of traditional material: a group of texts, sharing similarities that are not unique to them, was nevertheless regarded as worthy of being copied, commented on, updated, and transmitted and was instantiated in the canonical process.[42]

The process that led to the canonization of the Hebrew Bible is complex and included various factors, both external and internal, that are indicative of its formation and constitution. I have suggested elsewhere that there were different collections of authoritative texts used by the various Jewish communities before the Pharisaic canon became the majority canon of Rabbinic Judaism. These collections shared a common core of the Pentateuch with or without a loosely defined corpus of prophetic texts. The impetus of collecting and defining the authoritative books arose from the outside as Jews elevated the law as part of the Persian policy of provincial governance in the Achaemenid period. Other outside factors include

---

41. The metaphor of family resemblances has long been used by text critics to describe the family of text types, "bad genes," and so on. See now Yii-Jan Lin, *The Erotic Life of Manuscripts. New Testament Textual Criticism and the Biological Sciences* (Oxford: Oxford University Press, 2016), who investigates the epistemological underpinnings of the use of the biological metaphor in textual criticism.

42. See, inter alios, Michael Fishbane, *Biblical Interpretation in Ancient Israel* (Oxford: Clarendon, 1986); Philip R. Davies, *Scribes and Schools: The Canonization of the Hebrew Scriptures*, LAI (London: SPCK, 1998); Lim, "Origins and Emergence"; William M. Schniedewind, *How the Bible Became a Book: The Textualization of Ancient Israel* (Cambridge: Cambridge University Press, 2005); and David M. Carr, *Writing on the Tablet of the Heart: Origins of Scripture and Literature* (Oxford: Oxford University Press, 2009); and Carr, *The Formation of the Hebrew Bible: A New Reconstruction* (Oxford: Oxford University Press, 2011).

An Indicative Definition of the Canon   19

the standardization of the Homeric epics as "the Bible of the Greeks" in Alexandria and the emergence of the writings of the Christians.[43]

There were also internal factors. Texts were increasingly used to support the development of Jewish religion before and after the exile. The observance of laws and rituals, both at the Temple and in the family home, required the textualization and scripturalization of the traditional teachings. These teachings, once committed to writing, themselves became the object of interpretation and comment.

Several books recount the story from creation to the election of the patriarchs, the emergence of the people of Israel, the conquest of Canaan, the period of the judges, the establishment of the monarchy, the division of the monarchy and the eventual fall to the Babylonians, the exile of the Judeans, and the subsequent restoration in the Persian period. Whether one wishes to call this "credo," "confessional recital," "myth," or simply "the story of Israel," the origins of the people of God appear in several texts to support various aims.[44] The story of Israel is rehearsed in texts of the Second Temple period: for instance, in the call to separate from foreigners (Neh 9:6–14), in the idealization of the Davidic kingship (Chronicles), in the praise of the fathers of old (Sir 44–50), in the admonition of sectarian leaders to follow Jewish law correctly (4QMMT, section C), in the first-century canonical notice (Josephus, *Ag. Ap.* 1.38–41), and in the definition of faith (Heb 11).

The Deuteronomist prescribes the recitation of the narrative as part of the ritual of the firstfruits (Deut 26).

> 4 When the priest takes the basket from your hand and sets it down before the altar of the Lord your God, 5 you shall make this response before the Lord your God: "A wandering Aramean was my ancestor; he went down into Egypt and lived there as an alien, few in number, and there he became a great nation, mighty and populous. 6 When the Egyptians treated us harshly and afflicted us, by imposing hard labor on us, 7 we cried to the Lord, the God of our ancestors; the Lord heard our voice and saw our affliction, our toil, and our oppression. 8 The Lord brought us out of Egypt with a mighty hand and an outstretched arm, with a terrifying display of power, and with signs and wonders; 9 and he brought us into this place and gave us this land, a land flowing with milk and honey. (NRSV)

---

43. See my *Formation of the Jewish Canon.*

44. James Sanders, "Adaptable for Life: The Nature and Function of Canon," in *Magnalia Dei, The Mighty Acts of God: Essays on the Bible and Archaeology in Memory of G. Ernest Wright*, ed. Frank M. Cross, Werner E. Lemke, and Patrick D. Miller (New York: Doubleday, 1976), 531–60; David M. Carr, "Canonization in the Context of Community: An Outline of the Formation of the Tanak and the Christian Bible," in *A Gift of God in Due Season: Essays on Scripture and Community in Honor of James A. Sanders*, JSOTSup 225 (Sheffield: Sheffield Academic Press, 1996), 22–64.

20   *When Texts Are Canonized*

Gerhard von Rad famously described this and other passages as traditional material, a "credo," and reconstructed their origins within the setting of cultic worship. According to him, the original story of Israel in the Hexateuch did not include the giving of the law on Mount Sinai. The Sinaitic covenant of the Mosaic law was a secondary and later insertion into the book of Exodus.[45]

Von Rad was influenced by Julius Wellhausen's thesis of the regression of Israelite religion from prophecy to law, which is still important in Old Testament scholarship today.[46] Von Rad's reconstruction suffers from a number of difficulties: (1) verses 4–9 should not be extracted from its Deuteronomic context;[47] (2) his reconstruction depends upon a priori assumptions underlying his source-critical judgments of key biblical texts;[48] and (3) he does not give due weight to the various biblical contexts in reconstructing the core creed and its subsequent embellishments.[49]

Despite these caveats, it is widely agreed that von Rad's thesis identifies traditional material and accounts for the ways by which it was transmitted within Israel. The recitation of the story of Israel was an important factor in the canonical process. James Sanders built on von Rad's thesis and showed that the canon functions "to provide indications of identity as well as the life-style of the on-going community which reads it."[50] It had a pedagogical function in reminding generations of Israelites of the salvific acts of Yahweh and provided the rationale for the observance of the divine law.

---

45. Gerhard von Rad, *The Problem of the Hexateuch and Other Essays* (London: SCM, 1958), 7: "the events of Sinai are completely overlooked."

46. Von Rad, *Problem of the Hexateuch*, 14. This is not the place to offer a critique. An alternative history of Israel was advanced by Yehezkel Kaufmann (*The Religion of Israel: From Its Beginnings to the Babylonian Exile*, trans. Moshe Greenberg [London: Allen & Unwin, 1961]) that challenged, among other things, Wellhausen's dating of P to the postexilic period. See now Aly Elrefaei, *Wellhausen and Kaufmann: Ancient Israel and Its Religious History in the Works of Julius Wellhausen and Yehezkel Kaufmann*, BZAW 490 (Berlin: de Gruyter, 2016).

47. Calum Carmichael argues that Deuteronomy is compiling this creed for the first time, using the incident at Kadesh as a model (Deut 1; Num 13:20) ("A New View of the Deuteronomic Credo," *VT* 19 [1969]: 273-89).

48. Von Rad's argument, for instance, that there is no allusion to the events of Sinai in Exod 15 is based on the view that the poem was a cultic litany (*Problem of the Hexateuch*, 10–11). In the context of book, however, the Israelites have not yet arrived at Sinai, so it would make no sense to have a reference to an event that has yet to occur in the narrative.

49. A. D. H. Mayes, *Deuteronomy*, NCB (Grand Rapids: Eerdmans, 1979), 332–33; and Jan Christian Gertz, "Die Stellung des kleinen geschichtlichen Credos in der Redaktionsgeschichte von Deuteronomium und Pentateuch," in *Liebe und Gebot: Studien zum Deuteronomium*, ed. Reinhard G. Kratz and Hermann Spieckermann, FRLANT 190 (Göttingen: Vandenhoeck & Ruprecht, 2000), 30–45.

50. Sanders, "Adaptable for Life," 537.

When your children ask you in time to come, "What is the meaning of the decrees and the statutes and the ordinances that the LORD our God has commanded you?" 21 then you shall say to your children, "We were Pharaoh's slaves in Egypt, but the LORD brought us out of Egypt with a mighty hand. 22 The LORD displayed before our eyes great and awesome signs and wonders against Egypt, against Pharaoh and all his household. 23 He brought us out from there in order to bring us in, to give us the land that he promised on oath to our ancestors. 24 Then the LORD commanded us to observe all these statutes, to fear the LORD our God, for our lasting good, so as to keep us alive, as is now the case. 25 If we diligently observe this entire commandment before the LORD our God, as he has commanded us, we will be in the right." (Deut 6:20–25)

Joshua recites the same story in the covenant at Shechem. The people should serve the God of Israel, and not the gods of the Amorites, because Yahweh not only gave his people a land on which they did not labor, towns that they had not built, and the vineyards and olive groves that they had not planted, but he also had actively sought and protected the ancestors from the time that they left Ur of the Chaldees (Josh 24:2–13).

The same story is found in the earliest prophecies (e.g., Amos 2:9–11, 3:1–2, 4:10–11, 5:25, 9:7), in the history of the period of the Judges (e.g., Judg 2:1, 6:8–9:1) and in various psalms (e.g., Pss 78, 105, 106, 135, 136).[51] Not all elements appear in each version. Some begin with the exodus from Egypt; others start from the migration of Terah; and still others begin from creation. The variation affects the number and specific events mentioned. Some texts include the conquest and settlement of Israel in the promised land, and others confine themselves to the Yahweh's saving actions against the Egyptian army (Exod 15). The retelling of the story occurs at set times and on religious occasions (e.g., on Pesach, Exod 12; 13:15; on Sukkot, Neh 9). "It is clear," stated David Carr, "that such recognition of authority is community based, and as such involves significant debate around issues of authority of different types of texts, coordination of the authority of these different types, and the bearing of these texts on issues of central community concern."[52] The story of Israel is adapted to different textual and social contexts according to the needs of the community. Or, as Brevard Childs aptly sums up the canonical process, it "reflects an involvement which actively shaped both the oral and written traditions."[53]

---

51. See recently, Anja Klein, *Geschichte und Gebet: Die Rezeption der biblischen Geschichte in den Psalmen des Alten Testaments*, FAT 94 (Tübingen: Mohr Siebeck, 2014).

52. Carr. "Canonization in the Context of Community," 34.

53. Childs, *Introduction to the Old Testament*, 78.

22   *When Texts Are Canonized*

The Davidic Factor

Another contributing factor in the canonical process is the association of a text with the life and/or authorship of David. This can be seen in the way that scribes placed short notes at the head of some thirteen psalms (e.g., Pss 3, 34, 40, 51, 52, 54, 63). These secondary superscriptions are exegetical and refer to events in the life of David.[54] The increasing importance of the figure of David in the Second Temple period meant that a text gained greater authority by its association with the legendary king of Israel.

Moreover, some thirty-seven psalms claim Davidic authorship, using the so-called *lamed auctoris* מזמור לדוד (e.g., Pss 3, 12, 31, 68, 143).[55] The phrase should be translated as "by David" and is a statement of authorship rather than of possession. Implied is the view that Davidic authorship gives greater authority to the psalms. The attribution of Davidic authorship in these psalms should be seen as part of a trend in the Second Temple period of assigning the authorship of numerous psalms and songs to the greatest figure of Israel's monarchic past. The Great Psalm Scroll claims Davidic authorship for 3,600 psalms, 52 songs of the Sabbath offerings, 30 songs for festivals and holy days, and 4 songs for the stricken, a total of 4,050 compositions (11QPs^a XXVII, 2–11). Not all psalms that claim Davidic authorship were included in the canon, but those that were canonized frequently had this association.[56] Proverbs' attribution of authorship to "Solomon, son of David, King of Israel," is consistent with the Davidic factor, as is the putative authorship of the Song of Songs; and the book of Ruth anticipates the line of David in its epilogue.

Neither Necessary Nor Sufficient

The transmission of the story of Israel is an important factor in the canonical process. It was neither necessary nor sufficient. Not all texts that

---

54. See Brevard S. Childs, "Psalm Titles and Midrashic Exegesis," *JSS* 16 (1971): 137–50; Gene M. Tucker, "Prophetic Superscriptions and the Growth of a Canon," in *Canon and Authority: Essays in Old Testament Religion and Theology*, ed. George W. Coats and Burke O. Long (Philadelphia: Fortress, 1977), 56–70; Frank-Lothar Hossfeld and Eric Zenger, "Thoughts on the 'Davidization' of the Psalter," in Steinberg and Stone, *Shape of the Writings*, 119-30.

55. Albert Pietersma showed that לדוד was consistently translated in the Old Greek as τω δανιδ but was changed in the course of transmission to του δανιδ in order to clarify the Davidic authorship ("David in the Greek Psalms," *VT* 30 [1980]: 213–26). M. Kleer has argued that the portrayal of David in the books of Samuel was the impetus for the "Davidization" of the Psalter (*"Der liebliche Sänger der Psalmen Israels": Untersuchungen zu David als Dichter und Beter der Psalmen*, BBB 108 [Bodenheim: Philo, 1996]).

56. See my "All These He Composed through Prophecy," in *Prophecy after the Prophets? The Contribution of the Dead Sea Scrolls to the Understanding of Biblical and Extra-Biblical Prophecy*, ed. Armin Lange and Kristin de Troyer, CBET 52 (Leuven: Peeters, 2010), 61–76.

An Indicative Definition of the Canon 23

recounted the story were canonized. Conversely, not all texts that were canonized included the story; those that did not have the story of Israel must have been canonized for other disputed reasons. The rabbis continued to argue about the canonical status of Qohelet, Song of Songs, Ben Sira, Ezekiel, Ruth, and Proverbs well into the second century of the common era and beyond.[57]

The story of Israel was retold at set times and on religious and pedagogical occasions. The overwhelming majority of the texts that were eventually included in the canon contributed to this story, and it has been argued that that indicative canon is significant. The origins of the people of Israel are narrated in the Pentateuch, from Genesis to Deuteronomy. The story of Israel during the conquest, settlement, and monarchy are found in the books of Joshua, Judges, Samuel, and Kings and are retold and extended to the postexilic period in the book of Chronicles. The book of Ezra-Nehemiah overlaps with Chronicles and relates the return of the exiles to the Persian province of Yehud, the rebuilding of the Temple, and the restarting of the cultic worship.

Appended to this story of Israel are episodes of heroic acts of individuals:[58] the book of Ruth tells the story of a significant moment during the period of the judges when a Moabite woman becomes an Israelite and the mother of the Davidic kings; the book of Daniel recounts the wondrous exploits of a law-abiding Judean exile and his three companions in the royal court of the Babylonian kings; and the book of Esther valorizes the courageous efforts of a Jewish virgin who foils a murderous plot against the Jews in the court of the Persian king Ahasuerus.

Not all Jewish communities accepted these stories of individual heroism. Esther, as is well known, is absent from the collections of the Dead Sea Scrolls, which may indicate that the book was not considered author-

---

57. Philip Davies warned of the teleological fallacy in assuming the inevitable growth of the canon ("Loose Canons: Reflections on the Formation of the Hebrew Bible," in *Perspectives on Hebrew Scriptures: Comprising the Contents of the Journal of Hebrew Scriptures, vols. 1–4*, ed. Ehud Ben Zvi [Piscataway, NJ: Gorgias, 2006], 57). But earlier collections of authoritative Scriptures do to a large extent overlap with the lists of books in Josephus, 4 Ezra, Mishnah Yadayim, the church fathers, and Baba Batra (see my *Formation of the Jewish Canon*, 187). Eva Mroczek offers a critique of canon research and its supposedly anachronistic categories of "Bible" and "bibliography" ("The Hegemony of the Biblical in the Study of Second Temple Literature," *JAJ* 6 (2015): 2–35; and Mroczek, *The Literary Imagination in Jewish Antiquity* [Oxford: Oxford University Press, 2016]). I do not know anyone who has argued the concept of "bibliography" in canon research. She means "book." The irony of an overtly postmodern critique of the putative anachronism of previous scholarship seems to have been lost, as she underplays the centrality of the biblical texts in Second Temple–period literature.

58. According to the b. B. Bat. 14a–15b, Job lived in the days of Moses. Many of the prophetic books could also be assigned to a period in the history of Israel (e.g., Jeremiah in the period before and during the exile; Ezekiel in the exilic period; Zechariah and Haggai in the postexilic period; and so on).

itative. Instead, there are other stories of the Persian court included in the collections. The book of Daniel attracted further stories whose canonical status is debatable, one of which was the subject of a dispute between Africanus and Origen.[59]

The figure of David becomes an important factor in conferring authoritative status in the late Second Temple period. Several of the psalms are ascribed to the life and/or authorship of David. This Davidic factor is likewise not a necessary or sufficient condition for texts to be included in the canon. Its presence, however, among canonical texts of the psalms cannot be ignored.

Conclusions

In the foregoing discussion, I proposed rethinking the canonical process. I suggest that one cannot account for the books included in the canon by the use of a set of criteria. The search for criteria should give way to a different way of thinking, an indicative logic that is nonessentialist. The indicative definition points to a set of texts that came to be included in the canon without having to meet the criterion of uniqueness. Drawing on the game theory of analytical philosophy, I have suggested that the concept of family resemblances is a useful conceptual tool for thinking about the canon. The biblical books resemble one another in memorializing the history of Israel, and they also resemble other books that do the same but were not included in the canon. The fact that these, and not those, books were canonized is nonetheless significant. The indicative definition of the canon is a formal definition that recognizes that, in the canonical process, a group of texts transmitted the story of Israel and was eventually included on the list of authoritative books.[60]

---

59. Origen, *Sur les écritures: Philocalie 1–20*, ed. and trans. Marguerite Harl; and *La lettre à Africanus sur l'histoire de Suzanne*, ed. and trans. Nicholas de Lange, SC 302 (Paris: Cerf, 1983).

60. I have benefited from discussions on Wittgenstein and divine inspiration with my colleague David Fergusson, OBE. My wife, Laura Lim, has cast her critical eye on the whole argument and given guidance on what I say about family resemblances from a biological point of view.

The Way of God: Early Canonicity and the "Nondeviation Formula"

MANFRED OEMING

Scholarship typically assumes three stages of development regarding the biblical canon. Certain texts came to be regarded as authoritative and were written down. The collection of these authoritative scriptures and their arrangement began to stabilize. Finally, the "closed list of texts" emerged in the period between 400 BCE and 250 CE and set down the "canonical" status of the selected texts. It is this technical definition of the canon as a closed list that has captured scholarly attention, and research has focused primarily or even exclusively on the final stage of canonization.[1] Sustained analyses of the previous stages have been lacking.[2] I want to suggest that, since the technical meaning of the canon did not suddenly spring up nor did it develop in a vacuum, one needs to study the earlier, nontechnical sense of "canonicity," concepts that acted as precursors for or formed the backdrop of the biblical canon, in order to understand the emergence of the biblical canon.[3]

---

1. For terminological issues, see Timothy H. Lim, "Authoritative Scriptures and the Scrolls," in *The Oxford Handbook of the Dead Sea Scrolls*, ed. Timothy H. Lim and John J. Collins (Oxford: Oxford University Press, 2010), 303–22.

2. See, however, Peter Brandt, *Endgestalten des Kanons: Das Arrangement der Schriften Israels in der jüdischen und christlichen Bibel*, BBB 131 (Berlin: Philo, 2001). After an informative evaluation of modern canon research, Luc Zaman rightly observes that "the history of canon research teaches that studies predominantly start … from the perspective of the final phase of the canonization period" (*Bible and Canon: A Modern Historical Inquiry*, SSN 50 [Leiden: Brill, 2008], 207). His arguments are closely related to my own ideas. He argues extensively for the exile as the period of "canonical upsurge" (563). The evidence in Deuteronomistic historiography and Deuteronomistic reworking in prophetic books like Amos or Jeremiah in 560–521 BCE (212–537) confirms this dating. Nevertheless, Zaman also adds some convincing proposals about the oldest stages of the canonical process before the exile, which are visible in law, prophecy, and wisdom traditions (576–96).

3. The study of history has important dogmatic implications. See, e.g., Anton Ziegenaus, *Kanon: Von der Väterzeit bis zur Gegenwart*, Handbuch der Dogmengeschichte 1.3a (Freiburg im Breisgau: Herder, 1990); Donath Hercsik, *Die Grundlagen unseres Glaubens. Eine theologische Prinzipienlehre*, Theologie, Forschung und Wissenschaft 15 (Münster: LIT, 2005);

26   *When Texts Are Canonized*

This paper aims to shed light on the earlier stage of the canonization process. The first part will contend that the need for standardization already existed in preexilic Israel; the idea and the ideal of "Holy Scriptures" were developed before 400 BCE. While the canon as a closed list did not emerge until much later, the need for different "canons" already existed from early on, and multiple *Sitze im Leben* of ancient Israelite society imply this reality. The second part will take a specific formula, namely, the "nondeviation formula" ("do not turn from it to the right hand or to the left"), as a case in point and examine how the various ways in which the formula is applied reflect a neglected history of the biblical canon that needs to be written.

Earliest "Canons" in Material Culture

By the time of the establishment of the state of Judah and certainly under Assyrian and Babylonian imperial influence, discernible standardizations in different areas of material culture took place: measures of length, weight, and capacity were increasingly unified and standardized. Long before κανών became a technical term for a closed list of fixed texts, various "canons" (meaning "steady scales, fixed measures") existed in daily life and were used. Κανών was precisely the object that fulfilled the need for some kind of order or a shared standard in society. The need for some type of a fixed measure or standard did not suddenly appear in Second Temple Judaism but existed much earlier. A few representative examples would suffice to make the point.[4] The oldest example and the perfect visualization of a "canon" is the so-called Nippur-Elle, which is dated to circa 2750 BCE.[5] Other archaeological evidence comes from the time of the Babylonian ruler Nebuchadnezzar II (634–568 BCE). Documents from his time stipulate that one brick should be thirty-two to thirty-three centimeters.[6]

Ulrich H. J. Körtner, *Arbeit am Kanon: Studien zur Bibelhermeneutik* (Leipzig: Evangelische Verlagsanstalt, 2015).

4. On length, see, Rolf C. A. Rottländer, *Antike Längenmaße: Untersuchungen über ihre Zusammenhänge* (Braunschweig: Vieweg & Sohn, 1979). On volume, see Omer Sergi et al, "The Royal Judahite Storage Jar: A Computer-Generated Typology and Its Archaeological and Historical Implications," *TA* 39 (2012): 64–92. On weight, see Raz Kletter, "The Inscribed Weights of the Kingdom of Judah," *TA* 18 (1991): 121–63.

5. The Nippur-Elle is made of copper and measures 110 centimeters in length and weighs 45 kilograms. It is in the archaeological museum of Istanbul today. The *editio princeps* was published by Eckhard Unger, *Die Nippur-Elle: Publikationen der Kaiserlichen Osmanischen Museen, Konstantinopel 1916* (Constantinople: Ihsan, 1916).

6. For a general overview, see Marvin A. Powell, "Masse und Gewichte," in *RlA* 7: 457–530. In the biblical world, the human body represented the unit of measurement; one cubit was approximately 45 to 52 centimeters (royal cubit). Official instruments are not known in Israel and Judah, although we know from the text that there was a מדה (Job 11:9, 28:25) .

The Way of God   27

Measurement units for volume were less unified, although the oval storage jars (i.e., royal Judahite storage jars) reveal a trajectory toward standardization.[7] Most abundant are the remains of standardized weights, which are often inscribed with beca, pim, two shekels and *nṣp*.[8] These various forms of "canon" were crucial for the economy, trade, taxes, and building activities, and they formed the foundation for the later technical meaning. According to the literature of this period, all the different canons are protected by God himself and deviations from these standards are forbidden (e.g., Lev 19:35, Deut 25:15, Amos 8:5, Prov 20:10).[9]

Scribalism, Textual Reception, and Application

When the formation of authoritative texts took place is a question of debate in contemporary research. In my view this happened from the beginning of the establishment of Israel and Judah. Evidence of material standardization is, of course, not an argument for the early emergence of religious writings, but something like "canonization" was part of the increasingly networked society in Israel and Judah. It is fitting to assume that, with the rise of standardized literacy in the ninth century BCE or so,[10] something similar happened with written texts.[11]

---

7. The capacity of a biblical *bat* is not fixed but can range between thirty-nine and fifty-two liters. See Oded Lipschits et al., "The Enigma of the Biblical Bath, and the System of Liquid Volume Measurement during the First Temple Period," *UF* 42 (2011): 453–78. But "in the second stage [of their production], down to the early mid-8th century BCE, they developed gradually, as the standardized jars became more common than the non-standardized jars" (Sergi et al., "Royal Judahite Storage Jar," 88).

8. Abraham Eran, "Weights and Weighing in the City of David: The Early Weights from the Bronze Age to the Persian Period," in *Various Reports*, vol. 4 of *Excavations at the City of David 1978–1985 Directed by Yigal Shiloh*, ed. Donald T. Ariel and Alon de Groot, Qedem 35 (Jerusalem: Institute of Archaeology, Hebrew University of Jerusalem, 1996), 204–56. Curiously, these several concurrent standards of weight testify to the fact that the normalizing standards were linked to specific cultures and confined to certain localities in the ancient world. For example: (1) the southern levant system: 1 talent = 34.272 kg = 50 minas (= 0.57 kg) = 3000 sheqels (= 11.4 g) = 5000 pim (= 7.616 g) = 6000 beca (= 5.712 g) = 60.000 gerah (= 0.571 g); (2) the Babylonian sexagesimal system: 1 talent = 60 minas = 3600 sheqels = 86400 gerah; (3) the Hellenistic-Roman decimal system: 1 talent (41 kg) = 50 minas (818 g) = 2500 sheqels (16.3g).

9. Furthermore, it may be argued that these canons functioned as powerful identity markers, since recognizing and using a particular "canon" over against other ones indicated to which group one belonged. As the old adage states, "tell me what books you think are holy, and I will tell you who you are."

10. See Christopher Rollston, *Writing and Literacy in the World of Ancient Israel: Epigraphic Evidence from the Iron Age*, ABS 11 (Atlanta: Society of Biblical Literature, 2010).

11. Although I recognize that such a hypothesis requires a much more extensive treatment, I detect six important trajectories or streams of theological traditions that began

28   *When Texts Are Canonized*

Within the protracted and complex process of textual formation, scribes in every town contributed in significant ways to the formation of the biblical literature. Scholarship in the nineteenth century tended to attribute the formation of the canon to inspired individuals (e.g., Moses, Solomon, David, Ezra, and a few others) or small groups of elites. Recent insight into the complexity of the process, however, particularly the observation that multiple streams of traditions converged in the biblical canon, repudiates such a characterization of the process.[12] The canon was not an achievement of any single individual but the result of the collective production, interpretation, and selection process that lasted centuries.[13]

Production, however, is only one element of every theory of canonization; the other decisive part is reception and ongoing application. If the writings produced by a multiplicity of authors and scribes did not become meaningful and normative for a much larger group of religious people, they would have been forgotten. The places where these selections and applications took place were various: predominantly in Jerusalem and Samaria but not only in the capitals. By intensive use (in liturgical and pedagogical contexts)[14] a text became "biblical."[15] The repeated and renewed application from generation to generation, the memorization, and above all the daily practice of ethics, sacrifices, and prayers, influ-

---

already in the oral period (see below). This model is inspired by Odil H. Steck, "Theological Streams of Traditions," in *Tradition and Theology in the Old Testament*, ed. Douglas A. Knight (Philadelphia: Fortress, 1977), 183–214; Thomas Krüger, "Überlegungen zur Bedeutung der Traditionsgeschichte für das Verständnis alttestamentlicher Texte und zur Weiterentwicklung der traditionsgeschichtlichen Methode," in *Lesarten der Bibel: Untersuchungen zu einer Theorie der Exegese des Alten Testaments*, ed. Helmut Utzschneider and Erhard Blum (Stuttgart: Kohlhammer, 2006), 233–45.

12. This is an important point emphasized by Philip R. Davies, *Scribes and Schools: The Canonization of the Hebrew Scriptures*, LAI (Louisville: Westminster John Knox, 1998), but he thinks that behind this multilayered complexity there is no long history but a multiplicity of simultaneous scribal schools.

13. To be sure, some individual religious "geniuses" (receiver of revelation) gave the initial sparks of brilliance, but their basic insights were updated by many anonymous theologically minded scribes who rewrote and reorganized them into a larger whole.

14. See Manfred Oeming, "Die verborgene Nähe: Zum Verhältnis von liturgischer und exegetischer Schrifthermeneutik (mit besonderer Berücksichtigung des Alten Testaments in der christlichen Predigt)," in *Wort des lebendigen Gottes: Liturgie und Bibel*, ed. Alexander Zerfass and Ansgar Franz, Pietas Liturgica 16 (Tübingen: Francke, 2016), 181–206.

15. Eva Mroczek tries to downplay the importance of the term "biblical" ("The Hegemony of the Biblical in the Study of Second Temple Literature," *JAJ* 6 [2015]: 2–35; and *The Literary Imagination in Jewish Antiquity* [Oxford: Oxford University Press, 2016]). According to her, there existed no "book culture" in the First Temple period and also not in the Second Temple period; the texts have been much more fluid and open for different interpretations. I agree with her that the existence of a bookshelf in every religious house is an anachronistic "imagination," but I still believe that every pious person had contact with narrations, laws, prayers, songs, prophetic sayings, and wisdom proverbs "written on the tablets of the heart."

enced and controlled by the texts, were the sources and the filter for what became "classical" and "canonical."[16] Without a community and a praxis of faith no canon could have developed.[17] The process of canon formation was in some sense democratic.[18] This is not to imply that the texts were read by the common people. Indeed, only the elites would have had access to the treasure of tradition in the temples, "schools," palaces, or private "libraries" of priest, judges, or prophets. Daily life relied on oral tradition and custom.

If "canon" is understood as the scale that provides practical standards for a community—whether ethical guidance, cultic practice, or the like—then one can posit several *Sitze im Leben* in the early Israelite and Judahite society that required the existence of fixed and unchangeable texts. Surely certain social and liturgical settings must have necessitated *linguistic norms* or fixed texts. Indeed, various streams of traditions exhibit a proclivity to guarding and preserving ideas that were of central import, and this too implies that standardization of key texts was a desideratum.[19] Several settings come to mind:

1. The *law* aims to give shape to regulations that were already important for social order. It is no surprise that, according to historical-critical research, the Book of Covenant represents the earliest written text, a collection of rights.[20] Texts like the Decalogue or the

---

16. For a brilliant analysis of these processes, see Hans-Georg Gadamer, *Truth and Method*, 2nd ed. (London: Continuum, 2006).

17. This is the convincing argument of Brevard S. Childs, *Introduction to the Old Testament as Scripture* (Philadelphia: Fortress, 1979). For the discussion about his highly influential canonical approach, see Daniel R. Driver, *Brevard Childs, Biblical Theologian: For the Church's One Bible*, FAT 2/46 (Tübingen: Mohr Siebeck, 2010); and Dennis T. Olson, "Types of a Recent 'Canonical Approach,'" in *The Twentieth Century: From Modernism to Post-modernism*, vol. 3 pt. 2 of *Hebrew Bible, Old Testament: The History of Its Interpretation*, ed. Magne Sæbø (Göttingen: Vandenhoeck & Ruprecht, 2015), 196–218.

18. See Manfred Oeming, "Das Hervorwachsen des Verbindlichen aus der Geschichte des Gottesvolkes: Grundzüge einer prozessual-soziologischen Kanon-Theorie," *ZNW* 6 (2003): 52–58.

19. Even though there is no way of proving this, I think that the writers of the first scrolls were probably already familiar with the notion of canonicity. The subsequent redactors who added to the text (*Fortschreibungen*) probably saw themselves as playing a key role and even as inspired by God (see Hartmut Gese, *Zur biblischen Theologie: Alttestamentliche Vorträge*, BEvT 78 [Tübingen: Mohr, 1983], 9–30).

20. According to the widely accepted analysis of Ludger Schwienhorst-Schönberger (*Das Bundesbuch [Ex 20,22–23,33]: Studien zu seiner Entstehung und Theologie*, BZAW 188 [Berlin: de Gruyter, 1990]), the written form of the Book of the Covenant emerged already in the pre-state period and developed between the eleventh and eighth centuries as a casuistic law book, expressed in the third person. In the pre-Deuteronomistic era (maybe under Jehoshaphat), this secular text was theologized and transformed into a divine speech, with God speaking in first person and the person addressed in second person. Finally, the book

30   *When Texts Are Canonized*

series of moral exhortations in Lev 18–20 call the reader to learn these laws by heart, and they needed a fixed form.

2. In the *cult*, magical sayings, rituals, and spells that governed cultic celebrations were strictly formulaic, requiring precise wording and sequence.[21]

3. The *holy narrations* of some professional orators had astonishingly precise knowledge of the foundational myths and legends of Israel, which suggests that these myths and legends already had a fixed form. These highly educated storytellers knew of the decisive events of the early history of Israel, and they produced a religious and national story that shaped the identity and the ideology of "Israel." In the Persian and Hellenistic eras, the narratives became a unified stream of traditions.

4. The *sayings of the prophets* have been carefully stylized as "the poetry of perfection," which is anything but spontaneous free speech. Because they were written in opposition to the official propaganda, the words had to be selected with care in order for them to have a decisively subversive power.

5. Folkloric *proverbs* were initially produced by clever farmers but later became part of the royal state education, formulated by learned teachers. These proverbs had to be composed in such a way that they could be easily learned by heart: they had to be terse, clear, and memorable.

6. Since most *prayers* were songs that were apparently intended to be sung or performed by a choir, it would be absolutely necessary for the text to have a fixed form; otherwise the performance would fail.

All these settings in life required some kind of standardized text or form that was shared by people and was considered important, probably even authoritative.

I am well aware that this analysis is contested in current scholarship. Scholars argue that the production of "Holy Scriptures" started late—

---

underwent a Deuteronomistic revision with some characteristic insertions. Other scholars emphasize the original connection of the Book of Covenant with the Sinai narrative and date it after Deuteronomy, that is, in the sixth century (e.g., Cornelis Houtman, *Das Bundesbuch: Ein Kommentar*, DMOA 24 [Leiden: Brill, 1997]).

21. Konrad Schmid emphasizes that the development from oral traditions to fixed texts is explained by the crisis brought about by the disappearance of the Temple ("Der Kanon und der Kult: Das Aufkommen der Schriftreligion im antiken Israel und die sukzessive Sublimierung des Tempelkultes," in *Ex Oriente Lux: Studien zur Theologie des Alten Testaments; Festschrift für Rüdiger Lux*, ed. Angelika Berlejung and Raik Heckl, Arbeiten zur Bibel und ihrer Geschichte 39 [Leipzig: Evangelische Verlagsanstalt, 2012], 523–46). The Babylonian exile was an important reason for writing down scriptures, but hardly the source of canonicity.

The Way of God   31

during Hezekiah's reign or in the crisis of the Babylonian exile or up to four hundred years later—and was restricted to an elite that had power and economic means: the king and his court (so W. Schniedewind[22]) or the Levitical scribes at the Temple of Jerusalem with its different groups (so K. van der Toorn[23] and M. Satlow[24]). The main arguments for this late dating are based on the evidence of archaeology and the parallels of ancient Near Eastern practices. But the so-called archaeological evidence is very problematic.

As a field archaeologist, I am well aware of how rare it is to find documents of scribal activities. Writing materials like leather, papyrus, or wood deteriorate and disappear. The fact that leather scrolls survived two thousand years, as the Qumran scrolls did, is nothing short of miraculous. It is unrealistic to expect texts from the preexilic period to survive, but the absence of evidence is not "evidence of absence." The oldest epigraphic evidence on clay, dating between the tenth and eighth centuries, originates not from the royal court or the Temple but from farmers, travelers, and soldiers. It does not rule out the possibility that reading and writing in the tenth/ninth century were more widespread in Israel and Judah than is commonly believed. We have to take into account that, in an ethnological perspective, alongside a written form of canon there existed in many cases an oral tradition that was firmly anchored and widely fixed.[25]

The biblical texts testify to a widespread knowledge of reading and writing from the days of Moses and Joshua. For instance, Gideon caught a young man from Succoth who wrote down the names of the seventy-seven princes (Judg 8:14). David wrote a letter to Joab that put Uriah in harm's way (2 Sam 11:14–15). And Jeremiah dictated a letter to Baruch for the exiles (Jer 36:4, 18, 32; 45:1 [29:1]). There is no need to take all these biblical examples as late and fictitious. Furthermore, the view, widely held, that the Bible is the product of "scribal exercises" of postexilic officials is unlikely, because it does not fit the nature of the biblical texts that portray

---

22. William M. Schniedewind, *How the Bible Became a Book. The Textualization of Ancient Israel* (Cambridge: Cambridge University Press, 2003); and "Writing and Book Production in the Ancient Near East," in *From the Beginnings to 600*, ed. James N. B. Carleton Paget and Joachim Schaper, vol. 1 of *The New Cambridge History of the Bible* (Cambridge: Cambridge University Press, 2013), 46–62.

23. Karel van der Toorn, *Scribal Culture and the Making of the Hebrew Bible* (Cambridge: Harvard University Press, 2007).

24. Michael L. Satlow argues that, from the ninth to the fourth century BCE, most biblical texts were produced "by scribes for scribes" (*How the Bible Became Holy* [New Haven: Yale University Press, 2015]). They did not have real authority. Only beginning from the Hasmonean dynasty were scriptures promoted by groups with an ideological agenda.

25. See Jack Goody, *The Interface between the Written and the Oral*, Studies in Literacy, Family, Culture, and the State (Cambridge: Cambridge University Press, 1987).

32   *When Texts Are Canonized*

Yahweh and his revelations. The biblical texts cannot simply be explained by scribalism.

A fresh voice argues for the importance of wisdom traditions in Judah from Iron Age I onward.[26] Mark Sneed differentiates very convincingly among many types of scribes (e.g., heralds, teachers, preachers, administrators, muster officers, judges, prophetic scribes, priestly scribes, physicians) and assumes a long education and a variety of scribal exercises (from simple wisdom sayings, laws, or prayers to complex texts like the Song of Songs and Job). He concludes that a great deal of "the Bible" derives from the wisdom circles and that its formation started long before the Hasmonean period.

The "Nondeviation Formula" in the Hebrew Bible

In order to argue for the existence of the early concepts of "canonicity" and to analyze them, one has to look to texts that are more or less datable. This procedure, however, is fraught with methodological difficulties, since precise dating of biblical texts continues to be highly contested. One promising approach is to look for recurring formulas in the Hebrew Bible to discern their development in the light of the established compositional history.

Some of these have already been thoroughly investigated. Several scholars have studied the "canon formula" ("do not add anything to the word that I am commanding you, and do not take anything away from it"), for which contract law clearly forms its background.[27] Others have examined the "all generations formula" (לדר ודר; e.g., Gen 17:7, 9; Exod

---

26. Mark M. Sneed, *The Social World of the Sages: An Introduction to Israelite and Jewish Wisdom Literature* (Minneapolis: Fortress 2015), 161–82.

27. Bernard M. Levinson, "Die neuassyrischen Ursprünge der Kanonformel in Deuteronomium 13,1," in *Viele Wege zu dem Einen: Historische Bibelkritik; Die Vitalität der Glaubensüberlieferung in der Moderne*, ed. Stefan Beyerle, Axel Graupner, and Udo Rüterswörden, BThSt 121 (Neukirchen-Vluyn: Neukirchener Theologie, 2012), 23–59; Udo Rüterswörden, "Die sogenannte Kanonformel in Dtn 13,1," in *Juda und Jerusalem in der Seleukidenzeit: Herrschaft, Widerstand, Identität; Festschrift für Heinz-Josef Fabry*, ed. Ulrich Dahmen and Johannes Schnocks, BBB 159 (Göttingen: Vandenhoeck & Ruprecht, 2010), 19–29; Johannes Taschner, "'Fügt nichts zu dem hinzu, was ich euch gebiete, und streicht nichts heraus!' Die Kanonformel in Deuteronomium 4,2 als hermeneutischer Schlüssel der Tora," in *Kanonisierung—die Hebräische Bibel im Werden*, ed. Georg Steins and Johannes Taschner, BThSt 110 (Neukirchen-Vluyn: Neukirchener Theologie, 2010), 46–63; Antonius H. J. Gunneweg, "Weisheit, Prophetie und Kanonformel: Erwägungen zu Proverbia 30,1–9," in *Alttestamentlicher Glaube und biblische Theologie: Festschrift für Horst Dietrich Preuß zum 65. Geburtstag*, ed. Jutta Hausmann and Hans-Jürgen Zobel (Stuttgart: Kohlhammer, 1992), 253–60; Manfred Oeming, *Verstehen und Glauben: Exegetische Bausteine zu einer Theologie des Alten Testaments*, BBB 142 (Berlin: Philo, 2003), 121–37.

The Way of God   33

31:13; 40:15; Lev 17:7), which again emerged from the legal sphere—more specifically, from the law of inheritance.[28] Also relevant is the "eternal order formula" (חקת עולם; e.g., Exod 12:12, 17; 14:24; Lev 24:3; Num 15:15), which is informed by the theology of creation with eternal and unchangeable world orders and the priestly concern for eternal rules regarding the correct celebration of feasts and offerings. Lastly, the "authority of the scripture formula" (ככתוב; e.g., Josh 1:8; 8:31, 34; 23:6; 1 Kgs 2:3, etc.) is another germane consideration. This formula is taken from the world of contracts; it forbids changing whatever has been committed to writing and signed by both parties and makes it absolutely binding on both parties.[29]

I have chosen another key formula that relates to and informs the early idea of canonicity. I call this the "nondeviation formula" (hereafter NDF): "Do not turn from it to the right hand or to the left." The NDF reveals much about the history and the essence of "early high canonicity" in ancient Israel. Unlike other ancient religions, Israel already shows a marked tendency to fix a "way of God" as the only possible way to true piety in the preexilic and exilic periods.

The Profane Meaning

The NDF occurs sixteen times in the Hebrew Bible (most frequently in Deuteronomistic literature),[30] once in the Apocrypha (the LXX), and twice in Qumran texts, but there are no occurrences in the NT. At the most basic

---

28. Gese, *Zur biblischen Theologie*, 9–30; Brevard S. Childs, "Analysis of the Canonical Formula: 'It Shall Be Recorded for a Future Generation,'" in *Die Hebräische Bibel und ihre zweifache Nachgeschichte: Festschrift für Rolf Rendtorff zum 65. Geburtstag*, ed. Erhard Blum, Christian Macholz, and Ekkehard Stegemann (Neukirchen-Vluyn: Neukirchner Verlag, 1990), 357–64.

29. Thomas Willi, *Israel und die Völker: Studien zur Literatur und Geschichte Israels in der Perserzeit*, SBAB 55 (Stuttgart: Katholisches Bibelwerk, 2012), 101–22.

30. The classic theory of Martin Noth attributed the complex material from Deuteronomy to 2 Kgs 25 to one author who wanted to confess the sins of Israel against the law of Yahweh in view of its total destruction (*Die sammelnden und bearbeitenden Geschichtswerke im Alten Testament*, pt. 1 of Überlierferungsgeschichtliche Studien, Schriften der Königsberger Gelehrten Gesellschaft, Geisteswissenschaftliche Klasse 18.2 [Halle: Niemeyer 1943]). This explanation was criticized by the (re)construction of more and more redactional layers. For a good overview, see Christian Frevel, "Deuteronomistisches Geschichtswerk oder Geschichtswerke? Die These Martin Noths zwischen Tetrateuch, Hexateuch und Enneateuch," in *Martin Noth—aus der Sicht der heutigen Forschung*, ed. Udo Rüterswörden, BThSt 58 (Neukirchen-Vluyn: Neukirchener Verlag, 2004), 60–95; Markus Witte et al., *Die deuteronomistischen Geschichtswerke: Redaktions- und religionsgeschichtliche Perspektiven zur "Deuteronomismus"-Diskussion in Tora und Vorderen Propheten*, BZAW 365 (Berlin: de Gruyter, 2006); Hermann-Josef Stipp (ed.), *Das deuteronomistische Geschichtswerk*, ÖBS 39 (Frankfurt am Main: Lang, 2011), and, in this volume, especially the article by Thomas Römer, "Das deuteronomistische Geschichtswerk und die Wüstentraditionen der Hebräischen Bibel," 55–88.

34   *When Texts Are Canonized*

level, the NDF is a simple and literal directional reference that signifies the shortest and most direct route. Case in point, the NDF appears in the narrative of the ark of the covenant (1 Sam 6), which reports that the ark of the Lord fell into the hands of the Philistines.[31] But the ark brought them great calamities, so the Philistines sent it back to Israel as directly as possible along with offerings of atonement:

> The cows went straight in the direction of Beth-shemesh along one highway, lowing as they went; they turned [סרו] neither to the right nor to the left, and the lords of the Philistines went after them as far as the border of Beth-shemesh. (1 Sam 6:12 NRSV)

Similarly, the story of 2 Sam 2:12–32, which tells of the fratricidal war in Israel, expresses the tenacity of Asael's act with the NDF. Asael continually followed Abner like a shadow and would not leave Abner alone despite Abner's plea for Asael to go away.

> Asahel pursued Abner, turning [נטה] neither to the right nor to the left as he followed him. (2 Sam 2:19 NRSV)

The pentateuchal description of the conquest, which begins at Num 20:14, likewise employs the NDF as a directional reference.[32] The Israelites address the king of Edom as follows.

> Now let us pass through your land. We will not pass through field or vineyard, or drink water from any well; we will go along the King's Highway, not turning aside to the right hand or to the left [נטה] until we have passed through your territory. (Num 20:17 NRSV)

The Israelites did not want any conflict but wished only to pass from the desert to the middle of the promised land via the shortest way possible. Although they did not even ask for necessary supplies such as water, Edom showed hostility by denying them access to the passage.[33]

---

31. Since Leonhard Rost, this passage has been dated to the tenth century BCE (*Die Überlieferung von der Thronnachfolge Davids*, BWANT 42 [Stuttgart: Kohlhammer, 1926], 4–47). On the new late dating, see Albert de Pury and Thomas Römer, eds., *Die sogenannte Thronfolgegeschichte Davids: Neue Einsichten und Anfragen*, OBO 176 (Freiburg: Universitätsverlag; Göttingen: Vandenhoeck & Ruprecht, 2000).

32. In the first section of this text, Martin Noth finds such a close entanglement of J and E that no reasonable separation of sources is possible (*Überlieferungsgeschichte des Pentateuch*, 2nd ed. [Darmstadt: Wissenschaftliche Buchgesellschaft, 1960], 39). The present text comes from ᴿJE, but older material from around 800 BCE is used.

33. Because of this, the enmity began to grow between the peoples.

The Way of God   35

In the story of Balaam and his donkey, the NDF appears as a reference to a narrow, tube-shaped path without an escape route.[34]

> Then the angel of the LORD went ahead, and stood in a narrow place, where there was no way to turn [לנטות] either to the right or to the left. (Num 22:26 NRSV)

As in Num 20:17 above, the NDF in Deuteronomy designates a direct way without any diversion.

> If you let me pass through your land, I will travel only along the road; I will turn aside [אסור] neither to the right nor to the left. (Deut 2:27 NRSV)

Figurative Uses

Beyond a literal, directional reference, the NDF is used figuratively in several places, and two particular areas of development may be discerned. On the one hand, the NDF seems to have been imported into the realm of royal ideology, as its close association with the royal decree in the so-called Succession Narrative attests. In 2 Sam 14, Joab sends a wise woman from Tekoa to David to convince him to grant amnesty to Absalom.[35] She flatters the king as "the angel of God, so is my lord the king to discern good and evil."[36]

> The king said, "Is the hand of Joab with you in all this?" The woman answered and said, "As surely as you live, my lord the king, one cannot turn right or left [להמין ולהשמיל] from anything that my lord the king has said. For it was your servant Joab who commanded me; it was he who put all these words into the mouth of your servant." (2 Sam 14:19 NRSV)

The NDF is also found in the legal realm. In the so-called *Verfassungsentwurf* of Deut 16:18–18:22, the Jerusalemite central court (likely set in the late preexilic period) stipulates that any difficult legal case should be brought before the headquarters in Jerusalem. The NDF characterizes a kind of

---

34. According to Noth, this story belongs to J and dates to about 900 BCE (*Überlieferungsgeschichte des Pentateuch*, 34).

35. Both Rost's classic study and Erhard Blum's more recent study date the Succession Narrative to the early monarchy. See Erhard Blum, "Ein Anfang der Geschichtsschreibung? Anmerkungen zur sog. Thronfolgegeschichte und zum Umgang mit Geschichte im alten Israel," *Trumah* 5 (1996): 9–46.

36. The compliment is meant rather ironically. Typical man that he is, the old David imagines that he himself could determine everything!

36   *When Texts Are Canonized*

"Constitutional Court," which functions as the last resort and whose decisions are final and incontestable.

> You must carry out fully the law that they interpret for you or the ruling that they announce to you; do not turn aside [תסור] from the decision that they announce to you, either to the right or to the left. (Deut 17:11 NRSV)

In this case, the idea of absolute "binding" is linguistically condensed in the NDF and linked to the highest juridical authority.

Theological Use of the Formula

As noted above, the NDF appears most frequently in Deuteronomistic literature. The Deuteronomistic redaction—or more likely the latest insertions made by "DtrN"—uses the NDF to couple different text blocks at key points. The following passages probably all derive from a single hand or scribal circle. The NDF is used in the so-called royal law (Deut 17:14–20), which dates in its final form to the post-state era.[37]

> neither exalting himself above other members of the community nor turning aside [סור] from the commandment [המצוה], either to the right or to the left, so that he and his descendants may reign long over his kingdom in Israel. (Deut 17:20 NRSV)

Here המצוה means the copy of the legal text that the king is supposed "to read his entire life" (Deut 17:19) and from which he himself must not deviate.[38] For the first time, the NDF is explicitly linked to a written text.

The following exilic texts also make strategic use of the NDF. For instance, the NDF frames the Decalogue and obliges all Israel to live according to the Ten Commandments. It serves as a kind of *"general admonition* to the people to follow the complete instruction for life, given to them by their religion."[39]

> You must therefore be careful to do as the LORD your God has commanded you; you shall not turn [תסרו] to the right or to the left. You must follow exactly the path that the LORD your God has commanded you, so

---

37. Rüterswörden attributes the NDF here to Deuteronomy ("Die sogenannte Kanonformel in Dtn 13,1," 50–66). See the criticism of Eckart Otto, *Theologische Ethik des Alten Testaments*, Theologische Wissenschaft 3.2 (Stuttgart: Kohlhammer, 1994), 193-97, here 195.

38. It is unclear, however, if "his Torah" here (and, according to a Jewish tradition, in Ps 1:2 as well) is to be understood as a specific royal law, the compendium of the Deuteronomistic instruction for judicial and political authorities in Deut 16–26, the book of Deuteronomy, or even the Pentateuch as a whole.

39. Eduard König, *Das Deuteronomium*, KAT 3 (Leipzig: Deichert, 1917), 97.

The Way of God   37

that you may live, and that it may go well with you, and that you may live long in the land that you are to possess. (Deut 5:32–33 NRSV)

This admonition in Deut 5, which marks the beginning of a series of important revelations, corresponds to the command to safeguard the Torah:

The LORD will make you the head, and not the tail; you shall be only at the top, and not at the bottom—if you obey the commandments of the LORD your God, which I am commanding you today, by diligently observing them, and if you do not turn aside [תסור] from any of the words [מכל הדברים][40] that I am commanding you today, either to the right or to the left, following other gods to serve them. (Deut 28:13–14 NRSV)

In the programmatic keynote speech that marks the transition from Moses to Joshua, the Deuteronomistic redaction employs the NDF again.[41]

Only be strong and very courageous, being careful to act in accordance with all the law that my servant Moses commanded you; do not turn [תסור] from it to the right hand or to the left, so that you may be successful wherever you go. (Josh 1:7 NRSV)

Here the formula refers explicitly to *the complete written law*, which God revealed through Moses. Likewise, at the end of the book of Joshua, the NDF is employed with an oath that obliges the whole Israel to the book of the law of Moses.[42]

Therefore be very steadfast to observe and do all that is written in the book of the law of Moses, turning aside (סור) from it neither to the right nor to the left. (Josh 23:6 NRSV)[43]

Finally, a striking variation of the NDF concludes the Deuteronomistic History:

He [Josiah] did what was right in the sight of the LORD, and walked in all the way of his father David; he did not turn aside [סר] to the right or to the left. (2 Kgs 22:2 NRSV)

---

40. The words כל הדברים signify at least the whole Deuteronomy, as clearly indicated by the First Commandment.

41. That this verse is part of the Deuteronomistic redaction of the book of Joshua is shown in great detail by Edward Noort, *Das Buch Josua: Forschungsgeschichte und Problemfelder*, EdF 292 (Darmstadt: Wissenschaftliche Buchgesellschaft, 1998), esp. 331.

42. This book must include Deuteronomy at the very least, but it more likely includes the whole Pentateuch.

43. Recent research attributes this verse to DtrN. Noort (*Das Buch Josua*, 111, 188–90, 199ff.) enumerates the positions of V. Fritz, G. Auld, and R. Smend.

38   *When Texts Are Canonized*

In 2 Kgs 22, Josiah acted like Asael, who physically pursued Abner without veering to the right or to the left (2 Sam 2), except that the NDF here figuratively encapsulates Josiah's good character. Needless to say, Josiah did not physically follow David but perfectly emulated his exemplary behavior and qualities.[44]

Chronicles as a whole unambiguously extends the idea of David as the religious standard par excellence.[45] One telling example is found in 2 Chr 34, which repeats the statement of the Deuteronomistic History.

> He [Josiah] did what was right in the sight of the LORD, and walked in the ways of his ancestor David; he did not turn aside [סר] to the right or to the left. (2 Chr 34:2 NRSV)

As is evident from the preceding, at the most important compositional points (Deut 5:32, 17:20, 28:14, Josh 1:7, 23:6, 2 Kgs 22:2 = 2 Chr 34:2), the Deuteronomistic (fourth century BCE) and the Chronicler's (fourth century BCE) redactions insert the NDF to stress the authority of their Torah. They present the "book of the Torah of Moses"—along with the actions of David that supposedly conform to it—as an authoritative and binding written text. There simply is no other way to life. The Deuteronomistic school of theology programmatically raises these redacted texts to the

---

44. Apparently, David was viewed as a role model whom Josiah perfectly emulated. Ernst Würthwein attributes this variant to an editorial layer different from the layer that references Moses, namely, DtrN (*Die Bücher der Könige*, 2 vols., ATD 11 [Göttingen: Vandenhoeck & Ruprecht, 1977–1984], 2:445). Whether David's exemplary behavior conformed to the Torah of Moses—or perhaps to what extent—is not clear in this verse. DtrN seems to have harmonized them since no opposition or contradiction can be detected. In 1 Kgs 2, therefore, the dying David admonishes Solomon with the following words of testamentary grandeur: "and keep the charge of the Lord your God, walking in his ways and keeping his statutes, his commandments, his ordinances, and his testimonies, as it is written in the law of Moses, so that you may prosper in all that you do and wherever you turn" (1 Kgs 2:3 NRSV). One may ask, however, Does not the image of David as guarantor of unity and purity of the cult belong to Chronicles in the first place? Could it not be the case that the later revision of the books of Kings (and the whole Deuteronomistic History), which is often assumed by scholarship, is actually the Chronicler's redaction, which appraises the kings not only according to the criteria of the Torah—especially the first and second commandments—but also against David's exemplary "greatness"? The assessment of this question, however, requires a thorough study. See Uwe Becker and Hannes Bezzel, eds., *Rereading the relecture? The Question of (Post)chronistic Influence in the Latest Redactions of the Books of Samuel*, FAT 2/66 (Tübingen: Mohr Siebeck, 2014). Ernst Michael Dörrfuß tries to prove "that the inclusion of Moses aims essentially to criticize the Davidic monarchy and the Jerusalem Temple" (*Mose in den Chronikbüchern: Garant theokratischer Zukunftserwartung*, BZAW 219 [Berlin: de Gruyter, 1994], 279). Yet this theory is overly complicated and unlikely. The Chronicler clearly understands David as an attendant to the Torah of Moses.

45. Ehud Ben Zvi and Diana V. Edelman, eds., *What Was Authoritative for Chronicles?* (Winona Lake, IN: Eisenbrauns 2011).

The Way of God 39

rank of revelation.[46] Presumably, this insight would confirm that the Deuteronomistic school was indeed the creator of a fully developed "theology of scripture" and the progenitor of the biblical canon, although priestly and prophetic circles soon accepted and followed its lead.[47]

Uses in Wisdom Literature

In post-Deuteronomistic sapiential texts, the NDF appears twice. First, Wisdom cautions the addressees by means of the NDF.[48]

> Do not swerve [אל תט] to the right or to the left; turn [הסר] your foot away from evil. (Prov 4:27 NRSV)

Whoever leaves the narrow but correct path walks immediately in the way of sinners.[49] It must be highlighted, however, that the "right way" in

---

46. The theological significance of these processes cannot be overstated. This confirms the results of a previous inquiry into the so-called canon formula, "You shall not add anything and you shall not take away" (Deut 13:1), as well as other notions expounded in the narrative, for example, the statement that God wrote the Decalogue on the tablets of stone or that the Tablets of the Law were inscribed on both sides without any space for further additions (Exod 31:18, 34:1, Deut 4:13, 5:22, 9:10, 10:1–4). See Christoph Dohmen and Manfred Oeming, *Biblischer Kanon—warum und wozu? Eine Kanontheologie*, QD 137 (Freiburg: Herder, 1992), 68–90.

47. In the end, the Deuteronomistic notion of an obligatory text won out and became the cornerstone of the three world religions. One may assume that this process was influenced by Assyrian culture. Even if a direct influence is not detectable, it is very likely that the cultural politics of Assurbanipal (ca. 668–631 BCE) were known in Palestine. The king—erudite, aesthetic, and highly educated for his priestly career—states about himself that he had written down on tablets "the letters that recorded wisdom of Nebo (the god of writing) in neat cuneiform." He checked the text and then filed the documents in his palace, so that he "may behold [them] and read [them] again" (Hartmut Schmökel, *Ur, Assur und Babylon: Drei Jahrtausende im Zweistromland*, Grosse Kulturen der Frühzeit 2 [Stuttgart: Klipper, 1955], 97–99). This state-aided process of comparing and filing texts is similar to a process of canonization; see Stephen J. Lieberman, "Canonical and Official Cuneiform Texts: Towards an Understanding of Assurbanipal's Personal Tablet Collection," in *Lingering over Words: Studies in Ancient Near Eastern Literature in Honor of William L. Moran*, ed. Tzvi Abusch, John Huehnergard, and Piotr Steinkeller, HSS 37 (Atlanta: Scholars Press, 1990), pp. 305-36.

48. Arndt Meinhold, *Die Sprüche*, 2 vols., ZBK.AT 16 (Zurich: Theologischer Verlag, 1991), 1:99.

49. Moreover, the right way may not always be "the way through the middle," as suggested by Otto Plöger: "The straight way, which deviates neither to the right nor to the left, is the way through the middle, already recommended by Hesiod [who lived in the eighth century BCE] as desirable" (*Op.* 5.694: "Observe due measure: and proportion is best in all things"). See Plöger, *Sprüche Salomos (Proverbia)*, BKAT 17 (Neukirchen-Vluyn: Neukirchener Verlag, 1984), 50. The reference to the Greek cultural environment is not convincing in view of the younger wisdom tradition found here. The text is likely to be late postexilic. The Aristotelian definition of virtue as the middle ground is foreign to the Old Testament. The understanding of ἀρετή as μεσότης may be seen occasionally but Wisdom in general thinks

40   *When Texts Are Canonized*

wisdom literature is actually not governed by "the book of the Torah of Moses"! The context of Prov 4 and 5 is the parental admonition regarding prudence, and Wisdom appeals not to the Torah but to reason. As such, Wisdom should not be prematurely equated with Torah and certainly not with Torah piety. To be sure, one can observe the process of "sapiential-ization" of the Torah and the cult in the later period of the Old Testament, for example, in the book of Sirach. Yet the admonition of biological parents in Prov 4 and the call for marital fidelity in chapter 5 are not grounded in the Torah but exhibit a theological perspective that emerged quite independently of the Torah. This seems to suggest that wisdom literature derives from another theological tradition that sought to establish normativity through the help of the NDF but independent of the Deuteronomistic Torah-canonical concept.

Finally, the NDF is present in prophetic literature—though admittedly in a "sapientalized" later stratum of the book of Isaiah:[50]

> And your teacher[51] will not hide himself anymore, but your eyes shall see your teacher. Your ears will hear a word from behind you: This is the way; walk in it without turning to the right or to the left![52] (Isa 30:20b–21; my translation)

Isaiah 30:18–26 is written for an unsettled community that is struggling to grasp the best course of action. The addressees have to find comfort in the hope that they will receive a teacher—and a special one at that. Their present, hidden teacher is God himself! The fact that Yahweh is called מורה means that instructing the people was seen as Yahweh's crucial role (see Isa 2:3, 28:26, 48:17).

---

strictly in binary terms: good *or* bad, just *or* wicked; see Rüdiger Lux, "Der 'Lebenskompromiß'—ein Wesenszug im Denken Kohelets? Zur Auslegung von Koh 7,15–18," in Hausmann and Zobel, *Alttestamentlicher Glaube und biblische Theologie*, 267–78.

50. God is here "seen like a shepherd dealing with his herd," who would navigate his flock from behind, and in doing so, "the plight of missing guidance is remedied by God who becomes visible and audible" (Peter Höffken, *Das Buch Jesaja*, 2 vols., NSKAT 16 [Stuttgart: Katholisches Bibelwerk, 1993], 1:216). It is "expected that immediate communion with God, which will be reality on that day, enables correct decisions to be made *hic et nunc*" (Hans Wildberger, *Jesaja*, 3 vols., BKAT 10 [Neukirchen-Vluyn: Neukirchener Verlag, 1982], 3:1197).

51. The Great Isaiah Scroll from Qumran has a plural form. The Septuagint translates "your deceiver must not hide themselves anymore," and, therefore, likewise had a plural in its *Vorlage*. Many commentators follow this reading because even in the MT the form can be read as the suffixed form in the singular or the plural. The context, however, is a paraenesis for the community, not an encouragement for the "teachers." Therefore, I opt for the interpretation of the form as singular, which refers to Yahweh.

52. A verb is missing: the phrase כי ... וכי could be understood temporally, "walk in this way, while (walking) to the right and to the left"; so, e.g., Wildberger, *Jesaja*, 3:1189. In this case, there would be no NDF. Since the emphasis is on "*this* is the way," however, it makes the interpretation "neither ... nor" more likely.

The Way of God 41

To sum up, in both post-Deuteronomistic wisdom texts, the NDF is used in connection with ethical instructions. In contrast to the examples in DtrN, however, the NDF is not used as a canon formula that qualifies a *textual* corpus. Rather than as a reference to written texts, the NDF articulates, in keeping with independent sapiential theology, a type of "divergence," that is, the eschatological hope for God himself to act as the teacher who instructs them even without the book of Moses (cf. Jer 31:31–34, Joel 3).

Other Late Second Temple Uses

In the so-called apocryphal texts, the NDF is found only twice. One is a simple geographical reference (1 Macc 5:46), but the other is a highly charged and weighty theological declaration. In his speech, Mattathias, who was supposed to be the first in Modein to enact the reform of Antiochus IV Epiphanes in sacrificing to other gods, declares:

> We will not obey the commandment of the king; from our religion [τὴν λατρείαν ἡμῶν]; we will not deviate, neither to the right nor to the left. (1 Macc 2:22; my translation)

The NDF now governs not only some textual corpora but *the whole religion* with all of its rituals and everyday behavior.[53]

It is surprising that the NDF is scarcely used in the Dead Sea Scrolls, given the strict, elitist piety at Qumran.[54] Nevertheless, the formula is found in the opening passage of the Community Rule, which regulates the admission procedure to the *Yaḥad* and demands a wholehearted devotion to the community, especially regarding the festivals:

> All those who freely devote themselves to His truth shall bring all their knowledge, powers and possessions into the Community of God, that they may purify their knowledge in the truth of God's precepts and order their powers according to His ways of perfection and all their possessions according to His righteous counsel. They shall not depart from any command of God concerning their times; they shall be neither early nor late for any of their appointed times, they shall stray neither to the right nor to the left of any of His true precepts. (1QS I, 11–15)

> Let him [the novice] then order his steps [to walk] perfectly in all the ways commanded by God concerning the times appointed for him, stray-

---

53. Andreas Hahn, *Canon Hebraeorum, Canon Ecclesiae: Zur deuterokanonischen Frage im Rahmen der Begründung alttestamentlicher Schriftkanonizität in neuerer römisch-katholischer Dogmatik*, Studien zu Theologie und Bibel 2 (Münster: LIT 2009).

54. J. Alberto Soggin and Heinz-Josef Fabry, "ימין," *ThWAT* 3:658–63.

42   *When Texts Are Canonized*

ing neither to the right nor to the left [לסור] and transgressing none of His
words (1QS III, 9–11)[55]

Curiously, the formula is completely absent in the New Testament, even
though the idea is clearly present, especially in Matt 5:17, Gal 1:8, and
Jude 3. It seems as if the "fidelity to the letter" was replaced by the "fidelity to the person of Jesus Christ" (Acts 4:12) by this point.

Conclusion

In view of the foregoing analysis, we may now sketch a broad trajectory
of development. The earliest usage of the NDF was a literal, directional
reference to a clearly defined way. This directional reference came to be
used figuratively, particularly as a political and legal *last resort* (*Letztin-
stanz*). This itself was a very early development. Then Deuteronomistic
circles in the late seventh to mid-sixth century BCE began to employ the
NDF vis-à-vis the word of God. This distinct theological move was made
in combination with a host of related formulas: the "canon-formula" in
Deuteronomy (4:2, 13:1) determined the extent of the scriptures and pro-
scribed any alteration of the letters; the "all generations formula" emphasized the universal scope; the "eternal order formula" brought out the
perpetuity or timelessness of the divine orders; and the "authority of
scripture formula" stressed the crucial importance of a *written* text. This
last formula implies that Torah was seen not as a mere record of divine
opinions but as a fixed and binding contract, inscribed by authorities like
Moses, the king, or even God himself. All the associations and elements
of profane and metaphorical uses converge in the theological use of the
NDF and other related formulas. They testify that the very letter of the
Torah is the direct route to life and that deviating from it invariably incurs
grave consequences. These formulas constitute the idea of the canon as an
absolute norm. The NDF represents the self-understanding of Israel and
Judah, which were no longer independent states; that is, it represents the
self-understanding of the Judahite religion in its origins.[56]

---

55. Translation of 1QS are from Geza Vermes, *The Complete Dead Sea Scrolls* (London:
Penguin, 2011), 101 (for 1QS I, 11-15) and 103 (for 1QS III, 9-11).

56. This has methodological implications for exegesis; see Egbert Ballhorn and Georg
Steins, eds., *Der Bibelkanon in der Bibelauslegung: Methodenreflexionen und Beispielexegesen*
(Stuttgart: Kohlhammer, 2007). Theologically, the codification of "the letter" can be evaluated in various ways. One could classify the NDF *negatively* as an act of moral narrowing and
ossification caused by anxiety and also as an expression of terrifying intolerance. Certainly,
such a negative view contributed to the caricature of "Jewish legalism." One *could* fear it as
an early form of fundamentalism and as a lightening of oppressive religion and direct theological criticisms against it. Nevertheless, it is not necessary to evaluate it so negatively or

The NDF is also used in post-Deuteronomistic texts. Wisdom literature employs the NDF with reference to binding ethical obligations, rather than as a way of elevating the Torah. This sapiential usage seems to have developed apart from the Deuteronomistic school. Other late Second Temple texts also make use of the NDF in interesting ways. In 1 Maccabees, the NDF governs the whole religion, while the Qumran Community Rule applies it as a way to ensure wholehearted devotion to the regulations of the *Yaḥad*.

The formation of the canon, then, was not at all a late invention ex post. It was not devised by later authorities or synods ex nihilo; rather, it was part of the scripture itself from early on. Only minor parts of the canon were open and under discussion; the major part was clear from the preexilic beginnings.[57] The nondeviation formula, then, is an important marker of Hebrew Bible piety, which contributed significantly to the development of the later canonical list.[58]

---

unsympathetically. Already the use of the NDF in both wisdom texts, which show a very different theological outlook, shows that fundamentalism does not emerge within the canon of the Hebrew Bible; the repeated reference to the importance of experiential *reason* and to the *immediate instruction by God* counteract the move toward fundamentalism. I myself understand the NDF as a warmhearted exhortation of Deuteronomy and of honest and profound reflection of the Deuteronomistic History about the guilt of Israel as a necessary kerygma and as *a helpful call to commitment and active discipleship*. The NDF solicits responsibleness and seriousness. The NDF demands the concrete "way of life" to correspond to the "way of God." We should not be mere readers, listeners, and exegetes of the sacred words but doers. This idea, anachronistic though it may be in our postmodern situation, should be part of every good theology (cf. Matt 5:17–20).

57. Adolf Martin Ritter, *Charisma und Caritas: Aufsätze zur Alten Kirche*, ed. Angelika Dörfler-Dierken, Ralph Hennings, and Wolfram Kinzig (Göttingen: Vandenhoeck & Ruprecht, 1997), 265–80; Lee M. McDonald, *The Formation of the Christian Biblical Canon*, rev. and exp. ed. (Peabody, MA: Hendrickson, 1995); Hans P. Rüger, "Der Umfang des alttestamentlichen Kanons in den verschiedenen kirchlichen Traditionen," in *Die Apokryphenfrage im ökumenischen Horizont: Die Stellung der Spätschriften des Alten Testaments im biblischen Schrifttum und ihre Bedeutung in den kirchlichen Traditionen des Ostens und Westens*, ed. Siegfried Meurer, Bibel im Gespräch 3 (Stuttgart: Deutsche Bibelgesellschaft, 1993); Hans von Campenhausen, *Die Entstehung der christlichen Bibel*, rev. ed., BHT 39 (Tübingen: Mohr Siebeck, 2003).

58. Compared to other ancient Near Eastern traditions, the claim of the Deuteronomistic authors is amazing. The exclusivity with which this circle of theologically minded scribes presents its own writings as an unchangeable normative text and postulates it as God's instruction on the only way for humans to live seems to be almost unique.

Uses of Torah in the Second Temple Period

JOHN J. COLLINS

The canon of Hebrew Scriptures as we know it was not finalized until after the biblical period, not before the late first century BCE, arguably in the early rabbinic period.[1] The idea of authoritative, even normative, writings, however, emerged long before that time. In this paper, I want to explore the authority of the Torah of Moses in the Second Temple period by examining the way it is used. I will focus primarily on two case studies: first, the attempt in the books of Ezra and Nehemiah to ascribe legal authority to the Torah; second, the quite variable uses that we find in works that are often, although controversially, called "rewritten Bible."

Ezra

In the seventh year of Artaxerxes (probably 458 BCE, but possibly 398), a scribe named Ezra was commissioned by the Persian king "to make inquiries about Judah and Jerusalem according to the law of your God which is in your hand" (Ezra 7:14 NRSV). Or so at least the book of Ezra claims.[2] Ezra, we are told, was given wide-ranging authority. He is told to

> appoint magistrates and judges who may judge all the people in the province Beyond the River who know the laws of your God; and you shall teach those who do not know them. All who will not obey the law of your God and the law of the king, let judgment be strictly executed on them, whether for death or for banishment or for confiscation of their goods or for imprisonment. (Ezra 7:25–26 NRSV)

---

1. See the discussion by Timothy H. Lim, *The Formation of the Jewish Canon*, AYBRL (New Haven: Yale University Press, 2013), 178–88.

2. On the historical difficulties, see Lester L. Grabbe, *Yehud: A History of the Persian Province of Judah*, vol. 1 of *A History of the Jews and Judaism in the Second Temple Period*, LSTS 47 (London: T&T Clark, 2004), 324–31; Grabbe, *Ezra-Nehemiah*, OTR (London: Routledge, 1998), 125–53.

44

Uses of Torah in the Second Temple Period   45

This decree seems to grant Ezra authority over the entire satrapy, but, as Joseph Blenkinsopp remarks, "it seems tolerably clear that only those 'familiar with the law of our God' are intended, that is Jews and proselytes (*gerîm*) insofar as those came under the law."[3] In any case, the aim is to regulate Judean life as a whole and thereby prescribe a comprehensive way of life. The book that contains these laws is described as ספר תורת משה "the book of the Torah of Moses," in Neh 8:1.

It is apparent from the book of Ezra that the provisions of the Torah of Moses were unknown in Jerusalem before Ezra's arrival. For example, the idea that the people should live in booths during the festival of the seventh month comes as a surprise (Neh 8:13). Ezra 3 reports that a generation earlier Joshua son of Jozadak and Zerubbabel son of Shealtiel had "set out to build the altar of the God of Israel, to offer burnt offerings on it, as prescribed in the law of Moses, the man of God" (Ezra 3:2). Moreover, they had kept the festival of booths, as prescribed, and offered all the sacrifices "according to the ordinance." Michael Satlow is surely right when he suggests that this passage reflects the assumptions of the author of the book of Ezra, writing at least a generation later, rather than what actually happened in the late sixth century.[4] It would be remarkable indeed if the early returnees were guided by the law of Moses and yet it was forgotten by the middle of the following century.

It is generally assumed that Ezra's law book was something close to our Pentateuch, even if not in its final form.[5] Blenkinsopp concludes that "the law" in Ezra-Nehemiah, is basically "Deuteronomic law supplemented by ritual legislation in the Pentateuchal corpora conventionally designated P and H."[6] No doubt, this law had been in the process of formation for centuries, and earlier forms of it may have been regarded as authoritative in some communities, but the book of Ezra provides our earliest account of the imposition of the Torah as the official norm for life in Judah. The books of Ezra and Nehemiah, then, provide an early test case of what it might mean to have a canonical Scripture, in the sense of a written document that could serve as a rule of conduct.

Blenkinsopp goes on to say that the recognition of the law is "complicated by another factor: those indications in Ezra-Nehemiah of practice in accord with neither Deuteronomic nor Priestly law."[7] There are several discrepancies between the actions of Ezra and Nehemiah and the Torah as

---

3. Joseph Blenkinsopp, *Ezra-Nehemiah: A Commentary*, OTL (Philadelphia: Westminster, 1988), 151.

4. Michael L. Satlow, *How the Bible Became Holy* (New Haven: Yale University Press, 2014), 59.

5. See the discussion by Juha Pakkala, *Ezra the Scribe: The Development of Ezra 7–10 and Nehemia 8*, BZAW 347 (Berlin: de Gruyter, 2004), 284–90.

6. Blenkinsopp, *Ezra-Nehemiah*, 155.

7. Ibid.

46   *When Texts Are Canonized*

we have received it.[8] Stipulations regarding the Feast of Booths "according to the law" (Neh 8:13–18) are different from what we find in the Torah.
The prohibitions against intermarriage go beyond Deuteronomy (Neh
10:31), and making purchases on the Sabbath is not actually prohibited in
the Pentateuch (Neh 10:32). The institution of an annual temple tax and of
a wood offering (also in Neh 10) lack scriptural support. In the words of
Joachim Schaper, "Some [texts] that refer to torah, in fact *refer to no known
(quasi)-canonical or otherwise authoritative text.*"[9] Juha Pakkala finds "that
in no single case does the quotation or purported quotation correspond
exactly to a known pentateuchal text. Only in one case is it unequivocally clear which passage of the Pentateuch was used: Neh 13:1–2 is quoting Deut 23:4–6. Even in this case, the text in Neh 13:1–2 differs from the
known versions of Deut 23:4–6."[10] The most notable discrepancy is the
absence of Yom Kippur from the festivals of the seventh month in Neh
8, although there is a day of repentance and fasting on the twenty-fourth
(rather than the tenth) day of the month. It is apparent that the cultic calendar had not yet been finalized.

The issues raised by the other discrepancies are more complex.
Michael Fishbane has argued that at least some of them may have been
derived exegetically from the text as we know it.[11] So, for example, Neh
8:14, which says that "they found it written in the law … that the people
of Israel should live in booths during the festival of the seventh month,"
is "a verbatim citation" from Lev 23:42 ("you shall live in booths for seven
days"). Nehemiah differs from Leviticus with regard to *what* should be
gathered, the *kinds* of branches to be gathered, and *how* they should be
used.[12] Fishbane argues that the variations may be a matter of interpretation of Lev 23.[13] In the case of intermarriage, he argues that "the mech-
anism for prohibiting intermarriage with the Ammonites, Moabites, etc.
was an exegetical extension of the law in Deut. 7:1–3 effected by means of

---

8. Michael LeFebvre, *Collections, Codes, and Torah: The Re-characterization of Israel's Written Law*, LHBOTS 451 (London: T&T Clark, 2006), 103–31; Judson R. Shaver, *Torah and the
Chronicler's History Work: An Inquiry into the Chronicler's References to Laws, Festivals, and Cultic
Institutions in Relationship to Pentateuchal Legislation*, BJS 196 (Atlanta: Scholars Press, 1989),
100-103; Juha Pakkala, "The Quotations and References of the Pentateuchal Laws in Ezra-Nehemiah," in *Changes in Scripture: Rewriting and Interpreting Authoritative Traditions in the Second Temple Period*, ed. Hanne von Weissenberg, Juha Pakkala, and Marko Marttila, BZAW 419
(Berlin: de Gruyter, 2011), 193–221.

9. Joachim Schaper, "Torah and Identity in the Persian Period," in *Judah and the Judeans
in the Achaemenid Period: Negotiating Identity in an International Context*, ed. Oded Lipschits,
Gary N. Knoppers, and Manfred Oeming (Winona Lake, IN: Eisenbrauns, 2011), 32.

10. Juha Pakkala, "Quotations and References," 214.

11. Michael A. Fishbane, *Biblical Interpretation in Ancient Israel* (Oxford: Clarendon,
1985), 107–34.

12. Lefebvre, *Collections, Codes, and Torah*, 108–9.

13. Fishbane, *Biblical Interpretation*, 111–12.

Uses of Torah in the Second Temple Period   47

an adaptation and interpolation of features from Deut. 23:4–9."[14] Deuteronomy 23 bars Ammonites and Moabites from the assembly of God, but not Egyptians, who are also excluded in Ezra. Fishbane explains the ban on Sabbath purchases, which is admittedly not found in the Torah, by reference to Jer 17:21–22, which forbids carrying burdens on the Sabbath day. According to Neh 8:8, the Levites read from the Torah מפרש, an expression variously translated as "with interpretation," or "distinctly." We are also told that they gave the sense, so that the people understood the reading. Fishbane argues that "even though the precise meaning of the preceding terms remains in question, the way these activities are referred to leaves little doubt that they express developed and well-known exegetical procedures."[15] But as Michael Lefebvre has argued, "The fact remains, however, that nowhere in Ezra-Nehemiah is such exegetical activity actually indicated."[16] The reading by the Levites in Neh 8 is more easily understood as translation. Moreover, even Fishbane's ingenuity cannot explain away some discrepancies, such as the date of Yom Kippur. Lefebvre rightly concludes that the kind of exegetical procedure Fishbane assumes here is anachronistic and is not attested before the second century BCE.[17]

There is no doubt that the authors or editors of Ezra-Nehemiah regarded some form of the law of Moses as authoritative. It may be that the law known to them was different, at least in some cases, from that which has come down to us.[18] The cultic calendar is likely to be a case in point. It may also be, as Schaper has argued, that "the reference to an alleged written text simply seems to serve the aim of lending greater authority to a rule that actually has no support in authoritative texts."[19] The frequent use of the formula ככתוב ("as it is written") testifies to the new authority of written scripture as a point of reference for Judean practice in the mid to late fifth century BCE.[20] Nonetheless, the concern seems to be not with the letter of the law but with the general sense of the law, quite loosely interpreted in accordance with the wishes of the interpreting authorities.

The consensus of contemporary scholarship is that neither the great Mesopotamian law "codes," such as that of Hammurabi, nor the biblical

---

14. Ibid., 117.

15. Ibid., 108.

16. Lefebvre, *Collections, Codes, and Torah*, 129.

17. Ibid., 130–31.

18. So especially Cornelis Houtman, "Ezra and the Law: Observations on the Supposed Relation between Ezra and the Pentateuch," *OTS* 21 (1981): 91–115; Pakkala, "Quotations and References," 217.

19. Schaper, "Torah and Identity," 32.

20. L. Hänsel ("Studien zu 'Tora' in Esra-Nehemiah und Chronik" [PhD diss., Leipzig, 1999], cited by Schaper) finds that this formula is used only with reference to the Torah and that the references in Chronicles, unlike those in Ezra-Nehemiah, correspond to the Torah as it is known to us.

48   *When Texts Are Canonized*

law codes functioned as statutory law or were binding on judges.[21] Judges relied on their sense of the mores of a community rather than on written law. Written laws are never cited as decisive in trial scenes, and sometimes cases are decided in contradiction to what is written.[22] Law collections were descriptive rather than prescriptive. Bernard Jackson refers to the laws of Exodus as "wisdom laws," with the implication that they functioned in a way similar to Proverbs: they helped inform the wise person but did not determine right conduct automatically.[23]

Accordingly, Lefebvre has argued that the Torah in the time of Ezra was viewed in this period as "a collection of historic descriptions, not as a prescriptive code."[24] Yet it is clear that Ezra expects people to act in accordance with "what is written in the law of Moses," even if this does not always correspond to what we find in the text. The law is taken as prescriptive in some cases, but the enforcement is highly selective. Ezra focuses his attention on the festivals and then on the problem of intermarriage, which were issues of great symbolic importance.

Ezra's use of the Torah lends itself readily to analysis in terms of identity formation and boundary maintenance.[25] Coming from the Babylonian diaspora, Ezra was obsessed with maintaining clear boundaries between Judeans ("the holy seed") and others. (Not all Judeans in Babylon necessarily shared this obsession, but such concerns often arise in exilic communities).[26] Daniel Smith-Christopher argues that Ezra's use of

---

21. Joshua Berman, "The History of Legal Theory and the Study of Biblical Law," *CBQ* 76 (2014): 19–39; LeFebvre, *Collections, Codes, and Torah*, 1–54; Eckart Otto, "Aspects of Legal Reforms and Reformulations in Ancient Cuneiform and Israelite Law," in *Theory and Method in Biblical and Cuneiform Law: Revision, Interpolation and Development*, ed. Bernard M. Levinson, JSOTSup 181 (Sheffield: JSOT Press, 1994), 160–96, esp. 160–63; Otto, "Recht/Rechtswesen im Alten Orient und im Alten Testament," *TRE* 28:197–210; Konrad Schmid, *The Old Testament: A Literary History*, trans. Linda M. Maloney (Minneapolis: Fortress, 2012), 97; Jean-Louis Ska, *The Exegesis of the Pentateuch: Exegetical Studies and Basic Questions*, FAT 66 (Tübingen: Mohr Siebeck, 2009), 196–220.

22. Lefebvre, *Collections, Codes, and Torah*, 35.

23. Bernard S. Jackson, *Wisdom-Laws: A Study of the Mishpatim of Exodus 21:1–22:16* (Oxford: Oxford University Press, 2006).

24. Lefebvre, *Collections, Codes, and Torah*, 141

25. Philip F. Esler, "Ezra-Nehemiah as a Narrative of (Re-Invented) Israelite Identity," *BibInt* 11 (2003): 413–26; Katherine E. Southwood, *Ethnicity and the Mixed Marriage Crisis in Ezra 9–10: An Anthropological Approach*, Oxford Theological Monographs (Oxford: Oxford University Press, 2012); Donald P. Moffat, *Ezra's Social Drama: Identity Formation, Marriage and Social Conflict in Ezra 9 and 10*, LHBOTS 579 (London: Bloomsbury T&T Clark, 2013); and the essays in Christian Frevel, ed., *Mixed Marriages: Intermarriage and Group Identity in the Second Temple Period*, LHBOTS 547 (New York: T&T Clark International, 2011).

26. Ralf Rothenbusch, "The Question of Mixed Marriages: Between the Poles of Diaspora and Homeland; Observations in Ezra-Nehemiah," in Frevel, *Mixed Marriages*, 60–77, esp. 63; see also his fuller study, *"... abgesondert zur Tora Gottes hin": Ethnisch-religiöse Identitäten im Esra/Nehemiabuch*, HBS 70 (Freiburg im Breisgau: Herder, 2012).

Uses of Torah in the Second Temple Period   49

exclusive language and his strong action against intermarriage "all add up to a self-conscious community that is occupied with self-preservation, both as a pure community in a religious sense and also preservation in a material sense."[27] More specifically, Katherine Southwood attributes Ezra's concerns to the experience of "return migration."[28] She notes the frequency of references to "the children of the Exile, or Golah." The life of the exiled community (or a segment thereof) is regarded as definitive for what it means to be a Judean, and the community existing in Judah is measured and judged by reference to this ideal.[29]

The issue at stake in the mixed marriage crisis is characterized in the book of Ezra as one of purity. In a bold and innovative move it declares that Israelite "seed" is holy, and that it is defiled by intermarriage.[30] Saul Olyan attributes this move to "expansive and creative exegesis of earlier texts such as Lev 18:24–30, Deut 23:4–9, and Deut 7:1–6."[31] It is certainly true that Ezra invokes the authority of the Torah and that his position goes beyond what we find in the actual texts of the Torah. How far the justification of this position is exegetical seems to me questionable. Ezra seems to rely on the thrust of the older texts rather than on literal application. In doing so, he subordinates the text of the Torah to the perceived need for a clearly articulated Judean identity. Restrictions placed on outsiders can be generalized and expanded. He treats the Torah as a malleable instrument, a point that Olyan readily acknowledges.[32]

Over against the "holy seed" or "the people of the Golah/Exile," Ezra sets "the people of the land," identified as Canaanites, Hittites, and so on. Many scholars have suspected, with Daniel Smith-Christopher, that "some of these 'mixed' marriages … were probably not 'mixed' at all in any truly racial/ethnic sense of the term, and may well have represented marriages between Jews who were not a part of the exilic-formed 'Sons of the Golah' with those who were."[33] The "people of the Golah" set the

---

27. Daniel Smith-Christopher, *The Religion of the Landless: The Social Context of the Babylonian Exile* (Bloomington, IN: Meyer-Stone, 1989), 114.

28. Southwood, *Ethnicity and the Mixed Marriage Crisis*, 191–211.

29. Compare Peter R. Bedford, "Diaspora-Homeland Relations in Ezra-Nehemiah," *VT* 52 (2002): 147–65.

30. Christine Hayes, "Intermarriage and Impurity in Ancient Jewish Sources," *HTR* 92 (1999): 3–36.

31. Saul M. Olyan, *Social Inequality in the World of the Text: The Significance of Ritual and Social Distinctions in the Hebrew Bible*, Journal of Ancient Judaism: Supplements 4 (Göttingen: Vandenhoeck & Ruprecht, 2011), 159–72, here 160, following Fishbane, *Biblical Interpretation*, 114–29.

32. Olyan, *Social Inequality*, 159–72.

33. D. L. Smith-Christopher, "Between Ezra and Isaiah: Exclusion, Transformation and Inclusion of the 'Foreigner' in Post-Exilic Biblical Theology," in *Ethnicity and the Bible*, ed. Mark G. Brett, BibInt 19 (Leiden: Brill, 1996), 117–44; compare Smith-Christopher, "The Mixed Marriage Crisis in Ezra 9–10 and Nehemiah 13: A Study of the Sociology of the

50   *When Texts Are Canonized*

norms for what it means to be Judean. Those who did not belong to the community of returned exiles were not to be trusted and, indeed, could be labeled as "Canaanites" or other traditional enemies of Israel. Ezra depicts a struggle to refashion Judean identity by bringing it into conformity with the ideals and practices of one party of returned exiles.

Similar concerns are in evidence in Nehemiah, who tries to enforce strict observance of the Sabbath and expresses concern that the children of some Judeans could not speak "the language of Judah" (Neh 13:24). Nehemiah also appeals to the Torah (Deut 23:3) as a warrant for evicting Tobiah the Ammonite from quarters in the Jerusalem Temple, although Tobiah was surely a worshiper of Yahweh.[34] Needless to say, the Torah does not require adherence to "the language of Judah."

The authority of the Torah is fundamental to the reform of Ezra. In the matter of the mixed marriages, the people defer to the authority of Ezra and ask that things be done "according to the law" (Ezra 10:3). In Neh 8, Ezra reads to the people from the book, and the Levites, we are told, helped the people understand the law when it was read to them in public. But as Kyong-Jin Lee has observed: "There is no record that Ezra launched a massive educational campaign to inform the people of the content of the Torah."[35] Michael Satlow has emphasized that very few people in Persian Yehud could read.[36] In such a society, the general populace was heavily dependent on the word of the scribe and the priest. Conformity to the "law of Moses" was primarily a matter of cultic observance (including Sabbath observance in Nehemiah), which had great symbolic value, and matters of boundary maintenance (avoidance of mixed marriage, language) and was essentially a matter of conformity to the dictates of the religious authorities.

The Second Century BCE

The elevation of the Torah in the Persian period laid the foundation for a further development in the Hellenistic period. In the later period, however, we find much more sustained attention to the details of biblical law. It is generally agreed that the authority of the Torah had been clarified and

---

Post-exilic Judean Community," in *Temple and Community in the Persian Period*, ed. Tamara C. Eskenazi and Kent H. Richards, vol. 2 of *Second Temple Studies*, JSOTSup 175 (Sheffield: JSOT Press, 1994), 243–65, esp. 257; Southwood, *Ethnicity and the Mixed Marriage Crisis*, 114–15.

34. See Anne Fitzpatrick-McKinley, *Empire, Power, and Indigenous Elites: A Case Study of the Nehemiah Memoir*, JSJSup 169 (Leiden: Brill, 2015), 217–51.

35. Kyong-Jin Lee, *The Authority and Authorization of Torah in the Persian Period*, CBET 64 (Leuven: Peeters, 2011), 246.

36. Satlow, *How the Bible Became Holy*, 79.

Uses of Torah in the Second Temple Period   51

solidified considerably by the second century BCE. "Considerably," however, is not "absolutely." One of the revelations of the Dead Sea Scrolls has concerned the extent of textual variation in the Hebrew Scriptures, down to the turn of the era. It is now clear that textual traditions known to us from the Samaritan Pentateuch and the Septuagint were current in Hebrew in the land of Israel, as well as the precursors of the Masoretic Text, and there were other variations besides.[37] Variant editions of several biblical books were in circulation (Exodus, Jeremiah, Psalms).[38] This in itself presents an interesting problem, as it shows that authority resided in a book rather than in a particular textual form of that book. Scribal variation was not necessarily perceived as problematic. The variants include scribal errors but also intentional changes. Some of these consist of additions, rearrangements, and paraphrases, sometimes intended to clarify the text and sometimes tendentious.[39] There is a movement toward standardization of the text in the first century CE, as can be seen from the revisions of the Greek translation of the Minor Prophets and from the prevalence of proto-Masoretic texts at Masada, but there is still considerable evidence of textual variation in the New Testament and in Josephus.

Prior to the discovery of the Dead Sea Scrolls, it was easy enough to distinguish between a biblical text that was at variance with the MT (e.g., the Samaritan Pentateuch) and a book like Jubilees that retold the story of Genesis and part of Exodus but was clearly an independent composition. The distinction is blurred, however, in the text (or texts) known as 4QReworked Pentateuch (4Q158, 4Q364–367). This title refers to a group of five fragmentary manuscripts that were originally thought to make up a single, independent composition.[40] Since there are no significant overlaps, however, they are now increasingly viewed as distinct but related compositions.[41] All five manuscripts reflect pentateuchal texts, with vari-

---

37. For a concise summary, see Armin Lange, "'Nobody Dared to Add to Them, to Take from Them, or to Make Changes' (Josephus, *Ag. Ap.* 1.42): The Textual Standardization of Jewish Scriptures in Light of the Dead Sea Scrolls," in *Flores Florentino: Dead Sea Scrolls and Other Early Jewish Studies in Honour of Florentino García Martínez*, ed. Anthony Hilhorst, Émile Puech and Eibert Tigchelaar, JSJSup 122 (Leiden: Brill, 2007), 105-26, esp. 107–10; Lange, *Die Handschriften biblischer Bücher von Qumran und den anderen Fundorten*, vol. 1 of *Handbuch der Textfunde vom Toten Meer* (Tübingen: Mohr Siebeck, 2009).

38. See Eugene C. Ulrich, *The Dead Sea Scrolls and the Origins of the Bible*, SDSSRL (Grand Rapids: Eerdmans, 1999), 17–50, 99–120.

39. Michael Segal, "Between Bible and Rewritten Bible," in *Biblical Interpretation at Qumran*, ed. Matthias Henze, SDSSRL (Grand Rapids: Eerdmans, 2005), 12. See the discussion of the Samaritan Pentateuch by Magnar Kartveit, *The Origin of the Samaritans*, VTSup 128 (Leiden: Brill, 2009), 279–312.

40. Emanuel Tov and Sidnie White, "Reworked Pentateuch," in *Qumran Cave 4.VIII: Parabiblical Texts, Part 1*, ed. Harold Attridge et al., DJD XIII (Oxford: Clarendon, 1994), 187–351.

41. Michael Segal, "4QReworked Pentateuch or 4QPentateuch?" in *The Dead Sea Scrolls*

52 When Texts Are Canonized

ations, including rearrangements and additions (notably the Song of Miriam). In the words of Sidnie White Crawford, "these texts are the product of scribal interpretation, still marked mainly by harmonistic editing, but with one important addition: the insertion of outside material into the text, material not found in other parts of what we now recognize as the Pentateuch."[42] Many fragments correspond to the traditional text with minimal variation. The extant fragments do not suggest any changes of speaker or setting over against other forms of these texts. Consequently, they are increasingly viewed not as distinct compositions but as expansionistic variants of the text known from our Bible.[43] If this is so, it suggests that the there was still great freedom in copying the scriptural texts as late as the first century BCE.[44] How far these variant texts were accepted as authentic Scriptures, we do not know.

Rewritten Scriptures

There are other texts, however, that are closely based on the traditional text of the Torah but are generally recognized as distinct compositions in their own right. These texts are often categorized as "Rewritten Bible," a label introduced by Geza Vermes to describe such works as Jubilees, the Genesis Apocryphon, the Biblical Antiquities of Pseudo-Philo, and the *Antiquities* of Josephus.[45] The designation is problematic, since that which is rewritten was not yet "Bible," and so scholars increasingly refer to them as "rewritten scriptures."[46] The rewriting has much in common

---

Fifty Years after Their Discovery: Proceedings of the Jerusalem Congress, July 20–25, 1997, ed. Lawrence H. Schiffman, Emanuel Tov, and James C. VanderKam (Jerusalem: Israel Exploration Society, 2000), 391–99; George Brooke, "4Q158: Reworked Pentateuchᵃ or Reworked Pentateuch A?" *DSD* 8 (2001): 219–41; Sidnie White Crawford, *Rewriting Scripture in Second Temple Times*, SDSSRL (Grand Rapids: Eerdmans, 2008), 39; Molly M. Zahn, *Rethinking Rewritten Scripture: Composition and Exegesis in the 4Q Reworked Pentateuch Manuscripts*, STDJ 95 (Leiden: Brill, 2011).

42. White Crawford, *Rewriting Scripture*, 39–40.

43. For a list of scholars who hold this view, including now Emanuel Tov, see White Crawford, *Rewriting Scripture*, 56. See the discussion by Molly M. Zahn, "The Problem of Characterizing the 4QReworked Pentateuch Manuscripts: Bible, Rewritten Bible, or None of the Above?," *DSD* 15 (2008): 315–39; Zahn, "Rewritten Scriptures," in *The Oxford Handbook of the Dead Sea Scrolls*, ed. Timothy H. Lim and John J. Collins (Oxford: Oxford University Press, 2010); and her book, *Rethinking Rewritten Scripture*.

44. The manuscripts date from the late Hasmonean period (White Crawford, *Rewriting Scripture*, 40).

45. Geza Vermes, *Scripture and Tradition in Judaism: Haggadic Studies*, 2nd rev. ed., StPB 4 (Leiden: Brill, 1973), 67–126.

46. See, e.g., Anders Klostergaard Petersen, "Rewritten Bible as a Borderline Phenomenon – Genre, Textual Strategy or Canonical Anachronism?" in Hilhorst et al., *Flores Flo-*

Uses of Torah in the Second Temple Period 53

with what we find in expansionistic texts like 4QReworked Pentateuch. It involves harmonizing, rearranging, and expansion. Some scholars see a spectrum, which ranges from minor editorial changes in the received text to changes so extensive that the texts are considered independent works.[47] But, as Michael Segal has pointed out, the difference between "Bible" and "Rewritten Bible" is not simply quantitative.[48] If it were, the variant editions of Jeremiah that underlie the Masoretic Text and the Septuagint would be considered different compositions.

More important are differences in the literary frame, the authorial voice, and the scope of the composition. There has been extensive debate about the extent and definition of this category of writing.[49] It is not strictly a literary genre.[50] Individual compositions tend to follow the genre of the prototype.[51] A great amount of Jewish literature from the late Second Temple period is based on older scriptures in one way or another. For example, the fragments of Hellenistic Jewish literature preserve retellings of stories about the patriarchs and the exodus not only in narrative form but also in epic poetry and even in the form of a tragedy.[52] There is no question in these writings of replacing the original scriptures: they sim-

---

rentino, 284–306. Jonathan G. Campbell also objects to "rewritten scriptures"; he suggests terminology along the lines of "scripture" and "parascripture" ("'Rewritten Bible' and 'Parabiblical Texts': A Terminological and Ideological critique," in *New Directions in Qumran Studies: Proceedings of the Bristol Colloquium on the Dead Sea Scrolls, 8–10 September 2003*, ed. Jonathan G. Campbell, William John Lyons, and Lloyd Keith Pietersen, LSTS 52 [London: T&T Clark International, 2005] 43–68).

47. So White Crawford, *Rewriting Scripture*, 14.

48. Segal, "Between Bible and Rewritten Bible," 16. See also Zahn, "Rewritten Scriptures."

49. In addition to works already cited, see Moshe Bernstein, "'Rewritten Bible': A Generic Category Which Has Outlived Its Usefulness?," *Textus* 22 (2005): 169–96; George J. Brooke, "Rewritten Bible," in *Encyclopedia of the Dead Sea Scrolls*, ed. Lawrence H. Schiffman and James C. VanderKam, 2 vols. (Oxford: Oxford University Press, 2000), 2:777–81; Brooke, "The Rewritten Law, Prophets and Psalms: Issues for Understanding the Text of the Bible," in *The Bible as Book: The Hebrew Bible and the Judaean Desert Discoveries*, ed. Edward D. Herbert and Emanuel Tov (London: British Library, 2002), 31–40; Antti Laato and Jacques van Ruiten, eds., *Rewritten Bible Reconsidered: Proceedings of the Conference in Karkku, Finland, August 24–26, 2006*, Studies in Rewritten Bible 1 (Winona Lake, IN: Eisenbrauns, 2008).

50. Philip S. Alexander argues that the texts so classified by Vermes, Jubilees, the Genesis Apocryphon, the *Antiquities* of Josephus, and the Biblical Antiquities of Pseudo-Philo, do constitute a literary genre ("Retelling the Old Testament," in *It is Written: Scripture Citing Scripture; Essays in Honour of Barnabas Lindars, SSF*, ed. D. A. Carson and H. G. M. Williamson [Cambridge: Cambridge University Press, 1988], 99–121). These are all narrative texts, and do not include such compositions as the Temple Scroll.

51. Compare Brooke, "Rewritten Bible," 780: "Rewritten Bible texts come in almost as many genres as can be found in the biblical books themselves."

52. See further John J. Collins, *Between Athens and Jerusalem: Jewish Identity in the Hellenistic Diaspora*, 2nd ed., Biblical Resource Series (Grand Rapids: Eerdmans, 2000), 29–63; Emil Schürer, *The History of the Jewish People in the Age of Jesus Christ (175 B.C.–A.D. 135)*, ed.

54   *When Texts Are Canonized*

ply present (and often embellish) these stories in ways that render them more interesting for a hellenized audience and use them to reshape Jewish identity in a diaspora setting. They treat the scriptures as sources for their literary imagination. This is also true of Josephus's great retelling of biblical history in his *Antiquities*, which was one of the works originally categorized as "Rewritten Bible" by Vermes. These works may have an exegetical dimension, insofar as they sometimes try to resolve problems in the scriptures, but they are not primarily works of exegesis. They are new compositions that draw their source material from the traditional scriptures, supplemented by other sources. The same is arguably true of the Aramaic Genesis Apocryphon and Aramaic Levi Document. The fact that so much of Jewish literature in this period draws its source material from the Pentateuch is powerful testimony to the authoritative status of the narrative parts of the Torah. Authority in these cases means primarily literary authority. Genesis and Exodus are classic texts that are infinitely adaptable to new circumstances, just as the epics of Homer were classic texts for the Greeks.

In the case of legal texts, however, the issues were somewhat different. The book of Jubilees was one of the prototypical texts adduced by Vermes. It retells the narrative of Genesis and part of Exodus, but it supplies a new literary frame: the narrative is dictated to Moses by an angel on Mount Sinai. In this case, the rewriting is far more tendentious than anything we find in the fragments of 4QReworked Pentateuch. Much of it is concerned with a strict interpretation of halakic issues, including a 364-day calendar, which is injected into the retold narrative. The Temple Scroll is also presented as a revelation on Mount Sinai, but in this case God speaks directly to Moses. In contrast to Jubilees, it is entirely concerned with the legal texts of the Pentateuch. Both Jubilees and the Temple Scroll are likely to date from the second century BCE.[53]

There has been debate as to whether these books are intended to replace or supplement the traditional Torah. Hindy Najman has argued vigorously that they

> seek to provide the interpretive context within which scriptural traditions already acknowledged as authoritative can be properly understood. This is neither a fraudulent attempt at replacement, nor an act of impiety. It is rather, we may charitably assume, a pious effort to convey what is taken

---

Geza Vermes, Fergus Millar, and Martin Goodman, 3 vols. in 4 pts. (Edinburgh: T&T Clark, 1973–1987), 3.1:509–66.

53. On the date of Jubilees, see James C. VanderKam, *The Book of Jubilees*, Guides to the Apocrypha and Pseudepigrapha 9 (Sheffield: Sheffield Academic, 2001), 17–21; for the Temple Scroll, see Sidnie White Crawford, *The Temple Scroll and Related Texts*, Companion to the Qumran Scrolls 2 (Sheffield: Sheffield Academic, 2000), 24–26. VanderKam and White Crawford both favor dates before the middle of the second century BCE for their respective works.

Uses of Torah in the Second Temple Period   55

to be the essence of earlier traditions, an essence that the rewriters think is in danger of being missed.[54]

Moreover, she claims, "They claimed for their interpretations of authoritative texts the already established authority of the texts themselves."[55] Their goal is to solve interpretive problems in the older texts, and to appropriate the authority of the Torah for their interpretations. So, argues Najman, while they do not replace the existing Torah, they do claim the status of Torah for themselves. Najman is aware that there are significant differences between the two compositions.[56] I would suggest that these differences are important for the kind of authority claimed in each text and for the way in which their relationship to the older scriptures is conceived.

Jubilees

In the case of Jubilees, we are fortunate that the beginning of the work has been preserved. Both the short prologue and the opening chapter are attested in the fragments of 4Q216 and preserved in full in Ethiopic. From allusions to Exod 24:12–18, it appears that the setting is Moses's first forty-day sojourn on Mount Sinai.[57] Moses is told to write down

> everything I tell you on this mountain, the first things and the last things that shall come to pass in all the divisions of the days, in the law and in the testimony, and in the weeks of the *Jubilees* till eternity, till I descend and dwell with them through all eternity. (Jub. 1:26)[58]

The actual dictation is performed not by the deity but by the angel of the presence, who in turn derives the information from the heavenly tablets.[59]

Jubilees evidently presupposes that the story of the revelation on Sinai is familiar to readers, and so it can dispense with the narrative of the arrival at Sinai. It also clearly presupposes the existence, and authority, of "the first law." The most explicit reference is in Jub. 6:20–22, with

---

54. Hindy Najman, *Seconding Sinai: The Development of Mosaic Discourse in Second Temple Judaism*, JSJSup 77 (Leiden: Brill, 2003), 46.

55. Ibid., 45.

56. Ibid., 59.

57. See James C. VanderKam, "Moses Trumping Moses: Making the Book of *Jubilees*," in *The Dead Sea Scrolls: Transmission of Traditions and Production of Texts*, ed. Sarianna Metso, Hindy Najman, and Eileen M. Schuller, STDJ 92 (Leiden: Brill, 2010), 25–44.

58. Translation by R. H. Charles and revised by C. Rabin, "Jubilees," in H. F. D. Sparks, *The Apocryphal Old Testament* (Oxford: Clarendon, 1984), 1–139, here 13.

59. Hindy Najman, *Past Renewals: Interpretative Authority, Renewed Revelation, and the Quest for Perfection in Jewish Antiquity*, JSJSup 53 (Leiden: Brill, 2010), 39–71. This article was originally published in *JSJ* 30 (1999): 379–410.

56   *When Texts Are Canonized*

reference to the laws of Shavuoth: "for I have written in the book of the first law, which I have written for you, that you should celebrate it at its proper time." Again in Jub. 30:12, apropos of Dinah and the Shechemites: "I have written for you in the words of the law all the details of what the Shechemites did to Dinah." But in addition to the Torah, there was also the "testimony" תעודה, which, as VanderKam argues persuasively, should be identified with the contents of the book of *Jubilees* itself, although they may not exhaust the testimony contained in the heavenly tablets.[60]

Moses is not the speaker in Jubilees. His authority here is that of a mediator. More properly, Jubilees is angelic discourse, or even mediated divine discourse. The authority claimed for it is not ultimately that of Moses, as in Deuteronomy or the Testament of Moses, but that of divine revelation. Moses is important as guarantor of its transmission, but he is not its source. The fact that the traditional Torah is called "the first law" would seem to grant it priority, in a sense. But the "testimony" is also revealed on Mount Sinai, so for all practical purposes Jubilees and the "first law" are coeval and complementary.[61]

The body of Jubilees is made up of a rewritten narrative of Genesis and Exodus. Much of the rewriting can be explained as an exegetical attempt to resolve problems in the traditional text of the Torah, although some other traditions are also introduced, notably the Enochic story of the fallen angels.[62] But Jubilees is not presented as an exegetical text, and there is no acknowledgment that its authority derives in any way from other

---

60. VanderKam, "Moses Trumping Moses"; Cana Werman thinks that the "testimony" is "the preordained march of history." ("'The תורה and the תעודה': Engraved on the Tablets," *DSD* 9 [2002]: 75–103).

61. Compare Werman, "'תורה and the תעודה,'" 95: "Moses came down from Mount Sinai carrying two Torahs." Similarly Martha Himmelfarb, *A Kingdom of Priests: Ancestry and Merit in Ancient Judaism* (Philadelphia: University of Pennsylvania Press, 2006), 54–55: "*Jubilees* does not attempt to nudge the Torah out of its niche and replace it, but rather embraces the authority of the Torah even as it seeks to place itself alongside it." See also Himmelfarb, "Torah, Testimony, and Heavenly Tablets: The Claim to Authority in the *Book of Jubilees*," in *A Multiform Heritage: Studies on Early Judaism and Christianity in Honor of Robert A. Kraft*, ed. Benjamin G. Wright, Scholars Press Homage Series 24 (Atlanta: Scholars Press, 1999), 22–28.

62. Michael Segal, *The Book of Jubilees. Rewritten Bible, Redaction, Ideology and Theology*, JSJSup 117 (Leiden: Brill, 2007), 103–43. Gabriele Boccaccini construes the use of Enochic tradition in Jubilees as an attempt to merge two forms of Judaism ("From a Movement of Dissent to a Distinct Form of Judaism: The Heavenly Tablets in Jubilees as the Foundation of a Competing Halakah," in *Enoch and the Mosaic Torah: The Evidence of Jubilees*, ed. Gabriele Boccaccini and Giovanni Ibba [Grand Rapids: Eerdmans, 2009], 193–210). This construal entails assumptions about the social history of Second Temple Judaism that are not widely shared. See also John S. Bergsma, "The Relationship between Jubilees and the Early Enochic Books (Astronomical Book and Book of the Watchers)," in Boccaccini and Ibba, *Enoch and the Mosaic Torah*, 36–51, who notes that the influence of the early Enoch material in Jubilees is limited to the period from Enoch to Noah and does not come close to rivaling the importance of Moses.

Uses of Torah in the Second Temple Period   57

scriptures.[63] Its authority does depend on the setting at Sinai and the reader's acceptance that a foundational revelatory event occurred there. Verbal echoes of the older scriptures would probably have facilitated acceptance of Jubilees as a credible account of Sinaitic revelation. But this is not quite the same thing as appropriating the authority of the existing scriptures. Jubilees is presented as a distinct revelation. It is not intended to replace "the first law," but it does supersede it in some respects. Where it differs from or adds to the traditional Torah, there is no doubt in Jubilees as to which formulation has the higher authority.[64]

In view of the divine and angelic authority claimed for Jubilees, the appeal to the heavenly tablets may seem superfluous. For VanderKam, they simply add another layer of assurance of the reliability of the revelation: "These tablets are a written unchangeable, permanent depository of information under God's control."[65] James Kugel, in contrast, argues that the passages that refer to the heavenly tablets are interpolations, which stand in tension with the rest of the text in various ways.[66] The argument rests on perceived contradictions between these passages and the rest of the text, and some are more persuasive than others.[67] If Kugel is correct, however, this would explain why the interpolator has to trump even the angel of the presence by appealing to a still higher authority.

In any case, the heavenly tablets appear as a source of truth to which both the Torah and the Testimony are subordinate. Moreover, Enoch also "wrote his testimony and left it as a testimony on the earth for all the sons of men for every generation" (Jub. 4:19), and Noah is also cited as an author.[68] The testimony of Enoch and Noah is not explicitly associated with the heavenly tablets but is further evidence that revelation is not confined to the traditional Torah. As Martha Himmelfarb has observed, "This approach not only exalts *Jubilees* but also, less obviously, demotes

---

63. Najman says, "Jubilees claims that its teachings are the true interpretation of the Torah" and "derive their authority from that of the Torah" (*Past Renewals*, 40). But while the teachings of Jubilees are largely interpretations of the Torah, that is not how Jubilees presents itself.

64. Ben Zion Wacholder is correct that Jubilees trumps the traditional Torah in many places, even if it does not deny the Torah's authority ("Jubilees as the Super Canon: Torah-Admonition versus Torah-Commandment," in *Legal Texts and Legal Issues: Proceedings of the Second Meeting of the International Organization for Qumran Studies, Cambridge, 1995: Published in Honour of Joseph M. Baumgarten,* ed. Moshe Bernstein, Florentino García Martínez, and John Kampen, STDJ 23 [Leiden: Brill, 1997], 195–211).

65. VanderKam, "Moses Trumping Moses"; similarly Najman, *Past Renewals,* 50–62.

66. James Kugel, "On the Interpolations in the Book of Jubilees," *RevQ* 24 (2009): 215–72. Kugel is building on the work of Segal, *Book of Jubilees.*

67. A persuasive example is the contrasting roles of Mastema in *Jubilees* 48–49.

68. Jubilees 8:11, 10:13, 21:10; Himmelfarb, "Torah, Testimony, and the Heavenly Tablets," 27.

58   *When Texts Are Canonized*

the Torah, which must share its authoritative status with another text even as both are subordinated to the heavenly tablets."[69]

VanderKam and Kugel agree that the author of Jubilees could not just insert his new ideas into the received text of the Torah. For Kugel, this is why the interpolator made his insertions into Jubilees rather than into the Torah itself: "By the mid-second century BCE, any major, sectarian tampering with the Pentateuch would surely have been a controversial undertaking; its text was simply too widely known, and its study too well entrenched, across the spectrum of Jewish groups."[70] Whether this was already the case by the mid-second century BCE may be open to question, but at least the author of Jubilees chose not to change the text. He did not, however, subordinate his rewriting to the existing text by presenting it in the form of a commentary. Rather, he seems to have claimed for his "testimony" a status equal, at least, to that of the first Torah.

The Temple Scroll

In the case of the Temple Scroll, we do not have the opening column, and so there is some uncertainty as to how its revelation is presented. There is a passing reference to "Aaron your brother" in TS XLIV, 5, and another to "those things which I tell you on this mountain" in TS LI, 6. From these references, many infer that the discourse is addressed to Moses on Mount Sinai,[71] but these are the only nods to Moses in a lengthy text, and he is never mentioned by name. Najman argues that "by means of the second person singular pronoun, the reader is placed in the position of Moses, as the addressee of divine revelation on Mount Sinai."[72] But she also recognizes that the Temple Scroll is not about Moses: "Moses is nothing but the implicit, initial addressee and the implicit teacher of a Torah whose authority rests primarily on its direct revelation from God."[73] Lawrence Schiffman entertains the possibility that the allusions to Moses are mere lapses, where the author had not fully revised his sources, and that he did not intend to acknowledge the role of Moses at all.[74] Without the opening

---

69. Himmelfarb, *Kingdom of Priests*, 55; cf. Himmelfarb, "Torah, Testimony, and the Heavenly Tablets," 27–28. Note also Najman, *Past Renewals*, 71: "Jubilees' insistence on the pre-Sinaitic origin of its heavenly tradition could be seen to undermine the special authority that had been accorded to the Mosaic Torah." See also Boccaccini, "From a Movement of Dissent," 193–96.

70. Kugel, "On the Interpolations," 271.

71. So White Crawford, *Rewriting Scripture*, 86; White Crawford, *Temple Scroll and Related Texts*, 18.

72. Najman, *Seconding Sinai*, 68.

73. Ibid.

74. Lawrence H. Schiffman, "The Temple Scroll and the Halakhic Pseudepigrapha of

Uses of Torah in the Second Temple Period   59

column of the scroll, it is impossible to know for sure whether Moses had more than the incidental role he appears to have in the extant fragments.

There is no doubt, however, that the speaking voice in the Temple Scroll is that of God. Consequently, Schiffman is correct that this is a "divine" rather than a "Mosaic" pseudepigraphon. It is only "Mosaic discourse" insofar as its content resembles the discourse of Moses in Deuteronomy. It is actually presented as "divine discourse." As such, its claim to authority would seem to be unambiguous. It would be anachronistic to say that the Temple Scroll is "canonical," but it claims to be a direct revelation of divine law. It is true that large portions of the Temple Scroll follow the same kinds of procedures that we find in expansionistic "biblical" texts—rearranging passages and harmonizing them, to smooth out the tensions between them. But, unlike Jubilees, the Temple Scroll does not acknowledge any "first law." If the revelation is indeed set on Mount Sinai, then it would seem to be prior at least to Deuteronomy, perhaps even prior to the laws of Leviticus, which were allegedly given to Moses at the tent of meeting. Also unlike Jubilees, there is no appeal to the angel of the presence or to the heavenly tablets. No further authority is needed than the voice of God.

The claim to authority of the Temple Scroll is as strong as any we find in the Torah and stronger than many. There can be no doubt that it claims the status of Torah: several passages demand that the Israelites observe "the regulation of this law" (L, 5–9, 17), and it refers to itself as "this Torah" (LVI, 20–21, the law of the king; cf. LVII, 1, the law of the priests, LIX, 7–10).[75] The fact that it uses language familiar from the traditional Torah would probably make it easier to accept as the authentic revelation on Sinai. Moreover, TS LIV, 5–7 appropriates the stricture of Deut 13:1: "All the things which I order you today, take care to carry them out; you shall not add to them nor shall you remove anything from them." This could well be taken as a claim to exclusive authority. The strongest argument that the Temple Scroll presupposes the continued authority of other scriptures is that there are so many basic issues that it does not address. But even the traditional Torah does not address all aspects of the law—for example, there is no law regulating divorce, although the custom is clearly acknowledged in Deut 24. De facto, by the time the Temple Scroll was written, many laws, such as the Ten Commandments, must have been so

---

the Second Temple Period," in *Pseudepigraphic Perspectives: The Apocrypha and Pseudepigrapha in Light of the Dead Sea Scrolls; Proceedings of the International Symposium of the Orion Center for the Study of the Dead Sea Scrolls and Associated Literature, 12–14 January 1997*, ed. Esther G. Chazon and Michael E. Stone, STDJ 31 (Leiden: Brill, 1999), 121–31. See also Baruch A. Levine, "The Temple Scroll: Aspects of Its Historical Provenance and Literary Character," *BASOR* 232 (1978): 17–21, who argued that the Temple Scroll follows Priestly understanding of revelation, according to which all commandments are attributed directly to God.

75. Najman, *Seconding Sinai*, 52.

60   *When Texts Are Canonized*

familiar that they could be taken for granted. It would have been unrealistic, in any case, to seek to suppress books that were current and enjoyed authority. The whole biblical tradition is full of examples of material that corrects older scripture but does not erase it. It may be that "the *Temple Scroll* is meant to stand alongside the Torah, to supplement and explain it," like the book of Jubilees,[76] although it is then surprising that it does not explicitly acknowledge the existence of the older scripture. But there can be little doubt that the authors of the Temple Scroll intended that this law would be decisive on the matters it addressed.

The author of Jubilees may not have felt free to change the traditional text of scripture. The author of the Temple Scroll appears to have had no such inhibition. Jubilees may be a work based closely on traditional scripture; the Temple Scroll is more properly scripture rewritten. If the author of Jubilees, then, felt he had to acknowledge the "first law" as authoritative, this attitude was not universal. In the mid-second century BCE it was still possible to rewrite the Torah radically and present it as the Torah revealed by God on Mount Sinai.

This is not to say that such a rewritten Torah would necessarily be accepted. If the authors aimed to produce a normative text, there is little evidence that they succeeded. Unlike Jubilees, the Temple Scroll does not seem to have been translated into any other language. It survives in only a few copies—two that can be identified with certainty, a possible third and a manuscript that seems to contain a different, older form of the text (4QRP).[77] The fact that it was copied at all, at no small expense, suggests that some people accepted its claim to be divine revelation, but it is never clearly cited as an authority. To say that the authors did not succeed in having their work accepted, except by a few, is not to say that this was not their intention.

The authors of the so-called rewritten scriptures evidently handled their inherited scriptures with considerable freedom. The older scriptures were authoritative insofar as they framed the questions and provided a basic orientation, but the "rewriters" felt free to alter details in accordance with their own convictions. This is also true of other genres. Ben Sira famously declared that all wisdom is "the book of the covenant of the Most High God, the law that Moses commanded us" (24:23). Yet in his paraphrase of Genesis in chapter 17, he blithely declares that God "filled them [the primeval couple] with knowledge and understanding, and showed them good and evil," despite the fact that in Genesis God explicitly forbade them to eat the fruit of the tree of knowledge of good and evil. To the wisdom teacher, it was inconceivable that God would prohibit the

---

76. White Crawford, *Rewriting Scripture*, 87.
77. Ibid., 85.

quest for wisdom, and so he interpreted the text in a way that conformed with his sense of the truth.

Concluding Reflections

I would like to conclude with two more general reflections. First, the study of the scrolls, especially, has shown that the transmission of scriptures was a process, and that texts like Jubilees and the Temple Scroll were continuous with the kind of harmonistic editing that shaped the later stages of the biblical books.[78] Even when text and canon were stabilized in the common era, this kind of paraphrastic use of scripture did not cease. The editors of a recent journal issue devoted to Jubilees conclude that we do not need to choose between regarding Jubilees as a replacement for Genesis or as a commentary. "*Jubilees*," they write, "should not be understood either as a commentary on a static tradition, or as intended to replace an existing stage of that tradition. Rather, Jubilees is at once both new and part of the ongoing, dynamic tradition of Torat Moshe."[79] I would argue, however, that both Jubilees and the Temple Scroll not only extend the tradition of the Torah but revise it in decisive ways. This is not to say that they replace it. Jubilees still depends on "the first law" and the Temple Scroll assumes the Decalogue. But they are not simply reiterating tradition. They are revising it and, in the process, superseding it.

Second, the tendency, which we found already in Ezra, to subsume under "the Torah" or "the law" things that are not found in the written text, is by no means exceptional in ancient Judaism. At the end of the Second Temple period, Josephus wrote a summary of the Jewish law for the benefit of his Greek and Roman readers. While he claims to be summarizing the law, he makes several claims that are not found in the written text. "The woman, says the Law, is in all things inferior to the man. Let her accordingly be submissive.... The Law orders all the offspring to be brought up, and forbids women either to cause abortion or to make away with the foetus" and so forth (*Ag. Ap.* 2.200–203). But where does the law say these things? (Bear in mind that the Pastoral Epistles were not part of Josephus's Bible). Rather, as Seth Schwartz has written apropos of the legal papyri from the Judean Desert:

---

78. Compare Hindy Najman and Eibert Tigchelaar, "Unity after Fragmentation," *RevQ* 26 (2014): 497: "the writing and rewriting of Jubilees is continuous with the writing and rewriting of Genesis and other biblical traditions."

79. Ibid., 498.

62   *When Texts Are Canonized*

> "Torah" does of course refer to the Pentateuch, but it had a rather broader meaning too, referring to the entire body of traditional Jewish legal practice, which varied from place to place and time to time, and also in respect to the closeness of its relationship with the Pentateuch.... "Torah" was a set of negotiations between an authoritative but opaque text and various sets of traditional but not fully authorized practice.[80]

To be sure, this is not the whole story. We also find intensive halakic exegesis in the sectarian texts of the Dead Sea Scrolls from the first century BCE, and Alexandrian Jewish writers such as Philo developed their own allegorical way of reading the text. But what we find in Ezra and the so-called rewritten scriptures is broadly typical of Second Temple Judaism. Torah was not just the written text, despite the iconic importance that was increasingly attached to it. That text was usually read through a filter provided by tradition, in some cases, and in others by the ideological commitments of a particular author.

---

80. Seth Schwartz, *Imperialism and Jewish Society, 200 B.C.E. to 640 C.E.*, Jews, Christians, and Muslims from the Ancient to the Modern World (Princeton: Princeton University Press, 2001), 68.

Bad Prophecies: Canon and the Case
of the Book of Daniel

MICHAEL L. SATLOW

The composition of the Hebrew canon presents no shortage of puzzles. How, for example, did a book like Chronicles, much of which repeats, revises, and contradicts other biblical texts, attain a "holy" status? Why does the canon contain a seemingly impious book like Ecclesiastes while excluding Ben Sira and other more pious compositions? Why would the redactor include even in the single unified composition of the Torah multiple doublets and contradictions (e.g., Gen 1–2 and the Ten Commandments in Exod 20:1–17 and Deut 5:6–21)? None of these facts, however, is as puzzling as how and why false prophecies became part of the canon.

The Hebrew Bible contains several cases of prophecies that events had proven wrong already in antiquity. Some of these cases, such as the end of the book of Haggai (2:23, promising to make Zerubbabel "like a signet ring"), the later redactors and canonizers appear simply to have ignored.[1] In other cases, they revised the faulty prophecies, whether by changing original oracles or by restating them elsewhere.[2] While it is relatively easy to understand how later interpreters, who already accepted the authority and sanctity of the Hebrew Bible, freely reinterpreted these prophecies in ways that justified them (usually by claiming either that they were in fact fulfilled by later, less obvious events or that they remained unfulfilled), it is harder to understand how these incorrect prophecies gained authority to begin with. Given the significant and extreme rhetoric found in the

---

1. But see Robert C. Kashow, who argues that Zechariah indeed did offer a subtle response ("Zechariah 1–8 as a Theological Explanation for the Failure of Prophecy in Haggai 2:20–23," *JTS* 64 [2013]: 385–403).

2. Such is the case with 2 Sam 7:1–16, with an addition at v. 13 and a restatement in 1 Chr 17:1–14. See the discussion in William M. Schniedewind, *Society and the Promise to David: The Reception History of 2 Samuel 7:1–17* (New York: Oxford University Press, 1999), 17–71. For a discussion of the later reworking of the promise to David, see Jon D. Levenson, "The Last Four Verses in Kings," *JBL* 103 (1984): 353–61.

63

64   *When Texts Are Canonized*

Hebrew Bible itself that identifies the false prophet as one who utters a prediction in God's name that does not come to pass, why did authors, redactors, and canonizers revise or rework incorrect oracles rather than simply declare them false and erase them?[3]

In this essay, I attempt to bring these questions to bear on perhaps the false prophet par excellence, Daniel. Already by the late third century CE, the book of Daniel was labeled as a Maccabean-era pseudepigraphon by Porphyry, a charge that church fathers stridently fought.[4] Although Porphyry's precise interpretations were not always accurate, his fundamental insight largely coheres with modern critical research: Daniel contains prophetic oracles that did not come to pass and yet remain largely unproblematized in the book.[5] How and why were these relatively late, incorrect oracles seen as authoritative?

My goal here is to see whether paying close attention to the several incorrect oracles in Daniel and wondering how they not only survived but flourished might change our understanding of (1) the context of the original oracles, (2) the redaction of the book, and (3) the granting of authority to both.[6] To foreground my conclusion, I will argue that neither Daniel's oracles nor the book itself was known outside of small circles until the Roman period. Only after period sufficient to allow the haze of time to obscure their inaccuracy had passed were these oracles rediscovered and applied to the latest burning historical crisis, the relationship with Rome. More importantly, though, I hope that using Daniel as a test case might give us some purchase on the processes through which other bad prophecies eventually became part of the Jewish canon.

---

3. Passages that condemn "false" prophets include Deut 18:20–22 (cf. Deut 13:5), 1 Kgs 22:22–23, Jer 28:12–17, and Mic 3:5. See also Robert R. Wilson, *Sociological Approaches to the Old Testament*, GBS.OT (Philadelphia: Fortress, 1984), 67–80.

4. On Porphyry and his work, which is known only in fragments found among the early Christians who opposed him, see P. M. Casey, "Porphyry and the Origin of the Book of Daniel," *JTS* 27 (1976): 15–33. For a summary of early Christian responses to both Daniel and Porphyry, see Gerben S. Oegma, "The Reception of the Book of Daniel (and Danielic Literature) in the Early Church," in *The Pseudepigrapha and Christian Origins: Essays from the Studiorum Novi Testamenti Societas*, ed. Gerben S. Oegma and James H. Charlesworth, Jewish and Christian Texts in Contexts and Related Studies 4 (London: T&T Clark, 2008), 243–52.

5. For a modern treatment that references Porphyry, see Elias Bickerman, *Four Strange Books of the Bible: Jonah, Daniel, Koheleth, Esther* (New York: Schocken, 1967), 53–138.

6. This disaggregation of the different questions that are sometimes lumped together under the question of "canonization" follows several contemporary scholars. See, in particular, John Barton, *Oracles of God: Perceptions of Ancient Prophecy in Israel after the Exile* (London: Darton, Longman & Todd,), 35–95; Eugene C. Ulrich, "The Notion and Definition of Canon," in *The Canon Debate*, ed. Lee Martin McDonald and James A. Sanders (Peabody, MA: Hendrickson, 2002), 21–35; Timothy H. Lim, *The Formation of the Jewish Canon*, AYBRL (New Haven: Yale University Press, 2013).

Bad Prophecies   65

Canonization: Modeling a Process

As background to the argument I develop below, it is useful to review briefly the stages of canonization, with special attention to the prophetic books. Canonization of the Jewish and Christian Bibles, as is well recognized today, was a process rather than an event.[7] Texts were (usually?) not developed with the idea that they would immediately become part of an authoritative canon. Over time, some texts gained different kinds of authority, for different reasons, among different groups. Very roughly, one can distinguish four stages in this process:

1. *Oral delivery.* Nearly all Israelite and Jewish prophets—and here I am using the word generally to include both those who believe they were delivering authentic divine oracles and those whom others later come to accept as doing so—are described as having delivered their oracles orally.[8] This is not to deny that there were also literary prophets, but the vast majority of prophetic writings at least describe prophecies as having been orally delivered or performed, even if part of that performance involved writing (e.g., Ezek 2:6–3:3).[9] It is curious and significant that the oracles in Daniel, as discussed below, much more strongly suggest a literary rather than oral context.

2. *Literary expression.* Presumably the vast majority of orally delivered prophetic statements were lost. Some, though, were transcribed, typically, as in Jeremiah's case (Jer 36), by a scribe. We can presume that the scribe did not preserve the prophet's words verbatim or completely. We do not know if the initial literary production would have been simply a list of disconnected oracles, or whether the oracles were already massaged and arranged in their earliest stage of composition. We do not know how much time elapsed between the prophetic utterances and their transcription. We can be fairly

---

7. See especially the helpful summary in Lee Martin McDonald and James A. Sanders, "Introduction," in McDonald and Sanders, *Canon Debate*, 5–17.

8. Susan Niditch, *Oral World and Written Word: Ancient Israelite Literature*, LAI (Louisville: Westminster John Knox, 1996); Ehud Ben Zvi and Michael H. Floyd, eds., *Writings and Speech in Israelite and Ancient Near Eastern Prophecy*, SymS 10 (Atlanta: Society of Biblical Literature, 2000).

9. For more on literary prophecy, see recently Matthijs J. de Jong, "Biblical Prophecy—A Scribal Enterprise: The Old Testament Prophecy of Unconditional Judgement Considered as a Literary Phenomenon," *VT* 61 (2011): 39–70; Christoph Levin, "Zephaniah: How This Book Became Prophecy," in *Re-Reading the Scriptures: Essays on the Literary History of the Old Testament*, FAT 87 (Tübingen: Mohr Siebeck, 2013), 261–80.

66   *When Texts Are Canonized*

confident, though, that the literary prophetic work went through rounds of revisions and editing.[10] This, of course, raises the issue of the social context of these literary works. Were they intended to archive the words of prophets who were thought authentic, or were they used and transmitted as scribal literature? At what point did they receive the kind of authority that stopped the process of revision?

3. *Acquisition of textual authority.* We should probably presume—although this must also remain open to debate—not only that most prophetic oracles were not preserved in written form but also that most written prophetic books were themselves not copied and preserved. That is, it seems likely that at least some and probably most written prophecies were not preserved, probably because they either proved themselves wrong or irrelevant at a crucial moment in time. Those that did survive had achieved some kind of authority or status within a community, at which point revision would largely have ceased. This is the stage at which a text moves from being simply a text and becomes "authoritative scripture." The discussion of Daniel below will mainly focus on this stage.[11]

4. *Canonization.* In this final stage, the authoritative literary works are deemed canonical. Here again we presume that the canonizers picked from only a subset of authoritative works, works that would have proven themselves to be both true and useful. The move from stage 3 to 4, though, is one more of degree than of kind. There was no official rabbinic canon, after all, even though the rabbis considered all of the books that would eventually be included in the Hebrew Bible as authoritative.[12]

I want to be clear about how I am using this framework. I am not claiming, as in an old popular model, that Israelite prophecy evolved from a lower, oral form to a higher, written one. Nor would I make a sharp division between Israelite and post-Israelite prophecies.[13] Individual prophecies need not go through each of these stages, in sequence or not. A prophet, for example, might himself—unfortunately not herself in our extant Bible—have achieved authority well before his oracles were reproduced

---

10. Robert C. Culley, "Orality and Writtenness in the Prophetic Texts," in Ben Zvi and Floyd, *Writings and Speech in Israelite and Ancient Near Eastern Prophecy*, 45–64. For a nuanced approach that sees more fluidity between oral and written, see Joachim Schaper, "Exilic and Post-Exilic Prophecy and the Orality/Literacy Problem," *VT* 55 (2005): 324–42.

11. See Lim, *Formation of the Jewish Canon*, 1–16.

12. See the essays in McDonald and Sanders, *Canon Debate*, especially that of James A. Sanders, "The Issue of Closure in the Canonical Process," 252–63.

13. See, e.g., Paul D. Hanson, *The Dawn of Apocalyptic: The Historical and Sociological Roots of Jewish Apocalyptic Eschatology* (Philadelphia: Fortress, 1979).

Bad Prophecies   67

in written form. Rather, then, I see the usefulness of this framework to be heuristic. I hope to demonstrate this by applying it to the book of Daniel.

The Book of Daniel: Preliminaries

The book of Daniel is arguably one of the most redactionally complex books in the Hebrew Bible. It contains striking disjunctures of language, genre, and voice.

Daniel 1:1–2:3 is in Hebrew, and 2:4 is a transitional verse that means to account for the switch to Aramaic: "The Chaldeans said to the king [in] Aramaic, 'O king, live forever!'" The first half of the verse is in Hebrew and then the statement ("O king") switches to Aramaic. The language of the book stays in Aramaic through the end of chapter 7. Chapter 8 begins in Hebrew, which continues through the remainder of the book.

The differences of language do not discernibly map onto the genres found within the book. Chapter 1 is a tale about how Daniel got to the court of Nebuchadnezzar. Chapter 2 contains an oracle (vv. 31–45) embedded in a wisdom tale. Chapters 3–6 contain wisdom tales, although there is one fulfilled prophecy in chapter 4. Chapters 7–12 are primarily oracles, visions that Daniel had that are then interpreted by otherworldly beings.

There is also a noticeable, but less jerky, change of voice. While chapters 1–6 contain dialogue, they are written in the third person. Chapter 7 has a very light third person frame at the beginning and the end but purports to cite a written account penned by Daniel in the first person. It thus begins by saying that Daniel had a dream and that he "wrote the beginning of the words and said" (7:1).[14] A long oracle and its interpretation, all written with Daniel narrating, follow, and its ending is marked at the end of the account (7:28): "up to here is the end of the account" (עד כה סופא די מלתא). The rest of the book, which continues with Daniel relating in the first person other oracles, does not contain any other such markers.

These characteristics can be summed up in the following table:

---

14. This translation renders the MT, כתב ראש מלין אמר. The Old Greek differs somewhat: καὶ τὸ ἐνύπνιον ἔγραψεν. Ulrich suggests that the Hebrew clause was added later to balance 7:28, but the evidence from the manuscripts seems to me to be inconclusive. See Eugene Ulrich et al., *Qumran Cave 4.XI: Psalms to Chronicles*, DJD XVI (Oxford: Clarendon, 2000), 264. The difference in the two versions spills over into the next verse. The Hebrew of 7:2 begins, "and Daniel related and said ..." (ענה דניאל ואמר), whereas the Greek continues "I, Daniel...." These differences do not impact my observation that a first person account of the oracle is introduced here. I am focused here and throughout on the MT. While the Old Greek might in general deserve fuller consideration, such consideration would not seriously challenge the contours of the argument of this paper. See Amanda M. Davis Bledsoe, "The Relationship of the Different Editions of Daniel: A History of Scholarship," *CurBR* 13 (2015): 175–90.

68   *When Texts Are Canonized*

Hebrew	Aramaic	Tale	Oracle	First Person	Third Person
1:1–2:4		1:1–2:30			1–6
	2:4–7:28		2:31–45		
		2:46–6:28			
			7	7 (embedded)	
8–12			8–12	8–12	

While there are a few loose correspondences, the units that stand out as mostly coherent based on formal criteria are 2:4–6:28 (with the exception of the oracle at 2:31–45) and the oracular, Hebrew composition of chapters 8–12. These formal differences suggest a multistage redactional history of the book. In assessing the redaction of Daniel, though, and the time and degree to which the texts that comprised it were thought authoritative (canonical stage 3) we must consider in addition to the formal criteria both the content of the oracles and the reception history of the book.

Bad Prophecies

In the third century CE Porphyry already identified the book of Daniel as a pseudepigraphon of the Maccabean period. His argument for doing so rested on the identification of the so-called prophetic oracles. Daniel's prophecies were so precisely correct, he argued, up until the point that they went dramatically wrong, that they must have been written *ex eventu*, after the history that Daniel got right but before his predications went wrong. Even Jerome, who sought in the fifth century to repudiate Porphyry's dating of the work, admitted that much of Porphyry's historical identifications were correct. For Jerome, though, that only proved that Daniel was an authentic prophet and that the predictions that Porphyry identified as "wrong" really remained unfulfilled. The following oracles are the ones most contested:

1. The oracle of the four kingdoms in Daniel 2. This oracle, probably adapted from an original Persian one, foretells the succession of four kingdoms, probably Babylon, Media, Persia, and Greece. The reference to Greece is oddly specific. The Greek kingdom is represented by the feet and toes, made of a mix of clay and iron, of a statue. This mixture of clay and iron refers to the kingdom being held together by marriage, as the Ptolemies and Seleucids were. Yet,

Bad Prophecies   69

just as clay and iron do not mix, so too this kingdom was doomed to internal strife. "In the days of those kings" another kingdom will arise, one "that will never be destroyed, a kingdom that will not be transferred to another people. It will crush and wipe out all these kingdoms but will itself last forever—just as you saw how a stone was hewn from the mountain, not by hands, and that it crushed the iron, bronze, clay, silver, and gold" (2:44–45). Although Rome was the kingdom that ultimately did defeat these Greek kingdoms, this "stone" could hardly be a reference to it. Rather, some scholars understand the reference to be either to the Maccabees or to Israel more generally, and then the time must have been sometime prior to the demise of the Maccabees.[15] If so, though, it is clear that the Maccabees' success fell short of that attributed to the stone.

2. A more detailed oracle with a similar message appears in chapter 7. This is a vision of four beasts, probably representing Babylon, Media, Persia, and Greece. The fourth beast, which will "devour the whole earth" (v. 23), grew ten horns (representing the Seleucid line of succession) and then an eleventh, little horn appeared that blasphemed against the Most High, attempted to harass the "holy ones of the Most High," and attempted to change their festivals and law (v. 25). This is a relatively clear reference to Antiochus IV Epiphanes. Antiochus IV, though, is said to fall to the "holy ones" (the Maccabees or the people of Israel more generally), and the new kingdom will be "everlasting … and all dominions will serve and obey them" (v. 27). This oracle makes the most sense as having been composed sometime around the time of the Maccabean success in 167–164 BCE.[16] As in the previous oracle, the Maccabees hardly established a kingdom that all dominions obeyed.

3. Within this same oracle, and repeated elsewhere in the book, is a more specific prediction. This oracle makes a prediction that the Jerusalem Temple will remain desecrated, presumably under Antiochus IV, for about three and a half years. It is referred to differently in different places: "a time, times, and half a time" (7:25); twenty-three hundred evenings and mornings (8:14); half a week (9:27); and one thousand two hundred and ninety days (12:11). Yet, according to 1 Macc 1:54 and 4:52–54, the time was three years. I will return below to the fact that 1 Maccabees seems almost to go

---

15. Carol A. Newsom, with Brennan W. Breed, *Daniel: A Commentary*, OTL 21 (Louisville: Westminster John Knox, 2014), 80. Some scholars, though, are far less certain. See John J. Collins, *Daniel: A Commentary on the Book of Daniel*, Hermeneia 27 (Minneapolis: Fortress, 1993), 148–75.

16. Collins, *Daniel*, 323–24; Newsom, *Daniel*, 215–20.

70   *When Texts Are Canonized*

out of its way to emphasize this number, but for now it is worth noting that if it is to be believed, then Daniel's oracle is incorrect.[17]

4. Most of chapter 11 "prophesies" the history from the rise of the Seleucids to the desecration of the Temple. At verse 40, though, the prediction—correct to this point—veers wildly off course, predicting a culminating battle between the Seleucids and Ptolemies and the death of Antiochus in the land of Israel, none of which, of course, happened. It thus makes the most sense to date these prophecies too between 167 and 164 BCE, after which they became inaccurate.[18]

For writers like Jerome, these "incorrect" prophecies were hardly probative; they merely indicated that some of Daniel's prophecies from the sixth century BCE remained unfulfilled.[19] For most modern scholars, though, following Porphyry, they strongly suggest that at least these oracles were delivered within the rather tight time frame of 167–164 BCE. This, however, raises two difficult questions: What was the context in which these oracles were delivered, and did anybody believe them? And when they were shown to be incorrect, why did they continue to be preserved and given authority? In order to answer these questions we must first turn to the reception history of the book.

Reception History

"As soon as it was written," Steve Mason writes, "the book of Daniel became the definitive expression of apocalyptic hope."[20] Even if Mason's

---

17. On the other hand, it could also be the case that the author of 1 Maccabees is incorrect, a possibility rarely considered by scholars. For the sake of my argument, though, what really matters is simply the fact that they disagree. See below.

18. Porphyry already noticed this. See Jay Braverman, *Jerome's Commentary on Daniel: A Study of Comparative Jewish and Christian Interpretations of the Hebrew Bible*, CBQMS 7 (Washington, DC: Catholic Biblical Association of America, 1978), 115–18. See also Collins, *Daniel*, 388–89.

19. Jerome attributes to "the Hebrews" a line of interpretation that interprets Daniel's prophecies as applying to the Romans. Only some of these interpretations are attested in the extant rabbinic corpus. See, e.g., Braverman, *Jerome's Commentary on Daniel*, 120–23. I will argue below that the later Jewish application of Daniel's prophecies to Rome was, in fact, the primary reason that these texts acquired authority.

20. Steve Mason, "Josephus, Daniel, and the Flavian House," in *Josephus and the History of the Greco-Roman Period: Essays in Memory of Morton Smith*, ed. Fausto Parente and Joseph Sievers, StPB 41 (Leiden: Brill, 1994), 161–91, here 161. This view is widely shared. See, e.g., Lester L. Grabbe, "A Dan(iel) for All Seasons: For Whom Was Daniel Important?," in *The Book of Daniel: Composition and Reception*, ed. John J. Collins and Peter W. Flint, 2 vols., VTSup 83 (Leiden: Brill, 2001), 1:229–46.

Bad Prophecies 71

language is a bit overblown, it seems to me that he reflects more or less the consensus position. Nearly all commentators agree that Daniel became highly influential very quickly. Yet the very evidence that they cite to support this conclusion, which is all well known, is trickier to interpret and could lead to a more nuanced position.

The earliest somewhat-datable mention of Daniel occurs in 1 Maccabees, written around 100 BCE. The only direct mention occurs in 1 Macc 2:59–60, in Mattathias's deathbed speech to his sons recounting Israel's heroes. The author concludes this recitation of Israel's heroes' great deeds and their rewards with the following: "Hananiah, Azariah, and Misheal believed and were saved from the flame. Daniel, because of his innocence, was delivered from the mouth of the lions." Yet neither allusion conclusively shows that the author of 1 Maccabees was familiar with the book of Daniel in its present form. The three men in the oven recounted in Dan 3 are identified by three different names; the identification of those three with Daniel's companions, Hananiah, Azariah, and Mishael occurs in Dan 1:7 and might constitute a later gloss. The same problem appears to have been corrected in the Old Greek and Theodotion translations, which abruptly add the names Azarias and his companions to the account, along with their long prayer. There are three possibilities for how the author of 1 Maccabees made this identification: (1) the author made an exegetical connection between Dan 1:7 and chapter 3 working in the MT; (2) the author was working from the Old Greek (which is highly unlikely) or a text version on which the Old Greek is based; or (3) the author knew the story in some other way not directly dependent on the text. I suspect (3), which could also account for the allusion to the tale of Daniel's ordeal with the lion recounted in Dan 6. The author of 1 Maccabees clearly knew some of the wisdom tales that are also recorded in Daniel, but whether he knew them through the book of Daniel (or a section of the book that was circulating independently) is far less certain.[21]

It is also frequently argued that 1 Macc 1:54 (and less clearly 6:7) alludes to the book of Daniel through its notice that Antiochus had constructed the "abomination of desolation" (βδέλυγμα ἐρημώσεως) in the Temple.[22] This term (βδέλυγμα τῶν ἐρημώσεων) is mentioned in Dan 9:27 and 12:11 (with a close mention at 11:31). John J. Collins has argued that, because the term is rare, its appearance in 1 Maccabees demonstrates that its author was familiar with at least this particular oracle.[23] This is possible, although the words βδέλυγμα and forms of ἐρημώσεων are by themselves common,

---

21. On these court tales and their relationship to other such narratives, see Tawny L. Holm, *Of Courtiers and Kings: The Biblical Daniel Narratives and Ancient Story-Collections*, EANEC 1 (Winona Lake, IN: Eisenbrauns, 2013).

22. Collins, *Daniel*, 9.

23. Ibid., 72.

72   *When Texts Are Canonized*

with the former the standard translation in the LXX of the Hebrew תועבה. Yet, even if the author of 1 Maccabees was familiar with one or both of the oracles in Daniel, it is noteworthy that he (?) neither puts these oracles in Daniel's name nor even cites it as an authoritative oracle.[24]

The first certain attestations of the book of Daniel come from the Dead Sea Scrolls.[25] Fragments of four major manuscripts survive. 4QDan[a], a leather scroll about 15 cm high written in a skilled hand in script thought to be from the early Herodian period, contains fragments from most chapters of Daniel, indicating that the book was in its final redactional form at that time.[26] Although less complete, 4QDan[b] and 4QDan[d], also on leather in formal hands in the same script as 4QDan[a], contain fragments that cover a few of the redactional seams, again pointing to a completed redaction by this time. 4QDan[c] is an exception: it preserves only fragments of the Hebrew oracle collection (containing parts of chapters 10 and 11) and was written less carefully in a script that seems to date it to the second century BCE.[27] This might confirm the suggestion that the oracle collection (Dan 8–12) circulated independently prior to the final redaction of the book. Two other small fragments from cave 1 (1QDan[a] and 1QDan[b]) contain a few verses from chapters 1–3 and two other fragments (4QDan[e] and pap6QDan), written in the earlier script used in 4QDan[c], have a few verses from chapters 8–11.[28]

At Qumran there are also a number of texts that relate in some way to the figure of Daniel or to the tales found in the extant book of Daniel, but their relationship to the actual book, as well as their authority, is far from certain.[29] The Prayer of Nabodonius (4QPrNab), the Pseudo-Daniel texts, and the Four Kingdoms text all contain legends that seem related to those contained in the book of Daniel.[30] There is more debate about the relationship of 4Q246, the Aramaic "Son of God text," and the book of Daniel. The fragment, which does not mention Daniel by name, details a messianic vision that seems to culminate in the appearance of a divine figure and the advent of the eternal kingdom. Collins reads the fragment as "the earliest

---

24. See, in contrast, Matt 24:15 and Mark 13:14, where the term is cited but attached explicitly to Daniel's prophecies. These authors accepted the written oracle as authoritative. Luke 16:15 uses the word βδέλυγμα in a different context to mean simply an "abomination".

25. On a possible allusion in Sib. Or. 3 and its dating, see below.

26. Ulrich, *Qumran Cave 4*, 239–54.

27. Ibid., 269–77.

28. Ibid., 287–89; Eugene Ulrich, "The Text of Daniel in the Qumran Scrolls," in Collins and Flint, *Book of Daniel*, 2:573–85.

29. For one survey of these texts, see John J. Collins, "The Book of Daniel and the Dead Sea Scrolls," in *The Hebrew Bible in Light of the Dead Sea Scrolls*, ed. Nóra Dávid et al., FRLANT 239 (Göttingen: Vandenhoeck & Ruprecht, 2012), 203–17.

30. Ibid., 208–17. On the Pseudo-Daniel texts specifically, see John J. Collins, "Pseudo-Daniel Revisited," *RevQ* 17 (1996): 111–35, esp. 117–18.

Bad Prophecies   73

instance of the messianic interpretation of Daniel 7," but this is far from certain.[31] The community's approach to Daniel was so fluid that, in his survey of these texts, Loren Stuckenbruck concludes that

> one cannot be certain that members of the Qumran community and copyists of scrolls collected by the community would all have shared the same posture toward the book at any given time, and even more, that it was held in as much esteem at the inception of the community's existence during the second century B.C.E. as at the end in 68 C.E.[32]

There are, however, two sectarian texts that more clearly attribute authority to the book of Daniel. The first, 4QFlorilegium (usually dated, on the basis of its script, to the end of the first century BCE or beginning of the first century CE), introduces quotations from Daniel—both dealing with the notion of understanding and the *maśkîlîm*—with the phrase, "as it is written in the book of Daniel the prophet," a formula also used for other prophets such as Isaiah and Ezekiel (4QFlor II, 3-4).[33] The quotation itself, although fragmentary, appears to be a pastiche of three clauses: Dan 12:10, which is very close to the MT; 11:35, with significant grammatical differences from the MT; and 11:32, which adheres closely to the MT.[34] There are *vavs* connecting these three clauses, but it is not clear whether they are meant to string them together to look like one continuous passage or to distinguish them as individual fragments. In either case, the author of this text clearly assumed that Dan 11 and 12 were authentic oracles.

What is more significant is that the author of 4QFlorilegium already considered the two oracles he quotes to be *unfulfilled*. For 12:10, this makes some contextual sense; the verse in Daniel does seem to point to some future point. For 11:32 and 35, the writer appears to be drawing on the end of 11:35: "for an interval still remains until the appointed the time" (עד עת קץ כי עוד למועד). Daniel, then, is seen in this text as prophesying things that have yet to happen.

---

31. Collins, "Book of Daniel and the Dead Sea Scrolls," 215. Cf. Annette Steudel, "The Eternal Reign of the People of God—Collective Expectations in Qumran Texts," *RevQ* 17 (1996): 507–25.

32. Loren T. Stuckenbruck, "The Formation and Re-Formation of Daniel in the Dead Sea Scrolls," in *Scripture and the Scrolls*, ed. James H. Charlesworth, vol. 1 of *The Bible and the Dead Sea Scrolls: The Second Princeton Symposium on Judaism and Christian Origins*, ed. James H. Charlesworth (Waco, TX: Baylor University Press, 2006), 101–30, here 129.

33. See George G. Brooke, *Exegesis at Qumran: 4QFlorilegium in Its Jewish Context*, JSOT-Sup 29 (Sheffield: JSOT Press, 1985), 83–84, 124–25.

34. Annette Steudel, *Der Midrasch zur Eschatologie aus der Qumrangemeinde (4QMidr Eschat a.b): Materielle Rekonstruktion, Textbestand, Gattung und traditionsgeschichtliche Einordnung des durch 4Q174 ("Florilegium") und 4Q177 ("Catena A") repräsentierten Werkes aus den Qumranfunden*, STDJ 13 (Leiden: Brill, 1994), 48–49.

74   *When Texts Are Canonized*

The second explicit citation is in 11QMelchizedek (11Q13). Although quite fragmentary, this text introduces a prooftext (which one is not clear) with the clause, "as Daniel said" (באשר אמר ד). The formula is not as "authoritative" as the one in 4QFlorilegium, but it is unclear how much to read into that difference. Clearly the author of this text took Daniel, both as an individual prophet and (presumably) in some text attributed to him, to hold some kind of oracular authority.

There are, as Collins and others have pointed out, intriguing connections between the language of Daniel (primarily in chapters 7–12) and the Dead Sea Scrolls. The War Scroll (1QM) seems to allude to Daniel in several places.[35] The Dead Sea Scroll community use technical terms such as *maśkîl* and the *rabbîm*, assembly, which also occur in Daniel.[36] The use of the term "smooth" words or blandishments, *ḥălaqqôt*, in 11:32 also shows affinity with the scrolls, which sometimes apply this term to what many scholars suppose were the Pharisees.[37]

With the exception of Josephus, there are few other mentions of Daniel in Second Temple literature. Third Maccabees (6:6–7), probably from the first century CE, appears to know at least the tale of the boys in the furnace from the Old Greek text. A glancing reference to "ten horns" in the Sibylline Oracles (3:397) might also demonstrate acquaintance with the oracles in Daniel, but none of these works either explicitly recognizes the authenticity of Daniel's oracles or demonstrates familiarity with an actual book of Daniel.[38] Philo never mentions Daniel.

Josephus, like the members of the Qumran community, both knew of the book of Daniel and regarded Daniel as an authentic prophet.[39] In *Antiquities* he spends a great deal of time summarizing the stories in Dan 1–6. He shows no awareness of chapter 7, and then his account of Daniel's oracles becomes more selective. He lauds Daniel as a prophet:

---

35. Collins, *Daniel*, 73–74; Hanna Vanonen, "The Textual Connections between 1QM 1 and the Book of Daniel," in *Changes in Scripture: Rewriting and Interpreting Authoritative Traditions in the Second Temple Period*, ed. Hanne von Weissenberg, Juha Pakkala, and Marko Marttila, BZAW 419 (Berlin: de Gruyter, 2011), 223–45. Vanonen's study is limited but points to the importance of the later chapters of Daniel for the author of at least the first column of 1QM.

36. Collins, "Book of Daniel and the Dead Sea Scrolls," 206–7.

37. Albert I. Baumgarten, "Seeks after Smooth Things," in *Encyclopedia of the Dead Sea Scrolls*, ed. Lawrence H. Schiffman and James C. VanderKam, 2 vols. (New York: Oxford University Press, 2000), 2:857–59.

38. Rieuwerd Buitenwerf, *Book III of the Sibylline Oracles and Its Social Setting: With an Introduction, Translation, and Commentary*, SVTP 17 (Leiden: Brill, 2003), 229. The date of Sib. Or. 3 is much debated. Buitenwerf prefers a date between 80 and 40 BCE (126–30).

39. Josephus, *Ant.* 10.186–281; Geza Vermes, "Josephus' Treatment of the Book of Daniel," *JJS* 42 (1991): 149–66.

Bad Prophecies   75

For the books that he wrote and left behind are still read by us even now, and we believe from them that Daniel kept company with God, for not only did he keep prophesying the future, like other prophets, but he also determined the time when these things would come about. (*Ant.* 10.267)[40]

He demonstrates this by summarizing the oracle in chapter 8, harmonizing it with some later chapters, and asserting that it happened, down to the day, as Daniel foretold. Then he continues, "And in the same way Daniel also wrote about the empire of the Romans and that it would be laid waste by them" (*Ant.* 10.276).[41] In Josephus's reading, Daniel prophesied not only about the Roman Empire—which can be seen in his interpretations of the statue's iron feet in 2:33–34 and the Kittim in 11:30 (actually designated "Romans" in some Greek versions)—but also about the eventual Jewish defeat of it (*Ant.* 10.210).[42]

The identification of these references in Daniel with Rome during the Great Revolt and destruction of the Temple were probably not original to Josephus. Fourth Ezra 12:11–12 reads Daniel's vision as authentic but reinterprets it to refer explicitly to Rome. By the end of the first century, then, Daniel's oracles were not only accepted as authentic but were also being reinterpreted to refer not to the past but to the present and the future. An incorrect prophecy, having been granted authority, was transformed.

The larger point that emerges from this quick survey is that the authority of Daniel's oracles might not have been either definitive or immediate. In fact, the very texts used to show this authority suggest that Daniel's oracles gained traction only in the Roman period. If this is correct, it might help us to understand better when, how, and why the book of Daniel, with its incorrect prophecies, became authoritative.

A New Suggestion

Daniel, it is clear, was redacted in stages. Collins, in his magisterial commentary, presents a five-stage model:

1. The individual, Aramaic tales of chapters 2–6 circulated independently.

---

40. Translation from Christopher T. Begg and Paul Spilsbury, *Judean Antiquities Books 8–10*, Flavius Josephus, Translation and Commentary 5 (Leiden: Brill, 2005), 308.

41. Trans. Begg and Spilsbury, *Judean Antiquities*, 313–14.

42. See ibid., 283 nn. 893–94; Mason, "Josephus, Daniel, and the Flavian House," 172–73; Paul Spilsbury, "Flavius Josephus on the Rise and Fall of the Roman Empire," *JTS* 54 (2003): 1–24.

76   *When Texts Are Canonized*

2. Daniel 3:31–6:29 was probably the core initial collection of these tales.
3. The tales were collected in the Hellenistic period, and chapter 1, also in Aramaic at this point, was added.
4. Daniel 7 was composed in Aramaic at the time of the persecution of Antiochus Epiphanes and perhaps circulated briefly attached to chapters 1–6.
5. Finally, between 167 and 164 BCE, chapters 8–12 were composed (in Hebrew) and added to this preexistent collection of chapters 2–6, with chapter 1 translated into Hebrew to provide a narrative unity. Daniel 12:11–12, at the very end of the book, was added before the rededication of the Temple.[43]

This hypothesis is certainly plausible. In what follows, I will largely accept this reconstruction but expand on it in two important respects. First, by paying attention to the critical moment of the transition between orally delivered oracles and their written expression (the movement from canonical stage 1 to 2, outlined above), we can gain a better understanding of the social context of the "prophet." Second, focusing attention on the inaccurate prophecies—and asking when, why, and under what circumstances such inaccurate predictions would have been understood as genuine divine oracles—might help to shine a new light on Daniel's ascent to canonical status.

Collins does not consider the possibility that Daniel's oracles were originally delivered orally, and I think that he probably is correct not to: unlike the oracles of at least some of the classical Israelite prophets, the oracles of Daniel appear not to have had an oral beginning. This is reflected primarily in the nature of the prophecies themselves, which are delivered not as the word of God funneled through the prophet but as extended visions. In one case (Dan 9:1–2) the vision explicitly engages and interprets an earlier authoritative text. This, along with the heavy thematization of writing within the oracular part of Daniel, makes it more akin to books such as 2 Baruch and 4 Ezra than to Jeremiah and Ezekiel, even though the latter too contain some emphasis on the nexus between prophecy and writing.[44] In any event, in the case of Daniel there has most likely been a conflation of what I have called stages 1 and 2; the oracles

---

43. Collins, *Daniel*, 38.
44. See, e.g., Dan. 9:1–2, 12:1. For one study of the "textualization" of prophecy in preexilic Judah, see Joachim Schaper, "The Death of the Prophet: The Transition from the Spoken to the Written Word of God in the Book of Ezekiel," in *Prophets, Prophecy, and Prophetic Texts in Second Temple Judaism*, ed. Michael H. Floyd and Robert D. Haak, LHBOTS 427 (London: T&T Clark, 2006), 63–79; and, more generally, Schaper, "Exilic and Post-Exilic Prophecy," 324–42. My discussion emphasizes Daniel's oracles as generically similar to "prophets," although many scholars classify these oracles as "apocalyptic" instead. See the discussion in

Bad Prophecies 77

originated in written form. Given the knowledge of and engagement with Jeremiah and their use of Hebrew, the prophetic authors were almost certainly from the learned class.

Collins identifies this class as the *maśkîlîm*, mentioned several times in Daniel (1:4; 11:33, 35, 12:3). In 12:3 they are clearly glorified, destined to be radiant in resurrection, for which their martyrdoms in 11:35 prepare them. Daniel 11:33 spells out a teaching role for them: "The *maśkîlîm* among the people will make the many understand; and for a while they will fall by sword and flame, suffer captivity and spoliation." (The mention of the *maśkîlîm* in 1:4, incidentally, appears to be a gloss that connects the first set of Daniel tales to the later oracles.) Based on these references, Collins asserts "that Daniel's revelations were to be made public in the time of persecution, which was the time when they were actually composed."[45]

Collins certainly could be right, but it is difficult to reconstruct a historically plausible context in which this teaching to the masses would have occurred. Assuming that the oracles were composed around 168 BCE, do we imagine these *maśkîlîm* reading aloud these visions to the groups of Jews in Jerusalem as well as in other towns and villages? If so, in what language, the Hebrew in which they were written, or in Aramaic, a language in which most would likely have been more comfortable? Would the masses have even gotten the sense of such heavily scholastic visions? If so, would they believe them and how might they have acted upon them?

What might be more likely is that these written oracles instead had a more limited circulation, as a written scholastic work composed in Hebrew, which at this time was probably predominantly a scribal language.[46] The esoteric nature of the oracles might also be hinted at in the command to Daniel to keep the oracles secret and sealed in 12:4: "But you, Daniel, keep the words secret and the book sealed until the time of the end" (ואתה דניאל סתם הדברים וחתם הספר עד עת קץ). Collins is thus correct to view chapters 8–12 (more or less) as a coherent collection, but one that I think is best seen as a collection of written oracles created by and circulated among a scribal elite, the *maśkîlîm*. These *maśkîlîm* knew Jeremiah

---

John J. Collins, "Daniel," *The Oxford Handbook of the Reception History of the Bible*, ed. Michael Lieb, Emma Mason, and Jonathan Roberts (Oxford: Oxford University Press, 2011), 77–87.

45. Collins, *Daniel*, 342.

46. This is an admittedly controversial claim. The scholarly controversy over the use of Hebrew and Aramaic in the Second Temple period is ably summarized by Guido Baltes, "The Use of Hebrew and Aramaic in Epigraphic Sources of the New Testament Era," in *The Language Environment of First Century Judaea*, ed. Randall Buth and R. Steven Notley, Jerusalem Studies in the Synoptic Gospels 2, Jewish and Christian Perspectives Series 26 (Leiden: Brill, 2014), 35–65. Baltes argues for what is perhaps an emerging consensus of a bilingual and diglossic society, but the evidence is not decisive and, in any case, mostly applies later in the Second Temple period (or even beyond). Jewish scribes during this period appeared to work predominantly in Hebrew.

78   *When Texts Are Canonized*

and regarded his oracles as authoritative (Dan 9:1–2), even if they rein-terpreted them for their own purposes (9:24–27).[47] They were not writing for the masses; their oracles were only for the learned of their own circle. All of the earlier copies of Daniel found in the Dead Sea Scrolls might well have been this oracle collection, not a fragment of the entire book. This reconstruction also helps to explain the disappearance of the oracles from the historical record for the next century.

It is not unreasonable to assume that the highly educated, Hebrew-writ-ing intellectuals who foresaw and looked forward to the expulsion of the Seleucids from the Temple would have been aligned in some way with the Maccabees.[48] The alignment, though, would have been loose. Here 1 Maccabees, the later Hasmonean court history, is an intriguing witness. Although mentioning the tales found in the beginning of the book of Dan-iel, the author of 1 Maccabees does not mention the oracles at all. Nor do we find any such references in 2 Maccabees. One possibility is that these authors were not familiar with them. A second possibility, though, is that they were familiar with the oracles but they rejected their authenticity—perhaps because they were wrong. There might be some support for this second hypothesis in the insistence in 1 Macc 1:54 and 4:52–54 that the time of the defilement of the temple was three years, not three and a half years.[49] If the author of 1 Maccabees was familiar with the Daniel oracles, he appears to be rejecting them as inaccurate. Hence, although the *maśkîlîm* may have shared a common goal with the Hasmoneans, the Hasmonean

---

47. Jeremiah's oracle was already well known. Zechariah alludes to the seventy-year curse of the land (1:12). According to 2 Chr 36:22, Babylon's conquest by Persia was "in ful-fillment of the word of the Lord spoken by Jeremiah, until the land paid back its Sabbaths; as long as it lay desolate it kept Sabbath, till seventy years were completed." The author of 2 Chronicles was apparently not bothered by the fact that Jeremiah's numerical predic-tion was incorrect: no matter how you structure the chronologies, "seventy years" does not work. What was important to this author was that Babylon did fall, thus fulfilling Jeremiah's prophecy. To the author of Dan 9, though, Zechariah and the author of 2 Chronicles were wrong: the oracle in fact remained unfulfilled. Daniel knew this because Gabriel gave him the true meaning of Jeremiah's reference to "seventy years": it means seventy weeks of years, that is, 490 years. This almost certainly derives from some kind of knowledge and interpre-tation of 2 Chronicles and its reference to the Sabbath. The eschatological schema in Dan 9 shares the apparently incorrect dating of Antiochus's desecration of the temple with Dan 7:25, claiming it lasted "half a week," or 3.5 years, culminating with the establishment of the desolating abomination.

48. See Grabbe, "Dan(iel) for All Seasons"; and Philip Davies, "The Scribal School of Daniel," in Collins and Flint, *Book of Daniel*, 1:247–65. See further John J. Collins, "Daniel and His Social World," in *Interpreting the Prophets*, ed. James Luther Mays and Paul J. Achtemeier (Philadelphia: Fortress, 1987), 249–60.

49. Solomon Zeitlin makes a heroic but ultimately unconvincing case that the dates in Daniel and 1 Maccabees can be reconciled. See Sidney Tedesche and Solomon Zeitlin, *The First Book of Maccabees*, JAL 1 (New York: Harper & Brothers, 1950), 108, note to 4:54.

Bad Prophecies   79

neglect of Daniel might imply that there were tensions between the two groups.[50]

The oracle in Dan 7 appears to be an independent composition. Chronologically, form critically, and in terms of content it looks like chapters 8–12, but it is written in Aramaic like chapters 2–6. References in the chapter clearly make it contemporaneous with chapters 8–12, although some have argued that these are secondary additions.[51] Like the oracles in chapters 8–12, there is a concern with writing (7:10), but the redactor himself seems to mark this account as having had an independent written existence (7:1, 28). It is unclear if it circulated, as Collins suggests, together with chapters 1–6 or whether it was composed before or after the oracles of chapters 8–12. While form and contents suggest that chapter 7 had a different author from the oracles in chapters 8–12, the two authors shared expectations and most likely traveled in the same social circles.

In this reconstruction, the oracles in Daniel emerged from a small scribal circle prior to 164 BCE. Although it is again not unreasonable to assume that that same circle would survive the trauma of the Maccabean revolt and in fact gain some position of power or influence under the Hasmoneans, over the next few years it became increasingly clear that their oracular predictions did not come to pass. Just when one would expect a move to the granting of authority to these texts (canonization stage 3), they were instead shelved. That they were preserved at all, and probably copied, by the descendants of the *maśkîlîm* is somewhat remarkable. It is hard to know whether these later scribes saw in these texts authentic oracles, or whether they kept them around for antiquarian or didactic reasons. In any case, there is no evidence that they were known outside of these small circles.

The extant evidence suggests that the circulation of the Daniel oracles was quite limited for about a century after their composition. This absence of evidence, of course, cannot prove that they were in fact largely unknown, but there is no evidence to support the opposite supposition either. The oracles could well have been buried in unread books for a century, which is a long time indeed for memory of them to fade. Why, when it was quite possible that these oracles could have been buried and lost forever, did they instead emerge powerfully in the mid-first century BCE?

I would like to suggest that it was the penetration of Rome into Judea and, more specifically, the entrance of Pompey into the Jerusalem Tem-

---

50. Bickerman argues that the very pseudonymity of the oracles is due to hostility toward, or at least suspicion of, "new" seers by the Maccabees (*Four Strange Books*, 119–22). Simply slapping the name of an ancient sage on the oracles might not have helped very much.

51. Newsom argues that Daniel 7 was composed prior to the Antiochene persecutions, with those references added in later (*Daniel*, 215–17).

80   *When Texts Are Canonized*

ple in 63 BCE that gave these oracles new life and began the process that led to the final composition of the book of Daniel. To Jews in Jerusalem, whose views would have been shaped by the history of the Antiochene persecutions refracted through works such as 1 and 2 Maccabees and (perhaps) the Animal Apocalypse, Pompey's despoliation of the Temple would have been deeply disturbing.[52] Daniel's oracles, whose inaccuracies were erased by the forgetfulness of a century, were now applied to the Romans. Current events made the oracles relevant again. Unlike the later Porphyry, the circles that reread Daniel were not historians interested in fact-checking the oracles. The very antiquity of the oracles and the fact that they had been forgotten may have worked in their favor, adding to their authority in the eyes of those who found them.

The path from seeing these oracles as relevant to the redaction of the book of Daniel is relatively straightforward. With the oracles in chapters 7 and 8–12 as the core of the book, the tales of chapters 2–6, some of which were in any case well-known, were attached to provide historical context.[53] The redaction was not terribly artful and left multiple seams and discontinuities, as noted above. The redactors, who worked in Hebrew, may now have written chapter 1 and added a few connecting sentences (e.g., 7:1) throughout the work but did not bother to translate the Aramaic portions into Hebrew. Such a redaction could have been accomplished in less than a week.

The advantage of this reconstruction is that it makes better sense of both the historical context and the book's reception history. From the first appearance of Daniel among the Dead Sea Scrolls, the application of its oracles to Rome is taken for granted. At the same time, though, the authority of the book was still fluid. Other texts loosely connected to the book of Daniel floated around at the same time, suggesting that the book of Daniel was, in a sense, still in play; it was unclear what if anything could be done with it.

Clearly, though, by the first-century CE Daniel was known outside of Qumran. Josephus is the most obvious, but not the first, example not only of knowledge of Daniel but also of its connection with Rome. Similarly, the New Testament authors drew on Daniel in order to predict both the desecration of the Temple by the Romans and the identification of Jesus as the "son of man" (Matt 24:15).[54]

---

52. Jewish reaction to Pompey's "visit" to the Jerusalem Temple is scantly attested in ancient sources. See Josephus, *B.J.* 1.152, although there is a discrepancy between this and Josephus's description in *Ant.* 14.71. See Jane Bellemore, "Josephus, Pompey and the Jews," *Historia: Zeitschrift für Alte Geschichte* 48 (1999): 94–118.

53. Seeing the oracle collection as the core of the book follows, among others, H. J. M. van Deventer, "Another Look at the Redaction History of the Book of Daniel, or, Reading Daniel from Left to Right," *JSOT* 38 (2013): 239–60.

54. For an extended argument that Dan 7 played a critical role in early Christology, see Daniel Boyarin, *The Jewish Gospels: The Story of the Jewish Christ* (New York: New Press, 2012).

Conclusion

This paper has attempted to use Daniel as a test case for thinking about the ways prophetic texts gained authority. My focus has been on the issue of textual authority as a precondition for ultimate canonization. Daniel is a fascinating example precisely because it offers an extreme case: How can prophecies recognized, relatively close to the time of their delivery, as incorrect become authoritative, especially since the authenticity of the prophet in particular is judged according to the accuracies of his or her prophecies?

I have argued that the book of Daniel's path to authority was hardly straightforward. In fact, history—or, better, historical forgetfulness that led to rereading and reapplication of the oracles under new and distant conditions—and contingency were key factors. Throughout Israelite and early Jewish history there must certainly have been incorrect oracles that, discredited, were discarded. Others, though, may have sat on shelves, occasionally read or copied by scribes who later reinfused them with meaning. For the texts that would come to comprise the book of Daniel, historical circumstances (the entrance of Rome to the area) gave new life to an old set of oracles.

Is the case of Daniel unique, or might other texts have followed a similar journey to canonization? While the answer to that question is far beyond the scope of this paper, I hope that by providing an alternative model for thinking about authority and canon this paper contributes to such ongoing research.

Canon and Content

JOHN BARTON

This paper considers three loosely linked issues relating to canonical texts, all to do with the relation of canonicity and meaning. I want to argue that where biblical texts are concerned the relationship between form and content and that between content and status were significantly different in antiquity from how they are mostly seen nowadays, even given the variety of ways in which people today approach texts. I begin, though, with two brief prefatory comments.

First, I must say something about how I am using the word *canonical*. In line with several other scholars, I have argued for a distinction between the terms *canon* and *scripture*.[1] These are modern English terms that we are at liberty to use how we like, but it seems to me that it is sensible in scholarly contexts to distinguish them by using *scripture* for authoritative or official biblical texts but *canon* for definitive lists of such texts, so that one can have scriptures without having a canon though not vice versa. On that basis we can usefully say that there was a time—though people will disagree about when it was—when the Jewish people had scriptures but had not yet identified a canon, that is, had not yet closed their list of scriptural texts, so that (in principle at least) other texts might still be recognized as holy and authoritative. I have suggested, along these lines, that in the first century CE all the books now in the Jewish canon were already scriptural (including those about which many scholars think there was still dispute, notably Song of Songs and Qohelet, to which I shall return), but none was yet canonical, because other books might still be admitted. In this I follow the arguments of Albert C. Sundberg Jr.[2] Timothy Lim has recently argued very persuasively that, in fact, there was already a canon in the technical sense in the first century CE, espoused by the Pharisees and identified by

---

1. See John Barton, *Oracles of God: Perceptions of Ancient Prophecy in Israel after the Exile* (London: Darton, Longman & Todd, 1986; 2nd ed., London: Darton, Longman & Todd, 2007), chapters 1 and 2; Barton, *The Spirit and the Letter: Studies in the Biblical Canon* (London: SPCK, 1997; American ed., *Holy Writings, Sacred Text: The Canon in Early Christianity* [Louisville: Westminster John Knox, 1997]), chapter 1.

2. Albert C. Sundberg Jr., *The Old Testament of the Early Church*, HTS 20 (Cambridge: Harvard University Press, 1964).

Josephus.[3] If he is right, then the terminological distinction is still valid, but the advent of a fixed canon is earlier than Sundberg supposed.

I mention this issue here to get it out of the way, because in the present paper I shall use the term *canonical* in its more usual and looser sense as equivalent to what I call "scriptural." That is how most people use it, and though I see problems with it, they are not important in the present context. By "canonical texts," therefore, I here mean texts accepted by a given community as scripture, regardless of whether they form a fixed list. That is also how Brevard Childs used the term in his many publications on the "canonical approach," which he treated as synonymous with "reading the Bible as Scripture."[4]

Second, this paper is an empirical study of how canonical/scriptural texts were, or were probably, read in the past, rather than a programmatic proposal about how we ought to read them. I am very interested in that second question, but in the present context I am bracketing it out. I want to ask, what was the effect of recognizing a text as scriptural in biblical times and in antiquity, and to a lesser extent what is the effect of it now on most readers? I am not concerned to defend a particular thesis about the effect canonicity/scripturality ought to have on us as modern Christians, Jews, or interested readers of the Bible. In particular, I shall not be considering "theological interpretation of scripture" as a program in theology and biblical studies. I believe it is a fascinating and important line of thinking, but it is not my concern here.

To move, then, into my main point. Publishers nowadays distinguish between *books* and *content*. Books are particular objects or collections of objects in which a certain content is instantiated; but the same content can be instantiated in other media, for example, online or in audiobooks. If I am writing a work of scholarship or of fiction, it does not matter from the point of view of the work's significance what medium it is in: what matters is its content. An online version of, say, a Jane Austen novel is still that novel, provided it is accurate and complete, but a physical book version is not the novel if it has chapters missing or is very inaccurately copy-edited. Similarly, a film version that is faithful to the original content could be said to convey the meaning and contents of the novel better than a highly inaccurate printed edition. Accurate content matters more than the medium does. Even the most beautifully printed book containing only half of *Pride and Prejudice* is not the novel of that name, whereas the most unattractive online version that contains all the right words is. Though we may value beautiful books as objects, if we say we love *Pride and Prejudice*

---

3. Timothy H. Lim, *The Formation of the Jewish Canon*, AYBRL (New Haven: Yale University Press, 2013).

4. See Brevard S. Childs, *Introduction to the Old Testament as Scripture* (Philadelphia: Fortress, 1979).

84   *When Texts Are Canonized*

we do not usually mean that we love a particular edition for its physical beauty but that we love its content. My questions in this paper revolve around the validity of such a distinction in antiquity.

I

How far did content as opposed to outward form matter in thinking about scriptural/canonical books in antiquity? A classic case here is the book of Jeremiah. As is well known, the Septuagint version of Jeremiah contains considerably fewer words than the Masoretic Text, and the Qumran editions of the books seem to have been closer to the Septuagint in this respect. One can debate whether the longer or the shorter version is more original, though most scholars favor the theory that the MT is an expansion of the shorter version translated in the Greek text. But my question here is not which is more original but how far the difference mattered for anyone reading Jeremiah as a scriptural book. In recognizing Jeremiah as canonical, was anything being said about exactly what its content was? My impression is that this was probably not the case. People knew that there was a prophetic book called Jeremiah, but they accepted as authoritative whatever version of it they, or the community they belonged to, had inherited. "Jeremiah" did not mean a specific and accurate range of content but a physical book—a scroll, of course—entitled "The words of Jeremiah," whatever exactly was in it. As modern scholars, we can compare the longer and shorter recensions and can make many observations about the potential difference in meaning between them. But in antiquity most people could not do this; they were limited to the particular version they had available. Origen, of course, started to make comparisons of this sort with various recensions and versions of the Bible; but this was hardly something practiced by ordinary Bible readers.[5] As Eva Mroczek writes of the books in the Ethiopian Christian canon, "the *fact* of their inclusion in a list seems to hold more significance than their contents."[6]

This has an effect on a question often asked in modern biblical study about the significance of order in biblical texts. A whole volume

---

5. Of course, many Bible "readers" were in practice Bible "hearers," either illiterate or literate but knowing the text primarily through repeated hearings. Even learned scribes may often have recalled the text by heart rather than consulting it in a scroll.

6. Eva Mroczek, *The Literary Imagination in Jewish Antiquity* (Oxford: Oxford University Press, 2016), 158. This book is an invaluable discussion of the relation between texts and their meanings. See also William M. Schniedewind, *How the Bible Became a Book: The Textualization of Ancient Israel* (Cambridge: Cambridge University Press, 2006), tracing the route from oral fluidity to fixity of content.

Canon and Content   85

has recently been published on the order of the Writings, the Ketuvim,[7] and others have asked about the order within particular books, and even the order of the whole Bible. Where particular books are concerned, the order of the Psalms has become a major scholarly interest, with many theories about what meaning is conveyed through the way the Psalms are arranged. It is obvious that within the Psalter there are smaller collections in which juxtapositions are likely to be significant: for example, Pss 105 and 106, or 111 and 112, or 135 and 136. There may be arrangements on a larger scale than this, such as the last six psalms, or even, if one follows theories such as those of Michael Goulder, all the Psalms of Asaph or Korah or all the psalms in one of the five "books."[8] But a problem here is the evidence from Cave 11 at Qumran, where the Psalms, at least those later in the Psalter, have a quite different order. Thus, there is not a fixed content of the Psalter where order is concerned but only the order in particular editions of the Psalms. There cannot have been a *shared* belief that the Psalms had meanings dependent on their order, since that order varies and, presumably, people did not generally know that it did. At best, a given community might have made something of the order in the version that they happened to have, but it would not make sense to speak of *the* meaning of the Psalter on the basis of the order of the psalms. There is no fixed content to the Psalter, if by content we understand the order as well as the text of individual psalms.

On the macro-scale, I am very skeptical about finding meaning in the order of the whole Bible or even in one of its three divisions. There are, for example, many orderings of the Writings in which Ruth comes first, but I find it hard to think that any particular significance was attached to this. Or what about the fact that Chronicles traditionally comes last, despite its "natural" chronological position as preceding Ezra-Nehemiah? One can make much of the idea that it appears where it does so that the whole Bible ends with the word *ya'al*, "let him go up," and thus with hope for the restoration of Israel in its own land. But for whom was Chronicles the last book of the Bible in antiquity? It is very hard to think of a specific community that will have seen matters in that way, especially given that the Bible was a collection of scrolls rather than a codex. Nowadays of course we can read the text so, and from a literary perspective there is no problem at all in seeing meaning in the Bible as a whole: think of Northrop Frye's *The Great Code*, or Jack Miles's *God: A Biography*, where the Hebrew

---

7. Julius Steinberg and Timothy J. Stone, eds., *The Shape of the Writings*, Siphrut 16 (Winona Lake, IN: Eisenbrauns, 2015).

8. See, e.g., Michael D. Goulder, *The Prayers of David (Psalms 51–72): Studies in the Psalter, II*, JSOTSup 102 (Sheffield: JSOT Press, 1990); Goulder, *The Psalms of the Sons of Korah*, JSOTSup 20 (Sheffield: JSOT Press, 1982); Goulder, *The Psalms of Asaph and the Pentateuch: Studies in the Psalter, III*, JSOTSup 233 (Sheffield: Sheffield Academic, 1996).

86   *When Texts Are Canonized*

Bible is read as a kind of *Bildungsroman* in which the character of God develops throughout and eventually becomes more distant, not speaking again after his words to Job from the whirlwind.[9] Such an interpretation depends on the order that has now become traditional, but for a modern literary reading there is no problem about that. There is, however, if one wants to make historical claims about how the text was in reality read in ancient times. For Jewish communities before the advent of the codex, the order of the books was not part of their content in the way it is now.

Thus, it seems to me, the idea of a fixed content of biblical texts is something of a chimera: communities regarded as Holy Scripture whatever version they happened to possess. Biblical texts were holy books, not instantiations of holy content seen as existing independently of the actual manuscripts to hand. Isaiah or Jeremiah or the book of Psalms was sacrosanct, but exactly what those books contained was fuzzy, and it might be different in different communities.

II

My second point is also concerned with books as physical objects.[10] As is well known, there is a passage in m. Yadayim dealing with the issue of whether Song of Songs and Qohelet defile the hands:

> All the Holy Scriptures render the hands unclean. The Song of Songs and Ecclesiastes render the hands unclean. R. Judah says: The Song of Songs renders the hands unclean, but about Ecclesiastes there is dissension. R. Jose says: Ecclesiastes does not render the hands unclean, and about the Song of Songs there is dissension. R. Simeon says: Ecclesiastes is one of the things about which the School of Shammai adopted the more lenient, and the school of Hillel the more stringent ruling. R. Simeon b. Azzai said: I have heard a tradition from the seventy-two elders on the day when they made R. Eleazar b. Azariah head of the college, that the Song of Songs and Ecclesiastes both render the hands unclean. R. Akiba said: God forbid!—no man in Israel ever disputed about the Song of Songs [that he should say] that it does not render the hands unclean, for all the ages are not worth the day on which the Song of Songs was given to Israel; for all the Writings are holy, but the Song of Songs is the Holy of Holies. And if aught was in dispute the dispute was about Ecclesias-

---

9. C. Northrop Frye, *The Great Code: The Bible and Literature* (London: Routledge & Kegan Paul, 1982); Jack Miles, *God: A Biography* (London: Simon & Schuster, 1995).

10. For this section, see Timothy H. Lim, "The Rabbinic Concept of Holy Scriptures as Sacred Objects," in *Scribal Practices and the Social Construction of Knowledge in Antiquity, Late Antiquity and Medieval Islam*, ed. Myriam Wissa, OLA (Leuven: Peeters, forthcoming).

Canon and Content   87

tes alone. R. Johanan b. Joshua, the son of R. Akiba's father-in-law, said:
According to the words of Ben Azzai so did they dispute and so did they
decide. (m. Yad. 3:5)

This is almost universally taken to be an issue about the canonicity of
these two books, and it is said that Scripture was generally fixed before
the events at Jamnia/Yavneh except for these two books, which were still
a matter for debate. I have tried to show that the question of defiling
the hands arises only because these books were already scripture, and
there was something about them that made their ability to defile the
hands uncertain: I have argued that it was probably the fact that neither book contains the Tetragrammaton.[11] If I am right, then both books
were already agreed to be scriptural before Yavneh, so that there were no
books now in the canon that were doubtful; though this does not mean
the canon was *closed*: this, as we saw in one of my opening observations,
is a separate issue. The fact that a text as late as b. Megillah 7a can spec-
ulate that Esther might not defile the hands confirms to me that defiling
the hands cannot be about canonicity, since Esther by then had a complete feast to itself and was surely canonical if any non-Torah text was
canonical. But hardly anyone has accepted my suggestion, and the belief
that the question of whether books defile the hands is a question about
their canonicity persists and cannot be dislodged. So, for the sake of discussion, I propose to concede that this is the correct understanding of the
passage, but I then go on to ask what *kind* of canonicity is being attributed
to the books.

  We tend to assume, again, that it is a matter of content: the contents
of Song of Songs and Qohelet are divinely inspired, and hence the scrolls
in which they are instantiated defile the hands. (The oddity of *holy* things
causing defilement has been much debated since ancient times, but this is
not the place to go into it.) On my reading, it is rather the technical and
physical question whether these texts contain a particular set of graphic
signs, *yod-he-vav-he*. But even if I am mistaken about this, we should read
the passage in its context in the Mishnah. Immediately preceding it are
rulings about the power to defile attributed to the blank spaces within the
biblical books, and of the bits of them that are fixed to the rollers, and the
ribbons used to tie them up. If the books are "canonical," then so are the
physical attributes of the scrolls in which they appear. "The blank spaces
in a scroll [of the scriptures] that are above [the writing] and that are at the
beginning and the end render the hands unclean. R. Judah says: The blank
space at the end does not render [the hands] unclean until the roller is
joined to it" (m. Yad. 3:4). Furthermore, it is explicitly said that it is not the
content of the books that causes them to defile the hands, since the same

---

  11. See Barton, *Spirit and the Letter* (= *Holy Writings, Sacred Text*), 108–21.

88   *When Texts Are Canonized*

text that defiles in Hebrew does not do so in an Aramaic translation, and vice versa—a Hebrew version of the Aramaic portions of Ezra or Daniel, or of the two Aramaic words in the Torah, would not defile. Also the text must be written in the square script, not in any other version of the alphabet. M. Yadayim 4:5 thus reads:

> The Aramaic that is in Ezra and Daniel renders the hands unclean. If an Aramaic version was written in Hebrew, or if Hebrew was written in Aramaic, or in Hebrew script [i.e., paleo-Hebrew script], it does not render the hands unclean. The Scriptures render the hands unclean only when they are written in the Aramaic character, on leather, and in ink.

None of this has anything to do with the content of the texts, but with their external form.

What is more, it makes a difference how much of the text is present: there must be eighty-five letters, as many as there are in the text from Num 10:35–36, the passage that nowadays (we do not know how ancient the custom is) is used when the ark is opened to remove the Torah scroll during the synagogue liturgy: "Whenever the ark set out, Moses would say, "Arise, O LORD, let your enemies be scattered, and your foes flee before you." And whenever it came to rest, he would say, 'Return, O LORD of the ten thousand thousands of Israel.'" Thus the Mishnah says, "If the writing in a scroll was erased and yet there still remained eighty-five letters, as many as are in the paragraph *And I came to pass when the ark set forward* … it still renders the hands unclean. A [single] written sheet in which are written eight-five letters … renders the hands unclean" (m. Yad. 3:5)—this passage immediately precedes the discussion of Song of Songs and Qohelet. No fragment of the texts smaller than this has the power to defile the hands, even though it comes from a text even more obviously holy than Qohelet and Song of Songs, namely, from the Torah. Surely this is not most modern people's idea of a holy text; rather, it inhabits a rather different mental world. My suggestion, again, is that it can be explained in terms of a distinction between form and content. Where we would see the *content* of the Bible as holy, for this mentality it is its external *form* that is sacred and consequently "defiles the hands"—but only under certain conditions. There is also the matter of the so-called scroll of the Temple court, which is said not to defile the hands as long as it remains in the Temple (m. Kelim 15:6)—which shows clearly, in my view that "defiling the hands" is not equivalent to "being canonical." At any rate it shows that defiling the hands is a characteristic of texts as specific holy objects, rather than of the conceptual content of the texts.

Albert I. Baumgarten has recently argued that the idea that scriptures defile the hands is a peculiarity of Pharisaic belief. He suggests that it is

related to taking the text out of its special place in the Temple and into the community at large. While in the Temple, the scroll does not defile the hands because it is in some sense in its "proper" place and anyway would be handled only by ritually pure priests, but once outside the sanctuary it needed to be kept safe from profane use, and so the theory arose that it "defiled the hands."[12] This is very close to my own argument, put forward as long ago as 1997:

> Within the Temple, in its proper and natural place, the definitive Torah scroll had no power to convey uncleanness. It was only outside the precinct that the holiness of the Torah was a dangerous force. The holy book handled by ritually pure people in the holiest place on earth is not part of a structure of unbalanced forces pulling against each other, but is in perfect equlilibrium. Uncleanness occurs when the balance is disturbed.[13]

It is not the content of the scriptures that "defile the hands" but their physical presence within the profane everyday world.

II

My third point concerns how texts are read, once they are perceived as scriptural or canonical. One might expect that to canonize a text results in whatever the text means becoming authoritative for the community that does the canonizing; and that is indeed theoretically the case. But it is more complicated than that in practice. Canonizing texts tends to cause them to be read in accordance with what is already believed in the canonizing community. An example of this is the Gospel of John. If John had turned up among the Nag Hammadi texts, we should probably read it as an example of Gnosticism, with its concentration on the divine identity of Jesus, its interest in the descent of the Logos, its divine voices attesting to Jesus's divine status, and its discourses on the true vine, and so on. Now there is indeed much in John that does not lend itself to a gnostic reading; but it is surely much nearer to what we call Gnosticism than the Synoptic Gospels are. Given that it is canonical scripture for Christians, however, we read it as different from the Synoptics yet compatible with them; and that is how it has always been read in the church, ever since it

---

12. Albert I. Baumgarten, "Sacred Scriptures Defile the Hands," *JJS* 67 (2016): 46–67.

13. Barton, *Holy Writings, Sacred Text* (= *Spirit and the Letter*), 115. Like Baumgarten, I refer to the work of Mary Douglas. It is probably the inaccurate subtitle in the American edition—*The Canon in Early Christianity*—that has led to the book's comments on the Hebrew Bible not being noticed by scholars such as Baumgarten.

90   *When Texts Are Canonized*

was recognized as Holy Scripture. It is, however, a matter not of the content leading to canonization but more of the fact of canonization leading to a particular take on the content. John's Gospel, it can be argued, became scripture because it was thought to be by the Beloved Disciple; once that had happened, its content had to be read to make it fit with the emerging orthodoxy in the Christian churches. The same can be said in a less dramatic way of the Synoptics: from none of them can one extract exactly what Christians believed in the early second century, but once one knows what that is, the Synoptics can—and must—be read as according with it.

The basic point here is that what we read is in some measure the result of what we expect to read. A postmodernist perspective would say that this is always and necessarily true of the reading of all texts. But at any rate it is certainly true of texts that make a claim, or are claimed by others, to be sacred. There is a huge investment in reading them as compatible with the religion they are deemed to form part of, and this means they are read differently from how they would be read if they were newly discovered. Childs made the point by contrasting a text that is part of the canon with what he called "inert sherds" that have lain for centuries in the ground.[14] When texts are canonical, we are constrained to read them canonically, that is, as compatible with other canonical texts and with the religious system within which they are canonical. Childs regarded this as a very good thing; I am not making any value judgment on it but simply registering that it is generally true. It applies to the scriptures of many religions, not just to Jewish and Christian ones.[15]

This takes us much further afield, however, for a belief that all sacred texts are compatible with each other is the motive behind attempts at harmonization of texts in the Bible. The apparent discrepancies between whichever texts are to be harmonized are taken to be just that: apparent. In reality the texts are already wholly compatible. The task of the harmonizer, whether it is carried out by discussion of the texts or by producing a sequential version of them, is to demonstrate their compatibility. The harmony is not a substitute for or improvement on the original texts but a living demonstration that they do not conflict and are satisfactory as they stand. In the modern world such harmonization tends to be associated with an extremely conservative understanding of scripture. It implies that the Bible is regarded as a finished product that may not be changed in any way and seeks to demonstrate its complete self-consistency.

In Jewish tradition, one of the heroes of such harmonization is Hananiah ben Hezekiah. According to the Babylonian Talmud, Hananiah used

---

14. Brevard S. Childs, *Introduction to the Old Testament as Scripture* (Philadelphia: Fortress, 1979), 73.

15. See the discussion in Wilfred Cantwell Smith, *What Is Scripture? A Comparative Approach* (London: SCM, 1993), 35–50.

Canon and Content   91

three hundred barrels of oil to keep his lamp alight while he worked to show that there were no inconsistencies between Ezekiel and the Torah, as there appear to be (b. Šabb. 13b). But he had a predecessor in the Chronicler, who famously reconciled inconsistent regulations in the Pentateuch to produce a composite provision that included both. In Exod 12:9, the Passover sacrifice is to be roasted—neither raw nor boiled in water. But in Deut 16:7 boiling is actually commanded. In 2 Chr 35:11–13, the Chronicler shows that he cannot tolerate this discrepancy (known in rabbinic Hebrew as a *mahloket*). Accordingly, in recording how the Passover was celebrated under Josiah, he declares that the sacrifice was "boiled in fire." The practical effect of this is rather nonsensical, and it results in reporting an event that actually conforms to *neither* of the laws. But the important thing for the Chronicler was evidently that the laws had been harmonized, however ineptly. (Later rabbinic discussions produce other, more satisfactory, solutions to the problem.) As Benjamin Sommer puts it, the authors of Chronicles, unlike most modern scholars, "view the Torah not as an anthology of differing opinions (comparable to the Talmud) or as a compendium of different sources but as a single work, written by Moses.... Consequently, they deny that a legal disagreement or *mahloket* can occur in the Torah."[16]

Christian harmonization of the Gospels takes slightly different forms, though all share the conviction that there are no real discrepancies in the Gospels, only apparent ones. The classic example is Augustine's treatise *De consensu evangelistarum*. For the most part this work is not a Gospel harmony in the sense of a continuous retelling of the Gospel story in the words of scripture but rather a detailed discussion of apparent points of inconsistency in the Gospels—though Augustine does, as a sample of how the task could be accomplished, write out a harmonized birth narrative containing all the elements in both Matthew and Luke arranged in a coherent order. His discussion is so exhaustive that it established itself as definitive in the West over many centuries.

Augustine deploys two main strategies in dealing with discrepancies between the Gospels. Where similar incidents or sayings occur that nevertheless have significant differences, he tends to argue that they reflect two separate but similar occasions. Thus, Jesus twice told Simon that he would be called Peter: once early in his ministry, as recorded in John, and again at Caesarea Philippi, as reported in the Synoptics (*Cons.* 2.17). He preached two similar sermons, one on the Mount, one on the Plain (ibid.). At the tomb on the day of resurrection, Mark tells us there was an angel inside the tomb, Matthew that there was one outside, and both are correct; one

---

16. Benjamin Sommer, "Inner-biblical Interpretation," in *The Jewish Study Bible*, ed. Adele Berlin and Marc Zvi Brettler (New York: Oxford University Press, 2004), 1829–35, here 1832.

92   *When Texts Are Canonized*

account is not incompatible with the other (*Cons.* 3.24). From silence we may not infer absence, so that when Matthew tells us that two blind men were healed and Mark mentions only Bartimaeus, we may be sure that there were indeed two: Mark simply mentions the one who was known to his readers (*Cons.* 2.65). Thus, everything that we would regard as a variant tradition can be explained on the assumption that many similar things occurred or were said and that the evangelists were selective in which they reported—different evangelists making different selections. This strategy results in a very much elongated Gospel narrative and probably requires that the events of Jesus's life were spread over a longer period than any one Gospel suggests. To us that would imply that all the Gospels are wrong, rather than that they are all right, but Augustine did not see the matter in that way.

The second strategy Augustine adopts has a rather more modern appearance but still inhabits a precritical world. He suggests that neither the *order* of events nor the exact *wording* of sayings was particularly significant to the evangelists. So far as order is concerned, we find him dealing with the variation in the temptation stories between Matthew and Luke by arguing that the order simply did not matter to the evangelists: "this was nothing to the substance of the matter, since it is clear that all these things did happen" (*Cons.* 2.12). The basic matter of the story is not affected by the variation in order, since it is clear that all three temptations did happen. Probably each evangelist remembered things in a different order, but this does not detract from the historical facticity of each event:

> it is quite likely that each of the evangelists believed that he ought to tell the story in the order in which God had resolved to put into his mind the very things he was narrating, in those matters for which, after all, the order, whether this or that, in no way detracts from the authority and truth of the Gospel. (*Cons.* 2.14)

This is a bit like attitudes to the variety in a book such as Jeremiah. In a similar spirit, what matters in sayings of Jesus or others is not the exact words but the *res*, the content being communicated, and it does not matter if that is not recorded exactly. The *veritatis integritas*, the integrity of the truth, or as Augustine sometimes puts it the *sententia* where biblical texts are concerned—the meaning communicated—matters more than the precise words. This is rather the opposite of our example of the *mahloket* in the Hebrew Bible, where the exact wording is the problem. "We should understand," Augustine says, "that what is to be sought and embraced is not so much the truth of the *words* but of the *things* communicated" (*Cons.* 2.12). In the same chapter he discusses the words of John the Baptist: did he say he was unworthy to untie Jesus's sandals or to carry them? Perhaps he said both on different occasions, or perhaps he said both at the same

time, but in any case the same point (*sententia*) is made by the two sayings, viz., that John recognized his own inferiority to Jesus, and "we learn that we should seek only what John *intended* when he spoke, and not worry too much about the exact words" (ibid.). This is a slightly dangerous principle, which could lead to a certain indifference to the exact text of the Gospels; nevertheless it serves well enough to deal with a good many of the inconsistencies between them.

The types of harmonization I have been describing are related to the perceived need for a sacred text to be self-consistent. It seems obvious that this issue is indeed related to the status of the text. No one troubles about consistency in texts that have a low status: the drive for consistency results from the authoritative or prestigious character of the text in question. As William Graham puts it, one of the features many cultures expect in holy texts is what he calls "unicity."[17] They have to be read as speaking with a single voice, even though this may lead to the reader's twisting or distorting the natural sense of the text in the interest of establishing a coherent "canonical" meaning.

IV

Thus, the question of the content of holy texts in Judaism and Christianity turns out to be multifaceted. On the one hand, the content mattered down to the smallest details, and every effort had to be made to show that the text was harmonious. Furthermore, the text had to be read in such a way as to tally with the religious system as currently held and practiced: hence, John could not be read in a gnosticizing way but had to be read so as to reconcile it with the Synoptic, Gospels. The story told in each Gospel had to be reconcilable with that told in the others. Yet at the same time, there might be little concern for the exact *text*: one sees this especially in the Judaism of New Testament times, where certain books were regarded as sacred but their precise content was not specified. Jeremiah was canonical, but not any particular version of Jeremiah. The Psalms were canonical, but not in any particular order. And variety has always been tolerated in *New* Testament manuscripts anyway, which never in antiquity acquired a fixed and agreed form analogous to the Masoretic Text for the Hebrew Bible.

These two tendencies seem to pull in opposite directions, but what unites them is a tendency to see the relation of form and content differently from how we see it. Scriptural books may be seen as holy objects, regardless of what exactly is in them; or they may be regarded as exact

---

17. See W. A. Graham, "Scripture," in *The Encyclopedia of Religion*, ed. M. Eliade (New York: Macmillan, 1978), 13:131–41, here 141.

94　*When Texts Are Canonized*

transcripts of divine communication, and therefore flawless, needing to be shown to be self-consistent in every detail. They will generally be read as supporting the religious system to which the readers belong, so that their apparent sense may not be allowed to prevail over a sense dictated by that system. On the other hand, people may be quite unclear about what exactly constitutes the book of Genesis, say, or, as in the example I used, Jeremiah. They will simply assume that these books are their versions of these books and be unaware that others use different versions, or perhaps even know about it but not mind it. I draw no conclusions about how we should read the Bible but simply observe that there are some ways people used to do so that are fascinating precisely in their difference from most contemporary perspectives.

Jesus and the Beginnings
of the Christian Canon

CRAIG A. EVANS

Jesus quoted, paraphrased, or alluded to all of the books of Moses, most of the Prophets, and some of the Writings.[1] Superficially, then, the "canon" of Jesus is pretty much what it was for most religiously observant Jews of his time. Jesus also privileged certain books, such as Deuteronomy, Isaiah, and the Psalms, which again suggests that his usage of scripture was pretty much in step with what we observe at Qumran and in other circles.

But apparently Jesus did not privilege the Hebrew version as such, or at least the perspective of the Hebrew version.[2] He often paraphrased scripture, usually according to the Aramaic, which in his time, so far as we know, was emerging in an ad hoc fashion in the synagogue.[3] This study inquires into what influence Jesus's versional "openness" may have had on his disciples and the early church, which did not seem committed to one particular version, whether Hebrew, Aramaic, or Greek. This versional openness, I believe, had significant implications for the respective contents of scripture represented in the various canons of scripture in the Christian church.[4]

---

1. In speaking of Moses, the Prophets, and the Writings, I am not implying that a tripartite canon of scripture was recognized in the time of Jesus. I catalog the writings regarded as sacred this way only because it is convenient.

2. There is little doubt that the men of Qumran privileged Hebrew Scripture.

3. For a recent survey of the origin and function of the Targum, see Paul V. M. Flesher and Bruce D. Chilton, *The Targums: A Critical Introduction*, Studies in the Aramaic Interpretation of Scripture 12 (Leiden: Brill, 2011). For discussion of the Targum's relevance for Jesus and early Christianity, see 385–436.

4. For a survey and analysis of the canons of Christian Scripture, see Lee M. McDonald, *Formation of the Bible: The Story of the Church's Canon* (Peabody, MA: Hendrickson, 2012). See also Lee Martin McDonald and James A. Sanders, eds., *The Canon Debate* (Peabody, MA: Hendrickson, 2002). In the present study I discuss a number of passages that I think approximate authentic utterances of Jesus. Some scholars will no doubt object to one or more of my selections. Even so, the disqualification of one or two of my examples will not cancel out the principal point of the study. In saying this I do not imply that the language or versions of scripture to which Jesus made reference was actually discussed at Christian councils con-

96   *When Texts Are Canonized*

Jesus and the Announcement of the Kingdom of God

It is universally agreed that the single most important element in the preaching and teaching of Jesus was his announcement of the kingdom of God. The Markan evangelist sums it up as follows:

> πεπλήρωται ὁ καιρὸς καὶ ἤγγικεν ἡ βασιλεία τοῦ θεοῦ· μετανοεῖτε καὶ πιστεύετε ἐν τῷ εὐαγγελίῳ. (Mark 1:15)[5]
>
> The time is fulfilled, and the kingdom of God is at hand; repent, and believe in the gospel.

It is widely recognized that Jesus's announcement of the kingdom of God draws on the language and imagery of the prophet Isaiah, especially as some of these oracles had come to expression in the Aramaic paraphrases of the synagogue that in time would become the Targum.[6] References to the reign of God or to God acting in a kingly fashion are rendered in the Aramaic as "the kingdom of the Lord of hosts will be revealed" or "the kingdom of your God will be revealed [אתגליאת מלכות אלהיך / אתגליאת]," not only in Isaiah (Isa 24:23, 31:4, 40:9, 52:7) but in other prophets as well (Zech 14:9, Obad 21, and Mic 4:7b–8, where the Messiah is linked to the appearance of the kingdom).

The antiquity of the theological expression "kingdom of God" is partially attested in Hebrew Scripture, where we find "kingdom of the Lord [מלכות יהוה]" in Chronicles (1 Chr 28:5, 2 Chr 13:8), and in the Dead Sea Scrolls, especially in the Songs of the Sabbath Sacrifice, where more than twenty times we observe references to "his kingdom [מלכותו]" (4Q403 1 I, 8, 14, 32; 4Q405 3 II, 4; MasSS 2:20; etc.) or "the kingdom of your glory [מלכות כבודכה]" (4Q401 14 I, 6), including "the glorious kingdom of the king of all the g[ods]" (4Q405 24, 3). This encourages us to think that the expression, "kingdom of God," in Hebrew and Aramaic Jewish traditions and in the Aramaic-speaking Jesus was not idiosyncratic but a widely recognized theologoumenon in first-century Israel.

The kingdom, or rule, of God was the central datum in Jesus's procla-

---

cerned with questions of canon. It is only suggested that the observation of Jesus's and/or the evangelists' evident openness to different versions may well have played a part in the thinking of Christian teachers and authorities that in turn may have influenced decisions about canon.

5. The announcement is abbreviated and modified in Matthew: μετανοεῖτε· ἤγγικεν γὰρ ἡ βασιλεία τῶν οὐρανῶν (Matt 4:17). That Jesus proclaimed God's kingdom is widely accepted.

6. B. D. Chilton, *The Glory of Israel: The Theology and Provenience of the Isaiah Targum*, JSOTSup 23 (Sheffield: JSOT Press, 1982), 77–81; Flesher and Chilton, *Targums*, 81–82, 151–66. The extant Isaiah Targum, of course, did not exist in the time of Jesus. Rather, this later written text preserves some language, theological terms, and interpretive traditions that reach back to the time of Jesus and even earlier.

mation and teaching and remained central, even if qualified, in the preaching and teaching of the early church (e.g., Acts 1:3; 8:12; 14:22; 19:8; 28:23, 31; Rom 14:17; 1 Cor 4:20; 6:9; 15:50; Gal 5:21; Col 4:11; 2 Thess 1:5; 1 Clem. 42:3; 2 Clem. 9:6; 12:1; Ign. *Eph.* 16:1; Ign. *Phld.* 3:3; Barn. 21:1; Hermas 9.12.3–5 [89:3–5]). This language was rooted in the Aramaic paraphrase of Isaiah and other prophets and likely influenced the early church's appreciation of the Aramaic tradition. For example, Aramaic forms of scripture appear in the letters of Paul and elsewhere.[7]

Jesus and the Mystery of the Kingdom

Awkwardly between the parable of the sower (Mark 4:3–9) and its explanation (Mark 4:14–20), Jesus explains to his disciples why he speaks in parables:

> ὑμῖν τὸ μυστήριον δέδοται τῆς βασιλείας τοῦ θεοῦ· ἐκείνοις δὲ τοῖς ἔξω ἐν παραβολαῖς τὰ πάντα γίνεται, ἵνα βλέποντες βλέπωσιν καὶ μὴ ἴδωσιν, καὶ ἀκούοντες ἀκούωσιν καὶ μὴ συνιῶσιν, μήποτε ἐπιστρέψωσιν καὶ ἀφεθῇ αὐτοῖς. (Mark 4:11-12)

> To you has been given the secret of the kingdom of God, but for those outside everything is in parables; so that they may indeed see but not perceive, and may indeed hear but not understand; lest they should turn again, and be forgiven.

Jesus has paraphrased Isa 6:9–10 (in v. 12).[8] The language does not reflect either the Hebrew or the Greek, where the people refuse to turn back (or repent) and be *healed*; rather, the language reflects the Aramaic, which employs the prosaic, nonmetaphorical be "forgiven." But it is more than the diction itself that points to the Aramaic. It is also the perspective of the oracle.

In the Hebrew version, the prophet is commanded to speak thus:

> Go, and say to this people: "Hear and hear, but do not understand; see and see, but do not perceive." Make the heart of this people fat, and their ears heavy, and shut their eyes; lest they see with their eyes, and hear with their ears, and understand with their hearts, and turn and be healed. (Isa 6:9–10)

---

7. For a survey, see M. McNamara, *Targum and Testament Revisited: Aramaic Paraphrases of the Hebrew Bible*, 2nd ed. (Grand Rapids: Eerdmans, 2010).

8. Scholars are willing to accept the dominical origin of this utterance, but many suspect it was uttered on another occasion. For discussion, see R. T. France, *The Gospel of Mark: A Commentary on the Greek Text*, NIGTC (Grand Rapids: Eerdmans, 2002), 193–203; Adela Yarbro Collins, *Mark: A Commentary*, Hermeneia (Minneapolis: Fortress, 2007), 239–40, 247–50.

98   *When Texts Are Canonized*

The causative force is softened in the Septuagint, which transforms the Hebrew's imperatives into predictive futures: "You will hear and not understand, you will see and not observe." In the Greek the prophet is not to make the people obdurate (as in the Hebrew's השמן, "make fat"), for they already are obdurate: "For the heart of this people has grown thick [ἐπαχύνθη] ..." (LXX). But in the Aramaic, the harsh prophetic word is limited; it applies only to those who refuse to hear and see: "Go and speak to this people *who* hear but do not listen, and see but do not observe." The Hebrew's imperatives become descriptives. The Aramaic paraphrase appears to envision two groups: those in the company of the prophet, who do see, and those among the wicked, who refuse to see.

Jesus reflects both the diction of the Aramaic and its perspective: To his disciples the secret or mystery of the kingdom of God is given, but to outsiders everything is riddles. The Aramaic understanding and Jesus's understanding of Isa 6:9–10 may approximate that of the Great Isaiah Scroll's interesting reading, if William H. Brownlee's interpretation is accepted.[9]

Sitting on the Throne of Glory

In Q tradition Jesus assures his disciples that someday they will reign with him. The two versions of the utterance read as follows:

ἀμὴν λέγω ὑμῖν ὅτι ὑμεῖς οἱ ἀκολουθήσαντές μοι ἐν τῇ παλιγγενεσίᾳ, ὅταν καθίσῃ ὁ υἱὸς τοῦ ἀνθρώπου ἐπὶ θρόνου δόξης αὐτοῦ, καθήσεσθε καὶ ὑμεῖς ἐπὶ δώδεκα θρόνους κρίνοντες τὰς δώδεκα φυλὰς τοῦ Ἰσραήλ. (Matt 19:28)

Truly, I say to you, in the new world, when the Son of man shall sit on his glorious throne, you who have followed me will also sit on twelve thrones, judging the twelve tribes of Israel.

Ὑμεῖς δέ ἐστε οἱ διαμεμενηκότες μετ᾽ ἐμοῦ ἐν τοῖς πειρασμοῖς μου· κἀγὼ διατίθεμαι ὑμῖν καθὼς διέθετό μοι ὁ πατήρ μου βασιλείαν, ἵνα ἔσθητε καὶ πίνητε ἐπὶ τῆς τραπέζης μου ἐν τῇ βασιλείᾳ μου, καὶ καθήσεσθε ἐπὶ θρόνων τὰς δώδεκα φυλὰς κρίνοντες τοῦ Ἰσραήλ. (Luke 22:28–30)

You are those who have continued with me in my trials; and I assign to you, as my Father assigned to me, a kingdom, that you may eat and drink at my table in my kingdom, and sit on thrones judging the twelve tribes of Israel.

---

9. William H. Brownlee, *The Meaning of the Qumrân Scrolls for the Bible: With Special Attention to the Book of Isaiah*, James W. Richard Lectures in Christian Religion 1958 (New York: Oxford University Press, 1964), 186–88.

Jesus and the Beginnings of the Christian Canon   99

The dominical utterance appears to be based on Dan 7:9 ("thrones were placed"), 13 ("a son of man"), and, especially, Ps 122:3–5:

> Jerusalem, built as a city that is bound firmly together, to which the tribes go up, the tribes of the LORD, as was decreed for Israel, to give thanks to the name of the LORD. There thrones for judgment were set, the thrones of the house of David.

Not only is Dan 7 understood in an eschatological sense in Jewish interpretation,[10] as well as in dominical material (see also Matt 25:31, Mark 14:62), but Ps 122:3–5 is understood eschatologically in the Aramaic Psalter. Envisioned in the Aramaic version is the heavenly Jerusalem and end-time judgment.[11] In an early rabbinic midrash, Dan 7 and Ps 122 appear together in a depiction of eschatological judgment, in which the elders of Israel sit on twelve thrones in judgment upon the peoples (Midr. Tanh. Qedoshim §1 [on Lev 19:1–2]). The parallels with Jesus's saying are remarkable.[12]

The idea that the "son of man" figure in Dan 7 would sit on one of the thrones mentioned in verse 9 is found in 1 Enoch, in another book that likely originated in Aramaic, as the evidence from Qumran strongly suggests. Daniel's son of man figure appears in a number of places in the Similitudes of Enoch (i.e., 1 Enoch 37–71), where he is identified as the Messiah (48:10, 52:4) and Elect One (40:5, 49:2), who will "sit on the seat of glory" (45:3, 51:3) or "throne of glory" (54:3, 55:4, 61:8, 69:29). Although we have found no trace of 1 Enoch 37–72 among the many Aramaic fragments of Enoch in the Dead Sea Scrolls, it is probable that the Similitudes were composed in the first century and that the ideas contained in this collection were in circulation, at least in part, in the time of Jesus and his followers.[13] The Q saying once again shows Jesus's familiarity with scripture (i.e., Daniel, Psalms, Enoch) that was available in Aramaic.[14]

---

10. See b. Sanh. 38b (attributed to Akiva), 96b–97a, 98a; b. Ḥag. 14a.

11. For translation and notes, see David M. Stec, *The Targum of Psalms: Translated, with a Critical Introduction, Apparatus, and Notes*, ArBib 16 (Collegeville, MN: Liturgical Press, 2004), 220.

12. I treat the parallels in some detail in Craig A. Evans, "The Twelve Thrones of Israel: Scripture and Politics in Luke 22:24–30," in *Luke and Scripture: The Function of Sacred Tradition in Luke-Acts*, by Craig A. Evans and James A. Sanders (Minneapolis: Fortress, 1993), 154–70, esp. 162–64. For further discussion of the Matthean form of the tradition, see C. A. Evans, *Matthew*, New Cambridge Bible Commentary (Cambridge: Cambridge University Press, 2012), 346–48.

13. George W. E. Nickelsburg and James C. VanderKam, *1 Enoch 2: A Commentary on the Book of 1 Enoch, Chapters 37–82*, Hermeneia (Minneapolis: Fortress, 2012), 32: "an Aramaic original"; 60: "a date before 70 C.E. is almost certain."

14. In the case of Daniel, about one-half of the work, including chapter 7, originated and circulated in Aramaic. So far as we know, all of Enoch, including the Similitudes, orig-

100   *When Texts Are Canonized*

Resurrection "on the third day"

In the Synoptic tradition, Jesus is remembered to have predicted his suffering, death, and resurrection "after three days" or "on the third day."[15]

> δεῖ τὸν υἱὸν τοῦ ἀνθρώπου πολλὰ παθεῖν καὶ ἀποδοκιμασθῆναι ὑπὸ τῶν πρεσβυτέρων καὶ τῶν ἀρχιερέων καὶ τῶν γραμματέων καὶ ἀποκτανθῆναι καὶ μετὰ τρεῖς ἡμέρας ἀναστῆναι· (Mark 8:31)

> The Son of man must suffer many things, and be rejected by the elders and the chief priests and the scribes, and be killed, and after three days rise again.

> δεῖ αὐτὸν εἰς Ἱεροσόλυμα ἀπελθεῖν καὶ πολλὰ παθεῖν ἀπὸ τῶν πρεσβυτέρων καὶ ἀρχιερέων καὶ γραμματέων καὶ ἀποκτανθῆναι καὶ τῇ τρίτῃ ἡμέρᾳ ἐγερθῆναι. (Matt 16:21)

> He must go to Jerusalem and suffer many things from the elders and chief priests and scribes, and be killed, and on the third day be raised.

It is interesting to observe the variation of the prepositions μετά ("after") and ἐν ("on"). Both prepositions appear in Hos 6:2, the passage to which Jesus probably alluded in offering his disciples (and himself?) assurance that regardless of his fate in Jerusalem, he will be raised up. The Hebrew and Greek of Hos 6:2 read:

> יחינו מימים ביום השלישי יקמנו ונחיה לפניו[16]

> After two days he will revive us; on the third day he will raise us up, that we may live before him.

> ὑγιάσει ἡμᾶς μετὰ δύο ἡμέρας, ἐν τῇ ἡμέρᾳ τῇ τρίτῃ ἀναστησόμεθα καὶ ζησόμεθα ἐνώπιον αὐτοῦ.[17]

> After two days he will make us healthy; on the third day we will rise up and live before him.

---

inated and circulated in Aramaic. We do not know if Ps 122 was available in Aramaic in the time of Jesus, but understanding it in an eschatological sense, as we see in the later Targum, apparently was.

15. There is little doubt that the passion predictions have been edited, multiplied, and inserted into the narrative at key points. Even so, there are good reasons to think that they go back to warnings and assurances that Jesus gave his closest disciples. I discuss these reasons in "Did Jesus Predict His Death and Resurrection?" in *Resurrection*, ed. Stanley E. Porter, Michael A. Hayes, and David Tombs, JSNTSup 186, Roehampton Institute London Papers 5 (Sheffield: Sheffield Academic, 1999), 82–97.

16. The Hebrew text of Hos 6:2 is not preserved at Qumran.

17. The Greek text of Hos 6:2 is not preserved in 8ḤevXII gr.

The passion predictions in the Gospels echo the "after two days" (μετὰ δύο ἡμέρας) and "on the third day" (ἐν τῇ ἡμέρᾳ τῇ τρίτῃ), but it is the Aramaic version that makes the hint at resurrection explicit:

יחיינא ליומי נחמתא דעתידין למיתי ביום אחיות מיתיא יקימיננא וניחי קדמוהי

He will give us life in the days of consolations that will come; on the day of the resurrection of the dead he will raise us up and we shall live before him.[18]

The passion predictions of the Gospels do not reflect the diction of the Aramaic, but they do reflect the exegetical orientation of the Aramaic. The Hebrew's anticipation of national restoration becomes in the Aramaic an eschatological prophecy of future resurrection. Jesus accepts the eschatological framework of the Aramaic but narrows its focus when he applies the passage to himself.

The Vineyard and the Temple

Jesus begins his parable of the vineyard (Mark 12:1–9) with an obvious allusion to Isaiah's sharply critical song of the vineyard (Isa 5:1–7): "A man planted a vineyard, and set a hedge around it, and dug a pit for the wine press, and built a tower, and let it out to tenants, and went into another country" (Mark 12:1).[19] Some one dozen words are imported from Isaiah, inviting hearers and readers to think of the symbols and values of the old prophetic song as the parable unfolds. In its original setting, Isaiah's song offers a devastating critique of Israel's ruling elite, identified in verse 3 as the "inhabitants of Jerusalem and men of Judah" and in verse 7 as "the house of Israel, and the men of Judah." The description of the vineyard as planted on a "fertile hill" (v. 1) might have been viewed as a reference to Jerusalem and perhaps even to the hill on which the Temple was situated, but it is in the Aramaic that identification with the Temple becomes explicit and detailed. The relevant parts of the passage in the Targum read:

---

18. Translation from Kevin J. Cathcart and Robert P. Gordon, *The Targum of the Minor Prophets*, ArBib 14 (Wilmington, DE: Glazier, 1989), 41. See also the excursus, "Resurrection on the Third Day," in Hans W. Wolff, *Hosea: A Commentary on the Book of the Prophet Hosea*, Hermeneia (Philadelphia: Fortress, 1974), 117–18.

19. The authenticity of the parable of the vineyard is widely accepted. What is disputed is the originality of the allusions to Isa 5:1–7, which are found in Mark and Matthew but are not present in Luke and Thomas. Although there are advocates of Thomasine priority, most scholars view Thomas as secondary to the Synoptics and in this case probably dependent on Luke.

102   *When Texts Are Canonized*

> *I glorified them and I established them as the plant of a* choice vine; and I built *my sanctuary* in their midst, and I even gave *my altar to atone for their sins; I thought that they would do good deeds, but they made their deeds evil.…* And now I will tell you what I am about to do to my *people.* I will *take up my Shekhinah from them,* and they shall be for *plundering;* I will break down *the place of their sanctuaries.…* (Tg. Isa. 5:2, 5, with major alterations noted in italics)[20]

In the Aramaic paraphrase, the Hebrew's "hill" becomes a *high hill,* the "watchtower" becomes the *sanctuary,* and the "wine vat" becomes the *altar.* These identifications are explicit in the Tosefta (t. Me'il. 1:16; t. Sukkah 3.15). In the material that follows the song, we hear references to oppression (vv. 7–8), failure to pay tithes (v. 10), and ignoring the law (vv. 1–13), complaints that very much reflect complaints directed against the ruling priesthood in the decades leading up to the destruction of the Temple in 70. These complaints are found in later rabbinic literature (e.g., b. Pesaḥ. 57a; b. Yebam. 61a), but they are widely attested in earlier Jewish literature (such as the writings of Josephus), including literature that circulated prior to 70.[21]

The antiquity of the Temple-oriented interpretation of Isa 5:1–7 is attested in 4Q500. In this small fragment, the Temple is viewed positively (at least so far as we can discern), but the perspective found in Jesus, the Targum, and early rabbinic tradition shows that the negative interpretation was also in circulation in the pre-70 period[22] and that it was not distinctive to the early Christian movement, in reaction (say) to the ruling priests' opposition to Jesus.

The Rejected Stone as Rightful King

Jesus concludes the parable of the vineyard with a verbatim quotation of Ps 117:22–23 LXX.

οὐδὲ τὴν γραφὴν ταύτην ἀνέγνωτε· λίθον ὃν ἀπεδοκίμασαν οἱ οἰκοδομοῦντες, οὗτος ἐγενήθη εἰς κεφαλὴν γωνίας· παρὰ κυρίου ἐγένετο αὕτη καὶ ἔστιν θαυμαστὴ ἐν ὀφθαλμοῖς ἡμῶν; (Mark 12:10–11)

---

20. Translation from Bruce D. Chilton, *The Isaiah Targum,* ArBib 11 (Wilmington, DE: Glazier, 1987), 10–11. See also the discussion in Chilton, *A Galilean Rabbi and His Bible: Jesus' Use of the Interpreted Scripture of His Time,* GNS 8 (Wilmington, DE: Glazier, 1984), 111–14.

21. I have reviewed these materials in "Jesus' Action in the Temple and Evidence of Corruption in the First-Century Temple," in *Society of Biblical Literature 1989 Seminar Papers: One Hundred Twenty-fifth Annual Meeting, 18–21 November 1989, the Anaheim Hilton and Towers, Anaheim, California,* ed. David J. Lull, SBLSP 28 (Atlanta: Scholars Press, 1989), 522–39.

22. J. M. Baumgarten, "4Q500 and the Ancient Conception of the Lord's Vineyard," *JJS* 40 (1989): 1–6.

Jesus and the Beginnings of the Christian Canon   103

> Have you not read this scripture: "The very stone which the builders rejected has become the head of the corner; this was the Lord's doing, and it is marvelous in our eyes"?

Because the quotation follows the Greek, some scholars have argued or assumed that it cannot go back to Jesus.[23] Whatever Jesus's facility with Greek, I doubt very much that he quoted this passage from the Psalter in Greek. What is more likely is that Jesus quoted or paraphrased it according to the Aramaic, as he did other passages. But the popularity of this passage, as we see in a number of places in the Greek New Testament and early Christian Greek literature, in which Ps 118 [117]:22–23 is quoted in Greek (e.g., Acts 4:11; 1 Pet 2:4, 6–7; Barn. 6:4; Justin, *Dial.* 36:1),[24] led to assimilation to the Greek here in Mark 12:10–11. We see this very thing in the Gospels themselves, where, for example, the Matthean evangelist greatly reduces Jesus's paraphrase of Isa 6:9–10 in Mark 4:12, removing its Aramaic features, and then adds a formal quotation of Isaiah according to the LXX (Matt 13:13–15). Luke also reduces Jesus's paraphrase of Isaiah, and he too eliminates the Aramaic features (Luke 8:10). Like Matthew, the Lukan evangelist will quote Isa 6:9–10 LXX—only not in the parable context but at the end of the book of Acts (28:26–27).

What convinces me and others that the parable of the vineyard did originally conclude with a quotation of Ps 118 [117] as a prooftext (or *nimšal*, which normally concludes rabbinic parables) is, once again, its interpretive coherence with the Aramaic.[25] Whereas the Hebrew (MT) reads at Ps 118:21 (Heb. 22), "The stone that the builders rejected has become the head of the corner" (so also the Greek [Ps 117:22]), the Aramaic reads, "The builders abandoned the boy among the sons of Jesse, but he was worthy to be appointed king and ruler [למליך ושולטן]."[26] The Aramaic paraphrase, in which the *stone* is interpreted as *boy*, probably owes its inspiration to the play on words with אבן ("stone") and הבן ("the son").[27] The identification of the stone of Ps 118:22 with the son of Jesse, destined to become Israel's king, facilitated using Ps 118:22 as the concluding prooftext to the parable

---

23. As, e.g., in Eduard Schweizer, *The Good News according to Mark*, trans. Donald H. Madvic (Atlanta: John Knox, 1970), 239.

24. There are passages that speak of "stone" (λίθος) or "single stone" that are probably allusions to Ps 117:22 LXX (e.g., Hermas 10:6; 13:2; 86:7; Justin, *Dialogue with Trypho* 36).

25. Craig A. Evans, "On the Vineyard Parables of Isaiah 5 and Mark 12," *BZ* 28 (1984): 82–86; George J. Brooke, "4Q500 1 and the Use of Scripture in the Parable of the Vineyard," in *The Dead Sea Scrolls and the New Testament* (Minneapolis: Fortress, 2005), 235–60, esp. 253–56, with respect to Ps 118:22.

26. It is translated slightly differently in Stec, *Targum of Psalms*, 210.

27. Brooke, "4Q500 1," 254–55. The wordplay is at work in Josephus, *J.W.* 5.272.

104   *When Texts Are Canonized*

of the vineyard, in which focus is placed on the vineyard owner's rejected son.[28]

The Aramaic paraphrase merges Ps 118:19–27 with the story of the selection of Jesse's son David as Israel's new king (1 Sam 16:1–13) producing a remarkable antiphony, as David and his family wend their way up the holy hill to the waiting priests. The Aramaic paraphrase is part of a complex Jewish interpretive tradition, some of which was apparently known in the time of Jesus.[29] When Jesus recast Isaiah's song into a new parable, introducing novel elements that shifted the guilt from the fruitless vineyard to an avaricious and violent ruling priesthood, his opponents (i.e., the "builders") readily understood that "he had told the parable against them" (Mark 12:12).

The Aramaic tradition comes into play elsewhere in the dominical tradition, yet the evangelists themselves freely make use of other versions of scripture, either when they add prooftexts or when they paraphrase the dominical tradition itself. We observe the same thing elsewhere in the New Testament and early Christian writers, who make use of various versions of scripture or interpretations of scripture that depend on non-Hebrew versions. The evangelists Matthew and John make use of or presuppose scripture in Hebrew, Greek, and Aramaic.[30] So does Paul.[31]

Jesus and Books outside the Hebrew Scriptures

Jesus does not quote or formally appeal to writings outside the Hebrew Scriptures, but he does allude to several or at least to traditions also found in these writings. These include 1 Maccabees, 2 Maccabees, 4 Maccabees, Enoch, Psalms of Solomon, Sirach, Tobit, the Wisdom of Solomon, and perhaps some of the Testaments of the Twelve Patriarchs. Two examples may be discussed.

---

28. Klyne R. Snodgrass, *Stories with Intent: A Comprehensive Guide to the Parables of Jesus* (Grand Rapids: Eerdmans, 2007), 289–92.

29. For a detailed discussion of Ps 118's place in this interpretive tradition, see Timothy M. Edwards, *Exegesis in the Targum of the Psalms: The Old, the New, and the Rewritten*, Gorgias Dissertations 28 (Piscataway, NJ: Gorgias, 2007), 174–83.

30. On Matthew's knowledge of Hebrew, Aramaic, and Greek scriptural traditions, see Robert H. Gundry, *The Use of the Old Testament in St. Matthew's Gospel: With Special Reference to the Messianic Hope*, NovTSup 18 (Leiden: Brill, 1967), 172. For John, see Bruce G. Schuchard, *Scripture within Scripture: The Interrelationship of Form and Function in the Explicit Old Testament Citations in the Gospel of John*, SBLDS 133 (Atlanta: Scholars Press, 1992), 153–54. Schuchard finds that, although the Johannine evangelist was familiar with Hebrew, Aramaic, and Greek, when he quoted Scripture he drew on the Greek version, freely editing the text as necessary.

31. See E. Earle Ellis, *Paul's Use of the Old Testament* (Edinburgh: Oliver & Boyd, 1957), 10–16.

Jesus and the Beginnings of the Christian Canon 105

In his graphic warning of the dangers of temptation and how it is better to enter the kingdom of God without a hand or an eye than to be cast into Gehenna (Mark 9:42–48),[32] Jesus has probably alluded to the fearsome injuries suffered by the Maccabean martyrs (e.g., 2 Macc 6–7; 4 Macc 5, 10, 18).[33] This is probable, not simply because of the similarities of injuries (2 Macc 7:4, 4 Macc 10:5 [hands or feet], 4 Macc 5:30, 18:21 [eyes]) but because of comparable settings. Just as the Maccabean martyrs choose to lose limbs rather than risk loss of life in the world to come, so Jesus reasons that it is better to lose members of the body rather than be cast into Gehenna whole. The parallel is not exact,[34] but the point is very similar.

Jesus may also have alluded to the book of Enoch. In Matt 22:13a, an angry king in Jesus's parable of the marriage feast (Matt 22:1–14) commands, δήσαντες αὐτοῦ πόδας καὶ χεῖρας ἐκβάλετε αὐτὸν εἰς τὸ σκότος τὸ ἐξώτερον ("Bind him hand and foot, and cast him into the outer darkness"). David Sim has argued persuasively that the king's command alludes to 1 Enoch 10:4a: δῆσον τὸν Ἀζαὴλ ποσὶν καὶ χερσίν, καὶ βάλε αὐτὸν εἰς τὸ σκότος ("Bind Azael foot and hand, and cast him into the darkness").[35] The parallel is close enough that we probably should conclude that Matthew's wording has been influenced by a Greek version.[36] This of course does not rule out the possibility that the saying goes back to Jesus and that it was originally uttered in Aramaic,[37] the language in which Enoch circulated in Jewish Palestine in the time of Jesus (as amply attested by the many Aramaic Enoch scrolls from Qumran).[38]

In Jude, however, we seem to have a direct quotation of 1 Enoch 1:9. Jude 14a introduces the quotation, "It was of these also that Enoch in the seventh generation from Adam prophesied, saying," and then reads:

---

32. In this context Jesus appeals to Isa 66:24, and once again we have dictional coherence with the Aramaic, for only in the Targum is the unquenchable fire of Isa 66:24 specifically linked to Gehenna.

33. William L. Lane, *The Gospel of Mark: The English Text with Introduction, Exposition, and Notes*, NICNT (Grand Rapids: Eerdmans, 1974), 348.

34. The principal difference is seen in that the Maccabean martyrs suffer the loss of life and limb at the hands of tormentors, while Jesus speaks, hyperbolically of course, of self-inflicted loss.

35. David C. Sim, "Matthew 22.13a and 1 Enoch 10.4a: A Case of Literary Dependence?" *JSNT* 47 (1992): 3–19.

36. These options are discussed in ibid., 4–13. Sim concludes that the Matthean evangelist has used the form of the Greek text that is now extant in the sixth-century Panopolitanus Codex.

37. In rendering the Aramaic saying of Jesus into Greek, it is not surprising that the evangelist made use of a Greek version, as he does in other instances.

38. Unfortunately, only a few letters of 1 Enoch 10:4 are all that is extant in 4Q201 V, 5. What is extant agrees with the saying attributed to Jesus and the Panopolitanus Codex. First Enoch 10:4 is not extant in either 4Q202 or 4Q204.

106   *When Texts Are Canonized*

ἰδοὺ ἦλθεν κύριος ἐν ἁγίαις μυριάσιν αὐτοῦ ποιῆσαι κρίσιν κατὰ πάντων καὶ ἐλέγξαι πᾶσαν ψυχὴν περὶ πάντων τῶν ἔργων ἀσεβείας αὐτῶν ὧν ἠσέβησαν καὶ περὶ πάντων τῶν σκληρῶν ὧν ἐλάλησαν κατ᾽ αὐτοῦ ἁμαρτωλοὶ ἀσεβεῖς. (Jude 14b–15)

Behold, the Lord came with his holy myriads, to execute judgment on all, and to convict all the ungodly of all their deeds of ungodliness which they have committed in such an ungodly way, and of all the harsh things which ungodly sinners have spoken against him.

Jude's text closely matches the Greek text of 1 Enoch 1:9:

ἔρχεται σὺν ταῖς μυριάσιν αὐτοῦ καὶ τοῖς ἁγίος αὐτοῦ, ποιῆσαι κρίσιν κατὰ πάντων, καὶ ἀπολέσει πάντας τοὺς ἀσεβεῖς, καὶ ἐλέγξει πᾶσαν σάρκα περὶ πάντων ἔργων τῆς ἀσεβείας αὐτῶν ὧν ἠσέβησαν καὶ σκληρῶν ὧν ἐλάλησαν λόγων, καὶ περὶ πάντων ὧν κατελάλησαν κατ᾽αὐτοῦ ἁμαρτωλοὶ ἀσεβεῖς.

He comes with his myriads and with his holy ones, to make judgment against all, and he will destroy all the ungodly, and convict all flesh about all works of their ungodliness which they in an ungodly way committed and the harsh words which they have spoken, and about all which the ungodly sinners have spoken evil against him.

At first blush the text in Jude seems to be based on a Greek version of Enoch, such as we have extant in the Panopolitanus Codex. Although some of the differences in Jude's text can be plausibly explained in reference to the author's interest and the contextualization of the quotation in his epistle, other differences with the Greek suggest that he was acquainted with the Aramaic, for Jude's rendering of the Greek makes better sense of the Aramaic than what we see in the Panopolitanus Codex.[39]

Other examples could be discussed, in which either the *text* of scripture that is cited in early Greek Christian writings, or the *interpretation* of the text, reflects readings that are distinctive either to the Hebrew or the Aramaic. Exegetically as well as textually, then, appeals to scripture in early Christian literature reflect a trilingual reality in the early centuries of the church, which in turn influenced the very contents of canon.

Concluding Remarks

I suggest that the linguistic diversity that we observe in the quotations and interpretations of Israel's scripture was itself a factor in canonical forma-

---

39. For discussion, see Richard J. Bauckham, *Jude, 2 Peter*, WBC 50 (Dallas: Word, 1983), 94–96. Bauckham concludes that Jude "made his own translation from the Aramaic" (96). Others have reached the same conclusion. See Peter H. Davids, *The Letters of 2 Peter and Jude*, Pillar New Testament Commentary (Grand Rapids: Eerdmans, 2006), 77–79. A few words of the Aramaic text survive in 4Q204 I, 15–17; nothing survives of 1 Enoch 1:9 in 4Q201.

Jesus and the Beginnings of the Christian Canon   107

tion in the early church. The textual diversity—in the Christian community—originated with Jesus himself. There is little doubt that he regarded
the Hebrew text of scripture as sacred and authoritative, but this sacred-
ness and authority were not limited to the Hebrew. Jesus readily appealed
to readings and interpretations that originated in the Aramaic-speaking
synagogue that in time would come to expression as Targum. Following
the Master's example, early Christian teachers appealed to the Greek, as
well as to the Hebrew and Aramaic.

Of course, given the fact that the Greek literature of Christianity's
earliest writers formed the canon of scripture for the West, it is hardly
surprising that the Greek version of Scripture (i.e., the LXX and to a lesser
degree the recensions) dominates in the writings that make up this canon.
Accordingly, it is not surprising at all that the early Greek Christian Bibles
contained some of the books of the Apocrypha, particularly those that
were originally written in Greek or were translated into Greek.

The great disruption in this pattern was Jerome's decision to translate
into Latin not the Greek Old Testament but the Hebrew Bible. This decision, which was controversial, resulted in segregating the non-Hebrew
books (i.e., the Apocrypha) from the Hebrew books. This gave the Western
canon of scripture a distinctively Semitic orientation. The Greek Church,
of course, retained the Greek Old Testament, which included most of the
books of the Apocrypha.[40] The canons of the Eastern and Coptic Churches
were even less influenced by the West, with the result that books such as
Enoch or Jubilees continued to enjoy semicanonical authority (at least in
some branches and offshoots of these Eastern churches).

The "versional openness" of Jesus and his early followers left the
Christian church free to pursue either a Greek canon or a Hebrew-
Aramaic canon or a combination of the two. This the church did, with the
result that different canons emerged, reflecting languages, regional traditions, and historical and social vicissitudes. Canonical diversity should be
viewed not as a theological problem but rather as a hermeneutical asset
that facilitates the teaching and application of scripture in diverse cultural
and social settings.

---

40. For a convenient compilation of various canonical lists, see McDonald, *Formation of
the Christian Biblical Canon*, 439–51.

Canon and Religious Truth:
An Appraisal of *A New New Testament*

R. W. L. MOBERLY

I hope that some of the well-worn questions about the nature, purpose, and function of the biblical canon may be cast in a fresh light if we step back from familiar debates about canon in antiquity and choose a contemporary focus instead. Thus, I propose to consider the recent (2013) publication of *A New New Testament: A Bible for the 21st Century Combining Traditional and Newly Discovered Texts*, edited with a commentary by Hal Taussig.[1]

Every biblical scholar is familiar with collections of ancient documents that have been brought together to illustrate the wider world of the Bible. Most famous in relation to the Old Testament is probably James Pritchard (ed.), *Ancient Near Eastern Texts Relating to the Old Testament*, though there are numerous others,[2] while for the New Testament there are numerous titles along the lines of C. K. Barrett's *The New Testament Background: Selected Documents* or Bart Ehrman's *The New Testament and Other Early Christian Writings: A Reader*.[3] But such collections, however much they may emphasize similarities of genre and content between biblical and nonbiblical material, nonetheless conventionally preserve a basic distinction between biblical and nonbiblical: the Old or New Testament remains a distinctive collection, which is to be illuminated by being read alongside other documents and material remains from its wider world of origin.[4]

---

1. *A New New Testament: A Bible for the 21st Century Combining Traditional and Newly Discovered Texts*, edited with commentary by Hal Taussig, with a foreword by John Dominic Crossan (Boston: Houghton Mifflin Harcourt, 2013). Pagination of *A New New Testament*, abbreviated as *ANNT*, will be cited in parentheses in my main text.

2. James B. Pritchard (ed.), *Ancient Near Eastern Texts Relating to the Old Testament*, 3rd ed. (Princeton: Princeton University Press, 1969); see also, e.g., Christopher B. Hays, *Hidden Riches: A Sourcebook for the Comparative Study of the Hebrew Bible and Ancient Near East* (Louisville: Westminster John Knox, 2014).

3. C. K. Barrett, ed., *The New Testament Background: Selected Documents* (London: SPCK, 1956); Bart D. Ehrman, *The New Testament and Other Early Christian Writings: A Reader* (New York: Oxford University Press, 1998).

4. To be precise, collections whose purpose is purely historical not infrequently place

Now for the first time, however—to the best of my knowledge—we have a different kind of title. The title *A New New Testament: A Bible for the 21ˢᵗ Century Combining Traditional and Newly Discovered Texts* is placing new texts not *alongside* but *within* a canonical collection. With this title Taussig apparently wishes to claim for his volume the resonance, and presumably something also of the authority, of the time-honored and weighty terms *New Testament* and *Bible*, in a way that a descriptive title such as *Some Religiously Significant Documents from the Mediterranean World, 25–175 CE* might not manage. On any reckoning, this new volume is to some extent *competing* with the traditional New Testament and Bible—in Taussig's own words, this is "an explicitly alternative version of the New Testament" (509). Taussig has raised the stakes in a way that would not be possible with a more conventional title and presentation.[5]

A Profile of *A New New Testament*

In the preface, Taussig offers a brisk overall rationale for the new volume. There are two core notions that run through this preface and through the volume as a whole. On the one hand, there is *a fresh historical understanding* to be had from considering familiar New Testament documents alongside possibly unfamiliar documents that are illustrative of the rich diversity of ancient Christian (and other) life—so far this is similar to many existing collections of texts related to the New Testament. On the other hand, Taussig is no less concerned, and arguably even more concerned, for a contemporary experience of *spiritual renewal* that can come from carefully pondering the new material included in *ANNT*. A few sentences will show how these two concerns come together for Taussig:

---

biblical and nonbiblical documents alongside each other, as does Ehrman (see preceding note). He nonetheless preserves the distinction between biblical and nonbiblical in his title, presumably to increase the appeal of the collection.

5. There is some precedent in Elisabeth Schüssler Fiorenza, ed., *Searching the Scriptures*, vol. 2, *A Feminist Commentary* (London: SCM, 1995). Here familiar New Testament documents receive commentary according to genre alongside other ancient documents of similar genre; and these other documents have significant overlap with the new documents in *ANNT*. Schüssler Fiorenza offers the following as a rationale: "this commentary seeks to transgress canonical boundaries in order both to undo the exclusionary kyriarchal tendencies of the ruling canon and to renew the debate on the limits, function, and extent of the canon" (5). The text of none of these documents is printed, however, so there is no attempt to produce an actual Bible/New Testament. Moreover, there is no attempt to offer an explicitly alternative New Testament. As Schüssler Fiorenza puts it, "this transgressive approach ... does *not* seek to establish a new *feminist* canon. Its aim is not constructive but deconstructive.... Its goal is not a rehabilitation of the canon but an increase in historical-religious knowledge and imagination" (8-9).

110 *When Texts Are Canonized*

There are very few texts more influential on humankind than the
twenty-seven books that we know collectively as the New Testament....
But when placed in *A New New Testament* alongside ten new books from
the early Christ movements, this traditional literature springs to life in
new ways, sparkles with fresh comparisons and contrasts, and is supplemented where it has been found lacking.

It is not time to throw out the traditional New Testament, or to excise
those parts that offend. Rather, the moment has arrived to add to it and
rebind it.... We needed a new New Testament, one that benefited from
the discoveries of the past century and that reconsidered the choices
made (or not made) by bishops and councils of the fourth through sixth
centuries....

This fresh mix of early Christian books comes just in time. A deep spiritual longing has emerged over the past twenty-five years.... Innumerable
people are searching for alternative spiritual paths while still holding on
to traditions of the past.... They seek something grounded in the familiar
that they can nonetheless reinvent to call their own.

As both a professor of the New Testament and a pastor to an active,
engaged congregation, I have come to realize that the spiritual thirsts of
our day need more nourishment.... Here, then, is one new way of expe-
riencing scriptural heritage, a project conceived in response to genuine
yearning. (xvii, xvi, xviii, xix).

The layout of *ANNT* is that of two columns per page, as in most regular Bibles,[6] and all ten new documents have chapter and verse divisions
analogous to those of regular biblical documents. Thus, Taussig draws
on certain time-honored presentational conventions to give *ANNT* something of the "feel" of a familiar New Testament.

The final part of the introduction includes a section on "How to Read"
this new collection. There are four injunctions: "Read personally," "Read
thoughtfully," "Read imaginatively," and "Read meditatively or prayerfully" (xxviii–xxix). Taussig concludes, "The final advice on how to read
this book is to be open to the fresh spirit that brought it together and that
stood behind so much of this powerful literature. With a light and open
heart, approach this reading with joy, anticipation, and what beckons to
you in the process" (xxxi).[7] Thus, the concern for better understanding
of Christian origins is inescapably framed with the concern for contemporary spiritual nurture.

Taussig offers a striking personal testimony as a basis for readers'
trust in the content of *ANNT*:

---

6. To be precise, all the ancient documents are thus presented, while all commentary
and explanatory essays are laid out in the familiar manner of a modern book.

7. How the "fresh spirit" relates, or not, to the Holy Spirit Taussig does not clarify.

Canon and Religious Truth   111

A New New Testament springs from the thirty-plus years of my ministry within the local church and higher education. From listening to the spiritual thirst of people, preaching thousands of sermons, baptizing hundreds of people, teaching hundreds of professionals, marrying hundreds of couples, and teaching thousands of lay people, I have a solid impression of the needs of churched and non-churched individuals and what is at stake for them when they search for what to read for their own spiritual health. I know that there is no single answer for them, and that this spiritual journey has integrity in and of itself. I know that the material in *A New New Testament* is trustworthy." (551)

Although Taussig inaugurated, guided and wrote up the processes that have led to *ANNT*, he presents himself as a spokesperson for a group of nineteen people: the New Orleans Council. This is a "prestigious and experienced council of twenty-first-century spiritual leaders" (491), "spiritual leaders of national rank" (512), each of whom has "substantial experience in leading significant portions of the American public" (513), and who among themselves constitute a group of "bishops, denominational leaders, authors, and prestigious scholars" (489). This council was "modeled on early church councils of the first six centuries CE that made important decisions for larger groups of Christians" (555). To be sure, Taussig recognizes that the analogy with ancient councils is not exact: "The term *council* was perhaps a slight misnomer in that although many of its members were functioning authorities in various denominations and institutions, they were not official delegates from those organizations" (513); in other words, they represented only themselves. Needy times, however, call for unusual measures. Taussig observes, "My invitation to a range of national spiritual leaders to make the decisions about what books were added and my naming that group a 'council'—even when it was not sanctioned by any official church—are bold steps. I consciously took these actions because my pastoral and professorial experience had taught me that timid steps by religious leaders do not do justice to the crisis and potential of this moment in history" (552). Moreover, because they are a group of "wise and concerned leaders" (xix), who when they completed their work "were tingling with excitement" and "were confident of the integrity of their conversations and the literature they had just added to the traditional New Testament" (xxvii), it is clear that the reader is meant to feel able to have full confidence in the integrity both of the council members and of the new documents that are now presented as biblical and which Taussig is happy to depict as "inspired": "Both the heady enthusiasm for any new discoveries—whether the Gospel of Thomas or the Gospel of Judas—and the obvious defensiveness of Christian institutions have proven inadequate for this moment of sustained interest in the explosive diversity of inspired documents from the first two centuries of Christianity" (538).

112   *When Texts Are Canonized*

What is the precise profile and membership of the council? "I wanted the council to include leaders from a wide range of Christian perspectives. It eventually included Presbyterians (two), Roman Catholics (three), Episcopalians (three), United Methodists (four), United Church of Christ members (two), a Lutheran, two rabbis, and one representative of yogic traditions. Eleven members are ordained clergy and two are women religious. Nine are women and ten are men. Six are people of color. Two are bishops. Two are or were the head of their national denomination, and one is the national executive for a primary office of his denomination. Six are scholars and graduate teachers of New Testament" (515).

The council members, in alphabetical order, are Margaret Aymer; Geoffrey Black; Margaret Brennan, IHM; Lisa Bridge; John Dominic Crossan; Nancy Fuchs Kreimer; Bishop Susan Wolfe Hassinger; Bishop Alfred Johnson; Chebon Kernell; Karen L. King; Celene Lillie; Stephen D. Moore; J. Paul Rajashekar; Bruce Reyes-Chow; Mark Singleton; Nancy Sylvester, IHM; Hal Taussig; Barbara Brown Taylor; and Rabbi Arthur Waskow (555–58). Crossan, King, and Moore are probably the best-known New Testament scholars, while Barbara Brown Taylor may perhaps be the best known overall, as a famous preacher and writer of popular books on the spiritual life.

What, then, are the ten new books in *ANNT*?[8] Seven come from the 1945 discovery of material in Egypt at Nag Hammadi. Of these seven, by far the best known is the Gospel of Thomas;[9] the other six are the Prayer of Thanksgiving, the Gospel of Truth, the Thunder: Perfect Mind, the Prayer of the Apostle Paul, the Letter of Peter to Philip, and the Secret Revelation of John. Two other books, also discovered in modern times but of less certain provenance, are the Odes of Solomon and the Gospel of Mary. The tenth is the only one known from ancient times, the Acts of Paul and Thecla.

Taussig and the council are clear that this collection is provisional, not definitive, *A New New Testament* not *The New New Testament* (512). Although the council gave "primary attention to the spiritual value of documents for twenty-first-century North America" (517), different members of the council "had different ideas about what was spiritually important for the twenty-first century" (516), and, moreover, other places and times might require differing nurture. It is doubtful whether there is any limit in principle to adding other documents to other new New Testaments, though Taussig thinks it "important to allow time to see what real contributions this current *New New Testament* chosen by the New Orleans Coun-

---

8. For the Council's deliberations see esp. *ANNT*, 484–99.

9. Parts of this Gospel were already known from previously-discovered Greek fragments at Oxyrhynchus.

Canon and Religious Truth   113

cil can make in our time before moving too quickly to another version of a new New Testament" (546).

How best might one sketch the contours of this new collection? As should already be clear, Taussig positions the book within a Christian frame of reference, over against any rejection of Christianity. The idea of a new New Testament was apparently first proposed by the late Robert Funk, who is one of three to whom the book is dedicated (ix, 509). Funk, however, apparently "wanted the new New Testament to debunk conventional Christian authority, to be a vehicle for the truth of scholarship" (510). Taussig, by contrast, has kept all of the traditional books of the New Testament in the collection and sees his goal as "a larger reimagination of Christian self-understanding in our day" (546) through the putting together of old and new documents in the same Testament so as "to have similar and shared authority" (512).

Taussig is clear that a particularly influential voice on the council has been that of Karen King of Harvard,[10] who herself built on the work of Elaine Pagels: "The project of *A New New Testament* would not have been in any way possible without the courageous and brilliant work of Elaine Pagels" (535). What King and Pagels between them offer is "a new vision of the Early Christ movements" based on their extensive work especially on the Nag Hammadi documents: "There are startling challenges to rethink how the New Testament and Christianity itself came into being. There are beautiful prayers, stories, and proposals to nourish today's thirst for spirituality that are both grounded in tradition and new to almost everyone's experience" (519). This unsurprisingly requires setting aside a certain kind of traditional "master narrative" of "normative Christianity" in which the Nag Hammadi documents would typically be labeled with categories such as "heresy" and "Gnosticism" (xx, 526–36). Instead, there should be an openness to the intrinsic richness of this less-familiar material: "For this project we have avoided any assumptions that the new literature is somehow inferior or obscure" (xx).[11]

What are the criteria whereby the ten new documents were selected? Apart from a concern that the documents should be for the "spiritual welfare" of a large public, Taussig recognized that there was no unanimity in the council about "what was spiritually important for the twenty-first century" and so "refused to set special values or criteria for the group, implicitly acknowledging that such a range of spiritual leaders would have different criteria" (516, 517). The one fixed requirement was chronological, that any document proposed for inclusion should have been writ-

---

10. See *ANNT*, 513, 526–28.

11. This is the wording of Celene Lillie in her preface to the translations of the ancient documents.

114   *When Texts Are Canonized*

ten, or at least should have had a scholarly case made that it was written, between 25 and 175 CE.[12]

Despite the absence of specified criteria, one may nevertheless seek to infer from a careful reading which criteria of selection appear to have been operative. At least three related and recurrent concerns can be discerned. First, the role and voice of women are prioritized: "the New Orleans Council found itself drawn to a number of documents from outside the traditional New Testament that showed women in leadership in the first generations of the Christ movements" (334). The Acts of Paul and Thecla portrays a woman who stands up for herself in relation to government authorities and even to Paul; the Gospel of Mary (to which the New Orleans Council "gave ... its highest number of votes" [217]) focuses on Mary Magdalene as "an insightful and courageous leader" (220).[13]

Second, there is a challenge to gender and sexual stereotypes. For example, in the Thunder: Perfect Mind, the speaking divine voice is predominantly (though not exclusively) feminine, and this "offers readers today the chance to identify with Jesus and Thunder without rehearsing and reinforcing the long-held Western ideas of a defended and prescribed femininity and masculinity" (181). "[T]he eighth Ode of Solomon portrays Jesus as offering his breasts to his followers so that 'they could drink my own consecrated milk, that through it they might live'" (549). The Secret Revelation of John "is filled with imagery of God as the divine Mother, as well as the Father and Son" (465).

Third, there is a recurrent emphasis on the intrinsic value of human experience. For example, in the Gospel of Mary, "Jesus is the Savior because he teaches people how to welcome true humanity into themselves.... The good news is not in escaping one's human identity but in embracing it" (217, 218). In the Thunder: Perfect Mind, there is an identification of God "with suffering and especially dimensions of women's experience," and it helps "people feel a part of the larger universe and a belonging in the great 'I am' of God" (524, 525). In addition, "Thunder's divine and mostly feminine voice makes creative room for all kinds of human experience" (179).

But the main difference consequent upon whatever criteria the council used is eloquently summed up by Taussig thus:

---

12. "I chose 175 CE because this was the latest date any scholars have thought the documents of the existing New Testament had been written; 25 CE is the earliest possible date for similar reasons" (513).

13. A document featuring Mary Magdalene is not meant to give any credence to the fiction of Dan Brown and others: "There is no suggestion in the story of physical or sexual intimacy between Jesus and Mary. Indeed, the focus is on an intellectual and spiritual connection between them. The idea of a sexual relationship between Jesus and Mary is almost certainly a modern fixation, not an ancient notion" (219).

Canon and Religious Truth   115

In _A New New Testament_ there is simply more Jesus. In this book he is all that he is in the traditional New Testament, but he also bursts the boundaries of the traditional collection so that he is understood in many additional ways. These new portraits of Jesus alongside of the traditional ones offer both a wider spectrum of ways to relate to him and more perspectives with which to think about what the traditional images of him mean. So, as of _A New New Testament's_ advent, Jesus's future is simply bigger. (549)

To sum up: Taussig's and the New Orleans Council's compilation is addressing well-recognized issues. Modern biblical scholars have almost always sought to sharpen and deepen their understanding of biblical content by, among other things, setting it alongside other material from its world of origin; and the in-principle value of such an exercise is hardly controversial. Many contemporary believers undoubtedly can find the sheer familiarity of the biblical material to have a subtly dulling effect and can often be spiritually freshened and nourished by encountering less familiar, yet still comparable, material. Many people today clearly prefer to think of themselves as "spiritual," that is, open to a nonreductive view of the world where perhaps transcendent wholeness may yet be found, rather than "religious," that is, constrained by historic and institutional forms of belief and practice that may appear out of touch with the realities of today—even though this being spiritual is usually not uninformed by traditional religious content. So, some readers of this book might perhaps ask: What's not to like?

Toward Articulating a Critique of _A New New Testament_

The articulation of an appropriate critical appraisal of _ANNT_ seems to me to be unusually difficult.[14] There are perhaps two prime reasons for this.

The Challenge of a Dispassionate Response

First, and briefly, there is the difficulty posed by the fact that the book has an obvious edge to it, indeed a polemical agenda. A reader who does not share that agenda, especially one who feels targeted by it, may struggle to be suitably disciplined and dispassionate in evaluative response—as a little browsing of some of the blog responses to the book quickly indicates.

---

14. I will not discuss the translations of the documents in _ANNT_; all citations below from documents in _ANNT_ use the _ANNT_ translation.

116   *When Texts Are Canonized*

Insofar as I seek to be a loyal member of a particular historic (Anglican) church, where although I have my difficulties and discontents these do not take the form displayed by the New Orleans Council, how best can I as a reader of *ANNT* respond? I must confess that, despite my best efforts to read *ANNT* with an openness to being both historically informed and spiritually challenged, the excitement of the council members or of the church groups where Taussig tried out the material was simply not replicated in me. The new material certainly has its moments—for me especially in some of the prayer material of Odes of Solomon—and I enjoyed being reminded of the famous not-very-flattering description of Paul in the Acts of Paul and Thecla.[15] All too often, however, I found the new material somewhat puzzling, not to say disappointing; and sometimes it was downright off-putting. Maybe in part, of course, this is a problem of unfamiliarity that would be eased by prolonged encounter with the material. One learns to live with puzzles and difficulties in canonical texts and to become less bothered by them. But there is also no doubt a deeper, less articulate resistance within me to going along with *ANNT*, a resistance related to my Christian identity and my existing theological-cum-spiritual understanding. I do not think that this disqualifies me from attempting a critical appraisal or reduces to "You would say that, wouldn't you." But it is important that the reader of this essay have some sense of where the appraisal is coming from, especially since some dimensions of my response will clearly be articulated in my own voice in an attempt to express something of what I understand historic Christian faith to entail.

What Is the Genre of *ANNT*?

Second, and more fully, there is a difficulty posed by the identification of the genre and purpose of the book. Is it a contribution to scholarship? Is it a proposal for church reform? Is it a popular work? There are obvious elements of all three of these dimensions in the book, as also in the profile of the membership of the New Orleans Council. But what is the book overall? Is it is a sui generis attempt to be all three, and, if so, is it coherent?

Is *ANNT* a contribution to scholarship? There is an obvious scholarly framing of the book. Nonetheless, it is striking that there is no mention of what might be considered an obvious scholarly sine qua non, that is, a companion volume that provides a critical edition of the text of the ten new documents in their original languages, with an account of the decisions made about which textual readings to adopt and how best to

---

15. "A man small in stature, with a bald head and crooked legs, healthy, with knitted eyebrows, a slightly long nose, and full of kindness" (Acts of Paul and Thecla 3:2) (337).

Canon and Religious Truth   117

construe, divide, and arrange words where the manuscripts and texts are difficult.

The presentation of the dating of the documents in *ANNT* is also puzzling. As already noted, a fundamental criterion for inclusion is that these documents had to be datable by scholars between 25 and 175 CE. A full table is offered of the "range of possible dates for the composition of each book in *A New New Testament*" (496-97; cf. 503)—where the puzzling term is *possible*. On the one hand, the possibly earliest document of all is the Thunder: Perfect Mind, which, presumably because it does not mention Jesus, might have been composed as early as 25; and the Gospel of Thomas has an early possible initial date (ca. 60), earlier than any other Gospel (Mark, ca. 70; Matthew, Luke,[16] and John, ca. 90). On the other hand, the earliest possible date for the Acts of Apostles is said to be 90, while certain letters (Jude, 2 Peter, 1 and 2 Timothy and Titus) are placed unequivocally at varying points in the second century.[17] Yet some forty years ago John A. T. Robinson wrote *Redating the New Testament,* in which he argued that every book in the familiar New Testament canon was written prior to 70.[18] Robinson was a serious and nonpartisan scholar. If it be observed that Robinson was also something of a maverick who liked to be controversial, and that his datings have not generally persuaded other scholars, it can hardly be said that his datings are not *possible*. Similar things about being controversial and not generally persuading other scholars could also be said about Dominic Crossan with his confident "very, very early" dating of much of the Gospel of Thomas[19]—even if his work shows such dating to be *possible*. The truth is that we know less than we would like about the dating of all these documents, as Taussig himself in principle recognizes.[20]

---

16. There is some unclarity in the relation between the chart on pp. 496–97 and the table on p. 503, where, for example, the Gospel of Luke is assigned not to ca. 90 but to 100–125 CE.

17. An oddity is that Taussig's introduction to the two Letters to Timothy gives as "Recommended Reading" Luke Timothy Johnson, *The First and Second Letters to Timothy: A New Translation with Introduction and Commentary,* AB 35A (New York: Doubleday, 2001). The oddity is that Johnson considers the two letters to be authentically Pauline, and so written in either the 50s or 60s, an option for which Taussig does not even allow in his table of possible dates. This is suggestive of some carelessness of presentation on Taussig's part.

18. John A. T. Robinson, *Redating the New Testament* (London: SCM, 1976).

19. John Dominic Crossan, *The Historical Jesus: The Life of a Mediterranean Jewish Peasant* (Edinburgh: T&T Clark, 1991), 428. Crossan finds an early layer of the Gospel of Thomas that was "composed by the fifties CE," while a second layer was composed "possibly as early as the sixties or seventies" (*Historical Jesus,* 427).

20. Taussig twice sounds a caveat: "Estimating when an ancient document was written is a difficult and risky task.... There is little direct evidence for any proposed date, and the proposals—even those in this book—are open to challenge" (498). "Although dating when these documents were written is a very difficult, controversial, and inexact process ..." (513). It is surprising, then, that the range of dates given in the table and chart appears not to heed this caveat.

118   *When Texts Are Canonized*

But the scholarly reality of what can be considered *possible* dates for the documents is not well represented in *ANNT*.

There is also some unclarity about motive and goal in scholarly terms. It is striking that, of the book's three dedicatees, the first is Robert Funk, who founded the well-known and controversial Jesus Seminar, which made a considerable stir in the 1980s and 1990s; the foreword is contributed by John Dominic Crossan, who was one of the better-known members of the Jesus Seminar, and Taussig himself was also a member of that Seminar. At first sight the approach and concerns of the Jesus Seminar and of *ANNT* are markedly different. The Seminar focused on "historical Jesus" issues and voted on how much that is ascribed to Jesus in the canonical Gospels might be considered "historically authentic." The result was a distinctly slimmed-down Jesus. *ANNT*, by contrast, shows no interest whatever in "historical authenticity"—by which criterion, of course, the newly selected documents would consistently fare badly—but focuses rather on the spiritual richness and vitality of the newly included documents in the vision of life and worldview that they portray. The result, insofar as the documents focus on Jesus, is an expanded portrait ("simply more Jesus"). Arguably the one outcome that is common to both the Jesus Seminar and *ANNT* is a portrayal of Jesus that is other than that of the familiar New Testament. But since neither Taussig nor Crossan offers any account of why their scholarly judgments seem to be exercised by such vastly different criteria in the Jesus Seminar and in *ANNT*, it is hard to know to which, if any, scholarly debate they are contributing.

Is *ANNT* a proposal for church reform? To be sure, Taussig is emphatic that he is writing for a spiritually interested public who are dismayed by the "desperate clinging to past structures and tradition," which "has not helped churches thrive," and who are open to a "large reimagination of Christian self-understanding in our day" (546). Taussig reckons that "this reframing of what scriptures Christians might claim can act as a wedge into the tight and unhealthy structures of twenty-first-century church in order to prompt additional rethinking and action" (546).

Moreover, Taussig raises the issue of using *ANNT* not just in study groups but in formal Christian worship:

> One of the major challenges of this book to churches is the incorporation of the additional documents in worship. For pastors to begin preaching on these texts on Sunday morning seems an obvious possibility. Reading these texts in worship as additional readings or psalms are regularly read can easily be done. The many Odes of Solomon are obvious candidates for psalmlike worship, but every kind of text can be read as a second reading. Given the emphasis in this book on reading the new books alongside the traditional books, churches could have one traditional text read and then a new one. (545–46)

Canon and Religious Truth   119

Taussig seems to envisage actual reform of liturgical practice here and perhaps implies that such reform need not be too difficult.

And yet it is unclear what kind of reform is envisaged. There is no discussion of what might be involved in a serious proposal to existing churches to reconsider the extent of the New Testament canon or to revise liturgical and lectionary practices. Nor, of course, would the prospects for such proposals be likely to be promising. Even when a reformer of the stature of Martin Luther made strongly dismissive comments about the value of certain biblical books, the canon even within Lutheran churches remained and remains the familiar canon (although Lutherans developed a distinctive hermeneutic for reading it). Moreover, Taussig does not address the question of why ecclesial authorities today should be expected to heed a contemporary gathering of nineteen spiritually minded people of scholarly inclination, most but not all of whom are Christians, and who represent only themselves, when they propose that newly discovered documents should be received on the same level as the familiar New Testament documents and be read with similar expectations in terms of encountering truth about God and humanity in relation to Jesus. It no doubt makes for a simpler life not to engage with such an issue. But that then surely leaves *ANNT* looking rather like an idiosyncratic sectarian exercise.

Is *ANNT* a popular work? It has already been made clear that Taussig envisions *ANNT* as directed to a spiritually hungry (and ecclesially frustrated) public, who may not be scholars but who are open to learning more about Christian origins and to receiving fresh spiritual sustenance in the process. The popular nature of the work is on one level self-evident. Yet there are at least two difficulties here.

First, although there are general introductions to each document in *ANNT*, there is no guide for readers (other than the overall directions at the outset to read personally, prayerfully, and so on), no notes to help the reading of puzzling or difficult passages, no historical or theological commentary to assist possible appropriation (beyond what is given in the introductions). I will give two examples below of texts where lack of assistance must surely leave a general reader feeling baffled by what they read. This lack of assistance, at a time when mainstream churches are increasingly providing study Bibles with extensive assistance to readers in both verbal and pictorial form, must surely raise the question whether a real popular readership is envisaged and sought.

Second, it might be said that *ANNT* appears at times to be more populist than popular, that is it "dumbs down" and appeals to some extent to certain less healthy understandings and attitudes. For example, a foreword by John Dominic Crossan implicitly links "the traditional New Testament" with "indoctrination" rather than "education [which] is about knowing options" (xi). Taussig commends *ANNT* as offering "the chance

120   *When Texts Are Canonized*

to form new opinions about the earliest traditions of the Christ movements without the demands of later Christian doctrine or church organizations working to overwhelm with dogma or formal interpretations" (xviii), just as the work of Karen King enables one freshly to consider early Christianity "without canonical or creedal blinders" (526). Since any reader is presumably to suppose that indoctrination, being overwhelmed with dogma, and wearing blinders are not good things, the clear implication is that the churches that maintain the traditional canon are intrinsically hidebound and oppressive and do not really merit being taken seriously.

Elsewhere we read of "the conventional church presentation of Jesus as a superman" (62); we learn that "TV evangelists and popes alike portray humans as so thoroughly deserving of God's condemnation that only the bloody sacrifice of Jesus can make things right" (218); and the "joyous and ecstatic" Gospel of Truth "provides a stunning contrast to the kinds of twenty-first-century Christianity that feature condemnation and dark prophecies" (228). Where, one might wonder, are recognized biblical interpreters and theologians like, say, Karl Barth or Rudolph Bultmann or Raymond Brown or Rowan Williams? Where are popular spiritual writers like Thomas Merton, C. S. Lewis, Henri Nouwen, Jean Vanier, Richard Foster, Eugene Peterson? What would any or all of these have to say about "Jesus as a superman" or "condemnation and dark prophecies"?

No doubt certain facets of contemporary North American Christianity provoke dismay and distress among the members of the New Orleans Council (and elsewhere too!). Nonetheless, a presentation whose rhetoric depends at least in part on caricature and stereotyping of the mainstream churches raises questions about its real nature and purpose; and, among other things, such rhetoric could not unreasonably be considered populist.

A Bible without Israel's Scriptures/ the Old Testament?

A different kind of question to put to *ANNT* is: What has happened to Israel's Scriptures/the Hebrew Bible/the Old Testament? Although the book's main title keeps the terminology of *New Testament* and its subtitle includes the wording *A Bible*, I can find no discussion whatever, in the course of its 603 pages, of the greater part of the Christian Bible, the scriptures of Israel, whose common Christian designation is the Old Testament; nor can I find recognition that these documents are in part constitutive of what "Bible" means for Christians. There are occasional passing references to the Hebrew Bible/Scriptures;[21] but engagement with the signifi-

---

21. For example, "both books [Luke, Acts] refer to Hebrew Bible passages frequently" (86); "The closeness [of The Odes of Solomon] to the psalms of the Hebrew scriptures

Canon and Religious Truth 121

cance of this material as the canonical Christian Old Testament is lacking. To be sure, many Christians are ignorant of, and nervous about, the Old Testament, and it is a constant struggle genuinely to enable the Old Testament to be heard in the churches or in wider culture. But does this mean that the Old Testament should simply be ignored?

This silence about the Old Testament/Hebrew Bible becomes odd in various ways in the book, of which I will mention four. First, Taussig constantly emphasizes the possibilities for improved understanding when one reads the familiar New Testament documents alongside other documents ("the combination of documents sparks a wide range of fresh perspectives" [520]). On one level, this is unarguable. Nonetheless, it is unclear how better understanding of the early Jesus movements is facilitated by inattention to those documents that were scriptural for them before their own documents attained scriptural status. What has happened to the time-honored recognition that one constantly needs the Old Testament in order to understand the New Testament?

In one place (I think it is the only place) this point is recognized:

> In the Hebrew scriptures, God is revealed to Moses in the burning bush as "I am," "I am who I am," or "I am the one who is" (depending on how one translates the Hebrew in Exodus 3). Here God as the great "I am" can be understood as the one in whose being all other being exists or the one who is being itself. Some very early Christian traditions seem to have borrowed this vocabulary about the divine one who reveals "himself" and applied it to Jesus. The Gospel of John has Jesus speaking as a great "I am." (523)

Taussig then aligns well-known Johannine uses of "I am" with uses of "I am" in the Gospel of Thomas #77 ("I am the light which is above them all; I am the all ...") and especially in the Thunder: Perfect Mind, where "the 'I am' voice persists throughout almost the entire poem" (524). Whatever the merits of such an alignment, this raises the issue of the importance of the Old Testament/Hebrew Bible for understanding John, and other documents, in the first place. One would hope for at least some discussion or argument as to why the new Bible need not be considered diminished or incomplete without the Old Testament.[22]

Second, as already noted, one of the important concerns for Taussig and the council in *ANNT* is gender. Taussig summarizes:

---

suggests a 'Christ' movement with very strong ties to the traditions of Israel" (169); or Taussig commends Lee McDonald's *The Biblical Canon: Its Origin, Transmission, and Authority* (Peabody, MA: Hendrickson, 2007) as an "excellent source" that "covers the origins of both the Hebrew scriptures and the New Testament" (578).

22. There is, of course, ample precedent for the publishing practice of producing separate Old and New Testaments. But Taussig neither implicitly presupposes nor overtly recognizes the Old Testament as integral to the meaning of "Bible" for Christians.

122   *When Texts Are Canonized*

Gender identity from a Christian perspective has a broader future in *A New New Testament*. This book shows that the early Christ movements' vocabulary for thinking about who women and men are was far broader and deeper than that which the traditional New Testament reflects. To be sure, the traditional New Testament's breaking of gender boundaries still shines in Paul's proclamation that there is no longer "male and female," but that all are one in Christ. But the complexities and richness of new gender identity are multiplied in *A New New Testament*.

The powerful identity, self-understanding, and eloquence of Thecla in the Acts of Paul and Thecla and Mary Magdalene in the Gospel of Mary far outstrip the qualities of any woman in the traditional New Testament. These two books with an insulted yet powerful woman as the primary character expand the ways of thinking about who women are both in early Christianity and in the twenty-first century. (549–50)

Comparably, Crossan in his foreword commends even Thecla's adoption of celibate asceticism as a life-giving option on the grounds that this "proclaimed the right for women to choose their lives despite patriarchal ascendancy" (xii, xiv).

Yet Israel's scriptures contain two, or three, books named after women: Ruth and Esther, and maybe Judith (depending on which canon one is using). If, perhaps, the overall lifestyle of Ruth and Esther appears more at ease with traditional norms and so less promising for "expanded" options than some today might prefer,[23] there remains a host of other women in the pages of the Old Testament whose daring and unpredictability have unsurprisingly offered considerable resources for contemporary feminist reflection and appropriation. It is worth recalling that Judith goes single-handedly (apart from an accompanying maid) to face Holofernes, the commander of a large Assyrian army. There she uses her sexual attractiveness together with resolute lying to lull Holofernes and his officers, unflinchingly wields Holofernes's own sword to decapitate his drunken body, coolly carries out Holofernes's severed head in a bag, celebrates that the Lord has astonishingly given victory "by the hand of woman," and then refuses numerous offers of marriage for the rest of her life (Jdt 9:10, 13; 10:4; 13:6-8, 15; 14:14; 16:6; 16:22). This is surely a woman who is in confident control of her own sexuality and who consistently resists patriarchal power and expectations.[24]

---

23. Ruth, however, is open to markedly different readings. Ruth's famous commitment to Naomi has been taken as a normative expression for lesbian love today, while her nighttime encounter with Boaz at the threshing floor has been taken as affirming the validity of at least some extramarital sex.

24. Although Judith is not recognized as scripture by Protestant churches, the Thirty-Nine Articles of Religion in the Church of England's *Book of Common Prayer* commend "apocryphal" books to be used "for example of life and instruction of manners" (Article VI). In the case of Judith this makes for interesting hermeneutical options!

Canon and Religious Truth   123

Gender issues are also raised in relation to Odes of Solomon 33 and 36, in whose text the perfect Virgin speaks:

"Sons and daughters of humanity
Return yourselves and come.
Abandon the ways of the Corrupter,
And come near to me.
He led you into wrong, but I will bring you out from ruin,
And make you wise in the ways of Truth.
Do not be corrupted, nor perish.
Hear me and be saved ..." (33:6–10a)

On this Taussig comments (in his introductory remarks):

It is surprising to twenty-first-century readers to see these divine feminine characters integrated so seamlessly into the vocabulary of more familiar characters such as Son of God, the Most High, and the Spirit. The ancient world—both in general and with the early Christ movements—was much more comfortable with and interested in transgender identities than our twenty-first-century Western world. This ancient and early Christ movement blurring of what many modern sensitivities think of as firm sexual boundaries can be a major spiritual resource for twenty-first-century readers. Here the Son of God and the divine feminine Spirit of God are one, beckoning to the modern world with intimacy and an identity that is itself inherently cross-gendered. The fragile defensiveness of sexed identities in the twentieth and twenty-first centuries is offered a chance to relax and know a multisexual intimacy in God. (425)

Despite the confidence of Taussig's claims (which may be less straightforward than he makes them sound), there is one obvious lacuna in what he says. The voice of the Virgin in Ode 33 sounds strikingly similar to the voice of Wisdom in Prov 1–9, especially chapters 8–9. Here the female voice of Wisdom is very closely related to YHWH: she accompanied YHWH in the work of creation, and to find her is to find life (Prov 8:22–36). Moreover, there is substantial literature that discusses this relationship and role both in relation to its world of origin and in relation to Christian interpretation and appropriation. If one is looking for resources for discussing gender within canonical Scripture, why not look here?

My concern is simply that gender and gender identity are another area where one would not unreasonably expect the Old Testament as an existing part of Christian Scripture at least to be mentioned. Taussig celebrates the potential enrichment offered by *ANNT* in part through resolute ignoring of the potential already contained within the existing Christian canon of the Old Testament.

Third, it is striking that in the ten new documents overall there is far less either of explicit citation of, or of implicit working with, the content

124   *When Texts Are Canonized*

of Israel's scriptures than is characteristic of the familiar documents of the New Testament. To be sure, things vary from document to document, and the Odes of Solomon probably have the highest level of resonance with the Old Testament through affinities to the Psalter. But the new documents overall seem to work within a frame of reference other than that of Israel's scriptures; insofar as they allude to known documents, these are regularly the familiar documents of the New Testament. The possible significance of this distinctive frame of reference surely deserves some mention and analysis.

Fourth, in this persistent silence about the greater part of the Christian Bible, Taussig and the council would not, I presume, wish to be seen as in any way hostile to Judaism or Jewish spirituality. At any rate, there are passing comments in the course of the book that presuppose a positive stance toward Judaism. So, for example, the Gospel of Matthew receives editorial commendation for "its strong commitment to Judaism," since "in view of the many ways Christians have put down and done harm to Jewish people in the past 1,900 years, it is a treasure to have the New Testament include such an explicit endorsement and spiritually rich exploration of Judaism" (25). Despite such positive comments about Judaism, the decision by Taussig and the council to exclude Israel's scriptures from their *Bible for the 21st Century* at least raises the question whether they are promoting forms of spirituality that downplay the Hebrew and Jewish dimensions of Christian spirituality and diminish the common ground between Jews and Christians.

Two Examples of the Content of the New Documents

My appraisal thus far has not yet discussed any of the actual content of the new documents that have been included in *ANNT*. Some aspects of what I have already been trying to articulate may perhaps become clearer if we consider two examples of this content.

First, one of the striking features of the Thunder: Perfect Mind is that, as already noted, it does not refer to Jesus at all. Yet the first-person voice that speaks throughout is found highly suggestive:[25] "This great 'I am' never gives herself/himself a name, but the closeness of this 'I am' to the crucified 'I am' in the Gospel of John and the piece of wood in the Gospel of Thomas is striking,[26] even suggesting a primarily feminine Jesus" (524). But what do we find in the text? Consider, for example, this excerpt:

---

25. Much is also made of the use of citations from Thunder in contemporary literature, film, and music (*ANNT*, 179, 544).

26. The reference is to Gospel of Thomas 30:2//77:2: "Lift the stone, you will find me there. Split the piece of wood, I am there" (*ANNT*, 17, 21).

Canon and Religious Truth   125

I am the first and the last
I am she who is honored and she who is mocked
I am the whore and the holy woman
I am the wife and the virgin
I am he [*sic*] the mother and the daughter
I am the limbs of my mother....
I am the midwife and she who hasn't given birth
I am the comfort of my labor pains
I am the bride and the bridegroom
And it is my husband who gave birth to me
I am my father's mother,
My husband's sister, and he is my child....
You who deny me, confess me
You who confess me, deny me
You who speak the truth about me, lie about me
You who lie about me, speak the truth about me
You who know me, ignore me
You who ignore me, know me
I am both awareness and obliviousness
I am humiliation and pride
I am without shame
I am ashamed
I am security and I am fear
I am war and peace
Pay attention to me
I am she who is disgraced and she who is important.
                    (Thunder 1:5–6, 8–9, 2:4–10 [*ANNT*, 183])

How close are these "I am" sayings in Thunder to the "I am" sayings in John's Gospel? Not only are the "I am" sayings in Thunder far more numerous than anything in John's Gospel, but they also differ in both form and function. Instead of the Johannine predication of a resonant symbol together with the difference this makes for those who respond—"I am the bread of life ... whoever comes to me will never be hungry" (John 6:35); "I am the light of the world.... The person who follows me will not walk in darkness" (John 8:12)—there is a long flow of apparently paradoxical predication claims, with no clear implications for appropriate response. For straightforward form-critical reasons, the claimed "closeness" of Thunder's first-person sayings to the "I am" sayings of the Johannine Jesus looks entirely unpersuasive.

The interpretation of Thunder's paradoxical predication claims is also unclear. When is such language genuinely paradoxical in an attempt to articulate a rich and deep truth, perhaps a claim to be present in all human conditions? And when is such language a kind of rhetorical pirouetting that offers the spectacle of performance more than any substance? On any reckoning, some of the formulations, such as "I am the limbs of my mother

126   *When Texts Are Canonized*

… I am the comfort of my labor pains" or "You who deny me, confess me / You who confess me, deny me" are at least puzzling and may also, for some readers, repel rather than engage. This is one of those many places where the absence of notes or comment to assist readerly comprehension raises real questions about the intended audience, and what spiritually hungry readers who are not scholars of ancient texts might be expected to make of this material.

My second example is Jesus's well-known parable of the lost sheep, which comes not only in two of the familiar documents, but also in two of the new documents, and so becomes an obvious point of comparison:

So Jesus told them this parable: "Who among you who has a hundred sheep, and has lost one of them, does not leave the ninety-nine out in the open country, and go after the lost sheep until he finds it? And, when he has found it, he puts it on his shoulders rejoicing; and, on reaching home, he calls his friends and his neighbors together, and says, 'Come and rejoice with me, for I have found my sheep which was lost.' So, I tell you, there will be more rejoicing in heaven over one outcast who repents, then over ninety-nine good people, who have no need to repent." (Luke 15:3–7)

[Jesus is already speaking:] "What think you? If a person has a hundred sheep, and one of them strays, will the person not leave the ninety-nine on the hills, and go and search for the one that is straying? And, if he succeeds in finding it, I tell you that he rejoices more over that one sheep than over the ninety-nine which did not stray. So, too, it is the will of my Father who is in heaven that not one of these little ones should be lost." (Matt 18:12–14)

The versions of the parable in the familiar Synoptic Gospels vary in detail, in concluding pronouncement, and in implied referent. Perhaps most significantly, in Luke the lost sheep appears to be a "sinner," one of the undesirable and undeserving people the keeping of whose company brought criticism on Jesus's head (Luke 15:1–2), while in Matthew the straying sheep appears to be an errant member of the community of Jesus's disciples (cf. Matt 18:15). Nonetheless, both similarly emphasize the joy of the shepherd when he finds the one that was lost, a joy that is surprising, because joy for the one is greater than for the ninety-nine. The surprising joy in both contexts expresses the wonder of grace, the wonder of a love that resists, indeed overturns, conventional assumptions and expectations.

How does this parable appear in the two new documents? First, it comes in the Gospel of Thomas:

Jesus said: "The realm compares
to a shepherd who had a hundred sheep.
One of them, the largest, went astray. He
left the other ninety-nine, and he sought
after that one until he found it. After such
an effort, he said to the sheep: 'I love you
more than the other ninety-nine.'"

(Gos. Thom. #107)

Apart from the greater brevity of this version of the parable, there are two obvious differences. There is no mention of joy when the lost is found; and a particular explanation is provided for the shepherd's search for the lost sheep: the straying sheep was the largest and (maybe for this reason) the most loved. Whatever the purpose of this emphasis in the context of Thomas, the variation between this version and the familiar Synoptic version is striking: a search and an outcome that defy expectation and surpass calculation are now rational and calculable. The point of the parable is different.

Then there is a version in the Gospel of Truth:

He is the shepherd who left behind
the ninety-nine sheep that had not
strayed, and went and searched for the
one who had gone astray. He rejoiced
when he found it, for ninety-nine is a number
in the left hand which holds it. When the
one is found, the whole number moves
to the right hand. In this way, what is in
need of one—that is, the whole right
hand—draws that which it needs and
takes it from the left hand and moves it to
the right so the number becomes one
hundred. This is the sign of the sound of
the numbers. This is the Father.

(Gos. Truth 17:1–4)

There are at least two difficulties for any reader of this. First, what is the symbolism of the left and right hands with their respective numbers? Here one needs some knowledge of ancient conventions. For the text presupposes a well-known ancient method of counting, in which "the numbers up to 99 were reproduced by different positions of the fingers of the left hand, while 100 and the following hundreds were expressed with the right hand."[27] The point of the parable, then, lies in traditional negative

_____

27. W. C. van Unnik, "The 'Gospel of Truth' and the New Testament," in *The Jung*

128   *When Texts Are Canonized*

associations of the left hand (*sinister*) and in the numbers: "In 99 one unit is wanting ... whereby it is unfavorable, but if that 'one' = 'knowledge of God,' the One ... is added, then it passes over to the good side."[28] With that key, the main sense of the text is unlocked.

Second, however, what do its concluding words, "This is the sign of the sound of the numbers. This is the Father," mean? Part of the difficulty relates to how best to divide and construe the words of the text. For example, the reference to the Father might not belong to what precedes but might rather introduce the material that follows.[29] Nonetheless, the text that is presented in *ANNT* is presumably meant to make some sense. But what is that sense? As with knowing about the convention about counting, the lack of any notes or commentary, either to explain the nature of the scholarly judgments being incorporated in this division and reading of the text, or to clarify for the ordinary reader what kind of sense they might perhaps take from their reading, surely leaves the nature of *ANNT*'s readership unclear. Taussig's upbeat introduction to the Gospel of Truth stresses the overall value of the material: for example, "As it overflows with joy, fulfilment, and sensuousness, this gospel by turns sounds like a poem, a letter, or an ecstatic sermon" (227). And he notes that this Gospel includes "a strong awareness of Jesus as a teacher of parables" (228). But the reader receives no guidance on how best to handle problematic material.

The issue of theological vision—the vision of God—is also sharply posed by these two different versions of the well-known parable. Whatever the range of content in the ten new documents as a whole, the fact that here we have differing versions of the one parable, two in the familiar New Testament and two in the new documents of *ANNT*, does surely make this a particularly interesting focus for comparative theological evaluation. Both Thomas and Truth have a different point to their parable than the point in Matthew and Luke. At the heart of this difference (arguably a deliberate change) appears to be a desire to *rationalize* the attitude of the shepherd toward the lost sheep—the sheep is either more valuable or it brings completion to a deficit. The parable is no longer about a grace toward the lost that is amazing.

To return to the question of the genre and purpose of *ANNT*. As already noted, the work of the New Orleans Council is presented with a strong rhetoric: readers should be ready to set aside conventional understandings of early Christianity, not be constrained by ancient dogma, not

---

Codex: A Newly Recovered Gnostic Papyrus, ed. F. L. Cross (London: Mowbray, 1955), 79–129, here 97.

28. Ibid., 113.

29. See, e.g., Jacqueline A. Williams, *Biblical Interpretation in the Gnostic Gospel of Truth from Nag Hammadi,* SBLDS 79 (Atlanta: Scholars Press, 1988), 123.

assume that the new material is somehow inferior or obscure, be open-minded and ready to receive fresh spiritual challenge and illumination. One particular thought experiment is likely to be, indeed is clearly meant to be, difficult for the reader of *ANNT* to undertake. That is, what if one were to entertain the possibility that the ancient churches showed wise discernment in recognizing that some material on the edges of their mainstream was rightly relegated to the edges precisely because it diminished some of the wonder and mystery at the heart of the vision of God in Jesus Christ that the familiar New Testament is seeking to convey? And if such a thought were entertained, might it conceivably be followed with a question along the lines of: Are we being invited, in the name of open-mindedness, to sell a birthright of amazing grace for a mess of rationalized pottage?

To entertain that possibility is not necessarily to embrace it. But it means that a key issue for any appraisal of a *new* New Testament must surely be to try to understand the nature and logic of the *existing* New Testament. What might this look like?

Toward Seeing the Vision of the New Testament

Taussig appears uninterested in offering any account of the possible rationale of the traditional New Testament. To be sure, he emphasizes the fluidity of constituent books in the New Testament in antiquity,[30] and perhaps the implication is that this is all that needs to be said — the formation of the New Testament is a matter of flux and disagreement resolved by the winners in ecclesial politics. Yet the issue of the inner logic, the theological and spiritual vision, of the familiar New Testament is so important an issue that I shall attempt to offer some such rationale myself. In so doing I will not be trying to offer an account of the ancient or enduring applicability of the classic criteria of apostolicity, catholicity, and orthodoxy, at least not in those terms. For those classic criteria have been much critiqued by modern historically oriented biblical scholarship, and I have no wish to contest that critique on its own terms (and Taussig would no doubt align himself with that critique, even though he does not discuss it).[31] Rather, my concern is to offer an intrinsic rationale for the traditional New Testament in dialogue with some of those factors that characterize the new documents in *ANNT*, as articulated by Taussig.

---

30. See esp. *ANNT*, 500–509.

31. For a suggestive recent discussion, with bibliography, that seeks to reformulate the classic criteria downwind of typical modern critique, see Brevard S. Childs, *The Church's Guide for Reading Paul: The Canonical Shaping of the Pauline Corpus* (Grand Rapids: Eerdmans, 2008), 19–24.

130   *When Texts Are Canonized*

One way of putting this is that I want to offer some critical scrutiny of Taussig's assertion that "the picture of who Jesus is in *A New New Testament* is simply bigger, broader, and deeper than the picture of Jesus in the traditional New Testament" (549).

I would like to approach this by considering initially some of the issues raised by the Gospel of Thomas, not least because it is the newly discovered Gospel that has received the most widespread attention in recent years as a contender to be considered alongside the familiar canonical Gospels. How is Jesus portrayed here? In Taussig's words, "Although the Jesus in the Gospel of Thomas has many similarities with the Jesus in Matthew, Mark, and Luke, Thomas's Jesus is also stunningly different.... This Jesus never teaches about his crucifixion or resurrection, in contrast to the way that Jesus in Matthew, Mark, and Luke concentrates on this aspect of his identity" (549). "The picture of Jesus as teacher in Thomas does not include an emphasis on his saving death, his resurrection, or his healing. The meaning of Jesus comes from the wisdom he communicates, not from any special accomplishments, his position on earth or in heaven, or what fate or triumph he experiences" (12). One prime reason for this distinctiveness, of course, is that the Gospel of Thomas, in contrast to the traditional Gospels, though akin to the putative Q, is a sayings collection. Taussig finds positive meaning in this absence of narrative: "this exclusive concentration on Jesus's teachings is meant to convey a different meaning from a gospel of stories. Here the good news is the content of the sayings themselves. The meaning conveyed is that Jesus's words matter more than anything, and that to know Jesus best, one needs to know him as a teacher" (539–40).

No Christian, I imagine, would deny that Jesus's teaching is important and life-giving. The key issue, however, is Taussig's contention that "to know Jesus best, one needs to know him as a teacher". To this, classic Christian faith would reply, quite simply, "no"—a refusal that is as complex in its judgments as it is simple in its formulation. The basis in the four traditional canonical Gospels is nicely captured by the well-known observation that they are all, in one way or other, passion narratives with an extended prologue.[32] In other words, it is the death and resurrection of Jesus that is to be seen as the focus for understanding his life.

It is not just that the traditional Gospels combine sayings and story, for it is a particular kind of story that is presented. Jesus proclaims the

---

32. This famous statement comes from Martin Kähler in 1892 (in a footnote!) when he is commenting on "the way the figure of Jesus is actually reflected in the New Testament": "To state the matter somewhat provocatively, one could call the Gospels passion narratives with extended introductions" (*The So-Called Historical Jesus and the Historic Biblical Christ*, trans. Carl Braaten [Philadelphia: Fortress, 1964], 80 n. 11).

Canon and Religious Truth   131

kingdom of God and calls, teaches, and commissions disciples; he has memorable meetings with numerous ordinary people whom he heals, teaches, challenges, and forgives; alongside this there are also less fruitful encounters with others, not least religious authorities who are generally distanced and suspicious. It is this dual aspect of Jesus's ministry—both giving life and hope to people and also engendering misunderstanding, suspicion, and resistance—that leads into his passion and makes his passion a natural, as it were, culmination of his life and ministry (whatever the precise trigger that leads the authorities to arrest Jesus and put him on trial). Although the passion of Jesus is much less "theologized" or "explained" by the evangelists than one might perhaps have expected, Jesus's prime interpretation of his coming death in the context of his Passover meal with his disciples (in the three Synoptic Gospels) makes clear that what will happen to him, body broken and blood shed, is in some way a self-giving for others. In Paul's classic formulation, "Christ died for us," and this human self-giving is in fact an embodiment and outworking of divine love (Rom 5:8).

It is not just in Thomas that any account of Jesus's ministry and consequent passion is absent. It is also absent, or only low-key, in the other new documents in *ANNT*.[33] For example, in Thunder a divine voice speaks throughout. But this voice (which is not identified with Jesus) is not located in any particular time or place, it receives no narrative framing, and it does not speak of laying down its life for others.

The opening document of *ANNT* is the Prayer of Thanksgiving, which concludes with a brief mention of "eating holy food" (v. 13 [7]). About this Taussig says, "Here neither Jesus's last supper nor the imagery of body and blood are evoked as prayers around the early Christian bread and cup. Instead, in this meal prayer, the sharing of the bread and cup is experienced as a birth from the womb of God." Consequently, "the existence of first- and second-century communion prayers that do not tell the story of the last supper or use 'body' and 'blood' vocabulary could inspire twenty-first-century people to compose additional and different prayers for their sharing of bread and cup" (523). In this alternative language and imagery, birth can be celebrated instead of death.

The Gospel of Truth is perhaps the main exception to my general contention, as Jesus's ministry and passion are both represented. Here a narrator offers a sequential account of Jesus. But it is an account in which all specific places, times, and people are absent: no villages in Galilee, no synagogues, no lake, no Jerusalem, no temple, no festivals, no women or

---

33. This is not as such an issue in the Acts of Paul and Thecla, where one would hardly expect to find an account of the passion, even though what Thecla undergoes has certain ready resonances with the passion of Jesus.

132   *When Texts Are Canonized*

men coming to Jesus with their needs and hopes. Typical of the rather abstract portrayal of Jesus's ministry is this:

> This is the good news of the one whom they seek, revealed to those filled through the mercies of the Father. Through the hidden mystery, Jesus Christ shone to the ones in the darkness of forgetfulness. He enlightened them and showed them a way. The way he taught them is truth. Because of this Transgression was angry with him and pursued him. She was distressed by him and left barren. (4:1–4 [230])

To be sure, the death of Jesus is mentioned and is life-giving:

> He was nailed to a tree and became the fruit of the Father's knowledge. It did not cause destruction when it was eaten, but it caused those who ate it to come into being and find contentment within its discovery....
> He was nailed to a tree and published as the Father's edict on the cross. Oh, what a great teaching! He drew himself down from death, clothing himself in never-ending life. He stripped off the perishable rags and put on imperishable, which no one can take away from him. (4:5–6, 6:9–11 [230, 231])

Taussig commends this portrayal, in which Jesus's death is conceived as the fruit of the Father's knowledge and also as the publication of the book of life, as giving "a poetic twist" to familiar early Christian traditions (228). Fair enough. But one should also note that in this context one would no longer say of Jesus that he was "crucified under Pontius Pilate." There is no longer agony in Gethsemane or darkness at Golgotha, no fearful disciples, no brutal soldiers, no vacillating Roman prefect, no mocking onlookers; neither suffering and abandonment nor compassion for others any longer characterize Jesus's dying. Nor is there an empty tomb, bewildered women, and the risen Jesus appearing to his uncertain disciples.

Why should this matter? In traditional theological terms, it is a matter of the "full humanity" of Jesus—Jesus as a human being "like us" in every way, who was not spared the dark dimensions of the human condition.[34] He is thereby one with whom people can in important ways identify, one to whom people can become conformed, one into whose reality others can enter. The Christian imagination has always centered on a human life, which shows what life can and should truly be; but the context of this life is a graphic portrayal of human fear, greed, hatred, incomprehension, and brutality, realities whose power to get their own way is fully recognized even if they are ultimately overcome.

---

34. The classic limitation to this likeness is that Jesus alone was without sin (Heb 4:15, a point substantively developed by the church fathers); that is, Jesus was unique in the unbroken responsiveness and faithfulness of his relationship with his Father.

Canon and Religious Truth   133

Put differently, for all that Taussig emphasizes the joy and vitality of the new documents and their value as a resource for the spiritually hungry today, his account of the spiritual life engages neither the problems of human corruption and malice nor the problems of self-seeking and self-deception, the deep and recurrent human desires to harness God to human projects and priorities and to present this as goodness and piety. A key question is, What critical norms and practices are there to prevent the spiritual life degenerating into self-deception? In historic Christian life and liturgy (which accompany the reading of scripture) the two prime symbolic practices (the two undisputed sacraments) are baptism and Eucharist, both of which are understood in the light of the death and resurrection of Jesus: baptism symbolizes our own dying and rising to new life in Christ, while communion symbolizes a receiving of, and entering into, Jesus's self-giving for the life of the world. To be sure, it is easy for both of these sacraments to be misused and emptied of their reality; but, as ever, abuse does not remove right use. Christian spirituality, in its classic forms as rooted in the New Testament, is understood to be a constant process of dying to self-seeking and self-deceiving, so that one can receive true life in and through Christ crucified and risen. There is birth, but it comes through death.

Taussig's apparent lack of attunement to this dimension of the traditional New Testament and of the patterns of spirituality rooted in it is interestingly illustrated by his introductory remarks about 2 Corinthians. Taussig's choice of wording suggests that he does not much like the Paul of this letter ("... angry, sulking, or confused"), and its main value is for "understanding Paul as a person" because of "the uncensored and wildly emotional character of Paul's expression." Indeed, "if one wonders why such a letter was ever included in the traditional New Testament, the answer probably lies in its authentic connection to Paul himself, even if he wrote it while he was having a series of bad days" (281, 282).

One would not know from this that the presenting issue in 2 Corinthians is that the integrity of Paul's apostleship is being challenged. He responds by offering critical criteria for the discernment of apostolic authenticity, and these criteria focus entirely on following Jesus in the way of the cross: conformity to Jesus in his death and resurrection is *the* critical criterion for a would-be apostle to be recognized as genuine. Death and resurrection are the dominant images, the controlling metaphor, for Paul's life: "We always bear on our bodies the marks of the death that Jesus died, so that the life of Jesus may be exhibited in our bodies" (2 Cor 4:10).

My concern is in principle simple. Before one embraces the new documents in *ANNT* and new expressions of the spiritual life because of the deficiencies of the traditional New Testament and the spiritualities rooted in it, one needs to know what is at stake.

134   *When Texts Are Canonized*

Conclusion

Few would disagree with Taussig that there are numerous problems in contemporary North American churches (and European churches also), or that many churches struggle to engage meaningfully with contemporary culture and contemporary spiritual searching. The question, however, is what to do about it and whether this particular proposal to change and enlarge the canon of the New Testament is a good way ahead or a blind alley. I hope I have given sufficient reason for approaching *ANNT* with some caution in relation to its enthusiastic claims.

Of course, Taussig might counter by saying that the retention of all the traditional New Testament documents should obviate some of my concerns, on the grounds that nothing that has mattered in historic Christian faith is being lost—there is more ("simply more Jesus"), not less. But the rhetoric of "more" needs scrutiny. On the one hand, the absence of the Old Testament in *A Bible for the 21ˢᵗ Century* is real loss. On the other hand, if there is no longer a focus on Jesus in his life, death, and resurrection, there are hard but necessary questions about whether "more Jesus" may not in reality be, in Paul's words in 2 Cor 11:4, "another Jesus" who functions in a different mode with a different vision of God, humanity, and salvation.

In response to Taussig's enthusiasm for the new documents in *ANNT*, I have tried to indicate something of how the vision of the New Testament is focused on Jesus in his life, death, and resurrection. A human life in all its particularity and memorable qualities is the focus of the Christian imagination and its best way to God. The Christian understanding of Jesus as "fully human" is a way of saying that in this life we can in principle see the truth and potential of all human life, an ultimate norm for understanding life and recognizing what constitutes a good life. Moreover, the Christian understanding of Jesus as "fully divine" is not a way of turning him into some kind of superman. Rather, it is a way of saying that in what Jesus says and does, and in what he undergoes in suffering and dying and being raised from the dead, we see as fully and clearly as is possible the reality and qualities of the living God.

Are gender issues marginalized or skewed by such a focus on Jesus? It can hardly be denied that male perspectives are better represented than female perspectives within the familiar Bible. Moreover, it is unarguable that, for many today, there are problems with the use of masculine language for God and with the privileged roles reserved for males in the historic churches. But those churches that have most fully recognized women's leadership, and ordained women to positions of ministerial authority, have done so primarily because they have recognized that it is character (and gifts and abilities) rather than gender that should be determinative for leadership. Ironically, given Taussig's and the council's concern to promote women, the importance of Christian character may

Canon and Religious Truth   135

be diminished by thinking of Jesus as androgynous, rather than as a particular figure of the first century who lived as a faithful Jew, was crucified under Pontius Pilate, and was raised to an eternal divine life into which he calls people to enter still today.

Overall, the most serious editorial omission in *ANNT* is that Taussig says altogether too little about the larger issues that surround the recognition and privileging of certain documents as biblical, as canonical—questions of religious truth, questions of authority, questions of trust, questions of canon and community, questions of living with documents over time, questions of discernment and interpretation and appropriation. These are issues whose importance is probably matched only by the difficulty of handling them well.

In particular, the issue of the interrelationship between canon and community is perhaps an appropriate note on which to conclude. It is apparent that the dynamic interrelationship between the privileging of certain documents and the identity and vision and practices of groups of people remains a live issue today, as well as having been so in antiquity. Taussig envisages a readership profile of people (apparently mainly North American) who are sympathetic to, and perhaps still affiliated with, recognizable Christian identity, yet whose spiritual vision of Jesus and of life is set free from the apparent constraints of historic Christian belief. Perhaps the greatest contribution that *ANNT* can make and the best challenge it can offer to those who would more straightforwardly locate themselves within recognized Christian churches is to promote a more rigorous and searching engagement, both intellectual and existential, with questions of canon, community, and religious truth in relation to the knowledge of God through Jesus Christ.[35]

---

35. I am grateful for comments on draft versions of this paper from Richard Briggs, Wesley Hill, Francis Watson, my wife Jenny, and my informal postgraduate seminar (Jon Bentall, Paul Jones, Tom Judge, Jerry Lofquist, Zoltan Schwab).

Bibliography

Abraham, William J. *The Divine Inspiration of Holy Scripture*. Oxford: Oxford University Press, 1981.

Alexander, Philip S. "Retelling the Old Testament." Pages 99–121 in *It Is Written: Scripture Citing Scripture; Essays in Honour of Barnabas Lindars, SSF*. Edited by D. A. Carson and H. G. M. Williamson. Cambridge: Cambridge University Press, 1988.

Anthonioz, Stéphanie. *Le prophétisme biblique: De l'idéal à la réalité*. LD 261. Paris: Cerf, 2013.

Ballhorn, Egbert, and Georg Steins, eds. *Der Bibelkanon in der Bibelauslegung: Methodenreflexionen und Beispielexegesen*. Stuttgart: Kohlhammer, 2007.

Baltes, Guido. "The Use of Hebrew and Aramaic in Epigraphic Sources of the New Testament Era." Pages 35–65 in *The Language Environment of First Century Judaea*. Edited by Randall Buth and R. Steven Notley. Jerusalem Studies in the Synoptic Gospels 2. Jewish and Christian Perspectives Series 26. Leiden: Brill, 2013.

Barnett, Paul. "Jewish Sign Prophets—A.D. 40–70." *NTS* 27 (1981): 679–97.

Barr, James. Review of *The Divine Inspiration of Holy Scripture*, by William J. Abraham. *JTS* 38 (1983): 375.

Barrett, C. K., ed. *The New Testament Background: Selected Documents*. London: SPCK, 1956.

Barthélemy, Dominic. "L'état de la Bible juive depuis le début de notre ère jusqu'à la deuxième révolte contre Rome (131-135)." Pages 9–45 in *Le Canon de l'Ancien Testament: Sa formation et son histoire*. Edited by Jean-Daniel Kaestli and Otto Wermelinger. MdB 10. Geneva: Labor et Fides, 1984.

Barton, John. *Oracles of God: Perceptions of Ancient Prophecy in Israel after the Exile*. London: Darton, Longman & Todd, 1986. 2nd ed., London: Darton, Longman & Todd, 2007.

———. *The Spirit and the Letter: Studies in the Biblical Canon*. London: SPCK, 1997. American ed., *Holy Writings, Sacred Text: The Canon in Early Christianity*. Louisville: Westminster John Knox, 1997.

Bauckham, Richard J. *Jude, 2 Peter*. WBC 50. Dallas: Word, 1983.

Baumgarten, Albert I. "Sacred Scriptures Defile the Hands." *JJS* 62 (2016): 46–67.

138   *When Texts Are Canonized*

———. "Seeks after Smooth Things." Pages 857–59 in vol. 2 of *Encyclopedia of the Dead Sea Scrolls*. Edited by Lawrence H. Schiffman and James C. VanderKam. New York: Oxford University Press, 2000.

Baumgarten, Joseph M. "4Q500 and the Ancient Conception of the Lord's Vineyard." *JJS* 40 (1989): 1–6.

Baynes, Leslie. "Enoch and Jubilees in the Canon of the Ethiopian Orthodox Church." Pages 799–818 in vol. 2 of *A Teacher for All Generations: Essays in Honor of James C. VanderKam*. Edited by Eric F. Mason et al. JSJSup 153. Leiden: Brill, 2012.

Becker, Uwe, and Hannes Bezzel, eds. *Rereading the Relecture? The Question of (Post)chronistic Influence in the Latest Redactions of the Books of Samuel*. FAT 2/66. Tübingen: Mohr Siebeck, 2014.

Bedford, Peter R. "Diaspora-Homeland Relations in Ezra-Nehemiah." *VT* 52 (2002): 147–65.

Begg, Christopher T., and Paul Spilsbury. *Judean Antiquities, Books 8-10*. Flavius Josephus, Translation and Commentary 5 Leiden: Brill, 2005.

Bellemore, Jane. "Josephus, Pompey and the Jews." *Historia: Zeitschrift für alte Geschichte* 48 (1999): 94–118.

Ben Zvi, Ehud, and Diana V. Edelman, eds. *What Was Authoritative for Chronicles?* Winona Lake, IN: Eisenbrauns, 2011.

Ben Zvi, Ehud, and Michael H. Floyd, eds. *Writings and Speech in Israelite and Ancient Near Eastern Prophecy*. SymS 10. Atlanta: Society of Biblical Literature, 2000.

Bergsma, John S. "The Relationship between Jubilees and the Early Enochic Books (Astronomical Book and Book of the Watchers)." Pages 36–51 in *Enoch and the Mosaic Torah: The Evidence of Jubilees*. Edited by Gabriele Boccaccini and Giovanni Ibba. Grand Rapids: Eerdmans, 2009.

Berman, Joshua. "The History of Legal Theory and the Study of Biblical Law." *CBQ* 76 (2014): 19–39.

Bernstein, Moshe J. "'Rewritten Bible': A Generic Category Which Has Outlived Its Usefulness?" *Textus* 22 (2005): 169–96.

Bickerman, Elias J. *Four Strange Books of the Bible: Jonah, Daniel, Koheleth, Esther*. New York: Schocken, 1967.

Bledsoe, Amanda M. Davis. "The Relationship of the Different Editions of Daniel: A History of Scholarship." *CurBR* 13 (2015): 175–90.

Blenkinsopp, Joseph. *Ezra-Nehemiah: A Commentary*. OTL. Philadelphia: Westminster, 1988.

Blum, Erhard. "Ein Anfang der Geschichtsschreibung? Anmerkungen zur sog. Thronfolgegeschichte und zum Umgang mit Geschichte im alten Israel." *Trumah* 5 (1996): 9–46.

Boccaccini, Gabriele. "From a Movement of Dissent to a Distinct Form of Judaism: The Heavenly Tablets in Jubilees as the Foundation of a Competing Halakah." Pages 193–210 in *Enoch and the Mosaic Torah:*

The Evidence of Jubilees. Edited by Gabriele Boccaccini and Giovanni Ibba. Grand Rapids: Eerdmans, 2009.

Botterweck, G. J., H. Ringgren, and H.-J. Fabry, eds. *Theologisches Wörterbuch zum Alten Testament.* 10 vols. Stuttgart: Kohlhammer, 1973–2000.

Boyarin, Daniel. *The Jewish Gospels: The Story of the Jewish Christ*. New York: New Press, 2012.

Braaten, Carl, ed. *The So-Called Historical Jesus and the Historic Biblical Christ.* Philadelphia: Fortress, 1964.

Brandt, Peter. *Endgestalten des Kanons: Das Arrangement der Schriften Israels in der jüdischen und christlichen Bibel*. BBB 131. Berlin: Philo, 2001.

Braverman, Jay. *Jerome's Commentary on Daniel: A Study of Comparative Jewish and Christian Interpretations of the Hebrew Bible*. CBQMS 7. Washington, DC: Catholic Biblical Association of America, 1978.

Brooke, George J. "4Q158: Reworked Pentateucha or Reworked Pentateuch A?" *DSD* 8 (2001): 219–41.

———. "4Q500 1 and the Use of Scripture in the Parable of the Vineyard." Pages 235–60 in George J. Brooke, *The Dead Sea Scrolls and the New Testament*. Minneapolis: Fortress, 2005.

———. *The Dead Sea Scrolls and the New Testament*. Minneapolis: Fortress, 2005.

———. *Exegesis at Qumran: 4QFlorilegium in Its Jewish Context*. JSOTSup 29. Sheffield: JSOT Press, 1985.

———. "Rewritten Bible." Pages 777–81 in vol. 2 of *Encyclopedia of the Dead Sea Scrolls*. Edited by Lawrence H. Schiffman and James C. VanderKam. Oxford: Oxford University Press, 2000.

———. "The Rewritten Law, Prophets and Psalms: Issues for Understanding the Text of the Bible." Pages 31–40 in *The Bible as Book: The Hebrew Bible and the Judaean Desert Discoveries*. Edited by Edward D. Herbert and Emanuel Tov. London: British Library, 2002.

Brownlee, William H. *The Meaning of the Qumrân Scrolls for the Bible: With Special Attention to the Book of Isaiah*. James W. Richard Lectures in Christian Religion 1958. New York: Oxford University Press, 1964.

Buitenwerf, Rieuwerd. *Book III of the Sibylline Oracles and Its Social Setting: With an Introduction, Translation, and Commentary*. SVTP 17. Leiden: Brill, 2003.

Campbell, Jonathan G. "'Rewritten Bible' and 'Parabiblical Texts': A Terminological and Ideological Critique." Pages 43–68 in *New Directions in Qumran Studies: Proceedings of the Bristol Colloquium on the Dead Sea Scrolls, 8–10 September 2003*. Edited by Jonathan G. Campbell, William John Lyons, and Lloyd Keith Pietersen. LSTS 52. London: T&T Clark, 2005.

Campenhausen, Hans von. *Die Entstehung der christlichen Bibel*. Rev. ed. BHT 39. Tübingen: Mohr Siebeck, 2003.

140   *When Texts Are Canonized*

Carmichael, Calum M. "A New View of the Origin of the Deuteronomic Credo." *VT* 19 (1969): 273–89.

Carr, David M. "Canonization in the Context of Community: An Outline of the Formation of the Tanak and the Christian Bible." Pages 22–64 in *A Gift of God in Due Season: Essays on Scripture and Community in Honor of James A. Sanders.* JSOTSup 225. Sheffield: Sheffield Academic, 1996.

———. *The Formation of the Hebrew Bible: A New Reconstruction.* Oxford: Oxford University Press, 2011.

———. *Writing on the Tablet of the Heart: Origins of Scripture and Literature.* Oxford: Oxford University Press, 2009.

Carson, D. A., and John D. Woodbridge, eds. *Hermeneutics, Authority, and Canon.* Leicester: Inter-Varsity Press, 1981.

Casey, P. M. "Porphyry and the Origin of the Book of Daniel." *JTS* 27 (1976): 15–33.

Cathcart, Kevin J., and Robert P. Gordon, eds. *The Targum of the Minor Prophets.* ArBib 14. Wilmington, DE: Glazier, 1989.

Childs, Brevard S. "Analysis of the Canonical Formula: 'It Shall Be Recorded for a Future Generation.'" Pages 357–64 in *Die Hebräische Bibel und ihre zweifache Nachgeschichte: Festschrift für Rolf Rendtorff zum 65. Geburtstag.* Edited by Erhard Blum, Christian Macholz, and Ekkehard Stegemann. Neukirchen-Vluyn: Neukirchener Verlag, 1990.

———. *The Church's Guide for Reading Paul: The Canonical Shaping of the Pauline Corpus.* Grand Rapids: Eerdmans, 2008.

———. *Introduction to the Old Testament as Scripture.* Philadelphia: Fortress, 1979.

———. "Psalm Titles and Midrashic Exegesis." *JSS* 16 (1971): 137–50.

Chilton, Bruce D. *A Galilean Rabbi and His Bible: Jesus' Use of the Interpreted Scriptures of His Time.* GNS 8. Wilmington, DE: Glazier, 1984.

———. *The Glory of Israel: The Theology and Provenience of the Isaiah Targum.* JSOTSup 23. Sheffield: JSOT Press, 1983.

———. *The Isaiah Targum.* ArBib 11. Wilmington, DE: Glazier, 1987.

Cohen, Shaye J. D. *From the Maccabees to the Mishnah.* 3rd ed. Louisville: Westminster John Knox, 2014.

———. *Josephus in Galilee and Rome: His Vita and Development as a Historian.* Leiden: Brill, 2002.

Collins, Adela Yarbro. *Mark: A Commentary.* Hermeneia. Minneapolis: Fortress, 2007.

Collins, John J. *Between Athens and Jerusalem: Jewish Identity in the Hellenistic Diaspora.* 2nd ed. Grand Rapids: Eerdmans, 2000.

———. "The Book of Daniel and the Dead Sea Scrolls." Pages 203–17 in *The Hebrew Bible in Light of the Dead Sea Scrolls.* Edited by Dávid Nóra et al. FRLANT 239. Göttingen: Vandenhoeck & Ruprecht, 2013.

———. "Daniel." Pages 77–87 in *The Oxford Handbook of the Reception History of the Bible*. Edited by Michael Lieb, Emma Mason, and Jonathan Roberts. Oxford: Oxford University Press, 2013.

———. *Daniel: A Commentary on the Book of Daniel*. Hermeneia 27. Philadelphia: Fortress, 1993.

———. "Daniel and His Social World." Pages 249–60 in *Interpreting the Prophets*. Edited by James Luther Mays and Paul J. Achtemeier. Philadelphia: Fortress, 1987.

———. "Pseudo-Daniel Revisited." *RevQ* 17 (1996): 111–35.

Crawford, Sidnie White. *Rewriting Scripture in Second Temple Times*. SDSSRL. Grand Rapids: Eerdmans, 2008.

———. *The Temple Scroll and Related Texts*. Companion to the Qumran Scrolls 2. Sheffield: Sheffield Academic, 2000.

Crossan, John Dominic. *The Historical Jesus: The Life of a Mediterranean Jewish Peasant*. Edinburgh: T&T Clark, 1991.

Culley, Rober C. "Orality and Writtenness in the Prophetic Texts." Pages 45–64 in *Writings and Speech in Israelite and Ancient Near Eastern Prophecy*. Edited by Ehud Ben Zvi and Michael H. Floyd. SymS 10. Atlanta: Society of Biblical Literature, 2000.

Davids, Peter H. *The Letters of 2 Peter and Jude*. Pillar New Testament Commentary. Grand Rapids: Eerdmans, 2006.

Davies, Philip R. "Loose Canons: Reflections on the Formation of the Hebrew Bible." Pages 57–72 in *Perspectives on Hebrew Scriptures: Comprising the Contents of the Journal of Hebrew Scriptures, vols. 1-4*. Edited by Ehud Ben Zvi. Piscataway, NJ: Gorgias, 2006.

———. "The Scribal School of Daniel." Pages 247–65 in vol. 1 of *The Book of Daniel: Composition and Reception*. Edited by John J. Collins and Peter W. Flint. VTSup 83. Leiden: Brill, 2001.

———. *Scribes and Schools: The Canonization of the Hebrew Scriptures*. LAI. London: SPCK, 1998.

Deventer, H. J. M. van. "Another Look at the Redaction History of the Book of Daniel, or Reading Daniel from Left to Right." *JSOT* 38 (2013): 239–60.

Dohmen, Christoph, and Manfred Oeming. *Biblischer Kanon—warum und wozu? Eine Kanontheologie*. QD 137. Freiburg: Herder, 1992.

Dörrfuß, Ernst Michael. *Mose in den Chronikbüchern: Garant theokratischer Zukunftserwartung*. BZAW 219. Berlin: de Gruyter, 1994.

Driver, Daniel R. *Brevard Childs, Biblical Theologian: For the Church's One Bible*. FAT 2/46. Tübingen: Mohr Siebeck, 2010.

Edwards, Timothy M. *Exegesis in the Targum of Psalms: The Old, the New, and the Rewritten*. Gorgias Dissertations 28. Piscataway, NJ: Gorgias, 2007.

Ehrman, Bart D. *The New Testament and Other Early Christian Writings: A Reader*. New York: Oxford University Press, 1998.

142   *When Texts Are Canonized*

Eliade, Mircea, ed. *The Encyclopedia of Religion*. 15 vols. New York: Mcmillan, 1987–2005.

Ellis, E. Earle. *Paul's Use of the Old Testament*. Edinburgh: Oliver & Boyd, 1957.

Elrefaei, Aly. *Wellhausen and Kaufmann: Ancient Israel and Its Religious History in the Works of Julius Wellhausen and Yehezkel Kaufmann*. BZAW 490. Berlin: de Gruyter, 2016.

Eran, Abraham. "Weights and Weighing in the City of David: The Early Weights from the Bronze Age to the Persian Period." Pages 204–56 in *Various Reports*, vol. 4, pt. 4 of *City of David Excavations: Final Report*. Edited by Donald T. Ariel and Alon de Groot. Qedem 35. Jerusalem: Institute of Archaeology, Hebrew University,1996.

Esler, Philip F. "Ezra-Nehemiah as a Narrative of (Re-Invented) Israelite Identity." *BibInt* 11 (2003): 413–26.

Evans, Craig A. "Did Jesus Predict His Death and Resurrection?" Pages 82–97 in *Resurrection*. Edited by Stanley E. Porter, Michael A. Hayes, and David Tombs. JSNTSup 186. Roehampton Institute London Papers 5. Sheffield: Sheffield Academic, 1999.

———. "Jesus' Action in the Temple and Evidence of Corruption in the First-Century Temple." Pages 522–39 in *Society of Biblical Literature 1989 Seminar Papers: One Hundred Twenty-Fifth Annual Meeting, 18–21 November 1989, the Anaheim Hilton and Towers, Anaheim, California*. Edited by David J. Lull. SBLSP 28. Atlanta: Scholars Press, 1989.

———. "On the Vineyard Parables of Isaiah 5 and Mark 12." *BZ* 28 (1984): 82–86.

———. "The Twelve Thrones of Israel: Scripture and Politics in Luke 22:24–30." Pages 154–70 in *Luke and Scripture: The Function of Sacred Tradition in Luke-Acts*. Edited by Craig A. Evans and James A. Sanders. Minneapolis: Fortress, 2001.

Fishbane, Michael A. *Biblical Interpretation in Ancient Israel*. Oxford: Clarendon, 1985.

Fitzpatrick-McKinley, Anne. *Empire, Power, and Indigenous Elites: A Case Study of the Nehemiah Memoir*. JSJSup 169. Leiden: Brill, 2015.

Flesher, Paul V. M., and Bruce D. Chilton. *The Targums: A Critical Introduction*. Studies in the Aramaic Interpretation of Scripture 12. Leiden: Brill, 2011.

France, R. T. *The Gospel of Mark: A Commentary on the Greek Text*. NIGTC. Grand Rapids: Eerdmans, 2002.

Frevel, Christian. "Deuteronomistisches Geschichtswerk oder Geschichtswerke? Die These Martin Noths zwischen Tetrateuch, Hexateuch und Enneateuch." Pages 60–95 in *Martin Noth—aus der Sicht der heutigen Forschung*. Edited by Udo Rüterswörden. BThSt 58. Neukirchen-Vluyn: Neukirchner Verlag, 2004.

Bibliography   143

————, ed. *Mixed Marriages: Intermarriage and Group Identity in the Second Temple Period*. LHBOTS 547. New York: T&T Clark International, 2012.

Frey, Jörg. *Der Brief des Judas und der zweite Brief des Petrus*. THKNT 15.2. Leipzig: Evangelische Verlagsanstalt, 2015.

Frye, Northrop. *The Great Code: The Bible and Literature*. London: Routledge & Kegan Paul, 1982.

Gadamer, Hans-Georg. *Truth and Method*. 2nd ed. London: Continuum, 2006.

Gallagher, Edmon L. *Hebrew Scripture in Patristic Biblical Theory: Canon, Language, Text*. VCSup 114. Leiden: Brill, 2012.

Gertz, Jan Christian. "Die Stellung des kleinen geschichtlichen Credos in der Redaktionsgeschichte von Deuteronomium und Pentateuch." Pages 30–45 in *Liebe und Gebot: Studien zum Deuteronomium*. Edited by ReinhardG. Kratz and Hermann Spieckermann. FRLANT 190. Göttingen: Vandenhoeck & Ruprecht, 2000.

Gese, Hartmut. *Zur biblischen Theologie: Alttestamentliche Vorträge*. BEvT 78. Tübingen: Mohr, 1983.

Goody, Jack. *The Interface between the Written and the Oral*. Studies in Literacy, Family, Culture, and the State. Cambridge: Cambridge University Press, 1987.

Goulder, Michael D. *The Prayers of David (Psalms 51–72): Studies in the Psalter, II*. JSOTSup 102. Sheffield: Sheffield Academic, 1990.

————. *The Psalms of Asaph and the Pentateuch: Studies in the Psalter, III*. JSOTSup 233. Sheffield: Sheffield Academic, 1996.

————. *The Psalms of the Sons of Korah*. JSOTSup 20. Sheffield: JSOT Press, 1982.

Grabbe, Lester L. "A Dan(iel) for All Seasons: For Whom Was Daniel Important?" Page 229–46 in vol. 1 of *The Book of Daniel: Composition and Reception*. Edited by John J. Collins and Peter W. Flint. VTSup 83. Leiden: Brill, 2001.

————. *Ezra-Nehemiah*. OTR. London: Routledge, 1998.

————. *Yehud: A History of the Persian Province of Judah*. Vol. 1 of *A History of the Jews and Judaism in the Second Temple Period*. London: Continuum, 2004.

Graham, William A. "Scripture." Pages 131–41 in vol. 13 of *The Encyclopedia of Religion*. Edited by Mircea Eliade. New York: Macmillan, 1978.

Gray, Rebecca. *Prophetic Figures in Late Second Temple Jewish Palestine: The Evidence of Josephus*. Oxford: Oxford University Press, 1993.

Gundry, Robert H. *The Use of the Old Testament in St. Matthew's Gospel: With Special Reference to the Messianic Hope*. NovTSup 18. Leiden: Brill, 1967.

Gunneweg, Antonius H. J. "Weisheit, Prophetie und Kanonformel: Erwägungen zu Proverbia 30,1-9." Pages 253–60 in *Alttestamentlicher Glaube und biblische Theologie: Festschrift für Horst Dietrich Preuss zum 65*.

144　*When Texts Are Canonized*

Geburtstag. Edited by Jutta Hausmann and Hans-Jürgen Zobel. Stuttgart: Kohlhammer, 1992.

Hahn, Andreas. *Canon Hebraeorum, Canon Ecclesiae: Zur deuterokanonischen Frage im Rahmen der Begründung alttestamentlicher Schriftkanonizität in neuerer römisch-katholischer Dogmatik*. Studien zu Theologie und Bibel 2. Münster: LIT, 2009.

Halbertal, Moshe. *People of the Book: Canon, Meaning, and Authority*. Cambridge: Harvard University Press, 1997.

Hänsel, L. "Studien zu 'Tora' in Esra-Nehemiah und Chronik." PhD diss., Leipzig, 1999.

Hanson, Anthony Tyrrell. *Studies in the Pastoral Epistles*. London: SPCK, 1968.

Hanson, Paul D. *The Dawn of Apocalyptic: The Historical and Sociological Roots of Jewish Apocalyptic Eschatology*. Philadelphia: Fortress, 1979.

Hayes, Christine. "Intermarriage and Impurity in Ancient Jewish Sources." *HTR* 92 (1999): 3–36.

Hays, Christopher B. *Hidden Riches: A Sourcebook for the Comparative Study of the Hebrew Bible and Ancient Near East*. Louisville: Westminster John Knox, 2014.

Hercsik, Donath. *Die Grundlagen unseres Glaubens: Eine theologische Prinzipienlehre*. Theologie, Forschung und Wissenschaft 15. Münster: LIT, 2005.

Himmelfarb, Martha. *A Kingdom of Priests: Ancestry and Merit in Ancient Judaism*. Philadelphia: University of Pennsylvania Press, 2013.

———. "Torah, Testimony, and Heavenly Tablets: The Claim to Authority in the *Book of Jubilees*." Pages 22–28 in *A Multiform Heritage: Studies on Early Judaism and Christianity in Honour of Robert A. Kraft*. Edited by Benjamin G. Wright. Scholars Press Homage Series 24. Atlanta: Scholars Press, 1999.

Höffken, Peter. *Das Buch Jesaja*. 2 vols. NSKAT 16. Stuttgart: Katholisches Bibelwerk, 1933.

Holm, Tawny L. *Of Courtiers and Kings: The Biblical Daniel Narratives and Ancient Story-Collections*. EANEC 1. Winona Lake, IN: Eisenbrauns, 2013.

Hossfeld, Frank-Lothar, and Eric Zenger. "Thoughts on the 'Davidization' of the Psalter." Pages 119–30 in *The Shape of the Writings*. Edited by Julius Steinberg and Timothy J. Stone. Siphrut 16. Winona Lake, IN: Eisenbrauns, 2015.

Houtman, Cornelis. *Das Bundesbuch: Ein Kommentar*. DMOA 24. Leiden: Brill, 1997.

———. "Ezra and the Law: Observations on the Supposed Relation between Ezra and the Pentateuch," *OTS* 21 (1981): 91–115.

Isaacs, E. "1 (Ethiopic Apocalypse of) Enoch." Pages 5–89 in *Apocalyptic Literature and Testaments*. Vol. 1 of *The Old Testament Pseudepigrapha*.

Bibliography   145

Edited by James H. Charlesworth. Garden City, NY: Doubleday, 1983.

Jackson, Bernard S. *Wisdom-Laws: A Study of the Mishpatim of Exodus 21:1–22:16.* Oxford: Oxford University Press, 2006.

Johnson, Luke Timothy. *The First and Second Letters to Timothy: A New Translation with Introduction and Commentary.* AB 35A. New York: Doubleday, 2001.

Jong, Matthijs J. de. "Biblical Prophecy—A Scribal Enterprise: The Old Testament Prophecy of Unconditional Judgement Considered as a Literary Phenomenon," *VT* 61 (2011): 39–70.

Josephus. *Against Apion.* Translated by John M. G. Barclay. Flavius Josephus, Translation and Commentary 10. Leiden: Brill, 2007.

Kartveit, Magnar. *The Origin of the Samaritans.* VTSup 128. Leiden: Brill, 2009.

Kashow, Robert C. "Zechariah 1–8 as a Theological Explanation for the Failure of Prophecy in Haggai 2:20–23." *JTS* 64 (2013): 385–403.

Kaufmann, Yehezkel. *The Religion of Israel: From Its Beginnings to the Babylonian Exile.* Translated by Moshe Greenberg. London: Allen & Unwin, 1961.

Kelly, J. N. D. *Early Christian Doctrines.* 2nd ed. New York: HarperOne, 1960.

Kleer, Martin Kleer, *"Der liebliche Sänger der Psalmen Israels": Untersuchungen zu David als Dichter und Beter der Psalmen.* BBB 108. Bodenheim: Philo, 1996.

Klein, Anja. *Geschichte und Gebet: Die Rezeption der biblischen Geschichte in den Psalmen des Alten Testaments.* FAT 94. Tübingen: Mohr Siebeck, 2014.

Kletter, Raz. "The Inscribed Weights of the Kingdom of Judah." *TA* 18 (1991): 121–63.

König, Eduard. *Das Deuteronomium.* KAT 3. Leipzig: Deichert, 1917.

Körtner, Ulrich H. J. *Arbeit am Kanon: Studien zur Bibelhermeneutik.* Leipzig: Evangelische Verlagsanstalt, 2015.

Kraemer, David. "The Formation of Rabbinic Canon: Authority and Boundaries." *JBL* 110 (1991): 613–30.

Krüger, Thomas. "Überlegungen zur Bedeutung der Traditionsgeschichte für das Verständnis alttestamentlicher Texte und zur Weiterentwicklung der traditionsgeschichtlichen Methode." Pages 233–45 in *Lesarten der Bibel: Untersuchungen zu einer Theorie der Exegese des Alten Testaments.* Edited by Helmut Utzschneider and Erhard Blum. Stuttgart: Kohlhammer, 2006.

Kugel, James. "On the Interpolations in the Book of Jubilees." *RevQ* 24 (2009): 215–72.

Laato, Antti, and Jacques van Ruiten, eds. *Rewritten Bible Reconsidered: Pro-*

146 *When Texts Are Canonized*

ceedings of the Conference in Karkku, Finland, August 24–26, 2006. Studies in Rewritten Bible 1. Winona Lake, IN: Eisenbrauns, 2008.

Lane, William L. *The Gospel of Mark: The English Text with Introduction, Exposition, and Notes*. NICNT. Grand Rapids: Eerdmans, 1974.

Lange, Armin. *Die Handschriften biblischer Bücher von Qumran und den anderen Fundorten*. Vol. 1 of *Handbuch der Textfunde vom Toten Meer*. Tübingen: Mohr Siebeck, 2009.

———. "'Nobody Dared to Add to Them, to Take from Them, or to Make Changes' (Josephus, Ag. Ap. 1.42): The Textual Standardization of Jewish Scriptures in Light of the Dead Sea Scrolls." Pages 105–26 in *Flores Florentino: Dead Sea Scrolls and Other Early Jewish Studies in Honour of Florentino García Martínez*. Edited by Anthony Hilhorst, Émile Puech, and Eibert Tigchelaar. JSJSup 122. Leiden: Brill, 2007.

Lee, Kyong-Jin. *The Authority and Authorization of Torah in the Persian Period*. CBET 64. Leuven: Peeters, 2011.

LeFebvre, Michael. *Collections, Codes, and Torah: The Re-characterization of Israel's Written Law*. LHBOTS 451. London: T&T Clark, 2006.

Leiman, Sid Z. *The Canonization of Hebrew Scripture: The Talmudic and Midrashic Evidence*. Connecticut Academy of Arts and Sciences Transactions Series 47. New Haven: Connecticut Academy of Arts and Sciences, 1976.

———. "Inspiration and Canonicity: Reflections on the Formation of the Biblical Canon." Pages 56–63 in *Aspects of Judaism in the Graeco-Roman Period*, vol. 2 of *Jewish and Christian Self-Definition*. Edited by E. P. Sanders, Albert I. Baumgarten, and A. Mendelson. London: SCM, 1981.

Levenson, Jon D. "The Last Four Verses in Kings." *JBL* 103 (1984): 353–61.

Levin, Christoph. "Zephaniah: How This Book Became Prophecy." Pages 261-80 in *Re-Reading the Scriptures: Essays on the Literary History of the Old Testament*. FAT 87. Tübingen: Mohr Siebeck, 2013.

Levine, Baruch A. "The Temple Scroll: Aspects of Its Historical Provenance and Literary Character." *BASOR* 232 (1978): 5–23.

Levinson, Bernard M. "Die neuassyrischen Ursprünge der Kanonformel in Deuteronomium 13,1." Pages 23–59 in *Viele Wege zu dem Einen: Historische Bibelkritik; Die Vitalität der Glaubensüberlieferung in der Moderne*. Edited by Stefan Beyerle, Axel Graupner, and Udo Rüterswörden. BThSt 121. Neukirchen-Vluyn: Neukirchener Verlag, 2012.

Lieberman, Stephen J. "Canonical and Official Cuneiform Texts: Towards an Understanding of Assurbanipal's Personal Tablet Collection." Pages 305–36 in *Lingering over Words: Studies in Ancient Near Eastern Literature in Honor of William L. Moran*. Edited by Tzvi Abusch, John Huehnergard, and Piotr Steinkeller. HSS 37. Atlanta: Scholars Press, 1990.

Lim, Timothy H. "All These He Composed through Prophecy." Pages

61–76 in *Prophecy after the Prophets? The Contribution of the Dead Sea Scrolls to the Understanding of Biblical and Extra-Biblical Prophecy.* Edited by Armin Lange and Kristin de Troyer. CBET 52. Leuven: Peeters, 2010.

———. "Authoritative Scriptures and the Scrolls." Pages 303–22 in *The Oxford Handbook of the Dead Sea Scrolls.* Edited by Timothy H. Lim and John J. Collins. Oxford: Oxford University Press, 2010.

———. "The Defilement of the Hands as a Principle Determining the Holiness of Scriptures." *JTS* 61 (2010): 501–15.

———. *The Earliest Commentary on the Prophecy of Habakkuk.* Oxford: Oxford University Press, forthcoming.

———. *The Formation of the Jewish Canon.* AYBRL. New Haven: Yale University Press, 2013.

———. "Origins and Emergence of Midrash in Relation to the Hebrew Scriptures." Pages 592–612 in vol. 2 of *An Encyclopaedia of Midrash: Biblical Interpretation in Formative Judaism.* Edited by Jacob Neusner and Alan J. Avery-Peck. 2 vols. Leiden: Brill, 2004.

———. "The Rabbinic Concept of Holy Scriptures as Sacred Objects." In *Scribal Practices and the Social Construction of Knowledge in Antiquity, Late Antiquity and Medieval Islam.* Edited by Myriam Wissa. OLA. Leuven: Peeters, forthcoming.

———. "A Theory of the Majority Canon" *Expository Times* 124.8 (2013): 365-373.

Lin, Yii-Jan. *The Erotic Life of Manuscripts: New Testament Textual Criticism and the Biological Sciences.* Oxford: Oxford University Press, 2016.

Lipschits, Oded, "The Enigma of the Biblical Bath, and the System of Liquid Volume Measurement during the First Temple Period." *UF* 42 (2011): 453–78.

Lux, Rüdiger. "Der 'Lebenskompromiß'—ein Wesenszug im Denken Kohelets? Zur Auslegung von Koh 7,15–18." Pages 267–78 in *Alttestamentlicher Glaube und biblische Theologie: Festschrift für Horst Dietrich Preuss zum 65. Geburtstag.* Edited by Jutta Hausmann and Hans-Jürgen Zobel. Stuttgart: Kohlhammer, 1992.

Mason, Steve. "Josephus, Daniel, and the Flavian House." Pages 161–91 in *Josephus and the History of the Greco-Roman Period: Essays in Memory of Morton Smith.* Edited by Fausto Parente and Joseph Sievers. StPB 41. Leiden: Brill, 1994.

Mayes, Andrew D. H. *Deuteronomy.* NCB. Grand Rapids: Eerdmans, 1981.

McDonald, Lee Martin. *The Biblical Canon: Its Origin, Transmission, and Authority.* Peabody, MA: Hendrickson, 2007.

———. *Formation of the Bible: The Story of the Church's Canon.* Peabody, MA: Hendrickson, 2012.

———. *The Formation of the Christian Biblical Canon.* Rev. and exp. ed. Peabody, MA: Hendrickson, 1995.

148   *When Texts Are Canonized*

McDonald, Lee Martin, and James A. Sanders. "Introduction." Page 5–17 in *The Canon Debate.* Edited by Lee Martin McDonald and James A. Sanders. Peabody, MA: Hendrickson, 2002.

McNamara, Martin. *Targum and Testament Revisited: Aramaic Paraphrases of the Hebrew Bible; A Light on the New Testament.* 2nd ed. Grand Rapids: Eerdmans, 2010.

Meinhold, Arndt. *Die Sprüche.* 2 vols. ZBK.AT 16. Zurich: Theologischer Verlag, 1991.

Miles, Jack. *God: A Biography.* London: Simon & Schuster, 1995.

Moffat, Donald P. *Ezra's Social Drama: Identity Formation, Marriage and Social Conflict in Ezra 9 and 10.* LHBOTS 579. London: Bloomsbury T&T Clark, 2013.

Mroczek, Eva. "The Hegemony of the Biblical in the Study of Second Temple Literature" *JAJ* 6 (2015): 2–35.

———. *The Literary Imagination in Jewish Antiquity.* Oxford: Oxford University Press, 2016.

Müller, Gerhard, ed. *Theologische Realenzyklopädie.* Vol. 36. Berlin: de Gruyter, 2005.

Najman, Hindy. "Interpretation as Primordial Writing: Jubilees and Its Authority Conferring Strategies." *JSJ* 30 (1999): 379–410.

———. *Past Renewals: Interpretative Authority, Renewed Revelation, and the Quest for Perfection in Jewish Antiquity.* JSJSup 53. Leiden: Brill, 2010.

———. *Seconding Sinai: The Development of Mosaic Discourse in Second Temple Judaism.* JSJSup 77. Leiden: Brill, 2003.

Najman, Hindy, and Eibert Tigchelaar. "Unity after Fragmentation." *RevQ* 26 (2014): 495–500.

Newsom, Carol A., with Brennan W. Breed. *Daniel: A Commentary.* OTL 21. Louisville: Westminster John Knox, 2014.

Nickelsburg, George W. E., and James C. VanderKam. *1 Enoch 2: A Commentary on the Book of 1 Enoch, Chapters 37–82.* Hermeneia. Minneapolis: Fortress, 2012.

Niditch, Susan. *Oral World and Written Word: Ancient Israelite Literature.* LAI. Louisville: Westminster John Knox, 1996.

Noam, Vered. "Why Did the Heavenly Voice Speak Aramaic? Ancient Layers in Rabbinic Literature," in *From Text to Context in Ancient Judaism: Studies in Honor of Steven Fraade.* Edited by Michal Bar-Asher Siegal, Christine Hayes, and Tzvi Novick. Leiden: Brill, forthcoming.

Noort, Edward. *Das Buch Josua: Forschungsgeschichte und Problemfelder.* EdF 292. Darmstadt: Wissenschaftliche Buchgesellschaft, 1998.

Noth, Martin. *Überlieferungsgeschichte des Pentateuch.* 2nd ed. Darmstadt: Wissenschaftliche Buchgesellschaft, 1960.

———. *Überlierferungsgeschichtliche Studien.* Vol. 1, *Die sammelnden und bearbeitenden Geschichtswerke im Alten Testament.* Schriften der Königs-

berger Gelehrten Gesellschaft, Geisteswissenschaftliche Klasse 18.2. Halle: Niemeyer, 1943.

Oegema, Gerbern S. "The Reception of the Book of Daniel (and Danielic Literature) in the Early Church." Pages 243–52 in *The Pseudepigrapha and Christian Origins: Essays from the Studiorum Novi Testamenti Societas*. Edited by Gerbern S. Oegema and James H. Charlesworth. Jewish and Christian Texts in Contexts and Related Studies 4. London: T&T Clark, 2008.

Oeming, Manfred. "Das Hervorwachsen des Verbindlichen aus der Geschichte des Gottesvolkes: Grundzüge einer prozessual-soziologischen Kanon-Theorie." *ZNW* 6 (2003): 52–58.

———. "Die verborgene Nähe: Zum Verhältnis von liturgischer und exegetischer Schrifthermeneutik (mit besonderer Berücksichtigung des Alten Testaments in der christlichen Predigt)." Pages 181–206 in *Wort des lebendigen Gottes: Liturgie und Bibel*. Edited by Alexander Zerfass and Ansgar Franz. Pietas Liturgica 16. Tübingen: Francke, 2016.

———. *Verstehen und Glauben: Exegetische Bausteine zur einer Theologie des Alten Testaments*. BBB 142. Berlin: Philo, 2003.

Olson, Dennis T. "Types of a Recent 'Canonical Approach.'" Pages 196–218 in *The Twentieth Century: From Modernism to Post-modernism*. Vol. 3, pt. 2 of *Hebrew Bible, Old Testament: The History of Its Interpretation*. Edited by Magne Sæbø. Göttingen: Vandenhoeck & Ruprecht, 2015.

Olyan, Saul M. *Social Inequality in the World of the Text: The Significance of Ritual and Social Distinctions in the Hebrew Bible*. JAJSup 4. Göttingen: Vandenhoeck & Ruprecht, 2011.

Origen. *Sur les écritures: Philocalie 1–20*. Edited and Translated by Marguerite Harl; *La lettre à Africanus sur l'histoire de Suzanne*. Edited and Translated by Nicholas de Lange. SC 302. Paris: Cerf, 1983.

Otto, Eckart. "Aspects of Legal Reforms and Reformulations in Ancient Cuneiform and Israelite Law." Pages 160–96 in *Theory and Method in Biblical and Cuneiform Law: Revision, Interpolation and Development*. Edited by Bernard M. Levinson. JSOTSup 181. Sheffield: JSOT Press, 1994.

———. *Theologische Ethik des Alten Testaments*. Theologische Wissenschaft 3.2. Stuttgart: Kohlhammer, 1994.

Pakkala, Juha. *Ezra the Scribe: The Development of Ezra 7–10 and Nehemia 8*. BZAW 347. Berlin: de Gruyter, 2004.

———. "The Quotations and References of the Pentateuchal Laws in Ezra-Nehemiah." Pages 193–221 in *Changes in Scripture: Rewriting and Interpreting Authoritative Traditions in the Second Temple Period*. Edited by Hanne von Weissenberg, Juha Pakkala, and Marko Marttila. BZAW 419. Berlin: de Gruyter, 2011.

Pentiuc, Eugen J. *The Old Testament in Eastern Orthodox Tradition*. Oxford: Oxford University Press, 2014.

150   *When Texts Are Canonized*

Petersen, Anders Klostergaard. "Rewritten Bible as a Borderline Phenomenon—Genre, Textual Strategy or Canonical Anachronism?" Pages 284–306 in *Flores Florentino: Dead Sea Scrolls and Other Early Jewish Studies in Honour of Florentino García Martínez.* Edited by Anthony Hilhorst, Émile Puech, and Eibert Tigchelaar. JSJSup 122. Leiden: Brill, 2007.

Pietersma, Albert. "David in the Greek Psalms." *VT* 30 (1980): 213–26.

Plöger, Otto. *Sprüche Salomos (Proverbia).* BKAT 17. Neukirchen-Vluyn: Neukirchener Verlag, 1984.

Powell, Marvin A. "Masse und Gewichte." Pages 457–530 in *Reallexikon der Assyriologie,* vol. 7, ed. Dietz-Otto Edzard et al. Berlin: de Gruyter, 1987.

Pritchard, James B., ed. *Ancient Near Eastern Texts Relating to the Old Testament.* 3rd ed. Princeton: Princeton University Press, 1969.

Pury, Albert de, and Thomas Römer, eds. *Die sogenannte Thronfolgegeschichte Davids: Neue Einsichten und Anfragen.* OBO 176. Freiburg: Universitätsverlag; Göttingen: Vandenhoeck & Ruprecht, 2000.

Rad, Gerhard von. *The Problem of the Hexateuch and Other Essays.* London: SCM, 1958.

Ritter, Adolf Martin. *Charisma und Caritas: Aufsätze zur Alten Kirche.* Edited by Angelika Dörfler-Dierken et al. Göttingen: Vandenhoeck & Ruprecht, 1993.

Robinson, John A. T. *Redating the New Testament.* London: SCM, 1976.

Rollston, Christopher. *Writing and Literacy in the World of Ancient Israel: Epigraphic Evidence from the Iron Age.* ABS 11. Atlanta: Society of Biblical Literature, 2010.

Römer, Thomas. "Das deuteronomistische Geschichtswerk und die Wüstentraditionen der Hebräischen Bibel." Pages 55–88 in *Das deuteronomistische Geschichtswerk.* Edited by Herman-Josef Stipp. ÖBS 39. Frankfurt am Main: Lang, 2011.

Rost, Leonhard. *Die Überlieferung von der Thronnachfolge Davids.* BWANT 42. Stuttgart: Kohlhammer, 1926.

Rothenbusch, Ralf. *"… abgesondert zur Tora Gottes hin": Ethnisch-religiöse Identitäten im Esra/Nehemiabuch.* HBS 70. Freiburg im Breisgau: Herder, 2012.

———. "The Question of Mixed Marriages: Between the Poles of Diaspora and Homeland; Observations in Ezra-Nehemiah." Paged 60–77 in *Mixed Marriages: Intermarriage and Group Identity in the Second Temple Period.* Edited by Christian Frevel. LHBOTS 547. New York: T&T Clark International, 2012.

Rottländer, Rolf C. A. *Antike Längenmaße: Untersuchungen über ihre Zusammenhänge.* Braunschweig: Vieweg & Sohn, 1979.

Rüger, Hans P. "Der Umfang des alttestamentlichen Kanons in den verschiedenen kirchlichen Traditionen." Pages 137–45 in *Die Apokryphen-*

frage im ökumenischen Horizont: Die Stellung der Spätschriften des Alten Testaments im biblischen Schrifttum und ihre Bedeutung in den kirchlichen Traditionen des Ostens und Westens. Edited by Siegfried Meurer. Bibel im Gespräch 3. Stuttgart: Deutsche Bibelgesellschaft, 1993.

Rüterswörden, Udo. "Die sogenannte Kanonformel in Dtn 13,1." Pages 19–29 in *Juda und Jerusalem in der Seleukidenzeit: Herrschaft, Widerstand, Identität; Festschrift für Heinz-Josef Fabry.* Edited by Ulrich Dahmen and Johannes Schnocks. BBB 159. Göttingen: Vandenhoeck & Ruprecht, 2010.

Sanders, James A. "Adaptable for Life: The Nature and Function of Canon." Pages 531–60 in *Magnalia Dei, The Mighty Acts of God: Essays on the Bible and Archaeology in Memory of G. Ernest Wright.* Edited by Frank Moore Cross, Werner E. Lemke, and Patrick D. Miller. New York: Doubleday, 1976.

———. "The Issue of Closure in the Canonical Process." Pages 252–63 in *The Canon Debate.* Edited by Lee Martin McDonald and James A. Sanders. Peabody, MA: Hendrickson, 2002.

Satlow, Michael L. *How the Bible Became Holy.* New Haven: Yale University Press, 2014.

Schaper, Joachim. "The Death of the Prophet: The Transition from the Spoken to the Written Word of God in the Book of Ezekiel." Pages 63–79 in *Prophets, Prophecy, and Prophetic Texts in Second Temple Judaism.* Edited by Michael Floyd and Robert D. Haak. LHBOTS 427. London: Bloomsbury T&T Clark, 2006.

———. "Exilic and Post-Exilic Prophecy and the Orality/Literacy Problem." *VT* 55 (2005): 324–42.

———. "Torah and Identity in the Persian Period." Pages 27–38 in *Judah and the Judeans in the Achaemenid Period: Negotiating Identity in an International Context.* Edited by Oded Lipschits, Gary N. Knoppers, and Manfred Oeming. Winona Lake, IN: Eisenbrauns, 2011.

Schiffman, Lawrence H. "The Temple Scroll and the Halakhic Pseudepigrapha of the Second Temple Period." Pages 121–31 in *Pseudepigraphic Perspectives: The Apocrypha and Pseudepigrapha in Light of the Dead Sea Scrolls; Proceedings of the International Symposium of the Orion Center for the Study of the Dead Sea Scrolls and Associated Literature, 12–14 January 1997.* Edited by Esther G. Chazon and Michael E. Stone. STDJ 31. Leiden: Brill, 1999.

Schiffman, Lawrence H., and James C. VanderKam, eds. *Encyclopedia of the Dead Sea Scrolls.* 2 vols. New York: Oxford University Press, 2000.

Schmid, Konrad. "Der Kanon und der Kult: Das Aufkommen der Schriftreligion im antiken Israel und die sukzessive Sublimierung des Tempelkultes." Pages 523–46 in *Ex Oriente Lux: Studien zur Theologie des Alten Testaments; Festschrift für Rüdiger Lux.* Edited by Angelika Ber-

152   *When Texts Are Canonized*

lejung and Raik Heckl. Arbeiten zur Bibel und ihrer Geschichte 39. Leipzig: Evangelische Verlagsanstalt, 2012.

———. *The Old Testament: A Literary History.* Translated by Linda M. Maloney. Minneapolis: Fortress, 2012.

Schmökel, Hartmut. *Ur, Assur und Babylon: Drei Jahrtausende im Zweistromland.* Grosse Kulturen Der Frühzeit 2. Stuttgart: Klipper, 1955.

Schniedewind, William M. *How the Bible Became a Book: The Textualization of Ancient Israel.* Cambridge: Cambridge University Press, 2005.

———. *Society and the Promise to David: The Reception History of 2 Samuel 7:1–17.* New York: Oxford University Press, 1999.

———. "Writing and Book Production in the Ancient Near East." Pages 46–62 in *From the Beginnings to 600.* Edited by James N. B. Carleton Paget and Joachim Schaper. Vol. 1 of *The New Cambridge History of the Bible.* Cambridge: Cambridge University Press, 2013.

Schuchard, Bruce G. *Scripture within Scripture: The Interrelationship of Form and Function in the Explicit Old Testament Citations in the Gospel of John.* SBLDS 133. Atlanta: Scholars Press, 1992.

Schürer, Emil. *The History of the Jewish People in the Age of Jesus Christ (175 B.C.–A.D. 135).* Revised and edited by Geza Vermes, Fergus Millar, and Martin Goodman. 3 vols. in 4 pts. Edinburgh: T&T Clark, 1973–1987.

Schüssler Fiorenza, Elisabeth, ed. *A Feminist Commentary.* Vol. 2 of *Searching the Scriptures.* New York: Crossroad, 1994.

Schwartz, Seth. *Imperialism and Jewish Society, 200 B.C.E. to 640 C.E.* Jews, Christians, and Muslims from the Ancient to the Modern World. Princeton: Princeton University Press, 2009.

Schweizer, Eduard. *The Good News according to Mark.* Translated by Donald H. Madvic. Atlanta: John Knox, 1970.

Schwienhorst-Schönberger, Ludger. *Das Bundesbuch (Ex 20,22–23,33): Studien zu seiner Entstehung und Theologie.* BZAW 188. Berlin: de Gruyter, 1990.

Segal, Michael. "4QReworked Pentateuch or 4QPentateuch?" Pages 391–99 in *The Dead Sea Scrolls Fifty Years after Their Discovery: Proceedings of the Jerusalem Congress, July 20–25, 1997.* Edited by Lawrence H. Schiffman, Emanuel Tov, and James C. VanderKam. Jerusalem: Israel Exploration Society, 2000.

———. "Between Bible and Rewritten Bible." Pages 10–29 in *Biblical Interpretation at Qumran.* Edited by Matthias Henze. SDSSRL. Grand Rapids: Eerdmans, 2005.

———. *The Book of Jubilees: Rewritten Bible, Redaction, Ideology and Theology.* JSJSup 117. Leiden: Brill, 2007.

Semler, Johann. *Abhandlung von freier Untersuchung des Canon.* 4 vols. Halle: Carl Hermann Hemmerde, 1771–1776.

Sergi, Omer, et al. "The Royal Judahite Storage Jar: A Computer-Gener-

Bibliography   153

ated Typology and Its Archaeological and Historical Implication." *TA* 39 (2012): 64–92.

Shaver, Judson R. *Torah and the Chronicler's History Work: An Inquiry into the Chronicler's References to Laws, Festivals, and Cultic Institutions in Relationship to Pentateuchal Legislation*. BJS 196. Atlanta: Scholars Press, 1989.

Sim, David C. "Matthew 22:13a and 1 Enoch 10:4a: A Case of Literary Dependence?" *JSNT* 47 (1992): 3–19.

Ska, Jean-Louis. *The Exegesis of the Pentateuch: Exegetical Studies and Basic Questions*. FAT 66. Tübingen: Mohr Siebeck, 2009.

Smith, Wilfred Cantwell. *What Is Scripture? A Comparative Approach*. London: SCM, 1993.

Smith-Christopher, Daniel L. "Between Ezra and Isaiah: Exclusion, Transformation and Inclusion of the 'Foreigner' in Post-Exilic Biblical Theology." Pages 117–42 in *Ethnicity and the Bible*. Edited by Mark G. Brett. BibInt 109. Leiden: Brill, 1996.

———. "The Mixed Marriage Crisis in Ezra 9–10 and Nehemiah 13: A Study of the Sociology of the Post-exilic Judean Community. " Pages 243–65 in *Temple and Community in the Persian Period*. Edited by Tamara C. Eskenazi and Kent H. Richards. Vol. 2 of *Second Temple Studies*. JSOTSup 175. Sheffield: JSOT Press, 1994.

———. *The Religion of the Landless: The Social Context of the Babylonian Exile*. Bloomington, IN: Meyer-Stone, 1989.

Sneed, Mark M. *The Social World of the Sages. An Introduction to Israelite and Jewish Wisdom Literature*. Minneapolis: Fortress, 2015.

Snodgrass, Klyne R. *Stories with Intent: A Comprehensive Guide to the Parables of Jesus*. Grand Rapids: Eerdmans, 2007.

Soggin, J. Alberto, and Heinz-Josef Fabry. "ימין." Pages 658–63 in vol. 3 of *Theologisches Wörterbuch zum Alten Testament*. Edited by G. Johannes Botterweck and Helmer Ringgren. Stuttgart: Kohlhammer, 1982.

Sommer, Benjamin. "Inner-biblical Interpretation." Pages 1829–35 in *The Jewish Study Bible*. Edited by Adele Berlin and Marc Zvi Brettler. New York: Oxford University Press, 2004.

Southwood, Katherine E. *Ethnicity and the Mixed Marriage Crisis in Ezra 9–10: An Anthropological Approach*. Oxford Theological Monographs. Oxford: Oxford University Press, 2012.

Spilsbury, Paul. "Flavius Josephus on the Rise and Fall of Roman Empire." *JTS* 54 (2003): 1–24.

Stec, David M. *The Targum of Psalms: Translated, with a Critical Introduction, Apparatus, and Notes*. ArBib 16. Collegeville, MN: Liturgical Press, 2004.

Steck, Odil Hannes. "Theological Streams of Traditions." Pages 183–214 in *Tradition and Theology in the Old Testament*. Edited by Douglas A. Knight. Philadelphia: Fortress, 1977.

154　*When Texts Are Canonized*

Steinberg, Julius, and Timothy J. Stone. "The Historical Formation of the Writings in Antiquity." Pages 1–58 in *The Shape of the Writings*. Edited by Julius Steinberg and Timothy J. Stone. Siphrut 16. Winona Lake, IN: Eisenbrauns, 2015.

Steinberg, Julius, and Timothy J. Stone, eds. *The Shape of the Writings*. Siphrut 16. Winona Lake, IN: Eisenbrauns, 2015.

Steudel, Annette. "The Eternal Reign of the People of God—Collective Expectations in Qumran Texts (4Q246 and 1QM)." *RevQ* 17 (1996): 507–25.

———. *Der Midrasch zur Eschatologie aus der Qumrangemeinde (4QMidr Eschat a.b): Materielle Rekonstruktion, Textbestand, Gattung und traditionsgeschichtliche Einordnung des durch 4Q174 ("Florilegium") und 4Q177 ("Catena A") repräsentierten Werkes aus den Qumranfunden*. STDJ 13. Leiden: Brill, 1994.

Stipp, Hermann-Josef, ed. Das deuteronomistische Geschichtswerk. ÖBS 39. Frankfurt am Main: Lang, 2011.

Stuckenbruck, Loren T. "The Formation and Re-Formation of Daniel in the Dead Sea Scrolls." Pages 101–30 in *Scripture and the Scrolls*. Edited by James H. Charlesworth. Vol. 1 of *The Bible and the Dead Sea Scrolls: The Second Princeton Symposium on Judaism and Christian Origins*. Edited by James H. Charlesworth. Waco, TX: Baylor University Press, 2006.

Sundberg, Albert C., Jr. *The Old Testament of the Early Church*. HTS 20. Cambridge: Harvard University Press, 1964.

Taschner, Johannes. "'Fügt nichts zu dem hinzu, was ich euch gebiete, und streicht nichts heraus!' Die Kanonformel in Deuteronomium 4,2 als hermeneutischer Schlüssel der Tora." Pages 46–63 in *Kanonisierung— die hebräische Bibel im Werden*. Edited by Georg Steins and Johannes Taschner. BThSt 110. Neukirchen-Vluyn: Neukirchener Theologie, 2010.

Taussig, Hal, ed. *A New New Testament: A Bible for the 21st Century Combining Traditional and Newly Discovered Texts*. Boston: Houghton Mifflin Harcourt, 2013.

Tedesche, Sidney, and Solomon Zeitlin. *The First Book of Maccabees*. JAL 1. New York: Harper & Brothers, 1950.

Toorn, Karel van der. *Scribal Culture and the Making of the Hebrew Bible*. Cambridge: Harvard University Press, 2007.

Tov, Emanuel and Sidnie White. "Reworked Pentateuch." Page 187–351 in *Qumran Cave 4.VIII: Parabiblical Texts, Part 1*. Edited by Harold W. Attridge et al. DJD XIII. Oxford: Clarendon, 1994.

Tucker, Gene M. "Prophetic Superscriptions and the Growth of a Canon." Page 56–70 in *Canon and Authority: Essays in Old Testament Religion and Theology*. Edited by George W. Coats and Burke O. Long. Philadelphia: Fortress, 1977.

Bibliography 155

Ulrich, Eugene C. *The Dead Sea Scrolls and the Origins of the Bible.* SDSSRL. Grand Rapids: Eerdmans, 1999.

———. "The Notion and Definition of Canon." Pages 21–35 in *The Canon Debate.* Edited by Lee Martin McDonald and James A. Sanders. Peabody, MA: Hendrickson, 2002.

———. "The Text of Daniel in the Qumran Scrolls." Pages 573–85 in vol. 2 of *The Book of Daniel: Composition and Reception.* Edited by John J. Collins and Peter W. Flint. VTSup 83. Leiden: Brill, 2001.

Ulrich, Eugene C., et al. *Qumran Cave 4.XI: Psalms to Chronicles.* DJD XVI. Oxford: Clarendon, 2000.

Unger, Eckhard. *Die Nippur-Elle: Publikationen der Kaiserlichen Osmanischen Museen, Konstantinopel 1916.* Constantinople: Ihsan, 1916.

Unnik, Willem C. van. "The 'Gospel of Truth' and the New Testament." Page 79–129 in *The Jung Codex: A Newly Recovered Gnostic Papyrus.* Edited by F. L. Cross. London: Mowbray, 1955.

———. "De la regle μήτε προσθεῖναι μήτε ἀφελεῖν dans l'histoire du canon," *VC* 3 (1949): 1–36.

VanderKam, James C. *The Book of Jubilees.* Guides to Apocrypha and Pseudepigrapha 9. Sheffield: Sheffield Academic, 2001.

———. "Moses Trumping Moses: Making the Book of *Jubilees.*" Pages 25–44 in *The Dead Sea Scrolls: Transmission of Traditions and Production of Texts.* Edited by Sarianna Metso, Hindy Najman, and Eileen M. Schuller. STDJ 92. Leiden: Brill, 2010.

Vanonen, Hanna. "The Textual Connections between 1QM 1 and the Book of Daniel." Pages 223–45 in *Changes in Scripture: Rewriting and Interpreting Authoritative Traditions in the Second Temple Period.* Edited by Hanne von Weissenberg, Juha Pakkala, and Marko Marttila. BZAW 419. Berlin: de Gruyter, 2011.

Vermes, Geza. "Bible and Midrash: Early Old Testament Exegesis." Pages 199–231 in *Scripture and Tradition in Judaism: Haggadic Studies.* Leiden: Brill, 1961.

———. "Josephus' Treatment of the Book of Daniel." *JJS* 42 (1991): 149–66.

———. *Scripture and Tradition in Judaism: Haggadic Studies.* 2nd rev. ed. StPB 4. Leiden: Brill, 1973.

Vonach, Andreas. "Gottes Souveränität anerkennen: Zum Verständnis der 'Kanonformel' in Koh 3,14." Pages 391–97 in *Qohelet in the Context of Wisdom: Colloquium Biblicum Lovaniense XLVI (1997).* Edited by Antoon Schoors. ETL 136. Leuven: University Press, 1998.

Wacholder, Ben Zion. "Jubilees as the Super Canon: Torah-Admonition versus Torah-Commandment." Pages 195–211 in *Legal Texts and Legal Issues: Proceedings of the Second Meeting of the International Organization for Qumran Studies, Cambridge 1995; Published in the Honour of Joseph M. Baumgarten.* Edited by Moshe J. Bernstein, Florentino García Martínez, and John Kampen. STDJ 23. Leiden: Brill, 1997.

156   *When Texts Are Canonized*

Werman, Cana. "'The תורה and the תעודה': Engraved on the Tablets." *DSD* 9 (2002): 75–103.

Wildberger, Hans. *Jesaja.* 3 vols. BKAT 10. Neukirchen-Vluyn: Neukirchener Verlag, 1965–1982.

Willi, Thomas. *Israel und die Völker: Studien zur Literatur und Geschichte Israels in der Perserzeit.* SBAB 55. Stuttgart: Katholisches Bibelwerk, 2012.

Williams, Jacqueline A. *Biblical Interpretation in the Gnostic Gospel of Truth from Nag Hammadi.* SBLDS 79. Atlanta: Scholars Press, 1988.

Wilson, Robert R. *Sociological Approaches to the Old Testament.* GBS.OT. Philadelphia: Fortress, 1984.

Witte, Markus, et al. *Die deuteronomistischen Geschichtswerke: Redaktions- und religionsgeschichtliche Perspektiven zur "Deuteronomismus"-Diskussion in Tora und Vorderen Propheten.* BZAW 365. Berlin: de Gruyter, 2006.

Wittgenstein, Ludwig. *Philosophical Investigations: The German Text, with a Revised English Translation.* Edited and translated by Gertrude E. M. Anscombe. Revised 4th edition by P. M. S. Hacker and Joachim Schulte. Oxford: Wiley-Blackwell, 2009.

Wolff, Hans Walter. *Hosea: A Commentary on the Book of the Prophet Hosea.* Hermeneia. Philadelphia: Fortress, 1974.

Würthwein, Ernst. *Die Bücher Der Könige.* 2 vols. ATD 11. Göttingen: Vandenhoeck & Ruprecht, 1977–1984.

Zahn, Molly M. "The Problem of Characterizing the 4QReworked Pentateuch Manuscripts: Bible, Rewritten Bible, or None of the Above?" *DSD* 15 (2008): 315–39.

———. *Rethinking Rewritten Scripture: Composition and Exegesis in the 4QReworked Pentateuch Manuscripts.* STDJ 95. Leiden: Brill, 2011.

———. "Rewritten Scriptures." Pages 323–50 in *Oxford Handbook of the Dead Sea Scrolls.* Edited by Timothy H. Lim and John J. Collins. Oxford: Oxford University Press, 2010.

Zaman, Luc. *Bible and Canon: A Modern Historical Inquiry.* SSN 50. Leiden: Brill, 2008.

Ziegenaus, Anton. *Kanon: Von der Väterzeit bis zur Gegenwart.* Handbuch der Dogmengeschichte 1.3a Freiburg im Breisgau: Herder, 1990.

Zsengellér, József, ed. *Rewritten Bible after Fifty Years: Texts, Terms, or Techniques? A Last Dialogue with Geza Vermes.* JSJSup 166. Leiden: Brill, 2014.

Index of Passages

**OLD TESTAMENT/
HEBREW BIBLE**

Genesis

1–2	63
17:7	32
17:9	32
20:7	11

Exodus

3	121
12	21
12:9	91
12:12	33
12:17	33
13:15	21
14:24	33
15	21
20:1–17	63
24	7
24:3–7	11
24:12–18	55
24:12	7
31:3	32–33
31:18	39n46
34:1	39n46
40:15	33

Leviticus

17:7	33
18–20	30
18:24–30	49
19:1–2	99
19:35	27
23	46
23:42	46
24:3	33

Numbers

10:35–36	88

15:15	33
20:14	34
20:17	34, 35
22:26	35

Deuteronomy

2:27	35
4:2	42
4:13	39n46
5	37
5:6–21	63
5:22	39n46
5:32–33	37
5:32	38
6:20–25	21
7:1–3	46
7:1–6	49
9:10	39n46
10:1–4	39n46
13:1	39n46, 42, 59
13:5	64n3
16:7	91
16:18–18:22	35
17:11	36
17:14–20	36
17:19	36
17:20	36, 38
18:20–22	9, 64n3
18:22	9
23	47
23:3	50
23:4–6	46
23:4–9	47, 49
24	59
25:15	27
26:4–9	19, 20
28:13–14	37
28:14	38

Joshua

1:7	37, 38
1:8	33
8:31	33
8:34	33
23:6	33, 37, 38
24:2–13	21

Judges

2:1	21
6:8–9:1	21
8:14	31

1 Samuel

6	34
6:12	34
16:1–13	104

2 Samuel

2	38
2:12–32	34
2:19	34
7:1–16	63n2
7:13	63n2
11:14–15	31
14	35
14:19	35

1 Kings

2	38n44
2:3	33, 38n44
22	38
22:2	37, 38
22:22–23	64n3

1 Chronicles

17:1–14	63n2
28:5	96

158   *Index of Passages*

2 Chronicles		111	85	36:18	31
13:8	96	112	85	36:32	31
34	38	117:22–23	102	36:4	31
34:2	38	117:22	103, 103n24	45:1	31
35:11–13	91	118	104n29		
36:22	78n47	118:19–27	104	Ezekiel	
		118:21 [Heb. 22]	103	2:6–3:3	65
Ezra		118[117]:22–23	103		
3	45	118:22	103	Daniel	
3:2	45	122	99, 100n14	1–6	67, 68,
7:14	44	122:3–5	99		74, 76, 79
7:25–26	44	135	21, 85	1:1–2:30	68
10:3	50	136	21, 85	1:1–2:4	68
		143	22	1:1–2:3	67
Nehemiah				1	67, 76
8	47, 50	Proverbs		1:4	77
8:1–6	12	1–9	123	1:7	71
8:1	45	4	40	2–6	75, 76, 79, 80
8:8	47	4:27	39	2	67, 68
8:13–18	46	5	40	2:4–7:28	68
8:13	45	8–9	123	2:4	67
8:14	46	8:22–36	123	2:31–45	67, 68
9	21	20:10	27	2:33–34	75
9:6–14	19			2:44–45	69
10	46	Isaiah		2:46–6:28	68
10:31	46	2:3	40	3–6	67
10:32	46	5:1–7	101, 101n19,	3	71
13:1–2	46		102	3:31–6:29	76
13:24	50	5:1	101	4	67
		5:3	101	6	71
Job		5:7	101	7–12	67, 74
11:9	26n6	6:9–10	97, 98, 103	7	67, 68, 69, 73,
28:25	26n6	24:23	96		74, 76, 79,
		28:26	40		79n51, 80, 99
Psalms		30:18–26	40	7:1	67, 79, 80
3	22	30:20b–21	40	7:2	67n14
12	22	31:4	96	7:9	99
31	22	40:9	96	7:10	79
34	22	48:17	40	7:13	99
40	22	52:7	96	7:23	69
51	22	66:24	105n32	7:25	69, 78n47
52	22			7:27	69
54	22	Jeremiah		7:28	67, 67n14, 79
63	22	17:21–22	47	8–12	68, 72, 76,
68	22	28:12–17	64n3		77, 79, 80
78	21	29:1	31	8–11	72
105	21, 85	31:31–34	41	8	67, 75
106	21, 85	36	65	8:14	69

Index of Passages 159

9	78n47
9:1–2	76, 76n44, 78
9:24–27	78
9:27	69, 71
10	72
11	70, 72, 73
11:30	75
11:31	71
11:32	73, 74
11:33	77
11:35	73, 77
11:40	70
12	73
12:1	76n44
12:3	77
12:4	77
12:10	73
12:11–12	76
12:11	69, 71

Hosea

6:2	100, 100n16, 100n17

Joel 3	41

Amos

2:9–11	21
3:1–2	21
3:8	11
4:10–11	21
5:25	21
8:5	27
9:7	21

Obadiah

21	96

Micah

3:5	64n3
4:7b–8	96

Habakkuk

2:2d	8

Haggai

2:23	63

Zechariah

1:12	78n47
14:9	96

NEW TESTAMENT

Matthew

4:17	96n5
5:17–20	43n56
5:17	42
13:13–15	103
16:21	100
18:12–14	126
18:15	126
19:28	98
22:1–14	105
22:13a	105
24:15	72n24, 80
25:31	99

Mark

1:15	96
4:3–9	97
4:11–12	97
4:12	97, 103
4:14–20	97
8:31	100
9:42–48	105
12:1–9	101
12:1	101
12:10–11	102, 103
12:12	104
13:14	72n24
14:62	99

Luke

8:10	103
15:1–2	126
15:3–7	126
16:15	72n24
22:28–30	98

John

6:35	125
8:12	125

Acts

1:3	97
4:11	103
4:12	42
8:12	97
14:22	97
19:8	97
28:23	97
28:26–27	103
28:31	97

Romans

5:8	131
14:17	97

1 Corinthians

4:20	97
6:9	97
15:50	97

2 Corinthians

4:10	133
11:4	134

Galatians

1:8	42
1:11–12	9
3:1–4:13	9
5:1–15	9
5:21	97

Colossians

4:11	97

2 Thessalonians

1:5	97

2 Timothy

3:15	5n12
3:16–17	4
4:13	5n12

Hebrews

4:15	132n34
11	19

1 Peter

2:4	103
2:6–7	103

160   *Index of Passages*

2 Peter	
1:14	10
1:20–21	10, 11
3:4	10
3:16	10

Jude	
3	42
14a	105
14b–15	106

DEUTEROCANICAL WRITINGS

Judith	
9:10	122
9:13	122
10:4	122
13:6–8	122
13:15	122
14:14	122
16:6	122
16:22	122

Sirach	
17	60
24:23	60
44–50	19

1 Maccabees	
1:54	69, 71, 78
2:22	41
2:59–60	71
4:26	3
4:52–54	69, 78
5:46	41
6:7	71
9:27	3
14:41	3

2 Maccabees	
6–7	105
7:4	105

4 Maccabees	
5	105
5:30	105
10	105

10:5	105
18	105
18:21	105

OLD TESTAMENT PSEUDEPIGRAPHA

1 Enoch	
1:1–2	8
1:9	105, 106, 106n39
10:4	105n38
10:4a	105
37–72	99
37–71	99
40:5	99
45:3	99
48:10	99
49:2	99
51:3	99
52:4	99
54:3	99
55:4	99
61:8	99
69:29	99

4 Ezra	
12:11–12	75
12:36–38	6n15
14:21	6

Jubilees	
1:26	55
4:19	57
6:20–22	55
8:11	57n68
10:13	57n68
21:10	57n68
30:12	56

Odes of Solomon	
33	123
33:6–10a	123
36	123

Sibylline Oracles	
3	72n25, 74n38
3:397	74

DEAD SEA SCROLLS AND RELATED TEXTS

1QpHab	
XII, 1–5	9

1QS	
I, 11–15	41, 42n55
III, 9–11	42, 42n55

4Q201	
V, 5	105n38

4Q204	
I, 15–17	106n39

4Q401	
14 I, 6	96

4Q403	
1 I, 8	96
1 I, 14	96
1 I, 32	96

4Q405	
3 II, 4	96
24, 3	96

4QFlorilegium	
II, 3–4	73

4QMMT	
section C	19

11Q19	
Temple Scroll	
XLIV, 5	58
L, 5–9	59
L, 17	59
LI, 6	58
LIV, 5–7	59
LIX, 7–10	59
LVI, 20–21	59
LVII, 1	59
LXI, 2–4	9

11QPs^a XXVII, 2–11	22
CD XVI, 1–3	7
MasSS 2:20	96

JOSEPHUS AND PHILO

Josephus

Against Apion

1.38–41	3, 15–16, 19
1.38	17
2.200–203	61

Antiquities

10.186–281	74n39
10:210	75
10.267	75
14.71	80n52

Jewish War

1.152	80n52
5.272	103n27

Philo

Quis rerum divinarum heres sit

259	11

MISHNAH, TALMUD, AND RELATED LITERATURE

b. Baba Batra

14a–15b	22n58

b. Ḥagigah

14a	99n10

b. Megillah

7a	6, 87

b. Pesaḥim

57a	102

b. Šabbat

13b	91

b. Sanhedrin

38b	99n10
96b–97a	99n10

b. Yebamot

61a	102

m. Kelim

15:6	88

m. Yadayim

3:5	86–87, 88
4:5	88

t. Meʿilah

1:16	102

t. Soṭah

13:2	3

t. Sukkah

3.15	102

t. Yadayim

2:14	5

Midrash Tanhuma

Qedoshim §1	99

TARGUMS

Targum Isaiah

1–13	102
5:2	102
5:5	102
5:7–8	102
5:10	102

EARLY CHRISTIAN WRITINGS

1 Clement

42:3	97

2 Clement

9:6	97
12:1	97

Acts of Paul and Thecla

3:2	116n15

Augustine

De consensu evangelistarum

2.12	92
2.14	92
2.17	91
2.65	92
3.24	92

Barnabas

6:4	103
21:1	97

Eusebius

Historia ecclesia

6.25	2

Ignatius

To the Ephesians

16:1	97

To the Philadelphians

3:3	97

Justin

Dialogue with Trypho

36	103n24
36:1	103

Shepherd of Hermas

9.12.3–5	97
10:6	103n24
13:2	103n24
86:7	103n24
89:3–5	97

NAG HAMMADI

Gospel of Thomas

30:2	124n26
#77	121
77:2	124n26
#107	127

Gospel of Truth

4:1–4	132
4:5–6	132
6:9–11	132
17:1–4	127

Prayer of Thanksgiving

13[7]	131

Thunder: Perfect Mind

1:5–6, 8–9, 2:4–10	125

Index of Subjects and Authors

Acts of Paul and Thecla, 112, 114, 116, 122
Alexander, Philip S., on rewritten scriptures as literary genre, 53n50
all generations formula, 32, 33, 42
angelic authority, of Jubilees, 56, 57
Antiquities (Josephus)
  and Daniel (book and prophet), 74, 75
  as rewritten Bible, 52, 54
  use of canonical and noncanonical books, 15, 16
apocryphal texts, nondeviation formula in, 41
Aramaic
  in 1 Enoch, 99-100n14
  reflected in words of Jesus, 97, 98, 99, 101, 102, 103, 104
  use in Daniel, 67, 68, 75, 76, 79, 80, 88, 99-100n14
Aramaic "Son of God" text, allusions to figure of Daniel in, 72, 73
archaeology, and the canon, 31
Assurbanipal, and state-aided process of canonization, 39n47
Augustine, and harmonization of Gospel texts, 91, 92, 93
authoritative texts
  collections of, 18
  and indicative logic, 18-21
authorship, Davidic, 21

Baltes, Guido, on use of Hebrew and Aramaic in Second Temple period, 77n46
Barr, James, on divine inspiration and canonicity, 7

Barthélemy, Dominique, on cessation of prophecy, 16n37
Bauckham, Richard
  on prophecy in 2 Peter, 11
  on quotation of Enoch by Jude, 107n39
Baumgarten, Albert, on scriptures that defile the hands, 5n13, 88, 89
Baynes, Leslie, on Jubilees in Ethiopian church, 8n22
Bergsma, John, on use of Enochic material in Jubilees, 56n62
Bible, biblical texts
  content and form, 86, 87, 88
  harmonization of discrepancies in, 90, 91
  illustrated by nonbiblical texts, 108, 109
  meaning from literary perspective, 85, 86
  significance of order, 84, 85, 86
  See also authoritative texts; canon; canonical texts; Old Testament; New Testament; New Testament canon
Blenkinsopp, Joseph, on Torah in Ezra-Nehemiah, 45
Boccaccini, Gabriele, on use of Enochic material in Jubilees, 56n62
books and content, distinction between, 83, 84, 93
Brownlee, William H., and interpretation of Great Isaiah Scroll, 98
canon
  biblical, dating of, 30, 31
  as closed list, 25, 26
  criteria for inclusion in, 2

Index of Subjects and Authors   163

and defilement of the hands, 3n5, 5,
    5n13, 6, 86, 87, 88
and divine inspiration, 3-6
in Eusebius, 2
as fixed measure, 26, 27
formation of, in early church, 106,
    107
of Jesus, 95
and linguistic diversity, 106, 107
in material culture, 26-27
in Origen, 1, 2
and scripture, distinction between,
    82, 83
and validation by community,
    11-12
canon formula, 32, 39n46, 42
canonical, interpretation of, in antiq-
    uity, 83
canonical process. *See* canonization
canonical texts, consistency in, 93, 94
canonization
    Davidic factor in, 21, 24
    and false prophecy, 63-81
    and manner of reading texts, 89-93
    stages of, 65-67
    and stories of origins, 10, 20
Carr, David, on community basis of
    authoritative texts, 21
Childs, Brevard
    on canonical process, 21
    on reading canonical texts, 90
    and use of the term *canon*, 83
Cohen, Shaye, on divine inspiration
    and canonicity, 6
Collins, John J.
    on allusion to Daniel in 1 Macca-
        bees, 71, 72
    on the *maśkîlîm*, 77
    on messianic vision of Aramaic
        "Son of God" text, 72, 73
    on redaction of book of Daniel, 75,
        76, 77, 78
    on similarities of language between
        Daniel and Dead Sea Scrolls, 74
community
    and manner of reading canonized
        texts, 89-93
    role in formation of canon, 28, 29

Crawford, Sidnie White, on textual
    variation of Hebrew Scriptures
    in 4QReworked Pentateuch, 52
credo, 20
Crossan, John Dominic
    and the date of the Gospel of
        Thomas, 117, 117n19
    and *A New New Testament*, 117, 118,
        119, 122
cult, as setting for formation of author-
    itative texts, 29
cultic observance, and conformity to
    Torah, 50

Daniel (book)
    bad prophecies in, 68-70
    changes of voice, 67
    and Dead Sea Scrolls, similarities of
        language, 74
    language differences and genre, 67
    manuscript fragments in Dead Sea
        Scrolls, 72
    redactional history, 67, 68, 75-80
    in Second Temple literature, 74, 75
Daniel (prophet)
    allusions to, in Dead Sea Scrolls, 72,
        73, 74
    as false prophet, 64
David, as role model, 38n44
Davidic factor, in canonization of texts,
    22, 24
Davies, Philip, on development of
    canon, 23n57, 27n28
defiling the hands
    and canonicity, 3n5, 5, 5n13, 6, 86,
        87, 88
    and number of letters in text, 88
    and physical presence in profane
        space, 88, 89
Deuteronomistic literature, and non-
    deviation formula, 33, 33n30, 36,
    37, 38, 42, 43
Didymus Alexandrinus, 7
divine inspiration
    and canonicity, 3-6, 9-11
    and 2 Timothy, 4, 5
Dead Sea Scrolls
    attestation to Daniel in, 72-74

164   *Index of Subjects and Authors*

Dead Sea Scrolls (*continued*)
  nondeviation formula in, 41, 42
  textual variation of Hebrew Scriptures in, 51
  See also 11QMelchizedek; 4QFlorilegium; 4QReworked Pentateuch; Pesher Habakkuk; Prayer of Nabonidus; Pseudo-Daniel texts; Temple Scroll

11QMelchizedek, and authority of book of Daniel, 74
Enoch (book)
  allusions of Jesus to, 105
  claim to divine inspiration, 8
  direct quotation in Jude (book) to, 105, 106
  use by church fathers, 8
Epiphanius, 7
eternal order formula, 33, 42
Eusebius, on the canon, 2
Ezra (biblical book), on the Torah of Moses, 44-50

family resemblances
  and authoritative texts, 18
  and canonicity, 12-15
First Maccabees, allusion to Daniel (book), 71
Fishbane, Michael, on discrepancies in law book of Ezra-Nehemiah and Pentateuch, 46, 47
four beasts vision (Daniel), as false prophecy, 69
four kingdoms oracle (Daniel)
  allusions to figure of Daniel in, 72
  as false prophecy, 68, 69
4QFlorilegium, and authority of book of Daniel, 73
4QReworked Pentateuch, textual variation of Hebrew Scriptures in, 51, 52
Fourth Ezra, on divine inspiration and canonicity, 6
fundamentalism, and nondeviation formula, 42-43n56
Funk, Robert, and *A New New Testament*, 113, 118

Gallagher, Edmon, on Hebrew language and canonization of OT, 2
gender, as concern for *A New New Testament*, 114, 121, 122, 123, 134
Gospel of Mary, 112, 114, 122
Gospel of Thomas, 111, 112, 117, 121, 124, 126, 127, 130
  portrait of Jesus in, 130, 131, 132
Gospels, Christian harmonization of, 91, 92, 93
Goulder, Michael, on order of the Psalms, 85

Halbertal, Moshe, on rabbinic tradition and canonical criterion of divine inspiration, 5
Hanson, Anthony, on divine inspiration and 2 Timothy, 5
harmonization
  of canonized texts, 90, 91
  of Gospels, 91, 92, 93
heavenly tablets, in Jubilees, 55, 56, 57, 58, 59
Hebrew
  and canonization of Old Testament, 2, 3
  in Second Temple period, 77, 77n46
heroic acts of individuals, and canonical process, 23, 24
Himmelfarb, Martha, on authority of Jubilees and Torah, 57, 58
holy narrations, as setting for formation of authoritative texts, 30
Holy Spirit, and death of last prophets, 3, 4
human body, as unit of measurement, 26n6

"I am," in Thunder: Perfect Mind and Gospel of John, 124, 125
identity formation, and the Torah, 48, 49, 50
indicative logic
  and authoritative texts, 18-21
  and canon, 15-18
  and Josephus's understanding of canonicity, 17, 18
  and language games, 13, 14, 15

Index of Subjects and Authors 165

inspired individuals, and formation of
the canon, 28
Israel, stories of, and canonical
process, 19-23

Jackson, Bernard, on laws of Exodus as
wisdom laws, 48
Jeremiah (book), Hebrew and Greek
versions, 84
Jerome, 7
on Porphyry's interpretation of
Daniel, 68
translation of Hebrew Bible into
Latin, 107
on unfulfilled prophecies in Daniel,
70
Jerusalem Temple desecration (Daniel)
as false prophecy, 69, 70
Jesus
allusions to non-Hebrew writings,
104-6
announcement of the kingdom,
96-97
canon of, 95
full humanity of, 132, 134
and Jesus Seminar, 118
and the mystery of the kingdom,
97-98
portrayal in *A New New Testament*,
114, 115, 118
portrayal in Gospel of Thomas,
130
portrayal in New Testament Gospels, 130, 131
Jesus Seminar (on historical Jesus),
118
Johnson, Luke Timothy, and the date
of 1 and 2 Timothy, 118n17
Josephus
application of Danielic prophecies
to Rome, 75, 80
on authority of Daniel (book and
prophet), 74, 75
on canonical books, 15, 16
on prophetic succession and canonicity, 16, 16n38, 17
on trustworthiness of biblical and
extrabiblical texts, 17

Jubilees
as authoritative *perush* in Dead Sea
Scrolls, 7
on authority of Torah, 55-58
claim to divine inspiration, 7
as rewritten scriptures, 56, 57
Judah, Rab (250-290), on defilement of
the hands, 6

King, Karen, and *A New New Testament*, 112, 113, 120
kingdom, mystery of, and Jesus,
97-98
kingdom of God, Jesus's announcement of, 96-97
Kugel, James, on authority of Jubilees,
57, 58

law, as setting for formation of authoritative texts, 29
law book (of Ezra), and Pentateuch,
discrepancies, 45, 46
laws
prescriptive or descriptive, 47, 48
written, and mores of a community,
48; as binding, 47, 48
Lee, Kyong-Jin, on Torah in book of
Ezra, 50
Lefebvre, Michael, on law book of
Ezra-Nehemiah and Pentateuch,
47, 48
legal texts, and rewritten scriptures,
54
Leiman, Sid
on canonicity and divine inspiration, 3, 4
criteria for inclusion in canon, 2
Lim, Timothy, on fixed canon in first
century CE, 82, 83
linguistic diversity, and canon of early
church, 106, 107
literacy, early evidence for, 31, 32
literary expression, and canonization,
65, 66
lost sheep, parable of, in New Testament Gospels, Gospel of
Thomas, and Gospel of Truth,
126, 127, 128

166   *Index of Subjects and Authors*

Maccabean martyrs, allusion of Jesus to, 105
maśkîlîm, 77, 78
and the Maccabees, 78
Mason, Steve, on reception of book of Daniel, 70, 71
material culture, canons in, 26, 27
mixed marriages, and identity formation in book of Ezra, 48, 49
Mroczek, Eva
critique of canon research, 23n57
on Ethiopian canon, 84
on Second Temple Literature, 28n15

Nag Hammadi writings, in *A New New Testament*, 112, 113
Najman, Hindy
on authority of rewritten scriptures, 54, 55
on Moses in the Temple Scroll, 58
A New New Testament
audience for, 119
and Christian worship, 118, 119
criteria for selection of books, 114
critique of, 115-20
dating of documents in, 117, 118
genre of, 116-20, 128, 129
and Hebrew Bible/Old Testament, 120-24, 134
motive and goal, 118
new books in, 112, 113, 114
as populist work, 119, 120
rationale for, 109, 110
New Orleans Council, 111, 114, 115, 116, 120, 128
profile and membership, 112
New Testament
absence of nondeviation formula in, 42
alternate version of, 108, 109
New Testament canon, rationale for, 129-33
Nippur-Elle, 26, 26n5
Noam, Vered, on *bat qôl*, 4n8
nondeviation formula (NDF)
in apocryphal texts, 41
in Dead Sea Scrolls, 41, 42
figurative uses, 35, 35

and fundamentalism, 42-43n56
profane meaning, 33, 34, 35
in prophetic literature, 40
theological use, 36, 37, 38
in wisdom literature, 39, 40, 41
Noth, Martin, and composition of Deuteronomistic History, 33n30

Odes of Solomon, 112, 114, 116, 118, 120, 123, 124
Old Testament, and *A New New Testament*, 120-24, 134
Olyan, Saul, on purity and intermarriage, 49
oracles, in Daniel, literary context, 65
oral delivery, and canonization, 65
order of biblical texts, significance of, 84, 85, 86
Origen
on Old Testament canon, 1, 2
on various biblical recensions, 84
origins, stories of, and canonical process, 19, 20, 21

Pagels, Elaine, and *A New New Testament*, 113
Pakkala, Juha, on discrepancies in law book of Ezra-Nehemiah and Pentateuch, 46
parables, use by Jesus, 97
Pentateuch, as source material for second century BCE literature, 53, 54
Pentiuc, Eugen, on canon in Eastern Orthodox Church, 8n22
people of the Golah, 49, 50
Pesher Habakkuk, claim to divine inspiration, 8, 9
Philo, on divine origin of biblical prophecy, 10, 11
Pompey, despoliation of temple by, as cause of reinterpretation of Daniel's oracles, 80
Porphyry, on Daniel (book) as Maccabean-era pseudepigraphon, 64, 68
Prayer of Nabonidus, allusions to figure of Daniel in, 72

Index of Subjects and Authors   167

Prayer of Thanksgiving (Nag Hammadi), 131
prayers, as setting for formation of authoritative texts, 30
prophecies, false
application to Rome, 75, 79, 80
and canonical authority, 63-81
prophecy
textualization of, 76, 76n44, 77
true and false, 9, 10, 11
prophetic literature, nondeviation formula in, 40
prophetic succession, and canonicity, 16, 17
proverbs, as setting for formation of authoritative texts, 30
Psalms, ordering of, at Qumran, 85
Pseudo-Daniel texts, allusions to figure of Daniel in, 72
purity, and mixed marriages in Ezra, 49

Qohelet, canonical status of, 3, 9, 23, 86

rabbinic canon, and Pauline letters, 9
rabbinic literature
as canonical and inspired, 3, 4
on canonical criterion of divine inspiration, 5, 6
Rad, Gerhard von, on original story of Israel, 20
rationalization, ex post facto, and the canon, 2
reception by community, and formation of the canon, 28, 29
reception history, of book of Daniel, 70-75
rejected stone (Psalm 118), coherence with Aramaic interpretation, 102, 103, 104
resurrection on third day, 100-101
rewritten scriptures, 52-61
freedom of rewriters to alter, 60
as literary genre, 53, 53n50
Robinson, A. T., and date of New Testament books, 117
Rome, as cause of reinterpretation of Daniel's prophecies, 75, 79, 80

Sanders, James, on function of canon, 20
Satlow, Michael
on date of the author of the book of Ezra, 45
on literacy in Persian Yehud, 50
on production of biblical texts, 31n24
sayings of the prophets, as setting for formation of authoritative texts, 30
Schaper, Joachim, on law of Moses as authoritative in Ezra-Nehemiah, 47
Schiffman, Lawrence, on Moses in the Temple Scroll, 58, 59
Schmid, Konrad, on development from oral traditions to fixed texts, 30n21
Schüssler-Fiorenza, Elisabeth, and the limits and extent of the canon, 109n5
Schwartz, Seth, on Judean Desert legal papyri, 60, 61
Schwienhorst-Schönberger, Ludger, on written form of the Book of the Covenant, 29n20
scribalism, and formation of biblical canon, 27-32
Second Peter, and divine origin of biblical prophecy, 10, 11
Secret Revelation of John, 112, 114
Segal, Michael, on rewritten Bible, 53
Seleucid history (in Daniel), as false prophecy, 70
Semler, Johann, on closing of the canon, 4n9
Simeon b. Menasia, on defiling the hands, 5
Sitze im Leben, and formation of authoritative texts, 29, 30
Smith-Christopher, Daniel, on identity formation in book of Ezra, 48, 49
Sneed, Mark, on wisdom traditions and formation of the canon, 32
Sommer, Benjamin, on reading Torah as single work of Moses, 91

168   *Index of Subjects and Authors*

son of man figure, 98, 99
  in Similitudes of Enoch, 99
Song of Songs, canonical status of, 3, 5,
  9, 23, 86
Southwood, Katherine, on the return
  migration, 49
Stuckenbruck, Loren, on reception of
  Daniel in Qumran community,
  73
Sundberg, Albert C., Jr., on advent of
  fixed canon, 82, 83

Taussig, Hal
  and *A New New Testament*, 108-35
  on dating ancient documents,
    117n20
Temple Scroll
  authority of, 59, 60
  and authority of Torah, 59, 60
  and pentateuchal legal texts, 54
  on true and false prophecy, 9
textual authority, acquisition of, and
  canonization, 66
textual variation, of Hebrew Scriptures, in Dead Sea Scrolls, 51
throne of glory, and son of man, 98, 99
Thunder: Perfect Mind, 112, 114, 117,
  121, 124, 125, 131
Torah
  authority of: and Ezra's reform, 50;
    in second century BCE, 50-52; in
    Temple Scroll, 59, 60

in book of Ezra, 44-50
  traditional, as first law in Jubilees,
    56, 57
trustworthiness, of biblical and extra-
  biblical texts, 17

VanderKam, James
  on authority of revelation in Jubi-
    lees, 56, 57, 58
  on authority of Torah in Jubilees, 56
Vermes, Geza, on rewritten scriptures,
  52, 53, 54
versional openness, and canon of
  scripture, 95, 107
vineyard parable, coherence with
  Aramaic interpretation, 101, 102

weights and measures, and canon, 26,
  27, 27nn7, 8
Wellhausen, Julius, on Israelite religion
wisdom literature, nondeviation formula in, 39, 40, 41
Wittgenstein, Ludwig, on family
  resemblances and language,
  13-15
Writings, order of, 84, 85

Zaman, Luc, on canonical process,
  25n2